Y0-BRV-530

# The Management of Serials Automation

*Current Technology & Strategies for Future Planning*

Peter Gellatly is an editor, lecturer, library and editorial consultant, and business consultant. He is author of over 100 articles and reviews, and is co-author with Bill Katz of *Magazine and Serials Agents* (Bowker, 1960). Mr. Gellatly was for eighteen years head of the University of Washington's serials unit and has served on various ALA and PNLA committees.

# The Management of Serials Automation

## Current Technology & Strategies for Future Planning

*Edited with an Introduction by*
**PETER GELLATLY**

*A Monographic Supplement to* The Serials Librarian
*(Volume 6, 1981/1982)*

THE HAWORTH PRESS
New York

The Haworth Press, 28 East 22 Street, New York, New York 10010


**Library of Congress Cataloging in Publication Data**
Main entry under title:

The Management of serials automation.

"A monographic supplement to The serials librarian
(volume 6, 1981/1982)"
    Bibliography: p.
    Includes index.
    1. Serials control systems—Automation. I. Gellatly,
Peter. II. Serials librarian.
Z692.S5M32          025'.3432'02854          82-6166
ISBN 0-917724-37-2                          AACR2

Printed in the United States of America

*The Management of Serials Automation* is a monographic supplement to *The Serials Librarian*, Volume 6 (1981/1982). It is not supplied as part of the subscription to the journal, but is available from the Publisher at an additional charge.

*The Serials Librarian* is a quarterly journal devoted to all major aspects of serials librarianship in libraries of all types.

# The Management of Serials Automation

*Current Technology & Strategies
for Future Planning*

*A Monographic Supplement to*
The Serials Librarian, *Volume 6 (1981/1982)*

# THE MANAGEMENT OF SERIALS AUTOMATION

Librarian of Congress Boorstin, in warning against the temptation to accept uncritically the notion that the burgeoning presence of computer printouts represents an actual increase in the world's body of knowledge, nevertheless musters an almost lyrical enthusiasm for the computer itself:

> The last two decades have seen the spectacular growth of the information industry—the frontier spirit in the late twentieth century. A magic computer technology accomplishes the dreariest tasks in seconds, surpasses the accuracy of the human brain, controls production lines and refineries, arranges inventories, and retrieves records. All this makes us proud of the human imagination.[1]

Certainly the computer has over this period of time transformed both the look of libraries and the content of their operation. It is fair to say that the changes that have taken place in libraries, and that still take place, are of historical proportion. Libraries may wish for an occasional period of calm in the midst of all the upheaval, but have little time—and little enough regret—for the somnolent calm of pre-computer days.

Serials librarians, along with their colleagues in the circulation department, were, of course, pioneers in the library exploitation of the benefits of computerization. Even before the advent of the electronic computer, serials librarians, inured to the task of producing great lists of one sort or another, recognized that the laboriousness of the list-making task could be reduced to size through use of various mechanical devices; and so it is small wonder that they grasped quickly the implication of what the new computer technology might offer.

If few libraries have been left untouched by what is termed the "computer revolution," it is clear that serials automation has yet to come to full bloom. Some suggest that this eventuality must await other developments, such as the final firming up of bibliographical standards and conventions, and is consequently little closer to realization than is the intriguing vision of universal bibliographic control.

Reservations of this sort aside, however, the onlooker is bound to be impressed by the spate of activity surrounding the serials operation. If the serials corner of the library could ever have been considered quiet, that no longer is possible. Things are happening, and these for the most part are large and consequential.

This supplement to the *Serials Librarian* attempts to indicate what is in fact creating the stir, how this is affecting the life of libraries, and what its significance is for libraries in general.

First, an examination is made of the important literature of the 1970s that has to do with serials automation. Conclusions are drawn about the content and quality of the literature and an indication given of what paths it is likely to follow in the next few years' time. There follows a comprehensive, annotated list of items from the 1970s that are considered crucial to an understanding of the present state of the art in serials automation.

Next is a series of articles in which are described the workings of a number of automated serials systems in libraries in various parts of the country. The first article deals with the University of California, San Diego, system, which, as one of the first such systems in full and continuous operation, must be thought to have historic importance. Accounts follow of other systems, some fully operational, some still in transition from manual to computer mode. As conversion continues to occupy a good deal of effort and attention, conversion problems and techniques are given attention. The section ends with a description of a remarkable California experiment in cooperative conversion.

Following this are articles presenting a discussion of the various aspects of the cataloguing of serials in a machine environment. This section is preceded by an appraisal of the need for revised bibliographical and cataloguing standards. In the main body of the section consideration is given to such concerns as the adoption of AACR2, the use of the CONSER data base, and the availability of cataloguing information from OCLC.

Because serials librarians have an inveterate interest in union lists and their compilation, the following section is given over to an investigation of on-line union lists and what they will look like in the future.

No development in recent times has had a greater impact on the operation of serials departments (or, for that matter, the libraries they belong to) than has the growth in library networking. To provide an indication of the extent to which networking is affecting the work of serials librarians, the next section examines the serials packages offered by OCLC, RLG, and WLN and the plans the Library of Congress has for promulgating and supporting large-scale and national networking.

Finally, the supplement contains a miscellaneous section in which are discussed such peripheral, but nonetheless important, matters as the agent's use of the computer and the electronic journal.

It is recognized, of course, that short of producing an "Osborn" on computerization, no work can give comprehensive treatment to so vast and complex a subject as serials automation. The present work represents a start only in achieving this end. It may be that the final word awaits a further reemergence from retirement of the eminent author of *Serials Publications*.

The hope is that in the meantime this study will prove useful to anybody with an interest in the storing and retrieval of information on a mass scale.

*Peter Gellatly*

## REFERENCE

1. Daniel J. Boorstin, *Gresham's Law: Knowledge or Information* (Dallas: Somesuch Press, 1980).

# AUTOMATED SERIALS CONTROL:
# A BIBLIOGRAPHIC SURVEY

Anne Marie Allison

ABSTRACT. This review and selective bibliography span the 1970s with special emphasis on the latter half of the period. They cite publications on the National Serials Pilot Project, NSDP, ISDS, ISSN, CONSER, ANSI Z39, COMARC, CODEN, ISBD-S, NPC, and OCLC. They call attention to five periodicals, and a number of state-of-the art reports. They identify numerous independently developed applications. Relationships are emphasized. Together, they provide a framework for assessing the future.

Someone said that controlling serials is like nailing Jello to the wall. This paper and the bibliography which follows it provide a historical perspective on some of the recent nailing efforts, particularly on the use of automation for serials control with a special emphasis on developments in the last half of the 1970s. It should be useful to those wishing a foundation for developing other lists in the future, although experienced serialists may question inclusions, exclusions, and even arrangement. It should be most helpful to three groups: (1) reference, catalog, and acquisitions professionals, and library administrators seeking to increase their understanding of the challenges faced by serialists; (2) faculty members in graduate schools of library science, especially those developing courses in automation, serials, or technical services; and (3) university faculty who participate in library advisory committees, or trustees of larger public libraries wishing to familiarize themselves further with problems of automation and serials in libraries.

## Scope and Arrangement

The arrangement is chronological. Articles appearing in any given year may reflect activities completed several years prior to publication, and in some instances describe projects planned but not yet fully implemented. It follows that such an annual pattern results in an indicated, but not a precise chronological array. Within each year citations are given in alphabetical order and are numbered sequentially. For example, 1977-9, would be the number assigned to the ninth item listed among those published in 1977. Cited works discussed in this introductory essay are identified in parentheses, immediately after they are named, e.g., Pitkin (1976-16). Some references are made to published work that is not part of the bibliography and these are numbered in sequential order throughout the narrative and are listed together under "References," before the beginning of the bibliography itself.

The cutoff date is the end of 1979. The original intention was to begin with 1974, the last year covered by *Serials Automation in the United States: A Bibliographic History* by Gary Pitkin (1976-16). This annotated work spans the period 1951 through 1974 and cites publication indexed in *Library Literature* under carefully selected terms. Some materials published between 1970 and 1974 which do not appear in Pitkin are included on a selective basis, although works he lists are not repeated here. The period before 1970 was also covered by Elizabeth Pan's *Library Serials Control Systems: A Literature Review and Bibliography* (1970-3).

Preparation began with an examination of the annual year's work reviews in the summer issues of *LRTS* (*Library Resources and Technical Services*). It continued with an examination of *Library Literature, Library and Information Science Abstracts, ERIC*, plus the "Serials News," and "Current Abstracts on Serials" sections in the *Serials Librarian*. Additional information was obtained from bibliographies in materials found in these searches, and in some instances by telephone conversations with colleagues. The bibliography is selective and covers writing in the English language. It stresses activities in the continental United States with just a few references to reports published in other countries when the information seemed to have universal application. Brief news notes such as those announcing grants awarded, union lists planned, new institutions joining collectives, and so forth are not reported.

### Background

Much of the literature examined followed three conventions which seem as rigid as those of the classical ballet. The first is a mandatory statement on the significance of journals for learned communication. The second is a comment on the exponential growth of serials costs, with the corollary that such costs absorb a growing share of the total materials budget. The third is an acknowledgment that no library can possibly acquire more than a portion of the serials likely to be needed by its clientele.

These three statements are used to introduce a list of problems presented by serials. The problems center on control. They involve:

— *Control* of the physical items themselves as they are ordered, received, and become part of a library;
— *Control* of their own and related bibliographic records and holdings statements;
— *Control* of their contents.

The authors propose a variety of solutions to these control problems and they usually fall into one or more of the following categories:

1. Pleas for better discipline among authors. These articles express dismay over the sociology of academia and regret the "publish or perish" environment. They emphasize that only a small core of journals is really needed in many disciplines.
2. Coercion of publishers. They offer suggestions for externally or self-imposed restraints on the identity crises, marriages, births, cloning, and parthenogenesis that take place among serial publications.
3. Work toward agreement on standards for unique numeric or alphabetic identification codes.
4. Creation of international standards for choice and form of entries, for bibliographic formats, and for holdings statements.
5. Development of increasingly sophisticated hardware and programming capabilities to manipulate and exchange information about serials.
6. Initiation of new and strengthening of existing union lists, with collective sharing of materials themselves as well as the controlling apparatus.
7. Use of electronic systems for control and retrieval of citations, full bibliographic and holdings records, abstracts, and of actual text of individual articles.
8. Efforts toward regional, national, and international cooperation in all these endeavors.

Despite great interest in these problems, there is relatively scant attention to one important factor, the human element. An informal survey of employment opportunity listings in the professional journals was made simultaneously with the search for citations to be used in the bibliography. It showed that the number of advertisements for serial specialists was small in comparison to those for other areas of librarianship. This is surprising in light of the universal acceptance of the facts that serials constitute the single most important avenue for communication of research data; that serial costs represent the largest component of library budgets; and that these costs are growing on absolute and relative scales. This situation may call for study and action. Perhaps control problems will not be solved by the projects or techniques described in the bibliography. Their eventual resolution may depend on the willingness of the profession to build a system to identify and reward individuals with the necessary combination of skill and dedication to manage serials. Michael Gorman recently said, "Online catalogs will be a familiar feature of libraries long before good automated check-in systems are common."[1] Possibly the right people, in sufficient numbers and appropriately compensated, will prove he was wrong.

*Definitions*

The need to develop a meaningful construct creates its own need for definitions. The glossary of AACR2 (*Anglo American Cataloguing Rules*, 2d ed.) offers this definition of a serial:

> *Serial.* A publication in any medium issued in successive parts bearing numerical or chronological designations and intended to be continued indefinitely. Serials include periodicals; newspapers; annuals (reports, yearbooks, etc.); the journals, memoirs, proceedings, transactions, etc., of societies; and numbered monographic series. *See also* Series 1.

> *Series 1.* A group of separate items related to one another by the fact that each item bears, in addition to its own title proper, a collective title applying to the group as a whole. The individual items may or may not be numbered.[2]

Andrew Osborn says the "working definition at the Library of Congress and the Department of Agriculture"..."on practical grounds"...is "any item which lends itself to serial treatment in a library; that is to listing in visible indexes and specialized serial records."[3] In 1977 an article in the *Journal of Academic Librarianship* was entitled "What Is a Serial Publication?" It concluded that:

> It will be noted that chronological designation, or periodicity, is the exclusive characteristic of the serial. Application of this definition will include, as serials, periodicals, magazines, newspapers, yearbooks, and proceedings, transactions, and memoirs of societies if they have periodicity.[4]

Gorman says a serial is "any library material that can and does change."[5] Perhaps a serial is any item any serial librarian chooses to call a serial.

Having defined serials themselves, it is important to define automated control from the perspective of this review. Pitkin's work reveals a progression from earlier terms to automation, which has been used in *Library Literature* since 1958. Automation, for the purposes of this paper, is defined as reliance on electronic technology to capture, process, store, and manipulate serials-related data.

Control, as a criterion for selecting publications for the bibliography, was intended to mean management and planning for management of (1) the bibliographic and holdings records for serials; (2) the access points (both character strings and text) for serials; and (3) the physical serials themselves. Acceptance of these definitions led to development of guidelines for excluding certain broad classes of publications.

## *Exclusions*

It was decided not to include documentation issued by the three biblio-graphic utilities, OCLC, RLIN, and WLN (OCLC, Inc., formerly the Ohio College Library Center; the Research Libraries Information Network; and the Washington Library Network). Materials from OCLC's broker networks were also excluded. These publications constitute a universe in themselves and could well form the base for a separate bibliography. Papers dealing principally with cataloguing codes, their application, and cataloguing routines were too numerous to be included. Publications chiefly devoted to the development of the MARC-S machine-readable format for serials were excluded, along with editions of the format itself. The on-line reference data bases were similarly left out. Despite this seemingly solid framework of definitions and guidelines, the include/exclude decisions was frequently difficult because of the latticework nature of the literature. Nevertheless, the decisions were made and the review began with a search for bibliographies themselves.

## *Bibliographies*

The bibliography cites three significant earlier bibliographies. The first is Elizabeth Pan's *Library Serials Control Systems: A Literature Review and Bibliography* (1970-3). This was a product of the first among four planned phases of a joint serials control project for Cornell, the University of Rochester, and the State University of New York at Buffalo. The three were members of FAUL (Five Associated University Libraries). Through the consortium they undertook an effort that was to include a feasibility study, a system design, a pilot implementation of the system, and finally the operating system itself. The project ended with the completion of the report of Phase I (1971-4). At that time, FAUL set aside this effort toward serials control, elected to cast its collective lot with OCLC, and awaited developments on a network scale.

Pan's bibliography and introduction are models for clarity and precision. She identified and listed twenty-eight operating automated serials systems falling somewhere between simple listings and total control. She searched for serials projects that could be emulated or adapted. She lists the institution, the active areas of serials automation, and names a project director for each. Viewed from the vantage point of another decade, they invite a longitudinal study. She provides a historical overview, describes earlier bibliographies, and covers topics ranging from use studies through technology, standards, and costs, to control systems themselves and related research. Handling this work increases one's appreciation of the ERIC system for making such materials easily available.

The landmark bibliography for automated control of serials is the Pitkin book (1976-16). The work itself and five of its reviews are cited. In Pitkin's introduction he clearly outlines his objectives. They are to cite and annotate relevant items listed in *Library Literature* under the headings "Mechanical Aids" between 1949 and 1951, "Machines and the Library" between 1952 and 1957, "Automation" and "Mechanization of Library Procedures" between 1958 and 1960, "Mechanization of Library Processes" between 1961 and 1966, and "Automation of Library Processes" sub-heading "Serials Records" between 1967 and 1974. His lengthy annotations provide both the essence and the style of each work. A reader will certainly not finish the book knowing everything, but will gain a comprehensive understanding of trends, projects described, and concerns of those working with serials automation through 1974. The issues raised by the reviewers lend another dimension. Collectively, the reviews underscore the truism that it is impossible to please everyone.

Pitkin set himself a measurable goal, and admirably met his standard, but the reviewers were sometimes overly critical. Rather than rate him for his achievement of self-determined goals, some of them introduced other, more elaborate goals they felt he should have set. It can only be hoped that Pitkin or a colleague working under his direction can be persuaded to produce a sequel.

Another quality bibliography appeared in 1979. This is appended to Buell's work entitled *A Report on Serials List Activity in Nebraska's Metropolitan Library Network Area* (1979-5). She reported a survey of current union list activities and anticipated future needs. Her paper concentrates on one aspect of automated control in one state. However, the careful preparation, timeliness, and scope of her bibliography make it a valuable resource. She covers materials published between 1970 and 1977, with the majority in the last part of the period.

## Collections

There are two collections in this bibliography, and each contains a number of papers germane to the history of automated serials control. In each case the general work rather than the individual papers were cited. Richard Palmer compiled *Case Studies in Library Computer Systems* (1973-7). A faculty member at Simmons College, he addressed his book to library administrators. Eight of the systems he describes are serials-related. Two of them are also discussed in Pitkin. One of these is a system used at the library of the Arthur D. Little firm and the other is the San Francisco Public Library project. There is a contrast between reports of librarians actually involved with such programs and the presentations made by Palmer and his associates as theoreticians.

Another collection represents the proceedings of a Larc Institute on Automated Serials Systems (1973-2), edited by H. William Axford. Priscilla Mayden's "Problems of Entering a Computerized Serials Network," Paul Vassallo's "National Serials Data Program," and Glyn Evans' state-of-the-art review are notable. Discussion of the Larc (or LARC) symposium leads naturally to consideration of the organization itself. It was called The Library Automation Research and Consulting Association and The Association for Library Automation Research Communications. Toward the end of its existence it also named itself The Library and Information Science Division of WISE (World Information Systems Exchange).

The history of Larc is inviting as an area for further research. Work that would have been done had the Association survived has been absorbed by the American Library Association's ISAD, later LITA (Information Science and Automation Division, later Library and Information Technology Association). Larc's thrust was continued in part by the CCLN (Council on Computerized Library Networks), by NTAG (the National Technical Architecture Group), the three bibliographic utilities, and by the networks associated with OCLC. Perhaps Larc was an idea whose unique time came and went. Its series of reports, documenting data processing in individual libraries, forms a considerable archive. Larc initiated a *Computerized Serials Systems Series*. The first four items in this series, authored by Elsie Cerutti, Don Bosseau, John Demas, and William Corya, were cited by Pitkin. The fifth and final title in the series appeared after his deadline and is listed here. It is Nancy Olson's and Daniel Lester's *Management Information System for Serials and Continuations* (1974-8). Larc produced a newsletter and a journal, *Network* (1974-6), discussed later in this paper.

## Periodicals on Serials

The bibliography notes five periodicals germane to the serialist. Two are products of automated management activities in large subscription agencies. These are the *Serials Updating Service* issued by Faxon (1973-10) and the *Ebsco Bulletin of Serials Changes* (1975-8). Subscription agents and the continuation departments of the larger book jobbers such as Blackwell North America or Baker and Taylor surely handle more extended procurement orders and claims than even the largest library. It would seem worthwhile for librarians to learn more about automated control in these bibliographically oriented firms. Perhaps proprietary secrecy would make this impossible. If Macy's doesn't tell Gimbels, it might be assumed that Faxon will not tell Blackwell. Nevertheless, as an idea it may merit exploration.

Three new professional journals of interest for automated control appeared during the 1970s. The first to arrive on the scene was *Title Varies* (1973-11). Originating under the direction of David Taylor, it changed hands after he left the serials field to become Undergraduate Librarian at the University of North Carolina at Chapel Hill. It appeared sporadically. Once two volumes were issued as one, making it a good bad-example for a lecture on holdings statements. *Title Varies* is once again under Taylor's editorial supervision.

The idea behind the journal was an organized critique of the many changes publishers and learned societies make in their serial titles. These are usually unnecessary and always costly to libraries. *Title Varies* is a marketplace for the exchange of ideas about cataloguing, entry problems, and other issues related to automated serials control. There was one period when the CCRC (Catalog Code Revision Committee) was making decisions on corporate authorship and entries for serial titles. It considered the benefits of alternatives to existing protocols measured against one another, and against the worth of making any changes at all. While this was going on serialists communicated with one another in an exchange of articles and retorts in the pages of *Title Varies*. Their repartee is captured there for the dissertation writers of the future. The magazine is valuable because it stresses that access points do change. It underscores the relevance of identification codes designed to be fail-safe, and of computer power adequate to handle the changing and interrelated records for serials.

A second important journal was *Network: International Communications in Library Automation* (1974-6), issued by the Larc Association. Its pages offered a worldwide panorama of serials automation projects during the years it flourished. Libraries holding the few volumes of *Network* which were published possess a significant historical cache.

The two vendors' series provide information needed for day-to-day management. *Title Varies* offers a channel for sharing concerns in an informal setting. A third periodical appeared during the 1970s is the *Serials Librarian* (1976-19). It is significant as a forum for theoretical and practical papers possibly too specific for general journals. Nevertheless, their detail and comprehensiveness are essential to the serials manager. Almost one-third of the works cited in the bibliography during the period 1977 through 1979 were published in the *Serials Librarian*.

## Trends

Batch processing is not dead and the entire world has not gone on-line. The trend from local to regional, national, and international projects is obvious. Yet the independently generated application is very much alive and well. Thirty-five are listed. The total activity involving medical libraries or medical librarians seems inordinate when considered in relation to their numbers in the field. This may be a result of availability of computer power or funding in their parent institutions. It may be a factor of the compelling needs of health science professionals for recency in their periodical literature. Perhaps medical librarians are not significantly more concerned with automated serials control but instead are relatively more conscientious about reporting than are their counterparts in other types of libraries. Whatever the reason, there seems to be a noticeable trend in this direction, at least on the basis of materials assembled here.

Since titles of many articles reveal their contents, a simple scan of the bibliography gives a developmental overview of many areas during the years covered. While the titles provide history, the list of authors seems a veritable who's-who-in-serials-automation. Donald Johnson, Director of the National Serials Pilot Project, presented an informal summary of the Pilot Project at the January 1971 meeting of the Association of Research Libraries in Los Angeles. This almost conversational report would be an excellent point of departure for those wishing to begin their own search for trends.

The National Serials Pilot Project; NSDP (The National Serials Data Project); the ISSN (International Standard Serial Number); CODEN; the ISDS (International Serials Data System); the ISBD-S (International Standard Bibliographic Description-Serials); the NPC (National Periodicals Center) and their impacts can be traced. A number of well-crafted papers appeared as states of the art and yet, perhaps in this area more than anywhere else in librarianship, nothing is static. This is because of the volatile nature of serials, of computer science, and of the information community.

The evolution of the "Toronto Group" into the "Anable Group," which became the "Ad Hoc Discussion Group on Serials Data Bases" and finally produced CONSER, can be followed by reading the list, although some critical publications relating to CONSER are not title-revealing. Paul Fasana's "Impact of National Developments on Library Technical Services and Public Services (1974-9) was prepared for presentation at an ISAD/ASIS institute named Automated Serials Control—National and International Considerations. It offers insights on where-are-we, where-are-we-going, why, and shall-we. It should be considered part of the CONSER story. It is also valuable for tracing other facets of automated control. The effect of CONSER as its influence grew in a widening circle is revealed in Ross Bourne's article, called "Building a Serials File" (1978-1), in the British journal *Program*. As Head of the Serials Office at the British Library Bibliographic Services Division, Bourne considers CONSER, ISDS, ISSN, and ISBD-S and relates CONSER to the British BLAISE (British Library Automated Information Service).

OCLC issued a KWOC index to CONSER (1978-4). It remedied some problems caused by entry and title ambiguities inherent in any joint effort. The fact that it was available in microformat made its distribution less costly and provided an example of one technology's supporting the use of another. A deficiency in the KWOC index was that its information considerably predated its publication. The welcome announcement was made in mid-1980 that the National Library of Canada had developed a 1979 index supplement, incorporating new authentications, changes, and terminations. It is accompanied by a new set of cumulated indexes to the 1975–1978 base and to the supplement itself. They can be purchased from the Library of Congress.[6]

The discussion of CONSER involves a macrocosmic view of serials control during the 1970s. Nevertheless, there was no lack of attention to more specific areas of interest. Audrey Grosch's "Theory and Design of Serial Holding Statements in Computer-Based Serials Systems" (1977-4) elicited a response from Stephen Silberstein which became an article in itself (1978-17). This concern is one of the most contemporary and yet one of the oldest challenges to those who would design serials control systems. Glyn Evans, while in the library at the Royal Society of Medicine in the United Kingdom during the mid-1960s developed a system that addressed this issue.[7] He believes it was the first (or the first reported in the literature) to handle claiming by having the computer scan a holdings statement in its memory.[8] This is in contrast to the alternative of having reports of incoming materials matched against a file of predicted arrivals, typified by the early arrival card systems and their descendants.

Several authors touched on the OCLC serials-control subsystem. Anne Twitchell and Mary Sprehn forecast considerations prior to its implementation at the University of South Florida (1976-22). James Corey portrays the serials work flow and technical services environment at the University of Illinois as a background for a decision not to implement the subsystem (1978-3). Harry Kamens shares the conversion process and actualization of the subsystem at Kent State (1978-10 and 1979-11), while Nancy Buckeye reports its use at Central Michigan (1978-2). Tom Kilton describes the use of OCLC for pre-order verification (1979-12).

Throughout the period there was concern over development of standard codes. Finally, on November 16, 1979, the ANSI Standard Holdings Statement was approved. It was not published however, until 1980 and fell outside the scope of the bibliography.[9] This crucial document is a tribute to the efforts of those who contributed to its development.

## Conclusions

The decade saw the death of Larc; the completion of the National Serials Pilot Project; and the emergence of *Title Varies* and the *Serials Librarian*. CONSER, OCLC, and CRTs have become as commonplace as the date-due stamp. The 1970s began in the last days of the financial honeymoon libraries enjoyed with their funding agencies. The 1970s ended in an era of declining support and rising costs. Papers cited in the earlier years of the period sometimes repeated comments, typical of the 1960s, on the shortage of professionals. This is no longer true. Librarians compete in a buyers' market.

Now, more than ever, cataloguing variations demand standards and complex technology. Decisions on serials will have to be made with consideration of on-line catalogues and the proposed National Network. In the 1980s automated serials control will have to meet the needs of the cost-beleaguered administrator and the all-but-forgotten patron who only wants to read a journal and couldn't care less whether or not it is entered under an AACR or an AACR2 heading, or whether it has a generic title. Computers will play an increasingly major role in libraries, but optimism is tempered by caveats on the continued availability of electrical energy. No one seems to have proven, indeed no one seems to be trying anymore to prove, that automated processing costs less. Nevertheless, automated serials control is surely here to stay.

## REFERENCES

1. Michael Gorman, "Crunching the Serial," *American Libraries* 11 (July-August 1980):416.

2. *Anglo-American Cataloguing Rules*, 2d ed., Michael Gorman and Paul Winkler, editors (Chicago: American Library Association, 1978), p. 570.

3. Andrew D. Osborn, *Serial Publications: Their Place and Treatment in Libraries* (Washington, DC: American Library Association, 1970), pp. 16–17.

4. Doris M. Carson, "What Is a Serial Publication?" *Journal of Academic Librarianship* 3 (September 1977):206–209.

5. Michael Gorman, 416.

6. This is based on information issued by OCLC's G. Shiplee. Orders and inquiries should be sent to the Customer Service Section, Cataloging Distribution Service, Library of Congress, Building 159, Navy Yard Annex, Washington, DC 20541.

7. Glyn T. Evans, "Development of an Automated Periodical System at the Royal Society of Medicine Library," *Proceedings of the Royal Society of Medicine* 62 (August 1969):757–63.

8. Telephone conversation with Glyn Evans, August 1980.

9. American National Standards Institute, *American National Standard for Serial Holdings Statements at the Summary Level, ANSI Z39.42-1980* (New York: American National Standards Institute, 1980).

# AUTOMATED SERIALS CONTROL:
# A SELECTED BIBLIOGRAPHY

Anne Marie Allison
Janice E. Donahue

## 1970

*1970-1.* Burns, Robert W., Jr. *The Design and Testing of a Computerized Method of Handling Library Periodicals (Title III).* Fort Collins, CO: Colorado State University, University Libraries, 1970. Arlington, VA: ERIC Document Reproduction Service, ED 050 753.

*1970-2.* Martin, M.D., and Barnes, C.I. *Report on the Feasibility of an International Serials Data System, and Preliminary Systems Design.* Prepared... for *UNISIST/ICSU-AB Working Group on Bibliographic Descriptions.* London: INSPEC, the Institution of Electrical Engineers, 1970. Arlington, VA: ERIC Document Reproduction Service, ED 061 954.

*1970-3.* Pan, Elizabeth. *Library Serials Control Systems: A Literature Review and Bibliography.* Syracuse, NY: Five Associated University Libraries, 1970. Arlington, VA: ERIC Document Reproduction Service, ED 044 538.

*1970-4.* Stevenson, Chris G. "An Inexpensive Computer-Based System for Group-Routing Periodicals." *Special Libraries* 61 (October 1970):460–65.

## 1971

*1971-1.* American National Standards Institute. *American National Standard Identification Number for Serial Publications.* New York: American National Standards Institute, 1971.

*1971-2.* Association of Research Libraries. *Minutes of the Seventy-Seventh Meeting, January 17, 1971, Los Angeles, California.* Los Angeles: Association of Research Libraries, 1971.

*1971-3.* Evans, Glyn T., comp. *New PHILSOM System Documentation.* 2d ed. St. Louis: Washington University School of Medicine, 1971.

*1971-4.* Five Associated University Libraries. *Joint Serials Control System Project for the Libraries of Cornell University, University of Rochester and the State University of New York at Buffalo. Phase I Feasibility Study. Final Report.* Syracuse, NY: Five Associated University Libraries, 1971. Arlington, VA: ERIC Document Reproduction Service, ED 051 827.

## 1972

*1972-1.* Johnson, Donald W. *Toward a National Serials Data Program: Final Report of the National Serials Pilot Project.* Washington, DC: Association of Research Libraries, 1972. Arlington, VA: ERIC Document Reproduction Service, ED 063 009.

*1972-2.* Koltay, Emery L. "International Standard Serial Numbering (ISSN)." *Bowker Annual of Library and Book Trade Information* 17 (1972):197–200.

## 1973

*1973-1.* Anable, Richard. "The Ad Hoc Discussion Group on Serials Data Bases: Its History, Current Position, and Future." *Journal of Library Automation* 6 (December 1973):207–14.

*1973-2.* Association for Library Automation Research and Communications. *Proceedings of the Larc Institute on Automated Serials Systems, St. Louis, Missouri, May 24–25, 1973.* Edited by H. William Axford. Tempe, AZ: LARC Association, 1973.

*1973-3.* Grosch, Audrey N. "Minnesota Union List of Serials." *Journal of Library Automation* 6 (September 1973): 167–81.

*1973-4.* Grosch, Audrey N. "A Regional Serials Program under National Serials Data Program Auspices: Discussion Paper Prepared for Ad Hoc Serials Discussion Group." *Journal of Library Automation* 6 (December 1973):201–206.

*1973-5.* International Serials Data System. *Guidelines for ISDS.* Paris: UNESCO, 1973.

*1973-6.* Klein, Ann S., and Passiakos, Margaret. *Journal Control System by Batch Processing at Oak Ridge National Laboratory.* Oak Ridge, TN: Oak Ridge National Laboratory, 1973.

*1973-7.* Palmer, Richard P. *Case Studies in Library Computer Systems.* New York: Bowker, 1973.

*1973-8.* Pulsifer, Josephine S. "Comparison of MARC Serials, NSDP, and ISBD-S." *Journal of Library Automation* 6 (December 1973):193–200.

*1973-9.* Runkle, Martin. "Automated Serials Control Systems: The State of the Art." Master's thesis, University of Chicago, 1973.

*1973-10. Serials Updating Service,* vol. 1, August 1973– . Westwood, MA: F.W. Faxon, 1973– .

*1973-11. Title Varies,* vol. 1, no. 1, 1 December 1973– . Okemos, MI: *Title Varies,* 1973– .

## 1974

*1974-1.* Blum, Fred. "Standards Update: ANSI Committee Z39." *Library Resources & Technical Services* 18 (Winter 1974):25–29.

*1974-2*. Corya, William L., and others. "Indiana Union List of Serials Project." *Library Occurrent* 24 (August 1974):455–62.

*1974-3*. Fasana, Paul J. "Impact of National Developments on Library Technical Services and Public Services." *Journal of Library Automation* 7 (December 1974):249–62.

*1974-4*. Harp, Vivian, and Heard, Gertrude. "Automated Periodicals System at a Community College Library." *Journal of Library Automation* 7 (June 1974):83–96.

*1974-5*. International Federation of Library Associations. *ISBD(S): International Standard Bibliographic Description for Serials, Recommended by the Joint Working Group on the ISBD for Serials Set up by the IFLA Committee on Serial Publications*. London: IFLA Committee on Cataloguing, 1974.

*1974-6*. *Network: International Communications in Library Automation*, vols. 1–3, January 1974–Winter (?) 1976. Tempe, AZ: Association for Library Automation Research Communications, 1974–1976.

*1974-7*. Olson, Nancy B., ed. *Mankato State College Media System*. Computerized Serials Systems Series, vol. 1, no. 5. Tempe, AZ: LARC Association, 1974.

*1974-8*. Olson, Nancy B., and Lester, Daniel W. *A Management Information System for Serials and Continuations*. Mankato, MN: Mankato State College, Library, 1974. Alexandria, VA: ERIC Document Reproduction Service, ED 090 913.

*1974-9*. Pan, Elizabeth. *New York State Library Automated Serials Control System*. Albany: The University of the State of New York, The State Education Department, The New York State Library, 1974. Arlington, VA: ERIC Document Reproduction Service, ED 100 333.

*1974-10*. Saffady, William. "A Computer Output Microfilm Serials List for Patron Use." *Journal of Library Automation* 7 (December 1974):263–66.

*1974-11*. Upham, Lois. "CONSER: Cooperative Conversion of Serials Project." *Library of Congress Information Bulletin* 33 (29 November 1974): A245–48.

*1974-12*. Wesemael, A. L. van. "International Standardization of Serials Records: ISSN and ISDS." *Catalogue & Index* 34 (Summer 1974):15–16.

*1974-13*. Wilson, A., and others. "Automated Production of SALSSAH (Serials in Australian Libraries: Social Sciences and Humanities)." *LASIE* 5 (September 1974):36–40.

## 1975

*1975-1*. American National Standards Institute, Z39 Committee. "American National Standard Committee Z39 X/C 34 on Code Identification of Serial Articles, Draft Code Proposal, February 25, 1975." *Journal of Library Automation* 8 (June 1975):154–61.

*1975-2.* Anable, Richard. "CONSER: An Update." *Journal of Library Automation* 8 (March 1975):26–30.

*1973-3.* Anable, Richard. "CONSER: Bibliographic Considerations." *Library Resources & Technical Services* 19 (Fall 1975):341–48.

*1975-4.* Christ, Ruth, and others. "Alternative III." *Title Varies* 2 (September-November 1975):29.

*1975-5.* "Cooperative Conversion of Serials." *American Libraries* 6 (January 1975):10–11.

*1975-6.* "Cooperative Conversion of Serials." Comment by S. Michael Malinconico (Letter). *American Libraries* 6 (March 1975):128.

*1975-7.* Daniels, Mary Kay. "Automated Serials Control: National and International Considerations." *Journal of Library Automation* 8 (June 1975): 127–46.

*1975-8. Ebsco Bulletin of Serials Changes*, vol. 1, September 1975– . Birmingham, AL: Ebsco Industries, 1975– .

*1975-9.* Fasana, Paul James. "AACR, ISBD(S) and ISSN: A Comment." *Library Resources & Technical Services* 19 (Fall 1975):333–37.

*1975-10.* Hall, H. W. "Serials '74: A Review." *Library Resources & Technical Services* 19 (Summer 1975):197–205.

*1975-11.* International Organization for Standardization. *Documentation—International Standard Serial Numbering (ISSN)*. Geneva: International Organization for Standardization, 1975.

*1975-12.* Lim, Hong Too. "Developing a Computer-Based Periodicals Control System for the Specific Purposes of Listing and Accounting." *Singapore Libraries* 5 (1975):1–9.

*1975-13.* Livingston, Lawrence G. "CONSER Inter-Relationships." *Drexel Library Quarterly* 11 (July 1975):60–63.

*1975-14.* Livingston, Lawrence G. "The CONSER Project: Current Status and Plans." *Network: International Communications in Library Automation* 2 (March 1975):16.

*1975-15.* Loepprich, Joyce. "On-Line Serials Control in a Consortium Setting." Paper presented at the Annual Meeting of the Medical Library Association, Cleveland, Ohio, May 30–June 5, 1975. Arlington, VA: ERIC Document Reproduction Service, ED 115 222.

*1975-16.* Martin, Susan K. "Mixed Media for a Serial System: Hardcopy, Microform, and CRT's." In *Information Roundup: A Continuing Education Session on Microforms and Data Processing in the Library and Information Center: Costs/Benefits/History/Trends. Proceedings of the 4th ASIS Mid-Year Meeting. Portland Oregon, May 15-17, 1975*, edited by Frances G. Spiagi, Theodore C. W. Grams, and Julie Kawabata, pp. 111-18. Washington, DC: American Society for Information Science, 1975.

*1975-17.* Olson, Kenneth D. "Communications of a Bibliographer." *Special Libraries* 66 (May–June 1975):266–72.

*1975-18*. Pitkin, Gary M. *Serials Automation at Kearney State College*. Kearney, NE: Kearney State College, 1975. Arlington, VA; ERIC Document Reproduction Service, ED 116 683.

*1975-19*. Riggs, Donald E. *A Computerized Periodical-Retrieval System*. Athens, WV: Bluefield State College and Concord College, 1975. Arlington, VA: ERIC Document Reproduction Service, ED 101 745.

*1975-20*. Sauer, Mary. "National Serials Data Program." *Drexel Library Quarterly* 11 (July 1975):40–48.

*1975-21*. Silberstein, Stephen M. "Computerized Serial Processing System at the University of California, Berkeley." *Journal of Library Automation* 8 (December 1975):299–311.

*1975-22*. Vassallo, Paul. "The CONSER Project: An Analysis." *Drexel Library Quarterly* 11 (July 1975):49–59.

*1975-23*. Young, Barbara A. "Computer-Generated Routing Slips." *Special Libraries* 66 (February 1975):668–73.

## 1976

*1976-1*. Allen, Albert H., and Beirne, Eugene F. "On-line Logging in of Periodicals by CODEN Using Interactive Query Report Processor." *Journal of the American Society for Information Science* 27 (July–August 1976): 230–34.

*1976-2*. Bowden, Virginia M. "The PHILSOM System—One User's Experience." *Bulletin of the Medical Library Association* 64 (April 1976):219–33.

*1976-3*. Brodman, Estelle, and Johnson, Millard F. "Medical Serials Control Systems by Computer: A State of the Art Review." *Bulletin of the Medical Library Association* 64 (January 1976):12–19.

*1976-4*. Burke, Merilyn S. "CAHSL Union List of Serials: The Connecticut Experience." *Bulletin of the Medical Library Association* 64 (July 1976): 326–31.

*1976-5*. Darling, Louise, and Fayollat, James. "Evolution of a Processing System in a Large Biomedical Library." *Bulletin of the Medical Library Association* 64 (January 1976):20–24.

*1976-6*. Fasana, Paul J. "Serials Data Control: Current Problems and Prospects." *Journal of Library Automation* 9 (March 1976):19–33.

*1976-7*. Grosch, Audrey N. "Serial Arrival Prediction Coding: A Serial Predictive Model for Use by System Designers." *Information Processing and Management* 12 (1976):141–46.

*1976-8*. James, John R. "Serials '75—Review and Trends." *Library Resources & Technical Services* 20 (Summer 1976):259–69.

*1976-9*. Johnson, Millard F., Jr. "A Design for a Mini-Computer Based Serials Control Network." *Special Libraries* 67 (August 1976):386–90.

*1976-10*. Lee, Nancy Craig, and Hope, Dorothy H. "Biomedical Journal Holdings List: A Multi-Subject Approach." *Special Libraries* 67 (May–June 1976):261–64.

*1976-11*. Lewis, Gary A. *An Off-Line Serials System: A Practical First Step into Automation.* Radford, VA: Radford College Library, 1976. Arlington, VA: ERIC Document Reproduction Service, ED 150 980.

*1976-12*. National Serials Data Program. *ISSN: A Brief Guide.* Washington, DC: Library of Congress, NSDP, 1976.

*1976-13*. National Serials Data Program. *ISSN: Procedure for Requesting Assignment.* Washington, DC: Library of Congress, NSDP, 1976.

*1976-14*. National Serials Data Program. *ISSN: Publisher's Guide.* Washington, DC: Library of Congress, NSDP, 1976.

*1976-15*. Pan, Elizabeth. "Resources and Technical Services Division: Annual Reports, 1974/75; Serials Section Report." *Library Resources & Technical Services* 20 (Winter 1976):83–85.

*1976-16*. Pitkin, Gary M. *Serials Automation in the United States: A Bibliographic History.* Metuchen, NJ: Scarecrow Press, 1976.

*1976-17*. "RTSD Serials Section Executive Committee." *Library of Congress Information Bulletin* 35 (10 September 1976):553–54.

*1976-18*. Rice, Patricia. "CONSER from the Inside." *Title Varies* 3 (May–July 1976):13.

*1976-19*. *Serials Librarian*, vol. 1, no. 1, Fall 1976– . New York: Haworth Press, 1976– .

*1976-20*. Silberstein, Stephen M. "Computerized Serial Processing System at the University of California, Berkeley." "Erratum." *Journal of Library Automation* 9 (March 1976):77.

*1976-21*. Taylor, Betty. "Serials—Their Future in an Automated Library." LeCourt: Global Communications in Legal Information Technology 1 (Summer 1976):16–21.

*1976-22*. Twitchell, Anne, and Sprehn, Mary. *Implementation of the Ohio College Library Center's Proposed Serials Control Subsystem at the University of South Florida Library: Some Preliminary Considerations.* Tampa: University of South Florida, Library Science/Audiovisual Department, 1976. Arlington, VA: ERIC Document Reproduction Service, ED 124 220.

### 1977

*1977-1*. Ash, Joan, and Morgan, James E. "Journal Evaluation Study at the University of Connecticut Health Center." *Bulletin of the Medical Library Association* 65 (April 1977):297–99.

*1977-2*. Avram, Henriette D., and Anable, Richard. "Now, Add CONSER to Your Conversation: II. The Next Generation of CONSER." *American Libraries* 8 (January 1977):23–26.

*1977-3*. DeGennaro, Richard. "Wanted: A Minicomputer Serials Control System." *Library Journal* 102 (15 April 1977):878–79.

*1977-4*. Grosch, Audrey N. Review of *Serials Automation in the United States: A Bibliographic History*, by Gary M. Pitkin. *RQ* 16 (Summer 1977):358.

*1977-5*. Grosch, Audrey N. "Theory and Design of Serial Holding Statements in Computer-Based Serials Systems." *Serials Librarian* 1 (Summer 1977): 341–52.

*1977-6*. Hammer, Donald P. Review of *Serials Automation in the United States: A Bibliographic History*, by Gary M. Pitkin. *Library Journal* 102 (1 April 1977):778.

*1977-7*. Hawks, Jean. Review of *Serials Automation in the United States: A Bibliographic History*, by Gary M. Pitkin. *College & Research Libraries* 38 (May 1977):262.

*1977-8*. Howard, Joseph H. "Resources and Technical Services Division: Annual Reports, 1976/76; Serials Section Report." *Library Resources & Technical Services* 21 (Winter 1977):91–93.

*1977-9*. James, John R. "Serials in 1976." *Library Resources & Technical Services* 21 (Summer 1977):259–69.

*1977-10*. Klar, Rainer H. "The Integration of Library Functions Via Electronic Data Processing." In *On-Line Library and Network Systems: Symposium Held at Dortmund University, March 22–24, 1976. Organized by E. Edelhoff, W. Lingenberg, G. Pflug, and V. Wehefritz*, edited by E. Edelhoff and K.-D. Lehmann, pp. 22–38. Frankfurt am Main: Vittorio Klostermann, 1977.

*1977-11*. Louisiana State University, Baton Rouge. Library. *Serials Manual, L.S.U. Library*. Baton Rouge: Louisiana State University Library, Serials Manual Committee, 1977. Arlington, VA: ERIC Document Reproduction Service, ED 169 879.

*1977-12*. Martin, Susan K. "Experiences in National Networking: CONSER and COMARC." *Journal of Library Automation* 10 (June 1977):99–100.

*1977-13*. "National Periodicals System Roughed Out by NCLIS." *Library Journal* 102 (1 January 1977):17.

*1977-14*. Pan, Elizabeth. "Claiming—What and When." *Title Varies* 4 (March–May 1977):5.

*1977-15*. Paul, Huibert. "Serials Processing: Manual Control Vs. Automation." *Library Resources & Technical Services* 21 (Fall 1977):345–53.

*1977-16*. Plotnik, Arthur, and Bushman, Arlan G. "Now, Add CONSER to Your Conversation: I. A Brief Q & A Primer on CONSER." *American Libraries* 8 (January 1977):21–22.

*1977-17*. Sailer, Klaus, and Gruber, Peter. "System Explained Using a Data Base for Serials as an Example." In *On-Line Library and Network Systems: Symposium Held at Dortmund University, March 22–24, 1976. Organized by E. Edelhoff, W. Lingenberg, G. Pflug, and V. Wehefritz*, edited by E. Edelhoff and K.-D. Lehmann, pp. 48–52. Frankfurt am Main: Vittorio Klostermann, 1977.

*1977-18*. Saxe, Minna C. "Now, Add CONSER to Your Conversation: IV.

Great Faith and a Few Big Questions: Notes from a Librarian Using the CONSER Base." *American Libraries* 8 (January 1977):27.

*1977-19*. Simmons, Peter. Review of *Serials Automation in the United States: A Bibliographic History*, by Gary M. Pitkin. *Journal of Library Automation* 10 (March 1977):96.

*1977-20*. Sleep, Esther L. "Whither the ISSN? A Practical Experience." *Canadian Library Journal* 34 (August 1977):265–70.

*1977-21*. "The Solid Gold Computer." *Serials Librarian* 1 (Spring 1977):205–206.

*1977-22*. Taylor, David C. Review of *Serials Automation in the United States: A Bibliographic History*, by Gary M. Pitkin. *Serials Librarian* 2 (Fall 1977): 98–99.

*1977-23*. Upham, Lois N. "Now, Add CONSER to Your Conversation: III. Mixed Feelings: Taking Part in CONSER." *American Libraries* 8 (January 1977):26–27.

*1977-24*. Willmering, William J. "Northwestern University Library's NOTIS 3 Automated Serial Control System." In *Information Management in the 1980's: Proceedings of the 40th ASIS Annual Meeting. Chicago, Illinois, September 26–October 1, 1977*, p. 99. Compiled by Bernard M. Fry and Clayton A. Shepherd. White Plains, NY: American Society for Information Science, 1977.

*1977-25*. Willmering, William J. "On-Line Centralized Serials Control." *Serials Librarian* 1 (Spring 1977):243–47.

*1977-26*. Wittig, Glenn R. "CONSER (Cooperative Conversion of Serials Project): Building an On-Line International Serials Data Base." *Unesco Bulletin for Libraries* 31 (September–October 1977):305–310.

## 1978

*1978-1*. Bourne, Ross. "Building a Serials File." *Program* 12 (April 1978): 78–86.

*1978-2*. Buckeye, Nancy Melin. "The OCLC Serials Subsystem: Implementation: Implications at Central Michigan University." *Serials Librarian* 3 (Fall 1978):31–42.

*1978-3*. Corey, James F. "OCLC and Serials Processing: A State of Transition at the University of Illinois." *Serials Librarian* 3 (Fall 1978):57–67.

*1978-4*. *CONSER KWOC Index*. Columbus, OH: User Services Division, OCLC, Inc., 1978.

*1978-5*. Council on Library Resources. *A National Periodicals Center: Technical Development Plan*. Washington, DC: Council on Library Resources, 1978.

*1978-6*. Furlong, Elizabeth J. "Index Access to On-Line Records: An Operational View." *Journal of Library Automation* 11 (September 1978):223–38.

*1978-7.* Groot, Elizabeth H. "Unique Identifiers for Serials: 1977 Update." *Serials Librarian* 2 (Spring 1978):247–55.

*1978-8.* Gwinn, Nancy E. "A National Periodicals Center: Articulating the Dream." *Library Journal* 103 (1 November 1978):2166–69.

*1978-9.* James, John R. "Developments in Serials: 1977." *Library Resources & Technical Services* 22 (Summer 1978):294–309.

*1978-10.* Kamens, Harry H. "OCLC's Serials Control Subsystem: A Case Study." *Serials Librarian* 3 (Fall 1978):43–55.

*1978-11.* Kimzey, Ann C. "An Automated Book Catalog for a Learning Re sources Center Periodicals Collection." *Serials Librarian* 2 (Summer 1978): 405–10.

*1978-12.* McKay, Duncan J., and Alexander, Raymond A. "Bell College of Technology Library's Computer Serials System." *Program* 12 (July 1978): 139–52.

*1978-13.* Morton, Donald J. "Use of a Subscription Agent's Computer Facilities in Creating and Maintaining a Library's Subscription Profile." *Library Resources & Technical Services* 22 (Fall 1978):386–89.

*1978-14.* "The National Periodicals Center: A Castle in the Air Gets a Blueprint." *American Libraries* 9 (October 1978):511.

*1978-15..* New, Doris E. "Serials Agency Conversion in an Academic Library." *Serials Librarian* 2 (Spring 1978):277–85.

*1978-16.* Seba, Douglas B., and Forrest, Beth. "Using SDI's for Journal Acquisition." *Online: The Magazine of Online Information Systems 2 (January 1978):10–15.*

*1978-17.* Silberstein, Stephen M. "Audrey Grosch's Recent Article ("Theory and Design of Serial Holding Statements in Computer Based Serials Systems")...," in, "Letters to the Editor," *Serials Librarian* 3 (Fall 1978):3–4.

*1978-18.* Smith, Malcolm. "Evaluation of Computers for Library Applications." *LASIE* 9 (July–August 1978):2–14.

## 1979

*1979-1.* American National Standards Committee. *American National Standard for International Standard Serial Numbering (ISSN).* Rev. ed. New York: American National Standards Institute, 1979.

*1979-2.* "Benefits of CONSER Project Described." *Library of Congress Information Bulletin* 38 (24 August 1979):333–34.

*1979-3.* Bourne, Ross. "Building a Serials File." Comment by M. Jacob (Letter). *Program* 13 (January 1979):42.

*1979-4.* Bradley, Isabel. "International Standard Serial Numbers and the International Serials Data System." *Serials Librarian* 3 (Spring 1979):243–53.

*1979-5.* Buell, Carol Dick. *A Report on Serials List Activity in Nebraska's Metropolitan Library Network Area.* Lincoln, NE: Nebraska Library Commission, Metropolitan Library Network, 1979. Arlington, VA: ERIC Document Reproduction Service, ED 176 743.

*1979-6.* "The Creation of a National Periodicals Center...." In "Serials News." *Serials Librarian 3 (Spring 1979):338–42.*

*1979-7.* Glasby, Dorothy J. "Serials in 1978." *Library Resources & Technical Services* 23 (Summer 1979):203–12.

*1979-8.* Hayes, Florence. "CONSER Activities of the Five Associated University Libraries (FAUL)." In "Serials News." *Serials Librarian* 4 (Fall 1979): 119–21.

*1979-9.* "House Gives Initial Boost to Periodicals Center." *American Libraries* 10 (October 1979):509.

*1979-10.* "Indiana U. to Build Model OCLC-Based Serials List." *Library Journal* 104 (1 October 1979):2031–32.

*1979-11.* Kamens, Harry. "Serials Control and OCLC." In *OCLC: A National Library Network*, edited by Anne Marie Allison and Ann Allan, pp. 139–54. Short Hills, NJ: Enslow Publishers, 1979.

*1979-12.* Kilton, Tom D. "OCLC and the Pre-Order Verification of New Serials." *Serials Librarian* 4 (Fall 1979):61–64.

*1979-13.* Knight, Nancy H. "Forum Favors Concept of National Periodicals Center." *American Libraries* 10 (May 1979):229–30.

*1979-14.* Koenig, Michael E.D. "On-Line Serials Collection Analysis." *Journal of the American Society for Information Science* 30 (May 1979):148–53.

*1979-15.* "Library Announces Publication of CONSER Microfiche." *Library of Congress Information Bulletin* 38 (19 January 1979):19–20.

*1979-16.* Lupton, David Walker. "Tracking the ISSN." *Serials Librarian* 4 (Winter 1979):187–98.

*1979-17.* Morton, Donald J. "Use of a Subscription Agent's Computer Facilities in Creating and Maintaining a Library's Subscription Profile." "Erratum." *Library Resources & Technical Services* 23 (Spring 1979):129.

*1979-18.* Sabowitz, Norman. "Computer Assistance in Arranging Serials." *Canadian Library Journal* 36 (13 August 1979):211–13.

*1979-19.* Savage, Noël. "A National Periodicals Center: The Debate in Arlington." *Library Journal* 104 (15 May 1979):1108–15.

# THE UNIVERSITY OF CALIFORNIA, SAN DIEGO, AUTOMATED SERIALS SYSTEM, 1980

Roberta A. Corbin

ABSTRACT. Serials automation at the University of California, San Diego, began in 1961 and has proceeded through several stages of development and computer hardware. The system consists of three major subsystems. The receiving subsystem programs generate transaction, cumulated receipts, claims, and want lists. The updating subsystem consists of procedures which create, change, and update master records. Finally, the printing subsystem transforms information in the master file into more usable formats. The nearly 45,000 records in the file are updated monthly. In addition, auxiliary programs produce shelflists, keyword lists, subject lists, and others. Eventually the entire serials system may be subsumed by bibliographic, acquisitions, and circulation systems which are in various stages of planning and development.

In the summer of 1961, Melvin J. Voigt, then UCSD University Librarian, and Clay Perry, Jr., Director of the UCSD Computer Center, discussed the idea of automating serials control in the library. From their informal discussions came the germ of an idea which led to what is now a file containing nearly 45,000 serial entries representing active and inactive titles and cross references. The titles include journals, newspapers, monographic series, and many government documents. As part of the monthly update routines, the system records important bibliographic information and holdings, predicts expected issues, assists in claiming unreceived issues, and produces bindery lists and cards representing completed volumes. In addition, shelflists, keyword lists, want lists, subject lists, duplicate title lists, and many other forms of output can be produced on demand.

This system, which has operated regularly for almost twenty years, began on a small scale considering today's standards. With a grant of $10,000 the project was on its way.

Serials were chosen rather than monographs for this first major automation project in the library for several reasons:

1. Manual processing of serials consumes a large amount of staff time and is a costly operation.
2. Manual holdings are difficult to interpret and require staff intervention to be useful to patrons.

3. The repetitive nature of serials holdings makes them a prime condidate for automation.

Other criteria which made the project feasible were the relatively small size of the library and its close proximity to an excellent computer facility.[1]

After detailed analysis of the characteristics of serials and the contents of a serial record, existing scattered files were gathered together and the product goals of the project were defined. The following items were selected as products, with the first two having the highest priority:

1. Complete holdings lists of all serials
2. Lists of current receipts of periodicals by library location
3. Bindery lists of all serials received unbound
4. Nonreceipt lists for all serials
5. Expiration of subscription lists for all purchased serials

In order to provide a regularly updated, complete holdings list, a quick and easy method of checking in had to be developed. In addition there had to be a systematic way to add new records and to change records already in the file.[2]

In the beginning, 100 titles were converted into machine-readable form for developing and testing programs. Programs were originally written in FORTRAN 60 for use on a CDC 1604 computer. Later, to make more efficient use of the computer, a new program was written in FORTRAN 62 with subroutines in assembly language. As originally designed, the system was of the card-based batch type.

By mid-1962, 712 records had been input to the master file using the Intermediate Serial Record, a specifically designed form used to provide copy for the keypunch operators. Each record contained the location, call number, title, holdings statement, and inclusive dates for printing on the complete holdings list. In addition, the records contained information necessary for checking in and producing other lists. Other data elements included the date of subscription, currency of the serial, serial identification number, number of issues per volume, number of issues per year, regularity of appearance, latest continuous issue number, and a mnemonic title.

The production schedule for a complete holdings list was projected as every other month, but the list has, in fact, been produced every month since 1964.

In the past, current receipts lists were typed daily from alphabetized piles of periodicals. With the advent of automated check-in, it became apparent that receipt lists could be produced daily or as needed as a by-product of the updating procedures and could be issued in cumulative form as supplements to the complete holdings lists. Using the data elements input for each record, the computer produced punched IBM cards for each issue expected. Each card contained the call number, location, serial identification number, claims agent, code indicating shelving or special handling, issue designation and date, and a shortened version of the title (mnemonic). As an issue arrived, the card for it was pulled and used to produce the current receipts lists. At the end of the month, the card was used to update the master tape. Provision was also made for keypunching cards for those items which were received but not predicted.

In the early stages of development, continuous feedback was solicited and received from the check-in staff, and improvements were made as the system evolved and as additional programs were written. Refinements implemented in 1964 produced more sophisticated lists and instituted the bindery lists and cards. The bindery lists aided staff in pulling materials from the shelves for binding, and the cards served as input to the computer program, causing the appropriate completed, unbound volumes to be shown as bound in the holdings statement.

By 1968 the growth in activity of the system and hardware changes at the Computer Center had caused original provisions of the system to become inadequate, and the need for changes became apparent. By then there were over 17,000 entries in the master file, and the limit of 4,000 updates per month originally considered sufficient had been surpassed. To accommodate these larger regular monthly updates the bindery list and card system had to be deactivated, and a two-pass update was instituted. The increased volume made the process of interfiling the new monthly update cards with those remaining from the previous month extremely difficult and time-consuming. In addition, this increased activity, coupled with normal staff turnover, made the use of mnemonic titles in the check-in process more difficult. It became apparent that full titles were needed for checking in because the file grew so fast that the mnemonics could not be learned. These problems were compounded by a lack of programming maintenance due to sketchy documentation and insufficient programmer time available from the Computer Center. As a final impetus for change, about this time the Computer Center announced it was converting administrative and library applications from the CDC 3600 computer to the RCA Spectra 70 Model 45 and that as a result complete reprogramming would be required.[3]

Reprogramming for the new computer provided the opportunity for correcting the immediate problems and expanding and enhancing capabilities. By then the library had established its own systems department and hired a programmer who could begin the job of converting to the new equipment. Major changes in view included gradual decentralization of the check-in function to speed processing of received issues in the branch libraries, institution of full-title check-in lists, which included a newly developed twelve-month calendar showing actual arrival times of issues to assist in claiming, and the capability of handling a larger quantity of updates. A year after the RCA Spectra 70 Model 45 was installed, it was removed with only six weeks' notice. Those programs which had been converted were temporarily run on a commercially owned RCA Spectra 70 at an off-campus site.[4]

In May 1971, a Burroughs B6500 computer became operational at the Computer Center. Its larger memory, improved file handling, and more useful programming languages were extremely important in developing the current programs.[5] Since that time, the computer system has been upgraded twice. In 1972 the B6500 was replaced by a B6700, and in August 1979 a B7805 was installed. There has now been a period of stabiity, allowing time for refinements and continuous development of the serials system without the necessity of complete reprogramming.

The current UCSD serials system, like the preceding versions, is a batch system. However, IBM card files have given way to direct input via computer terminals. The basic programs are in COBOL, while some of the auxiliary programs utilize PL/I and ALGOL programming languages.

There are three major files in the system: the serials master file, the transaction file, and the edit file. These three files are stored on magnetic tape, freeing large disk areas for other uses and saving the cost of disk space rental. The serials master file contains nearly 45,000 fixed-length, blocked records. Each record is 480 characters long and consists of a fixed field and a variable field. The fixed field has codes which denote:

1. Active or inactive status of the title
2. Serial identification number (a unique number assigned to each new entry by the computer)
3. Issues per volume/volumes per year
4. Issues per year
5. Cancellation code
6. Regularity (reflection of the publication pattern of the serial)
7. Library location
8. Location in library
9. Fund
10. Status (how the serial is obtained)
11. Document (whether or not the entry is a government document)
12. Continuous issue number
13. Source
14. Claim (whether or not the normal claim procedures are to be followed)
15. Bindery data
16. Suppress (suppression of certain program functions for a record)

The variable field consists of the entry, call number, a miscellaneous field used to record the International Standard Serial Number (ISSN) and/or the OCLC number, detailed holdings information, inclusive years, and an information field which contains notes for both public lists and expected arrivals or transaction lists. Not all information is required for each record, but certain basic elements must be present for each entry.

The transaction file, about half the size of the master file, contains variable-length records composed of small fixed-length segments which are used as needed. This file contains some elements of the master file and additional data elements required to predict and record issues as they arrive. It is accessed repeatedly during the update process.

The third major file, the edit file, contains variable-length records which are packed into a fixed-length block until the next record will not fit. It contains records from the master file reformatted for production of public holdings lists.[6]

The system consists of three subsystems:

1. Receiving: this subsystem records the arrival of serials issues in the library.
2. Updating: this subsystem maintains a current record of serials held by the library, including location and holdings.
3. Printing: this subsystem produces printed and microfiche lists of serials for users and staff of the library.[7]

From the newly updated master file and the last updated transaction file, a new transaction file is produced. Serials are checked in using an expected arrivals or transaction list (Example 1) which is produced from the transaction file. Each of six check-in stations has its own list. Transaction numbers are assigned to each predicted issue. The list is marked as each issue arrives, and the transaction numbers are later keyed at a terminal to create a receipts file (Example 2). Issue information may be changed by keying the correct information following the transaction number. Unexpected arrivals are input using the serial identification number followed by the issue information. Methods have also been devised for recording notes or comments, indicating a claimed issue, binding a complete volume, and removing a prediction or comment. Each week the receipts files are run against the transaction file, received issues are flagged, comments are added, and a cumulative receipts list is generated for each of the libraries in the system. At the end of the update cycle, a file of received issue data is created for transfer to the updating subsystem. When a new master file has been produced, new active records are programmatically added to the transaction file, deactivated and deleted records are removed, and a new transaction list with the latest predictions is printed for use in checking in.

In addition to producing the transaction lists and cumulative receipts lists, the receiving subsystem programs can be used to generate lists of issues claimed and lists of those issues predicted before a given date but still not received. Another option allows the production of a missing issues or want list for aid in filling in holdings.

The updating subsystem consists of manual and automated procedures necessary to create, change, and update master records. As new titles are catalogued,

06999   ACADEMIA ESPANOLA.MADRID.BOLETIN.   .   .   .   .   .   .   .   .   .   .   .   .   .   PC4008          --1--1--1
GB  S                                                                                           A3              C5B 39  5 X2
            C.U.L.   PC4008   A3                                                                                 0303   3+
                                       900113  U61N222.APR1981                                   061981

39820   ACADEMIA ESPANOLA.MADRID.BOLETIN.ANEJO.   .   .   .   .   .   .   .   .   .   .   .   .   XXX
GT  O                                                                                                            ───────── ASX
            NOTE- HOLD UNREC.SAE S171Q                                                                           0000   X+
            C.U.L.  XXX

33349   ACADEMIA NACIONAL DE LA HISTORIA.BUENOS AIRES.BOLETIN.   .   .   .   .   .   .   .   .   F2801
GA  O                                                                                           A22                        G9
            C.U.L.   F2801   A22                                                                                 ───────── 
                                       900114  B48.       1975              101976              0001   V+
                                       900115  ADGT CHG W/51                101980
                                       900116  B51.       1977              011982
                                       900117  U51.       1977              021982

01803   ACADEMIA NACIONAL DE LA HISTORIA.CARACAS.BOLETIN   .   .   .   .   .   .   .   .   .   .   F2301          --1--1--1
GB  G                                                                                             A15            9 A3 28
            C.U.L.   F2301   A15                                                                                 0404   3+
                                       900118  U63N251.SEP1980                101980
                                       900119  U63N253.MAR1981                091981

23941   ACADEMIA SINICA(FOUNDED 1927).INSTITUTE OF ETHNOLOGY.BULLETIN.   .   .   .   .   .   .   DS730
GA  E                                                                                           C47              ─────────
            C.U.L.   DS730   C47                                                                                 0000   V+
                                       900120  U33.      1971                061973  .X

30738   ACADEMIA SINICA(FOUNDED 1927).INSTITUTE OF ETHNOLOGY.MONOGRAPH.   .   .   .   .   .   .   DS730
GX  E                                                                                            C472            ─────────
            C.U.L.   DS730   C472                                                                                0000   C+
                                       900121  B20.      1970                031973  .X
                                       900122  B23.      1974                121980

30739   ACADEMIA SINICA(FOUNDED 1927).INSTITUTE OF ETHNOLOGY.MONOGRAPH SERIES B.   .   .   .   .   DS730
GX  E                                                                                             C472B          ─────────
            C.U.L.   DS730   C472B                                                                               0000   C+
                                       900123  B5.       1970                121972  .X

EXAMPLE 1: Transaction List

EXAMPLE 2.  Receipts Disk File

```
L  GEATRANS/AE/RECD8002
#FILE (LB8)GEATRANS/AE/RECD8002 ON ADMINPACK
100   99995 TANK LOCATION A-E 800130
200  900002
300  900003PUL
400  900019
500  900035
600   39430U58N11,NOV1979
700  900074
800   07786U176N2,AUG1979
900  900101
1000  900119U289N4,17SEP1979
1100  900120U289N5,24SEP1979
1200   48604U289N5,24SEP1979
1300   48604U289N4,17SEP1979
1400  900153
1500  900154
1600  900204XXX
1700   16958S5U65N1-2, 1979
1800   4193U1980N88,JAN1980
1900  900237
2000   39827U6N12,DEC1979
2100  900278
2200  900285
2300  900345
2400   00008U34N102, 1979
2500  900372
2600   04274U51N2,DEC1979
2700  900437
2800  900563
2900  900617
3000  900618
3100  900708
3200  900722
3300  900766
3400  900767
3500  900780
3600  900796
3700  900873PUL
3800  900874PUL
3900  900918
4000  900928
4100   17961U96, 1979
4200  900965
4300  900966PUL
4400   45640U43N2, 1978
4500  901060PUL
4600  901063
#
```

the appropriate data are keyed from source documents into the computer at terminals by staff in the individual cataloguing units to create a disk files of input data (Example 3). Corrections are made by using individual field and subfield identifiers. These records can be input directly as the new titles are (Example 4), but they are generally hand-written or typed onto a Serials Data Entry Form (Example 5) and forwarded to the computer center for keying. At the end of the update cycle, disk files of new titles and corrections are brought

EXAMPLE 3. New Titles Disk File

```
L NT/JANLOCK/GEAJP 9200-13500
#FILE (LB8)NT/JANLOCK/GEAJP ON ADMINPACK
9200  ##T=LIBRARY OF CONGRESS,LIBRARY OF CONGRESS OFFICE,NAIROBI.ACCESSIONS
9300 LIST,EAST AFRICA#
9400  C=Z3516L5#
9500  H=U14N1-2,(1981-APR1981)#
9600  M=N:0090-371X[A],OC:2403577#
9700  F=(+)F(0606)R(1)L(GB.F)D(O)#
9800  ##T=ACCESSIONS LIST,EASTERN AFRICA#
9900  Z=SEE LIBRARY OF CONGRESS,LIBRARY OF CONGRESS OFFICE,NAIROBI.ACCESSIONS
10000 LIST,EASTERN AFRICA#
10100 F=L(G)#
10200 ##T=CREDITWEEK#
10300 Z=SEE STANDARD AND POOR'S CREDITWEEK#
10400 F=L(G)#
10500 ##T=STANDARD AND POOR''S CORPORATION.CREDITWEEK#
10600 Z=SEE STANDARD AND POOR'S CREDITWEEK#
10700 F=L(G)#
10800 ##T=STANDARD AND POOR''S CREDITWEEK#
10900 C=REFHG4501S766#
11000 M=OC:7910037#
11100 Z=HOLDINGS UNRECORDED.PLEASE SEE SHELVES.CONTINUES STANDARD AND POOR'S
11200 FIXED INCOME INVESTOR WITH NOV.2,1981.INCLUDES SUPPLEMENT,CREDITWATCH
11300 AND INDEXES.LIBRARY RETAINS CURRENT TWO YEARS ONLY/RET LAT 2 YRS ONLY
11400 HOLD UNREC#
11400 HOLD UNREC#
11500 F=(+)F(0152)R(X)L(GCDS)D(O)S(Z9)#
11600 ##T=FIXED INCOME INVESTOR#
11700 Z=SEE STANDARD AND POOR'S FIXED INCOME INVESTOR#
11800 F=L(G)#
11900 ##T=FOLKLORE BIBLIOGRAPHY#
12000 C=REFGR66(Z)F6#
12100 H=B1973-1976,(1973-...1976)#
12200 M=N:0272-8494[A],OC:6346982#
12300 F=(+)F(0001)R(C)L(GCDO)D(O)S(W5X)#
12400 ##T=SIMMONS,MERLE EDWIN,1918- .FOLKLORE BIBLIOGRAPHY#
12500 Z=SEE FOLKLORE BIBLIOGRAPHY#
12600 F=L(G)#
12700 ##T=FOLK LORE#
12800 Z=FOR TITLES BEGINNING WITH THESE WORDS,SEE ALSO FOLKLORE#
12900 F=$(GA)#
13000 ##T=ORGANISATION FOR ECONOMIC CO-OPERATION AND DEVELOPMENT.CATALOGUE
13050 OF PUBLICATIONS#
13100 C=REFHC24107622(Z)#
13200 H=B1965-1980,(1965-...1980)#
13300 I=MICROFORM EDITION.CONTINUES ITS GENERAL CATALOGUE OF PUBLICATIONS
13400 WITH 1965#
13500 F=L(GC)D(O)#
#
```

together. Three programs assist in editing the data and preparing it for input to the updating process.

Three programs run simultaneously to update the master file. New titles are added, corrections are made to existing titles, and received issues are processed and added to the holdings. A file of completed volumes is generated during the update run, from which a list and punched cards are produced to aid in binding and updating the holdings in the master record to reflect changes to bound status.

Once a new master file is created, the printing subsystem transforms that information into more usable forms. Master lists (Example 6), for staff use, and public lists (Example 7), housed at reference desks, are produced on microfiche. As mentioned earlier, new transaction lists are printed (Example 1). In addition, individual branch lists (Example 8) are produced which contain records for serials held in one or more branches. These are distributed to various locations. In order to hold costs down, and for convenience, printed lists are

EXAMPLE 4. Corrections Disk File

```
L COR/JANLOCK/GEACT
#FILE (LB8)COR/JANLOCK/GEACT ON ADMINPACK
100 ##40503  EXTRA VERSE   (CUL)
200 C=PR1170E9#
300 M=N:0531-6243,OC:3250143#
400 Z=U15-17,(1965-...1966)#
500 F=L(GF)D(O)#
600 ##28619  ENVIRONMENT AND PLANNING   (CUL)
700 C=HT166E55#
800 M=N:0013-9173,OC:1568066#
900 I=SPLIT INTO ENVIRONMENT AND PLANNING A WITH VOL.6,1974 AND ENVIRONMENT
1000 AND PLANNING B WITH VOL.1,JUNE 1974#
1100 F=L(GA)#
1200 ##40109  NOUVELLE CRITIQUE   (CUL)
1300 M=N:0048-0967,OC:2620165#
1400 H=S1B73-74,S2B70-92,S2U93,S2B94-129,S2U130,(#
1500 I=ISSUED IN SERIES,SER.1,NO.1-181,DEC.1948-JAN.1967,NOUVELLE SERIE
1600 (SER.2),NO.1-130,FEB.1967-JAN//FEB.1980.CONTINUED BY REVOLUTION
1700 (PARIS,FRANCE:1980)IN MAR.1980#
1800 Y=1956-FEB1980#
1900 F=L(GA)D(O)#
2000 ##49156  URBAN DESIGN   (CUL)
2100 C=NA9000D4#
2200 M=N:0267-0339[A],OC:2826437#
2300 I="CONTINUED BY URBAN DESIGN NEWSLETTER IN JUNE 1979"51>#
2400 F=L(GA)#
2500 ##31172   (CUL)
2600 T=DESIGN AND ENVIRONMENT#
2700 C=NA9000D4#
2800 M=N:0011-930X[A],OC:877104#
2900 H=B1-7,(#
2950 Y=1970-OCT1976#
3000 I=CONTINUED BY URBAN DESIGN WITH VOL.7,NO.4,1976#
3100 F=L(GA)#
3200 ##38222  MUSIC AND MAN   (CUL)
3300 I=CONTINUED BY JOURNAL OF MUSICOLOGICAL RESEARCH WITH VOL.3,OCT.1979#
3400 M=N:0306-2082[A],OC:1794039#
3500 ##33627  EMILY DICKINSON BULLETIN   (CUL)
3600 C=PS1541Z5E4#
3700 M=N:0046-1881,OC:1912461#
3800 H=B1-33,#
3900 I="CONTINUED BY DICKINSON STUDIES WTIH NO.34"38#
4000 Y=1968-JUN1978#
4100 F=L(GA)#
4200 ##58193  SOCIOLOGY OF LEISURE AND SPORT ABSTRACTS   (CUL)
4300 C=REFGV1(Z)S6#
4400 ##07841  COLLEGE ENTRANCE EXAMINATION BOARD.COLLEGE HANDBOOK   (CUL)
4500 D=DELETE#
#
```

journal d'urologie et de mephrologie        ew 6/23/80

Serials Data Entry Form

# #  02404  f= (=) f(.) r(.) ℓ(ms) s(.)#     (deactivate)

i=,continues journal d'urologie medicale ét

chirurgicale with vol.67,1961.supplements accompany

some issues.continued by journal d'urologie#  (change note)

m=η:0021-8200#          (add issn)

LS 6 (Rev. 9/77)

UCSD Libr.

EXAMPLE 5.  Serials Data Entry Form

```
ABDOMINAL SURGERY. SEE JOURNAL OF ABDOMINAL SURGERY$
  21002 (UNIV HOSP)                          <M> $        <C> $        <Z> *

ABERDEEN PHILOSOPHICAL SOCIETY TRANSACTIONS$
  51422 (CUL)
  = FREQ:F( )   REG:R( )   LIB/LOC/FUND/STATUS:L(GA    <C> AS122A3$   HNDLG:H( )   <H/Y> .B1-4.(1840-  1910)*   CONTIS:C( )
    SRC/CLM:S( )      CAN:N( )        BIND:B( )          SUPPL/TP/IDX/TC:I( )   DOC:D( )        SPECCD:X( )   (113)

ABERDEEN UNIVERSITY STUDIES$
  55017 (SID)
  = FREQ:F( )   REG:R( )   LIB/LOC/FUND/STATUS:L(IIT   <C> XXX$       HNDLG:H( )   <H/Y> .B41.B154.(1906-  1978)*   CONTIS:C( )
    SRC/CLM:S( )      CAN:N( )        BIND:B( )          SUPPL/TP/IDX/TC:I( )   DOC:D(O)        SPECCD:X( )   ( 97)

ABERTURA CULTURAL$
  48757 (CUL)                                <C> F45$   <M> $   <Z> HOLDINGS UNRECORDED.PLEASE SEE SHELVES*
  = FREQ:F( )   REG:R( )   LIB/LOC/FUND/STATUS:L(GR )  HNDLG:H( )                               CONTIS:C( )
    SRC/CLM:S( )      CAN:N( )        BIND:B( )          SUPPL/TP/IDX/TC:I( )   DOC:D(O)        SPECCD:X( )   (102)

ABHANDLUNGEN AUS DEM GEBIET DER AUSLANDSKUNDES
  24540 (CUL)   .B53.B64.B71.B74.(1922-  1975)  <I>.SUPERSEDES HAMBURG KOLONIAL INSTITUT ABHANDLUNGEN ALSO NUMBERED IN VA
                RIOUS SUBSERIES.ATLAS FOR VOL.23 SHELVED IN EXTRA OVERSIZE/IP S675*
  = FREQ:R( )   REG:R( )   LIB/LOC/FUND/STATUS:L(GA )  <C> AS182H31$   <M> $   <H/Y> .B10-11.B14.B16.B23.B25.B41.B46   HNDLG:H( )
    SRC/CLM:S( )      CAN:N( )        BIND:B( )          SUPPL/TP/IDX/TC:I( )   DOC:D(O)        SPECCD:X( )   (294)

ABHANDLUNGEN AUS DER GEBURTSHUELFE UND GYNAEKOLOGIE UND IHREN GRENZGEBIETEN$
  29847 (BIOMED)   <H/Y> .B1-5.B7.(1927  1936)  <I>.SUPPLEMENT TO MONATSSCHRIFT FUER GEBURTSHUELFE UND GYNAEKOLOGIE.CONTINUED BY BI
                BLIOTHECA GYNAECOLOGICA WITH VOL.8,1948*                      <C> W1AB367/GY$   <M> $
  = FREQ:F( )   REG:R( )   LIB/LOC/FUND/STATUS:L(MA )  HNDLG:H( )                DOC:D(O)        CONTIS:C( )
    SRC/CLM:S( )      CAN:N( )        BIND:B( )          SUPPL/TP/IDX/TC:I( )                   SPECCD:X( )   (270)

ABHANDLUNGEN DER AKADEMIE DER WISSENSCHAFTEN IN GOETTINGEN,PHILOLOGISCH-HISTORISCHE KLASSE$
  56888 (CUL)   <M> OC.14787I3$   <H/Y> .S2B1-25.S3B1-12.S3B15-19.S3B21.S3B23-24.S3B33.S3B35-36.S3B41-42.S3B46.S3B49.S3B58-59.S3B66   <C> AS182A311$
                .S3B70.S3B74-106.S3U107-118.S3U121.(1896-  1981)  OL.1,1932-SUPERSEDES.IN PART SOCIETY'S ABHANDLUNGEN/IP S265V.ISSUED IN SERIES.SER.2.VOL.1-25.1896-1931.SER.3.V
  + FREQ:F(OOOO)  REG:R(V)  LIB/LOC/FUND/STATUS:L(GXDO) HNDLG:H( )               DOC:D(O)        CONTIS:C( )
    SRC/CLM:S(IADX)   CAN:N( )        BIND:B( )          SUPPL/TP/IDX/TC:I( )                   SPECCD:X( )   (402)

ABHANDLUNGEN EINER PRIVAT GESELLSCHAFT IN BOEHMEN SEE CESKA SPOLECNOST NAUK.PRAGUE.ABHANDLUNGEN$
  31358 (CUL)                                <C> XXX$                           <M> $        <Z> *           <C> $

ABHANDLUNGEN FUER DIE KUNDE DES MORGANLANDES$
  27888 (CUL)   <C> PJ5A2$   <I>./I.P.S325V*    <M> $        <H/Y> .B1-42.U43.U43.B43P1.B43P3-4.U44N2.
  + FREQ:F(O4O4)  REG:R(2)  LIB/LOC/FUND/STATUS:L(GXDO) HNDLG:H( )               DOC:D(O)        CONTIS:C( )
    SRC/CLM:S(IADX)   CAN:N( )        BIND:B( )          SUPPL/TP/IDX/TC:I( )                   SPECCD:X( )   (176)
                B44P3-4.U45N1-2.U45N4.U46N2.(1857-  1981)

ABHANDLUNGEN FUER DIE KUNDE DES MORGANLANDES$
  27889 (CUL)   <C> PJ5A2C.2$   <M> $   <H/Y> .U1N2.U2N3-4.U6N3.U9N2.U15N2.U1
                9N3.U22N3.U23N6.U25N1.U25N4.B30.U32N2.U35N3.B43P1-2N4.B44P1.(1857-  1964)*
  = FREQ:F( )   REG:R( )   LIB/LOC/FUND/STATUS:L(GX )  HNDLG:H( )                DOC:D(O)        CONTIS:C( )
    SRC/CLM:S(IADX)   CAN:N( )        BIND:B( )          SUPPL/TP/IDX/TC:I( )                   SPECCD:X( )   (200)

ABHANDLUNGEN DEN WIRTSCHAFTLICHEN STAATSWISSENSCHAFTEN$
  39816 (CUL)                                <C> XXX$                           <M> $        <H/Y> STO WITH N2-.(1970-
  + FREQ:F(OOO)   REG:R(X)   <Z>./HOLD UNREC.SAE SO12T*  HNDLG:H( )              DOC:D(O)        CONTIS:C( )
    SRC/CLM:S(IADX)   CAN:N( )   LIB/LOC/FUND/STATUS:L(GTDO)  SUPPL/TP/IDX/TC:I( )              SPECCD:X(H)   (153)
```

EXAMPLE 6. Master Format Microfiche

EXAMPLE 7.  Public Format Microfiche

S I 0

A.A.A.R.E.SCIENTIFIC REPORTS.

SEE AUSTRALIAN NATIONAL ANTARCTIC
RESEARCH EXPEDITIONS.PUBLICATION.


S & E
Q                A.A.A.S.BULLETIN.                              STACKS
1                   1942-MAY1974 (LIBRARY MAY NOT HAVE
A111             ALL YEARS)--LIBRARY HAS:
                 B1-5, U6N1-2, U6N4, U7N1-3, U8N2-4,
                 U9, U10N1, U10N3-4, U11-18, U19N1-3.

                 NOTE: SUSPENDED WITH VOL.19NO.3,1974.


S I 0
S10              A.A.A.S.BULLETIN.                              STACKS
1                   1961-SEP1974 (LIBRARY MAY NOT HAVE
A26              ALL YEARS)--LIBRARY HAS:
                 B6-16, U17-18, U19N1-3.

                 NOTE: CEASED WITH VOL.19,NO.3,SEP1974.
                 VOLS.14-16 IN OVERSIZE.


BIOMED
                 A.A.A.S.SCIENCE BOOKS AND FILMS.

                 SEE SCIENCE BOOKS AND FILMS.


CENTRAL
MICRO            A.A.COMMUNE.                                   MICROFORM
F
45                  NOTE: HOLDINGS UNRECORDED,FOR HOLDINGS
                 SEE SHELVES.


CENTRAL
Z                A.A.L.L.INSTITUTE FOR LAW LIBRARIANS.          ALL VOLUMES
675              PROCEEDINGS.                                   ON FLOOR 6
L2                  1959-1963 (LIBRARY MAY NOT HAVE ALL         (ANALYZED)
A3               YEARS)--LIBRARY HAS:
                 B4-6.

                 NOTE: VOLS.FOR 2 EARLIER INSTITUTES
                 1937-38 AND THE FIRST 3 HELD AFTER ITS
                 PROGRAM WAS REACTIVATED IN 1953 WERE
                 NOT PUBLISHED BUT APPEARED IN LAW
                 LIBRARY JOURNAL.NOS.4-6 ALSO ISSUED IN
                 A.A.A.L.PUBLICATIONS SERIES AS NO.1,3,
                 7.EACH VOL.HAS ALSO A DISTINCTIVE
                 TITLE.

EXAMPLE 8. Branch List

REF
767Z
A2
ABORTION BIBLIOGRAPHY.
1970-1978 (LIBRARY MAY NOT HAVE ALL YEARS)--LIBRARY HAS:
B1970--1978.
+ REFERENCE

HQ
767
A23
ABORTION RESEARCH NOTES.
1978-1981 (LIBRARY MAY NOT HAVE ALL YEARS)--LIBRARY HAS:
U7N1-2, U8, U9N1-4, U10N1-2.
+ B=BOUND VOLS ON FLOOR 6 U=UNBOUND ON FLOOR 2-MAIN

MICRO
F
45
ABOUT FACE.
1969-JUL1969 (LIBRARY MAY NOT HAVE ALL YEARS)--LIBRARY HAS:
B1P1-5.
MICROFORM

ML
5
A22
ABOUT THE HOUSE.
1962-1976 (LIBRARY MAY NOT HAVE ALL YEARS)--LIBRARY HAS:
B1P1-5, B1P3-7, B1P10-11, B2P1-2, B3P4-5, B2P8-11, B3P1-5, B3P7-8, B3P10-12, B4.
ALL VOLUMES ON FLOOR 4

SP COLL
AP
2
A241
ABOVE GROUND REVIEW
1970-1972 (LIBRARY MAY NOT HAVE ALL YEARS)--LIBRARY HAS:
U2, U3N1.
SPECIAL COLLECTIONS

PJ
3001
A2
ABR-NAHRAIN
1955-1976 (LIBRARY MAY NOT HAVE ALL YEARS)--LIBRARY HAS:
B1-16.
ALL VOLUMES ON FLOOR 7

SP COLL
PS
580
A3
ABRAXAS(MADISON,WIS).
1980-1981 (LIBRARY MAY NOT HAVE ALL YEARS)--LIBRARY HAS:
U1-7, U9-12, J20.
NOTE: LIBRARY HAS INDEX TO NOS.1-10 INCLUDED IN NO.10.
SPECIAL COLLECTIONS

B
1
A42
ABRAXAS,SOUTHAMPTON,NEW YORK
1970-1971 (LIBRARY MAY NOT HAVE ALL YEARS)--LIBRARY HAS:
B1P1, B1P3.
NOTE: SUSPENDED WITH VOL.1,NO.3. APR1971.
B=BOUND VOLS ON FLOOR 5 U=UNBOUND ON FLOOR 2-MAIN

REF
DK
266
A2
A2
ABSEES.
1970-JAN1981 (LIBRARY MAY NOT HAVE ALL YEARS)--LIBRARY HAS:
B1-8, U9N1-2, U10, U11N1-2.
NOTE: SUPERSEDES SOVIET STUDIES INFORMATION SUPPLEMENT AND IS ALSO CALLED NO.27- IN CONTINUATION OF ITS NUMBERING.NOS.1-4 ARBITRARILY CALLED VOL.1-BEGINNING WITH VOL.2.INCLUDES AS A SUPPLEMENT SOVIET EUROPEAN AND SLAVONIC STUDIES IN BRITAIN,WHICH IS CATALOGED SEPARATELY.VOL.8,1977- INCLUDE MICROFICHE IN POCKETS.
+ REFERENCE

REF
HV
40Z
A2
ABSTRACTS FOR SOCIAL WORKERS.
1965-MAR1977 (LIBRARY MAY NOT HAVE ALL YEARS)--LIBRARY HAS:
B1-12, B13P1-.
NOTE: CONTINUED BY SOCIAL WORK RESEARCH AND ABSTRACTS WITH VOL.13,NO.2,SUMMER 1977.
REFERENCE

REF
GN
A13
ABSTRACTS IN ANTHROPOLOGY.
1970-1981 (LIBRARY MAY NOT HAVE ALL YEARS)--LIBRARY HAS:
B1-4, U5, B6-7, U8.
+ REFERENCE

REF
GN
1
A134
ABSTRACTS IN GERMAN ANTHROPOLOGY.
1980-1980 (LIBRARY MAY NOT HAVE ALL YEARS)--LIBRARY HAS:
U1.
REFERENCE

GN
281
A2
ABSTRACTS IN HUMAN EVOLUTION.
1975-1976 (LIBRARY MAY NOT HAVE ALL YEARS)--LIBRARY HAS:
B1.
NOTE: CEASED WITH VOL.1,NO.6,1976.
ALL VOLUMES ON FLOOR 6

AS
343
S693
A2
ABSTRACTS OF BULGARIAN SCIENTIFIC LITERATURE.PHILOSOPHY,PSYCHOLOGY AND PEDAGOGICS.
1963-1968 (LIBRARY MAY NOT HAVE ALL YEARS)--LIBRARY HAS:
U6N2-, B7, U8N2, U9, B10, U11N2, B12-18.
NOTE: TITLE VARIES ISSUING AGENCY VARIES.
B=BOUND VOLS ON FLOOR 5 U=UNBOUND ON FLOOR 2-MAIN

AS
343
S693
A2
ABSTRACTS OF BULGARIAN SCIENTIFIC LITERATURE.PHILOSOPHY.SOCIOLOGY. SCIENCE OF SCIENCE.PSYCHOLOGY AND PEDAGOGICS.
1970-1978 (LIBRARY MAY NOT HAVE ALL YEARS)--LIBRARY HAS:
B13-21.
NOTE: CONTINUES ABSTRACTS OF BULGARIAN SCIENTIFIC LITERATURE.PHILOSOPHY AND PSYCHOLOGY AND PEDAGOGICS WITH VOL.13, 1970.
* LATEST ISSUES UNDERGOING TECHNICAL PROCESSING.
ALL VOLUMES ON FLOOR 5

ABSTRACTS OF BULGARIAN SCIENTIFIC LITERATURE.PHILOSOPHY AND PEDAGOGICS.
SEE ABSTRACTS OF BULGARIAN SCIENTIFIC LITERATURE.PHILOSOPHY.PSYCHOLOGY AND PEDAGOGICS.

REF
GN
A14
ABSTRACTS OF DOCTORAL DISSERTATIONS IN ANTHROPOLOGY (LIBRARY MAY NOT HAVE ALL YEARS)--LIBRARY HAS:
B1969-1971.
* * REFERENCE

* * NOTE: SEE MICROFICHE FOR COMPLETE LIST OF PERIODICALS IN THE UCSD LIBRARIES * *

EXAMPLE 8. Branch List

KWIC INDEX TO SERIAL TITLES IN THE BIOMEDICAL LIBRARY - JANUARY 1982

| Leading context | Keyword title | Call no. |
|---|---|---|
| ARCHIVES DES INSTITUTS PASTEUR DE L | AFRIQUE DU NORD | W1AR328 |
| SOCIETE MEDICALE D | AFRIQUE NOIRE DE LANGUE FRANCAISE.BULLETIN | W1SO529 |
| INTERNATIONAL UNION | AGAINST CANCER.ACTA | W1IN945 |
| INTERNATIONAL UNION | AGAINST CANCER.BULLETIN | W1IN945B |
| INTERNATIONAL UNION | AGAINST TUBERCULOSIS.BULLETIN | W1IN947 |
|  | AGE | W1AG171 |
|  | AGE AND AGEING | W1AG180 |
| AGE AND | AGEING | W1AG180 |
| MECHANISMS OF | AGEING AND DEVELOPMENT | W1ME104 |
| FEDERAL AVIATION | AGENCY.OFFICE OF AVIATION MEDICINE.AVIATION | W1FE143 |
|  | AGENTS AND ACTIONS | W1AG201.1 |
|  | AGENTS AND ACTIONS SUPPLEMENTS | W1AN956 |
| ANTIMICROBIAL | AGENTS AND CHEMOTHERAPY.ANN ARBOR,MICH,1961-1970 | W1AN957 |
| ANTIMICROBIAL | AGENTS AND CHEMOTHERAPY.WASHINGTON,D.C.1972- | W1AG223 |
|  | AGGIORNAMENTI CLINICOTERAPEUTICI | W1AG493 |
|  | AGGRESSIVE BEHAVIOR | W1AG550 |
| INTERNATIONAL JOURNAL OF | AGING AND HUMAN DEVELOPMENT | W1IN767 |
| NEUROBIOLOGY OF | AGING | W1NE434 |
| EXPERIMENTAL | AGING RESEARCH | W1EX434 |
|  | AGRESSOLOGIE | W1AG804 |
|  | AGRICULTURAL AND BIOLOGICAL CHEMISTRY.TOKYO | W1AG834 |
|  | AGRICULTURAL CHEMICAL SOCIETY OF JAPAN.BULLETIN | W1AG835 |
| CALIFORNIA ATTRIBUTED TO PESTICIDES AND OTHER | AGRICULTURAL CHEMICALS    OCCUPATIONAL DISEASE IN | W1OC217 |
| JOURNAL OF | AGRICULTURAL RESEARCH | W1JO222 |
| BIBLIOGRAPHY OF | AGRICULTURE | ZW1B581 |
| SOTILASLAAAKETIETEELLINEN | AIKAKAUSLEHTI.ANNALES MEDICINAE MILITARIS FENNIAE | W1SO727 |
| INTERNATIONAL JOURNAL OF | AIR AND WATER POLLUTION | W1IN768 |
|  | AIR POLLUTION CONTROL ASSOCIATION.JOURNAL | W1AI450 |
|  | AIR REPAIR | W1AI600 |
| REVUE DES CORPS DE SANTE DES ARMEES.TERRE.MER. | AIR | W1RE886 |
| DE SANTE DES ARMEES DE TERRE.DE MER ET DE L | AIR          REVUE INTERNATIONALE DES SERVICES | W1RE949 |
| MEDICINA.BUENOS | AIRES | W1ME480 |
| OFFICIAL | AIRLINE GUIDE.NORTH AMERICAN EDITION | REFTL720.8031 |
| POMORSKA ... SMIERCZEWSKIEGO.SZCZECIN.ROCZNIK | AKADEMIA MEDYCZNA IM.GENERALA KAROLA | W1PO538 |
| POLSKA | AKADEMIA NAUK.BULLETIN.SERIE DES SCIENCES | W1PO288 |
| POLSKA | AKADEMIA NAUK.WYDZIAL NAUK MEDYCZNYCH ANNALS | W1PO290 |
| POLSKA | AKADEMIA NAUK.WYDZIAL NAUK MEDYCZNYCH.ROZPRAWY | W1PO291 |
| SCHWEIZERISCHE | AKADEMIE DER MEDIZINISCHEN WISSENSCHAFTEN.BULLETIN | W1SC367 |
| DE WIS- EN NATUURKUNDIGE WETENSCHAPPEN.PROCE- | AKADEMIE VAN WETENSCHAPPEN.AMSTERDAM.AFDELING VOOR | W1NE193 |
|  | AKADEMIIA MEDITSINSKIKH NAUK SSSR.MOSCOW.VESTNIK | W1AK190 |
| BULGARSKA | AKADEMIIA NA NAUKITE.INSTITUT PO FIZIOLOGIIA | W1BU257 |
| BULGARSKA | AKADEMIIA NA NAUKITE.MIKROBIOLOGICHESKIIA INSTITUT | W1BU264 |
| SECTIONS | AKADEMIIA NAUK SSSR.DOKLADY.BIOCHEMISTRY SECTION | W1AK383 |
| SECTIONS | AKADEMIIA NAUK SSSR.DOKLADY.BIOLOGICAL SCIENCES | W1AK384 |
|  | AKADEMIIA NAUK SSSR.DOKLADY.BIOPHYSICS SECTION | W1AK385 |
|  | AKADEMIIA NAUK SSSR.DOKLADY.BOTANICAL SCIENCES | W1AK386 |
| DEIATELNOSTI.WORKS.PATHOPHYSIOLOGICAL SERIES | AKADEMIIA NAUK SSSR.INSTITUT VYSSHEI NERVNOI | W1AK456 |
| DEIATELNOSTI.WORKS.PHYSIOLOGICAL SERIES | AKADEMIIA NAUK SSSR.INSTITUT VYSSHEI NERVNOI | W1AK464 |
| BIOLOGICHESKAIA | AKADEMIIA NAUK SSSR.IZVESTIIA.SERIIA | W1AK390 |
| MEDICINSKIH NAUKA.GLAS ... SRPSKA | AKADEMIJA NAUKA I UMETNOSTI.BELGRAD.ODELJENJE | W1SR614 |
|  | AKTUELLE CHIRURGIE | W1AK789 |
|  | AKTUELLE PROBLEME IN DER ANGIOLOGIE | W1AK891 |
| NEUROCHIRURGIE | AKTUELLE PROBLEME IN DER PSYCHIATRIE.NEUROLOGIE. | W1AK893 |

EXAMPLE 9. Keyword List

generated on 8-½ × 11 inch paper directly from tape on the Honeywell Page Printing System through an off-campus vendor (Examples 1 and 8).

Of the nearly 45,000 master records the system is now handling, 35,000 are serial entries (over 15,000 are active) and 10,000 are cross references. Each month approximately 150 new titles are added, 1,000 corrections are processed, and 6,000–8,000 new issues are received. Currently, computer charges, microfiche production, and printing costs are a little over $2,000 per month for a complete cycle of the system.

Another article could be written on the range of auxiliary lists which can be produced from the master file. Vendor lists, branch master lists, gifts and exchange lists, active title lists, lists by specific location in library, and combinations thereof are produced readily by using the fixed-field codes of the master record. Additional programs have been written to extract records with specific data in the variable-field portion of the record. These include LC classification lists, shelflists, and subject lists. Reference librarians find keyword lists (Example 9) of particular value, especially since UCSD's serials cataloguing does not include subject access. In a multi-branch system such as this, the duplicate titles lists help determine how many active orders there are for each title and where they are located. In addition to the programs mentioned above, there is one which converts UCSD master serial records into MARC format for production of the *University of California Union List of Serials*.

Future developments planned include implementation of a feature which programmatically passes missing issue information from the transaction file to the missing issues file. It is hoped that the timely transfer of this information will increase the chance of locating needed issues. Currently, the keyword lists can be produced only on a branch-by-branch basis. With some reprogramming it will be possible to have more flexibility so that a science libraries keyword list can be produced showing the branch location for each individual title. At the present time the location in library code reprsents both shelving locations and special handling instructions. If an item requires both shelving and special handling instructions (e.g., oversized and routed), it is frequently necessary to add an information statement to the transaction list to represent one of the instructions. By developing a fixed-field location and codes for special handling and using the current location in library only for shelving locations, the problem would be solved. In addition, the removal of the information statements would help shorten the variable-field data in many records.

Further in the future there are plans to do more on-line data entry, possibly by moving records to be corrected to a disk file to simulate an on-line situation. There are also plans to upgrade the master records by including more data elements and expanding the length of each record. As the Library grows so does the number of titles which require more than one 480 character record to accommodate the holdings field.

Some of these developments require more than programming. Since the

B7805 was installed, the Computer Center has experienced problems in that peripheral equipment has caused down time, a condition interfering with on-line processing. There have also been some problems with the concentrator through which several of the library's terminals access the computer. Finally, more terminals distributed throughout the library will be needed to implement some of the changes.

Eventually the entire serials system may be subsumed by a total inventory/circulation system in which holdings would be recorded. Bibliographic records would be in the University of California On-line Library Catalog with links between the two systems. UCSD is currently evaluating various acquisitions/book fund accounting systems which could provide another link in the chain.

On a broader scale the University of California's Division of Library Automation has produced regular editions of the *University of California Union List of Serials* since 1976. The 1979 microfiche edition includes 502,000 serial records representing 322,400 titles in machine-readable form contributed by the nine campuses of the University of California and nineteen campuses of the California State University and Colleges. The list is a Key Term Index in Key Word Out of Context (KWOC) format. The 1980 edition in preparation will be entitled *California Academic Libraries List of Serials* and will include, in addition to records from those campuses already mentioned, the serial records from Stanford University. Negotiations are underway for inclusion of records from the University of Southern California in the 1981 edition.

The Division of Library Automation is currently designing a user-friendly interface for the planned University of California On-line Library Catalog. This bibliographic data base for the University of California will eventually include the serial records from the file described above and monographic records from the nine UC campuses.

## REFERENCES

1. Vdovin, George, et al., "Computer Processing of Serial Records," *Library Resources & Technical Services* 7, no. 1 (Winter 1963):71–80.

2. See note 1.

3. Bosseau, Don L., "The University of California at San Diego Serials System—Past, Present and Future" (a paper presented at the University of Oregon Workshop on Library Automation, July 16, 1968).

4. Bosseau, Don L., "The University of California at San Diego Serials System—Revisited," *Program* 4, no. 1 (January 1970):1–29.

5. Balch, Earl, "Serials Processing System Reference Manual," *The Larc Reports* 5, no. 3 (1972).

6. See note 5.

7. See note 5.

# AUTOMATED SERIAL RECORDS IN THE ON-LINE CATALOG: THE NORTHWESTERN LUIS SYSTEM

William J. Willmering

ABSTRACT. On-line catalogs should be able to provide more data for serials than was possible with catalogs in card format because an electronic file can be updated instantaneously and manipulated rapidly. If constructed as an integrated file, it can bring more data to the catalog than was possible with card format. The Northwestern University Library LUIS serial display described here demonstrates how the bibliographic, holdings, and location function of a catalog may be enhanced through use of an electronic medium.

How and where to display serial holdings for public use has always been a major concern for serial librarians. Ideally, holdings should be integrated with the bibliographic description of serials because, unlike a monograph search, a search for a serial must not only answer what titles the library has, but also what volumes it owns. Historically, even those libraries which integrated the catalog for serials with the catalog for monographs usually were not able to list holdings at all access points in their catalog; often holdings appeared only on the main entry or the shelf list. During the publication explosion of the last two decades, even this practice was frequently abandoned as impractical. Users were referred from the catalog to a separate serial list. This expedient—to reduce the librarian's work—made the user's search longer because often two sources had to be consulted to complete a search.

With the advent of on-line catalogs, it becomes possible, as never before, to integrate the bibliographic and holdings functions of a catalog. Unlike a file of paper records, an electronic file can be updated rapidly, displayed immediately, even at remote locations. An electronic file can gather data from separate files into one display and can provide this display at all access points. Combining the bibliographic and holdings functions of a catalog will be a major benefit of an on-line catalog.[1]

LUIS (Library User Information System), a public use version of the Northwestern University Library's NOTIS (Northwestern On-line Total Integrated System), provides both bibliographic and volume holdings data for all serial titles, both active and dead, at all access points. A modular automated serials system, developed first for acquisitions and cataloguing, now interfaces with the LUIS on-line catalog. Because the NOTIS serials subsystem combines the bibliographic, holdings, and order data in one system, it makes possible the complete display of both bibliographic data and volume holdings. It now gives bound holdings in the shelflist tradition and will soon give current issue receipts, a service impossible with a paper catalog.

From the beginning of its development in 1970, the automated serial records in the NOTIS serials subsystem were available to anyone with access to a NOTIS terminal. In reality, the first version of the system, NOTIS-2, was not generally available to the public, or even to nontechnical service librarians, because the limited numbers of terminals and the single access point by key search code based on main entry made searching difficult.[2]

In 1977 Northwestern implemented its NOTIS-3 system. This development, together with a wider distribution of terminals in public service areas, increased the use of the automated serial records by nontechnical service staff. The NOTIS-3 system's index, based on full word strings, and giving author and title access from both main and nonsubject added entries, immediately and dramatically increased use in public areas. Skill at constructing complex search keys from main entries derived from a variety of complex and changing cataloguing rules no longer was a prerequisite for access.[3]

With the problem of access solved, the next apparent problem was how to integrate the various components of the serial record into one comprehensive and coherent screen for the patron version. As the NOTIS-3 system is structured, linked segments sharing the same data, but displaying as different screens, hold bibliographic data, copy and volume holdings, and current orders separately.[4] The answer to this problem of integrating the separate screens is LUIS—a subsystem of NOTIS-3 which draws together a variety of data from the various record components to make a comprehensive, yet concise and readily understood public use display of all the Library's 400,000 on-line records, including some 50,000 serial records.

Access to LUIS is through an index similar in data elements, to that designed for the technical service programs of NOTIS, but with a different display structure. A patron starts with the LUIS constant screen shown in Figure 1. As this screen shows, a user may choose between an author or a title search. If the search argument is specific and there is only one record, the program displays that record. For example, using the title search term: "library resources and technical" results in a display of the title LIBRARY RESOURCES AND TECHNICAL SERVICES, as shown in Figure 2. If the search term if broader, such as "library resources" the program gives an index display as shown in Figure 3. Here the user may select whatever record matches his needs. Secondary terms based on personal or corporate main entry and imprint place for serials or imprint date for monographs help qualify the title for easier identification. If the search should be so broad as to result in more than seventeen index terms, the program goes to a guide display. This is shown in Figure 4. Here the search term "library" results in 380 entries. The guide screen shows

LUIS CATALOG ACCESS BY TITLE OR AUTHOR
This program can be used to find catalog information for most library materials received since 1970 and for all periodicals.

| TO SEARCH BY TITLE: | EXAMPLES: |
|---|---|
| 1. Type t= | t = 158 pound marriage |
| 2. Type title or portion of title; | t = world according to |
| omit: initial article, punctuation, | t = journal of marriage and the fam |
| symbols, accent marks | t = past present NOT past & present |
| 3. Press ENTER and wait for response | t = mr sammlers pl NOT mr. sammler's pl |
| TO SEARCH BY AUTHOR: | EXAMPLES: |
| 1. Type a= | a = eliot thomas s |
| 2. Type author's name or portion of | a = eliot t NOT eliot t s |
| name; last name first; omit | a = ohara NOT o'hara |
| punctuation and accent marks | a = kubler ross NOT kubler-ross |
| 3. Press ENTER and wait for response | a = american psychological assoc |

If you make a mistake, press BACKSPACE and type over the mistake, OR press CLEAR to start over. If you need help, ask a library staff member.

VALID COMMANDS ARE: a t e                    (FOR HELP TYPE ? AND PRESS ENTER)
TYPE YOUR COMMAND:

FIGURE 1

LUIS CATALOG ACCESS T = LIBRARY RESOURCES AND TECHNICAL
      1 ENTRY FOUND—BIBLIOGRAPHIC DISPLAY
Library resources and technical services. v. 1- winter 1957- —Fulton, Mo.
→ COPY IN: main,pr 025.05;L697
      VOLUMES: 1-23(1957-79)
VALID COMMANDS ARE: a t e b                  (FOR HELP TYPE ? AND PRESS ENTER)
TYPE YOUR COMMAND:

FIGURE 2

seventeen intervals within that array. The user then selects the term which most closely precedes the title he wants. The program goes into the index display of those entries, and the user then selects the specific entry he needs. The guide technique differs from the linear index used in technical service applications of NOTIS in order to approximate the browsing capability of a traditional card catalog.

LUIS provides added entry access as well as main entry access. If searched under "american library association," the title LIBRARY RESOURCES AND TECHNICAL SERVICES may be found under the index term "american library association resources and technical services division" as shown in Figure 5. Series-added entries also index. Figure 6 shows the entry "northwestern university studies in geography" as a main entry in line 18, followed by added entries for the analytics on lines 19 through 23.

LUIS CATALOG ACCESS T = LIBRARY RESOURCES
   12 ENTRIES FOUND—INDEX DISPLAY
1 NU:LIBRARY RESOURCES AND TECHNICAL SERVICES (FULT
2 NU:LIBRARY RESOURCES FOR AFRICAN STUDIES IN GHANA *KOTEI S I A (1974
3 HS:LIBRARY RESOURCES FOR THE BLIND PHYSICALLY HANDICAPPED (WASH
4 NU:LIBRARY RESOURCES HOW TO RESEARCH AND WRITE A P *LEE CLARENCE
   PEND (1971
5 NU:LIBRARY RESOURCES IN GREAT BRITAIN ON LATIN AMERICA *STEELE COLIN
   (1974
6 NU:LIBRARY RESOURCES IN LONDON AND SOUTH EAST ENGLAND (1979
7 NU:LIBRARY RESOURCES IN PSYCHOLOGY *LONDON UNIVERSITY BIRKBECK
   COLLEG (1974
8 NU:LIBRARY RESOURCES IN SCOTLAND (GLAS
9 NU:LIBRARY RESOURCES IN SOUTH WEST ENGLAND AND THE *LIBRARY
   ASSOCIATI (1978
10 NU:LIBRARY RESOURCES ON LATIN AMERICA *LAUERHASS LUDWIG (1978
11 NU:LIBRARY RESOURCES ON LATIN AMERICA RESEARCH GUID *LAUERHASS
   LUDWIG (1978

VALID COMMANDS ARE: a t e i b        (FOR HELP TYPE ? AND PRESS ENTER)
TYPE YOUR COMMAND

FIGURE 3

LUIS CATALOG ACCESS T = LIBRARY
   380 ENTRIES FOUND—GUIDE DISPLAY
   1 NU:LIBRARY (
 40 NU:LIBRARY B
 55 NU:LIBRARY C
 73 NU:LIBRARY D
 81 NU:LIBRARY G
 86 NU:LIBRARY H
 98 NU:LIBRARY J
102 NU:LIBRARY L
109 NU:LIBRARY M
118 NU:LIBRARY N
125 NU:LIBRARY O
311 NU:LIBRARY P
320 GE:LIBRARY Q
322 NU:LIBRARY R
344 NU:LIBRARY S
371 NU:LIBRARY T
377 NU:LIBRARY W
VALID COMMANDS ARE: a t e g i        (FOR HELP TYPE ? AND PRESS ENTER)
TYPE YOUR COMMAND:

FIGURE 4

LUIS CATALOG ACCESS A = AMERICAN LIBRARY ASSOCIATION
151 ENTRIES FOUND—INDEX DISPLAY OF 130-146
130 NU:AMERICAN LIBRARY ASSOCIATION REFERENCE AND ADUL + NOTABLE
    BOOKS 197 (1974
131 NU:AMERICAN LIBRARY ASSOCIATION REFERENCE AND ADULT SERVICES DIVI
    + RQ (CHIC
132 NU:AMERICAN LIBRARY ASSOCIATION REFERENCE AND SUBS + PURCHASING
    AN ENC (1979
133 NU:AMERICAN LIBRARY ASSOCIATION REFERENCE AND SUBS + REFERENCE
    AND SUB (CHIC
134 NU:AMERICAN LIBRARY ASSOCIATION REPRODUCTION OF LI I DIRECTORY OF
    LIBR (1974
135 NU:AMERICAN LIBRARY ASSOCIATION REPRODUCTION OF LI + DIRECTORY OF
    LIBR (1976
136 NU:AMERICAN LIBRARY ASSOCIATION REPRODUCTION OF LI + DIRECTORY OF
    LIBR (1978
137 NU:AMERICAN LIBRARY ASSOCIATION RESOURCES AND TECH + LIBRARY
    RESOURCES (FULT
138 NU:AMERICAN LIBRARY ASSOCIATION RESOURCES AND TECHNI + RTSD
    NEWSLETTER (CHIC
139 NU:AMERICAN LIBRARY ASSOCIATION RESOURCES SECTION + INTERNATIONAL
    SUBS (1974
140 GE:AMERICAN LIBRARY ASSOCIATION RESOURCES SECTION + THIRD WORLD
    BOOKDE (1975
141 NU:AMERICAN LIBRARY ASSOCIATION RESOURCES SECTION + THIRD WORLD
    BOOKDE (1975
142 NU:AMERICAN LIBRARY ASSOCIATION SERIALS SECTION + INTERNATIONAL
    SUBSCR (1974
143 NU:AMERICAN LIBRARY ASSOCIATION SOCIAL RESPONSIBIL + WOMEN IN
    LIBRARIE (NEW
144 GE:AMERICAN LIBRARY ASSOCIATION SOCIAL RESPONSIBILI + GAY
    BIBLIOGRAPHY (1974
145 NU:AMERICAN LIBRARY ASSOCIATION SOCIAL RESPONSIBILITIES R
    + NEWSLETTER (BROO
146 NU:AMERICAN LIBRARY ASSOCIATION STAFF DEVELOPMENT + NEW
    DIRECTIONS IN (1971
VALID COMMANDS ARE: a t e g i b m          (FOR HELP TYPE ? AND PRESS ENTER)
TYPE YOUR COMMAND:

FIGURE 5

As seen in Figure 2, the actual record display for a serial in LUIS picks up
from the NOTIS bibliographic record, the title (MARC field 245), the date
field (362), and the imprint (260). The location, call number, and completed
volumes data from the NOTIS-3 copy and volume holdings records display
below the bibliographic data. If there are multiple copies, such as shown in
Figure 7, holdings display for each copy.

LUIS is also able to suppress data not suitable for public display. If a title

LUIS CATALOG ACCESS T = NORTHWESTERN UNIVER
76 ENTRIES FOUND—INDEX DISPLAY OF 18-34
18 NU:NORTHWESTERN UNIVERSITY STUDIES IN GEOGRAPHY (EVAN
19 NU:NORTHWESTERN UNIVERSITY STUDIES IN GEOGRAPHY + DIFFUSION OF
   RELATIV (1976
20 NU:NORTHWESTERN UNIVERSITY STUDIES IN GEOGRAPHY + FESTSCHRIFT
   ARTHUR E (1971
21 NU:NORTHWESTERN UNIVERSITY STUDIES IN GEOGRAPHY + ONE DIMENSIONAL
   CENT (1974
22 NU:NORTHWESTERN UNIVERSITY STUDIES IN GEOGRAPHY + POPULATION
   MOBILITY (1978
23 NU:NORTHWESTERN UNIVERSITY STUDIES IN GEOGRAPHY + SPECIFICATION
   AND ES (1978
24 NU:NORTHWESTERN UNIVERSITY STUDIES IN HISTORY *NORTHWESTERN
   UNIVERSIT (EVAN
25 NU:NORTHWESTERN UNIVERSITY STUDIES IN HISTORY *NORTHWESTERN
   UNIVERSIT (EVAN
26 NU:NORTHWESTERN UNIVERSITY STUDIES IN PHENOMENOLOG + ADVENTURES
   OF THE (1973
27 NU:NORTHWESTERN UNIVERSITY STUDIES IN PHENOMENOLOG + ANATOMY OF
   DISILL (1967
28 NU:NORTHWESTERN UNIVERSITY STUDIES IN PHENOMENOLOG + COGITO IN
   HUSSERL (1972
29 NU:NORTHWESTERN UNIVERSITY STUDIES IN PHENOMENOLOG + COGNITION
   OF THE (1973
30 NU:NORTHWESTERN UNIVERSITY STUDIES IN PHENOMENOLOG + CONFLICT OF
   INTER (1974
31 NU:NORTHWESTERN UNIVERSITY STUDIES IN PHENOMENOLOG
   + CONSCIOUSNESS AND (1973
32 GE:NORTHWESTERN UNIVERSITY STUDIES IN PHENOMENOLOG + EDMUND
   HUSSERL PH (1973
33 NU:NORTHWESTERN UNIVERSITY STUDIES IN PHENOMENOLOG + EDMUND
   HUSSERL PH (1973
34 NU:NORTHWESTERN UNIVERSITY STUDIES IN PHENOMENOLOG + EXPERIENCE
   AND BE (1969
VALID COMMANDS ARE: a t e g i b m          (FOR HELP TYPE ? AND PRESS ENTER)
TYPE YOUR COMMAND:
H

FIGURE 6

is withdrawn, the entry does not display for public use. If the library receives
copies not for public use, they are suppressed in the LUIS program. An example is shown in Figure 8. Here in the upper portion—the technical service mode
—there are six copies, four of which are either withdrawn or for desk use. In
the public use display, shown in the lower portion of Figure 8, only the two
copies available for public use display.

LUIS is able to explode many encoded messages to natural language for ease of interpretation by the public. Thus in Figure 8, the code "ci:pr" under copy 1 is exploded by LUIS to read "CURRENT ISSUES IN PERIODICALS ROOM." Many other messages assist users in locating material. When the current edition is elsewhere than the location given in the call number, such as when the latest edition is in reference for an item catalogued for the main collection, the message "LATEST VOLUME IN REFERENCE" appears. Titles on-order and in-process display with appropriate messages. If a subscription is cancelled, but not completely withdrawn, a "Subscription cancelled" message appears to alert the user that the run is not current. This is shown in Figure 9.

A major problem in planning public use of serial records is how to encode the volume holdings so that the statement may be readily understood, and yet not become unwieldy. Working with a system which has evolved over ten years' time, LUIS also had to cope with notation introduced not necessarily for ease of interpretation but for compact data entry. Fortunately, the volume holdings conventions developed for NOTIS-3 could be expanded in LUIS for easier user interpretation.

The volume holdings notation in NOTIS-3 is not enumerative, but it is issue specific. Several conventions used in paper serial lists carry over into the electronic notation. For example, commas separate issue level notation; semicolons, volume notation. When notation is not included at the issue level, the volume is assumed to be complete.

Lacking issues may be indicated in two different ways. The first method

```
LUIS CATALOG ACCESS T = FORTUNE
       31 ENTRIES FOUND—BIBLIOGRAPHIC DISPLAY OF 1
Fortune. v. ]- Feb. 1930- —Chicago, Time.
— COPY IN:  main,pr L381.005;F745
   VOLUMES:  1-100(1930-79)
              INDEX:1-10(1930-34)(1v)
              INDEX:1-16(1930-37)(1v)
              INDEX:83-88(1971-73)
              (ALSO AVAILABLE IN MICROFORM)
→ COPY IN:  main/2 L381-005;F745
   VOLUMES:  1-73(inc)(1930-)
              INDEX:1-10(1930-34)
              LACKS:61,no.5(1960,may);64,no.2(1961,aug)
              LACKS:68,no.5(1963,dec);72,no.1,5(1965,july,nov)
→ COPY IN:  schf/3 L381.005;F745
   VOLUMES:  41-99(1950-79)
→ COPY IN:  main/4 L381.005;F745
   VOLUMES:  (CURRENT ISSUES ONLY)
VALID COMMANDS ARE: a t e g i b          (FOR HELP TYPE ? AND PRESS ENTER)
TYPE YOUR COMMAND:
```

FIGURE 7

used in the initial conversion of the Library's shelflist gives general holdings, followed by specific issues which are lacking. The general holdings line has either the term "inc" or "I" for incomplete in a parenthetical note. Originally, the lacks fields were headed by an upper-case indicator "L." In LUIS the program explodes this to read "LACKS" in highlight. The second notation indicates the missing issues of a volume by explicit gaps in the numerical sequence, punctuated by commas. Both types of lacks notation are shown in Figure 9, the public display version shown below the technical service mode. In addition to explicit volumes held, NOTIS volume holdings notation also displays cumulative index and supplements statements. Figures 7, 8, and 10 show this. Linking notation is also given in LUIS. For example, in Figure 7, the notation "ALSO AVAILABLE IN MICROFORM" guides the user to check on microform holdings.

LCAT DONE AAK2755                                    LI818—NUL CATALOGING L8NR
SERL AAK2755 ISSN 0363-0277 S/STAT c FREQ s S/T p REPRO CFR 22/1/3
Library Journal. v. 1- Sept. 1876- —New York, R. R. Bowker.
STATUS h DT 01/01/77 AD NONE
NOTES 1a - 1a r2:LRW:1/13/76
001 2D CN 1A main,pr 1b 020.5;L69 1v v.                              1d 01/01/77
        NOTES 1a ci:pr
002 2Z CN 1a core/2                                                  1d 01/01/00
        NOTES 1a desk copy 1a lv only retained
003 2Z CN 1a main/3                                                  1d 01/01/00
        NOTES 1a - 1a lv:ref 1a lv only retained
004 2Z CN 1a x                                                       1d 01/01/00
        NOTES 1a wd = main/4
005 2D CN 1 a schf/5                                                 1d 01/01/00
        NOTES
006 2Z CN 1a mus/6                                                   1d 01/01/00
        NOTES 1a desk copy 1a lv only retained

*TECHNICAL SERVICE DISPLAY*

LUIS CATALOG ACCESS T = LIBRARY JOURNAL
        3 ENTRIES FOUND—BIBLIOGRAPHIC DISPLAY OF 2
Library journal. v. 1- Sept. 1876- —New York, R. R. Bowker.
→ COPY IN:  main,pr 020.5;L69
  VOLUMES:  1-104(1876-1979)
                INDEX:1-22(1876-97)
  CURRENT  ISSUES IN PERIODICALS ROOM.
→ COPY IN:  schf/5 020.5;L69
  VOLUMES:  60-104,pt.1(1935-79)

*PUBLIC DISPLAY*

FIGURE 8

LCAT DONE AAM5935                              LI850—VOLUME HOLDINGS L8NR
SERL AAM5935 S/STAT c FREQ m S/T p REPRO
Forecast for home economics. v. 1- 1956- —Dayton, O., School Division of
  Scholastic Magazines.
→ 001 2D CN 1a main 1b L640.5;P8951 1v v. 1d 000101
    VH001  1a 1-18(I)(1956-1973,May/June)                              1d 12/10/73
    VH002  1a L = 2,no.4(1956,Dec.);6,no.8(1960,Apr.);12,no.6(1967,Feb      1d 02/23/71
    VH003  1a L = 13,no.1-5(1967,Sept.-1968;Jan.1)                        1d 12/28/71
    VH004  1a 19(no.1-2,5-6,8-9)(1973,sept-oct,1974,jan-feb,apr-may)      1d 05/07/80

*TECHNICAL SERVICE DISPLAY*

LUIS CATALOG ACCESS T = FORECAST FOR HOME ECO
  1 ENTRY FOUND—BIBLIOGRAPHIC DISPLAY
Forecast for home economics. v. 1- 1956- —Dayton, O., School Division of
  Scholastic Magazines.
→ COPY IN:  main L640.5;P8951
  VOLUMES:  1-18(I)(1956-1973,May/June)
          LACKS:2,no.4(1956,Dec.);6,no.8(1960,Apr.);12,no.6(1967,Feb
          LACKS:13,no.1-5(1967,Sept.-1968,Jan.1)
          19(no.1-2,5-6,8-9)1973,sept-oct,1974,jan-feb,apr-may)
  Subscription cancelled.
VALID COMMANDS ARE: a t e b                    (FOR HELP TYPE ? AND PRESS ENTER)
TYPE YOUR COMMAND:

*PUBLIC DISPLAY*

FIGURE 9

When a serial repeats its numbering in various series, the notation can become quite complex. Originally, the NOTIS notation was interpreted in conjunction with the series statements in the 362 field. For easier interpretation in
LUIS, these volume holdings statements are being revised to indicate by head-
ers at the beginning of each field what series it records. An example of multiple series in a volume holdings statement is shown in Figure 10.

The LUIS version of NOTIS thus extends the benefits of the automated
serial record beyond the library staff and makes detailed holdings data available to the public at all access points in the on-line catalog. Future enhancements of LUIS call for display of current issue receipts from the NOTIS-3
order records so that users will have up-to-the-moment data on all titles. This is
possible because the NOTIS serials subsystem includes on-line issue-by-issue
check-in of each title. The index will soon be expanded so that abbreviated
terms, such as those shown in Figure 5, will be displayed completely. Like-
wise, the bibliographic display will be expanded to include all note fields, as
well as the linking preceding title (780) and later title (785) fields. Authority
records will be integrated into the index to provide "see" and "see also" ref-

```
LUIS CATALOG ACCESS T = ANNALES
    242 ENTRIES FOUND—BIBLIOGRAPHIC DISPLAY OF 1
Annales. t. 1-10, 1929-38; ⟨n.s.⟩ t. 1-3; 1939-41; ⟨ser. 3⟩ t. 1-8, 1942-45;
    ⟨ser. 4⟩ 1.- annee, 1946- —Paris, A. Colin.
→ COPY IN:main 305;A6131
    VOLUMES: ⟨1ST SER⟩:v.1-10(1929-38)
             ⟨1ST SER⟩:INDEX:1-10(1929-1938)(bw = v.10)
             ⟨NEW SER⟩:v.1-3(1939-41)
             ⟨SER 3⟩:v.1-8(1942-45)
             ⟨SER 4⟩:v.1-33(1946-78)
    CURRENT ISSUES IN PERIODICALS ROOM.
VALID COMMANDS ARE: a t e g i b              (FOR HELP TYPE ? AND PRESS ENTER)
TYPE YOUR COMMAND:
```

FIGURE 10

erences. Eventually, series authority records may be incorporated into the index also.

Even as currently developed, the LUIS component of NOTIS makes possible a full integration of serial records in the public on-line catalog. Thus the library is able to provide the user with the ideal serial record—one source of all data relating to a serial, be it bibliographic, holdings, or location.

## REFERENCES

1.  Most discussions of serials in an on-line catalog dwell on the problems of entry and names arising from adoption of AACR II. Jean S. Decker in her article "Catalog Closing and Serials," *Journal of Academic Librarianship* vol. 5, no. 5 (Nov., 1979), pp. 261–65, notes: "Serial users in all likelihood suffer more frustration from inadequate indexing and inaccurate holdings records than from catalog deficiencies."

2.  For a description of the NOTIS-2 serial system see Willmering, William J. "On-line Centralized Serial Control," *Serials Librarian* vol. 1, no. 3 (Spring, 1977), pp. 243–49.

3.  For a full discussion of this development and its impact see Furlong, Elizabeth J. "Index Access to On-line Records: An Operational View," *Journal of Library Automation* vol. 11, no. 3 (Sept. 1978), pp. 223–38.

4.  A complete description of the NOTIS-3 serial subsystem is given in Willmering, William J. "Northwestern University Library's NOTIS-3 Automated Serial Control System," *Proceedings of the 1977 Annual Meeting, American Society for Information Science*, 1977.

# SERIALS AUTOMATION AT THE UNIVERSITY OF ILLINOIS AT URBANA: PRESENT BENEFITS FROM INVENTORY CONTROL; FUTURE PLANS FOR ACQUISITION CONTROL

Tom D. Kilton

ABSTRACT. The attainment of automated serials inventory control has been a major first step in serials automation for the University of Illinois Library at Urbana. The success of this control through the library's Library Computer System (LCS) has greatly assisted both library patrons and library staff members as a short bibliographic record circulation system providing on-line circulation data as well as on-line capabilities for searching the library shelflist. The library's plans for realizing complete automated serials control involve serials acquisition control and full bibliographic control.

While plans for automated acquisition control and full bibliographic control of serials at the University of Illinois Library have not yet been realized, automated inventory control of serials has been successfully accomplished by the conversion of holdings from the central serial record of both live and dead titles to machine-readable form. The realization of this massive conversion of serial holdings to the library's automated Library Computer System (LCS) is thoroughly described in the accompanying article by Lenzini and Koff. From the standpoint of both library patrons and members of the library staff, LCS has proven its worth as an efficient on-line automated circulation system featuring inventory control over bound volumes of periodicals, continuations, and analyzed serials. Because LCS is designed as a short-record circulation system and not as an on-line full bibliographic record catalog, complete descriptive cataloguing data is not contained in the records for individual serial titles. However, by virtue of various access points currently available (general searches by author/title or title, and specific searches by call number and multiple detailed search options) together with an increasing amount of data being continually added, such as successive title notes, the system does provide remote catalog access sufficient to enable library patrons and members of the library staff to conduct very thorough searches of serials at terminals throughout the library system. Full bibliographic on-line catalog access to serials through additional secondary added entry points will be available within a year or so when the library's full bibliographic record on-line catalog becomes operative. Featured together with the on-line catalog will be a machine-readable authority file and cross-reference structure to insure complete standardization of serial entries.

Although the major part of the library collections at Illinois are classed by the Dewey classification scheme, certain departmental libraries, namely Law, Asian, and Music, classify their materials by the Library of Congress classification scheme, and United States federal documents received on deposit are classed by the Superintendent of documents classification scheme. Fortunately, LCS is equipped to pull up matches in any of these schemes, and shelflist position searches can be made on all of them.

## Remote Access

Serial publications at Illinois are distributed over a wide area consisting of the main library building housing the general bookstacks area, the undergraduate library, and fifteen departmental libraries. There are also some twenty additional departmental libraries located throughout a very large campus area. Since each of these separate library locations is equipped with at least one LCS terminal, a patron at any one of the locations is now able to quickly ascertain holdings and circulation information for serials held at any of the other locations without consulting the central serial record in the main library building. Bound volumes of periodicals and continuations in a given location can be electronically charged on LCS to a patron, the charge then being recorded next to the record for the volume borrowed in the LCS holdings display. At the present time there are four public terminals in the central card catalog area (three cathode ray tubes and one printer), and one cathode ray tube terminal in the adjacent main reading room. Assistance in the use of LCS, the central serial record, and the card catalog is provided each day from 10:00 A.M. to 9:00 P.M. by library staff members, and written guides to assist patrons in the searching of serials are present at each terminal. Although serial holdings ceased to be posted in the central serial record on January 1, 1980, control cards and cross-reference cards will continue to be entered into the serial record until the library's full bibliographic record on-line catalog becomes operational, a provision which insures the continued availability of complete and up-to-date descriptive cataloguing information for all serials.

## Reconciliations and Conversions

The library's total count of serial titles (i.e., live and dead periodicals, continuations, analyzed serials, and newspapers) is approximately 140,000. Of this total count, there are currently 100,000 records complete with holdings in LCS. This discrepancy is accounted for in part by the fact that approximately 40,000 records for dead serial titles were never reconciled from the main card catalog to the serial record following its establishment in 1956. Entries for these unreconciled titles can be called up on LCS; however, holdings for them are still available only in the card catalog shelflist. A major project has been underway for several years to reconcile all of these dead titles, whose holdings are systematically being added to the LCS data base.

An additional ongoing conversion project aims at making circulatable through LCS on-line charging all serial volumes in the library system which can be circulated through the manual charging system. Because bibliographic holdings statements in the central serial record and LCS do not in all cases match the contents of single circulatable physical volumes, there are presently many volumes which must still be manually charged and discharged. Unfortunately, many holdings records entered into the serial record in years past were based on bibliographic units, not physical circulatable units. For example, volume 2, parts 1 and 2 of a continuation may appear on a serial record holdings card as well as in LCS as one physical unit recorded simply as volume 2, while in fact the volume as it stands on the shelf may be divided and separately bound into parts 1 and 2. Upon completion of this conversion project it will be possible for a patron in one departmental location to remotely charge out a serial volume from another location on campus in the same fashion that monographs can currently be remotely charged between locations.

## Serial Searching Options

To locate information on a given serial, LCS provides for two basic types of searches: general and specific. General searches (author/title, and title) call up holdings and circulation information for all copies of a serial beginning with the most recent issues of copy 1. A general search is used when a searcher does not know the call number of a title. When a call number of a serial is known in advance of a search, several search keys may be used to call up various data elements, such as a specific issue by year or volume number, the location of all current unbound issues, the copies and holdings of the serial in one specific departmental library location, and the holdings of a specific copy.

The search keys required to perform these detailed searches are extremely simple. Following the letters DSC (detailed search by call number), the call number of the serial is typed. Following are the major types of detailed searches used by patrons and staff members.

| *Type of detailed search* | *Search Key* |
|---|---|
| For complete holdings and circulation information for all copies of a serial (simple detailed search by call number): | DSC/051TIM |
| For the location of all copies of a particular year: | DSC/A050P418,Y = 1971 |

For the location of all copies of a particular
    volume:                                      DSC/A050P418,B = 15

For the location of all current subscription
    copies together with a complete holding
    statement for each copy:                     DSC/A020C226B3,B = 99999

For the holdings of all copies in a particular
    location (such as the Undergraduate
    Library Stacks):                             DSC/A050P418,LOC = UGX

Foɪ the holdings of a particular copy:           DSC/A050P418,C2

For the total number of copies and the
    numbers of those copies:                     DSC/051TIM,ALL

For volumes of a serial currently charged out
    together with their circulation records and
    error override charges:                      DSC/A050P418,ALLC

## *Detailed Search Display for a Continuation*

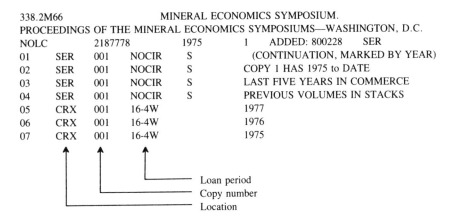

338.2M66                    MINERAL ECONOMICS SYMPOSIUM.
PROCEEDINGS OF THE MINERAL ECONOMICS SYMPOSIUMS—WASHINGTON, D.C.
NOLC        2187778         1975        1     ADDED: 800228    SER
01    SER   001   NOCIR     S                 (CONTINUATION, MARKED BY YEAR)
02    SER   001   NOCIR     S                 COPY 1 HAS 1975 to DATE
03    SER   001   NOCIR     S                 LAST FIVE YEARS IN COMMERCE
04    SER   001   NOCIR     S                 PREVIOUS VOLUMES IN STACKS
05    CRX   001   16-4W                        1977
06    CRX   001   16-4W                        1976
07    CRX   001   16-4W                        1975

                                             Loan period
                                             Copy number
                                             Location

## *Detailed Search Display for a Periodical*

051A                    ATLANTIC$BOST           4-12666   41433   5   ADDED:      771120
      SER               PER
01    SER   004   NOCIR     S                 (PERIODICAL, MARKED BY VOLUME)
02    SER   004   NOCIR     S                 COPY 4 HAS VOLUME 1 TO DATE
03    SER   004   NOCIR     S                 VOLUME 165 TO DATE IN UNDERGRAD
04    SER   004   NOCIR     S                 PREVIOUS VOLUMES IN STACKS
05    STX   004   NOCIR     S                 1-5    1857N-1860JE
06    UGX   004   NOCIR                        244    1979    JY-D
07    UGX   004   NOCIR                        243    1979    JA-JE
08    UGX   004   NOCIR                        242    1978    JY-D

When particular bound volumes are snagged, withdrawn, reported lost, or
reported returned by borrowers, appropriate abbreviations denoting these

statuses can be entered next to the volumes. Individual volumes can be shown in a display as charged out to borrowers, to reserve collections, or to various locations in the technical services departments. Some elements recently introduced into the data base which are of special use to both patrons and staff members include marking instructions, the paper order files where titles are checked in (periodical or continuation), successive title notes, incomplete back volumes of periodicals awaiting claimed issues before being sent to binding, and the search option B = 99999 to retrieve the holdings statements (earliest volume to date for live titles or inclusive holdings for dead titles) for each copy and location of a serial. This feature spares a user from having to work through page after page of holdings for the various copies of a title in order to become aware of the extent of holdings for those copies.

Since no uniform library-wide policy exists for the loan periods of monographs, continuations, and bound volumes of periodicals, the student and faculty loan periods are stated in the fourth column of each LCS display. The 16-4W notation in the first display example above, for instance, indicates that the faculty loan period is 16 weeks and the student loan period is 4 weeks.

## Library Staff Use of the System

Even though the University of Illinois Library to date has neither an automated serial check-in system nor an automated acquisition system for the ordering, claiming, receipt, and payment of serials, the LCS inventory control in its present form assists all serials operations in one way or another. Although Illinois no longer has a separately administered serials department, the various functions of serials work continue to be performed efficiently by several separately organized library divisions: Collection Development (searching, verifying, and preparing orders); Order, Claiming, and Receiving (typing of purchase orders, vendor selection, maintenance of order and receipt paper files, check-in, invoice approval, claiming and noting, and processing of volumes received); Automated Records (OCLC rapid cataloguing and LCS updating); the Original Cataloguing Department (cataloguing of titles for which no OCLC copy exists); and the Binding Division.

The remote on-line access to LCS serials data has been of great assistance to work routines in all of these divisions. For examples, the amount of time required for the preorder searching of serial orders in the Collection Development Division has been substantially reduced since searchers in that division can quickly ascertain through LCS a wealth of information on titles owned and catalogued by the library. Prior to the availability of remote access to this information the serials searchers had to consult the various paper serial order files in the Order, Claiming, and Receiving Division as well as the central serial record. These paper files still must be consulted for information on titles ordered but not yet received and catalogued. However, plans are currently underway to commence entering all order records for both monographs and serials into LCS—a feature which will even further expedite the preorder searching procedures by completely eliminating the necessity of checking the paper order files except for information on current unbound issues of periodicals. Even that information will become available on-line as soon as Illinois develops an on-line check-in system as part of its program for automated acquisition control.

Within the state of Illinois there are currently seventeen academic institutions using LCS as an automated circulation system for their own collections.* The data bases of these institutions are mutually accessible on-line, and remote interlibrary loan transactions are operational between them. In addition to these LCS participating libraries, eighteen regional library systems comprising public and academic libraries throughout the state known as ILLINET (Illinois Library and Information Network) own LCS terminals and are able to borrow materials through LCS from the collections of the University of Illinois Urbana campus. Moreover, a pilot project to use LCS as a transmitter of photocopy requests for serials from the ILLINET system to the Urbana campus is currently underway.

### Future Plans

The attainment of serials inventory control has been a major first step in serials automation for Illinois. Complete bibliographic control will be realized with the establishment of the full bibliographic record on-line catalog, which should be implemented sometime in 1981. Following this implementation the last major automation project will be acquisition control: on-line records for the ordering, receipt, claiming, binding, invoice payment, and full-fund accounting for serials and monographs alike.

Although the data bases of LCS and the on-line full bibliographic record catalog will be distinct and separate one from another, their respective records will be made to interface so that data from each system will be accessible on a single set of terminals with uniform access protocol to retrieve data from each system. Consequently, an automated on-line periodical check-in system could be integrated into either data base depending on preferred electronic design and cost factors. Regardless of the data base chosen for the check-in function, two separate records will exist—one for the on-line posting of periodical issues and continuation volumes as they are received together with claiming and invoice payment data, and one for the circulation records of these pieces.

---

*The Catholic Theological Union at Chicago, Chicago State University, DePaul University Governors State University, Illinois Institute of Technology, Illinois State University, Judson College, Kankakee Community College, Lake Forest College, Millikin University, Northern Illinois University, Saint Xavier College, Sangamon State University, Triton College, the University of Illinois at Urbana, the University of Illinois Chicago Circle Campus, and the University of Illinois Medical Center (Campuses at Chicago, Peoria, Rockford, and Urbana).

Ultimately, these two records might be displayed separately or as two different fields in one single record.

As part of an automated acquisitions control system to reflect on-line the ordering, claiming, receipt, and invoice payment of serial and monograph orders, prospects for placing serial orders on-line through subscription agents featuring on-line order capabilities are presently under consideration; however, there are no immediate plans for contracting with agents for on-line acquisition systems.

One aspect of automated acquisitions control which the library has been developing over a period of years is that of full-fund accounting. Although none of the budget accounting records have been put on-line, monthly print-outs produced by an automated fund accounting system developed for the library in the early 1970s are sent every month to each departmental librarian or area studies bibliographer having discretion over monograph and serial funds. Sorted according to internal departmental funds, such as the Modern Languages Library's French continuation fund or Spanish periodical fund, these printouts state each fund's free balance, all encumbrances for outstanding orders, payments made for orders received, and previous payments made during the current fiscal year. Bibliographic entries for all orders referred to are supplied. The library hopes to soon replace this system with an on-line system which in the future could be linked to an acquisition-control data base.

The University of Illinois Library at Urbana–Champaign has not yet attained full automated control of its serials operations. However, with an efficiently operating on-line inventory control system which assists both librarians and patrons involved with all aspects of serials control, it is concertedly aiming at the day when all of its serials operations will be fully automated.

# ON-LINE SERIALS
# AT BRIGHAM YOUNG UNIVERSITY

H. Kirk Memmott
K. Paul Jordan
John R. Taylor

ABSTRACT. A brief account of the automation of Brigham Young University's serial's activities is presented. The system is a computerized on-line approach to the processing of the 42,000 serial titles held by the University's libraries. Several functions are discussed including the main functions of check-in, claiming, and notification for binding.

## Introduction

Brigham Young University's Harold B. Lee Library has developed an on-line serials system that has been in use since July 1978. Early in the development of this system, the J. Ruben Clark, Jr. Law School Library became a partner in the effort. An earlier, shorter report of this system appeared in *Utah Libraries*, volume 21, number 2 (Fall, 1978).

The system was developed around three main functions: (1) check-in, (2) claiming, and (3) bindery preparation notification. These components of the system, which are still receiving minor modifications, comprise the core of the working system. Lesser but related parts of the developing system are the accounting and exchange phases. Eventually, accounting will be a major component.

The developed components of the system are completely on-line and interactive as far as serials work is concerned. This means the files are available through computer terminals and the data in any field can be input, changed, or deleted through terminal access.

This paper will discuss briefly the following areas: (1) history of the development, (2) a description of the operation, (3) developed system functions, (4) projected system functions, (5) patron service, and (6) some management concerns. The final portion will anticipate the future somewhat and discuss general advantages and disadvantages of the operation.

*History*

Before automation, Brigham Young University (BYU) Library functioned on a kardex system. The kardex became the main source of input to the computer file.

Discussions of serials automation began at BYU in rather general, wishful terms in 1968. By May 1971, these discussions had become serious, and the Library Administration gave approval for the automation of the files and functions of the Serials Department.

Actual work on the process of automation began in 1973. The launching event was the dumping of the machine-readable patron catalog onto a computer disk. (Prior to 1973, the patron's catalog was printed from a computer tape, which was updated by punched cards.)

A decision was made to model the emerging BYU system after the system developed by James Fayollat at UCLA Biomedical Library. The idea originally came from reports of the UCLA system in the literature and was examined more closely during consultations with Mr. Fayollat.

When work began at BYU, it soon became apparent that the BYU system had needs which differed from those at the UCLA Biomedical Library. BYU's Lee Library is a general library acquiring titles in all fields and for levels of use from freshmen to doctoral students as well as for faculty. The UCLA system was adapted by BYU to accommodate these general needs.

In October 1971, James Fayollat very kindly provided BYU with complete programs and documentation describing the UCLA system. The UCLA programs were written in the PL/I language. It was necessary to translate these programs to COBOL because the BYU Computer Center provided only a COBOL interface for this kind of effort.

BYU followed the UCLA programs closely for direction and general purposes. As would be expected, and as alluded to above, a substantial amount of revision and original programming was necessary to meet local needs. However, there is no way of expressing the value of having a framework for the developing system. To have started from scratch would have prolonged development considerably.

It was easy to underestimate the time required to develop the system. An extremely optimistic forecast of three months from start to finish somehow developed into a project that lasted five years. Ideas for modification and improvement seemed to generate spontaneously. The main conversion activity centered in loading different data elements from the kardex and other files to the computer files. The final kardex to computer pass, the one that converted holdings to the UCLA format, required six months. Usually, from four to eight hours per day were dedicated to building the files. Time for this effort came from people whose main duties were maintaining the manual kardex system.

Initially, it was expected that a period of operating the kardex and automated systems simultaneously would be necessary. This was not done, however, due to lack of time and personnel to accomplish it. When the time came to begin using the automated system, it was initialized alphabetically kardex section by kardex section. The kardex ceased to function section by section as up-to-date holdings were added to the computer file.

## Operation Description

When conversion began, there were approximately 34,000 serial titles on the kardex system. Slightly less than half of these titles were being received on an active, ongoing basis. Presently there are some 38,900 titles on the record, of which approximately 17,200 are active in Lee Library.

The system has the support of one full-time library systems analyst and one full-time programmer. These people presently devote a total of about twenty-five hours per week to the maintenance of the system. Two part-time programmers contribute to developing new system components. All of these people are on the library staff. They support the systems of both Lee and Law Libraries.

The Lee Library Serials Department consists presently of nine full-time employees and nine half-time employees. Of these people, approximately five are interacting with the system at any single point of time within a normal work day. However, all serials personnel work with the system from time to time in discharging their duties.

The system is operated by an IBM 4341 computer, and its files reside on over 140 cylinders of CALCOMP 3330 discspace. The programming language, as mentioned, is COBOL. The data is accessed and manipulated by six terminals. Four of these are used for check-in and problem solving; one is used for accounting and bindery preparation, and one is located in the current periodicals reading room to assist in patron services. It is expected that eventually terminals will exist in all public services areas. This will be especially important when the library operates an integrated automation system where circulation, cataloguing, serials, and other subsystems are accessible from the same terminals. The Law Library, which operates on the same system but with separate files, has three terminals. The Law Library contributes to the developing system and is an important part of it.

The four terminals in BYU Lee Library check in about 500 issues per day total. During the check-in procedure, one title per minute is processed. Without stopping to solve problems, the check-in rate can be doubled. As indicated, these four terminals are also used for other than check-in purposes. Approximately one half of their use comes from general problem solving and access, preorder searching, and so on.

The operation requires eleven on-line files, some of which are automatically produced index files. The main files are the master file, the claims file, the check-in, bindery, keyword, and cross-reference files. (The cross-reference file is automatically accessed when the form of title being sought does not exist on the master file but does exist on the cross-reference file.)

The master file contains some seventy separate fields. Some of these are title, call number, ISSN, holdings, notes, language, source, and bindery preparation fields. All of these fields are machine-addressable and can be changed and keyed on for computer-generated lists.

The title is accessed in the main files by four methods: (1) first thirty-one characters of the title, (2) ISSN, (3) keyword—the first four characters of the first three significant words in the title, and (4) an accession number peculiar to BYU's automated system.

Some important products of the system are the claim letters, dropped claim reports, listings of titles for which there are no claim responses, bindery tickets, bindery status reports, binding packing lists, serials catalog (on microfiche), and historical accounting.

*Main Functions*

*Check-In*

As issues are received through the mail, they are sorted into four alphabetical groups. This is necessary because each of the four terminals serves a portion of the alphabet.

The first attempt to access the title is by ISSN if the ISSN is attached to the piece. After this, access is attempted by title or keyword. When accessing by title, the cross-reference algorithm comes into effect, as explained previously.

When the proper record for the issue in hand is accessed, the clerk examines the expected information fields. (The system automatically predicts the next issue to arrive when the issue in hand is checked in. This feature is necessary for the claiming and binding notification processes.) If the expected information matches the piece in hand, the issue number is keyed into the displayed holdings string manually. As the update is made, the computer then automatically predicts the next expected issue.

*Claims*

Claims are initiated automatically by the computer or manually by the operator. The computer activates the claiming process when the issue in hand does not match the expected issue information, or when activity for an otherwise active title ceases for a predetermined number of weeks. The operator can key a claim into the system for an issue at any time depending upon the need.

Once entered into the system, all claims follow the same pattern. The claim appears on a list that is generated weekly for normative review by the claims clerk. If the claims clerk approves of the claim, it enters a new phase where claim letters are generated. (The claim letter program is run twice a week.) The record is checked against the claim letters before they are sent. This seems to be a necessary repeat of the list check. If there is no response to the first claim, second and third claim letters are sent when predetermined times have elapsed. The intervals between letters are set automatically by the computer, and can be set or altered at the terminal to match an individual serial's circumstance. If there is no response to the third claim, it is automatically dropped from the claiming process and presented to the Serials Librarian on a list for a decision for further action.

The computer-generated claim letters are worded differently depending upon the following criteria: (1) Is this claim for a paid subscription/standing order? (2) Is this claim for a gift item? (3) Is this claim for an exchange item? (4) Is this a first, second, or third claim for the issue? (5) Is the publication pattern regular or irregular? Irregular publications are queried rather than claimed.

Studies were accomplished on the kardex claiming system prior to automation. Studies have also been done since automation. The automated system produces fifty-six percent more claims than the manual system did. Fifty percent of the automated claims are successful as compared to a twenty-five percent success rate for the manual claims on the kardex system. This means the present claiming system acquires approximately three times more missing material than the manual system did. This is attributed mostly to the greater timeliness of the computer-generated claims. The system presently issues approximately 360 first claims per week.

## Binding

Information relevant to the binding process is loaded into the computer record for each active title. The computer, taking its cues from the check-in module, initiates the binding activity.

The system normally allows patrons to use the last issue of a binding for three weeks before beginning the binding process. This use period can be shortened or lengthened depending upon the library users' needs as expressed by public services librarians. At the end of the three week use period, the computer automatically embarks upon an eight-step binding process:

*Step one*—Identifies the title and the specific issues ready for binding to employees in the bindery preparation unit.

*Step two*—Indicates the need for entry of binding information into the computer, if none has been entered. This is a one-time activity for each title.

*Step three*—Performs two main functions: It notifies bindery preparation's people that they need to locate indexes, tables of contents, and the like for the binding in question, and indicates where these items can be found. This step also prompts employees to check the number of issues received on an irregular title to insure that an acceptable size of binding will result. For irregular titles, the computer counts issues received and notifies only when a preset number of issues have arrived.

*Step four*—Produces bindery pick-up lists which are used by library personnel in various areas of the library to retrieve the material indicated as ready for binding by the computer. If bindery preparation people agree that issues should be bound, the process moves on to step five. If problems are identified, they are resolved before proceeding.

*Step five*—Loads a code indicating that issues have been removed from direct patron access and entered into the binding process. In this step, a three-part bindery instruction ticket is produced by the computer based upon bindings permitted to proceed through the process by employees interacting with the lists in step four. The first part of the ticket provides "tear down" and issue preparation information for the use of bindery preparations personnel. This amounts to preparing the material for the commercial binder. The second part of the slip provides instructions to the commercial binder and is sent with the issues for binding. The third part is used for library control.

*Step six*—Signifies that volumes are ready for binding and are waiting in the Serials Department to be picked up by the commercial binder. When this stage is reached, a binding shipment packing list is produced by the computer.

*Step seven*—Produces a code which indicates the material is at the commercial bindery.

*Step eight*—Results in a code indicating the material has returned from the commercial binder and has been processed back into the library's collection.

A control list called the "Binding Status Report" is produced weekly and distributed to everyone within the library who desires it. This list indicates the binding stage of each binding in process and is used by the subject librarians to retrieve an issue from the process for emergency patron use.

The system is controlled to produce an average of 250 binding tickets each week. Some of these tickets are used for temporary bindings, which are accomplished by the library's in-house repair unit. This "temporary" process closely follows the eight-step process described above.

## Other Features

### Accounting

The accounting module involves an "Accounting Master File," which exists on computer tape. The Accounting Master File is updated by machine-readable invoices provided by serial vendors and by invoice files created manually via the computer terminal. (Not all serial vendors provide machine-readable invoicing.) The Accounting Master File is produced periodically on microfiche for Serials Department use. The microfiche contains such information for each title as invoice amount, number and date, payment number and date, years and/or volumes of material for which payment is issued. Purchase order transactions are also recorded on the Accounting Master File.

Academic department budget codes have been loaded onto the main serials file for each title. As the system develops, these codes will be used to break down total expenditures for each budget (fund accounting). This is a very promising segment of the emerging system. Through it, prices can be monitored for changes relating to extravagant price fluctuations, departmental expenditures can be compared and reported for control purposes, and much other useful information can be obtained. Also, the general subscriptions budget can be divided into departmental or subject budgets to effect better evaluation of titles and greater control.

## Vendor File

In order to automatically produce claim letters, the system requires an extensive vendor file. The vendor file in use at BYU currently lists approximately 7,500 addresses. Vendors and addresses are entered into a data entry terminal and dumped from there onto a computer tape.

The system is controlled by a vendor number which exists on the main record for each title. The vendor file is used by the system to automatically address claim letters. It will be used shortly to produce mailing labels for the library's gift and exchange program.

An ambitious effort is required to maintain the vendor file. As the serials program expands, the file grows constantly. At the same time, changes occur that necessitate file updating.

## New Serials

An order "in-process" segment is available through the automated system. This segment controls on-order and in-cataloguing titles. It automatically produces claims for overdue orders and lists for overdue material from cataloguing.

## Exchange

Considerable progress has been made in developing the automation of exchange records and procedures. When complete, the exchange master files will be available through the computer terminals and on lists produced by the computer. These files will show serial and miscellaneous publications involved in exchange programs from both the sending and receiving ends.

*Patron Services*

The library's Current Periodicals Reading Room, which is a public-access area, has a computer terminal with direct reading access to all segments of the system. This terminal assists public services personnel in providing up-to-the-minute information to the library patron. It is expected that computer terminals will eventually be available for patron services at all reference desks.

The *BYU Periodicals and Serials Catalog* is the most important product produced for the library patron. This microfiche catalog is a union list of publications held by the Lee Library and by the Law Library.

Prior to the summer of 1980, a hard copy of the *Catalog* was produced for patron use. In June 1980, however, the hard copy was replaced by microfiche.

Two editions of the catalog will be produced: (1) a patron's edition with an abbreviated, simplified holdings statement similar in format to statements seen in the serials catalogs of most libraries, and (2) a listing with a comprehensive holdings statement that shows the exact library holdings for every title. This copy will be used by public services librarians in their work with the patron. (The library has found that patrons do not do well with the comprehensive holdings statement.)

When computer terminals are available at all reference desks, the comprehensive holdings lists will not be needed for reference. The list of holdings on the terminal is comprehensive. It is translated by the computer to produce the simplified holdings listing for the patron.

*System Management Assistance*

Most experienced librarians agree that serials management is one of the more difficult of library tasks. This is partly because serials change constantly. Titles, prices, frequencies, publishers, and many other important elements of serials are subject to change. Other problems include service cessations or interruptions, unwanted duplicates, piles and piles of gifts, and binding slowdowns owing to nonreceipt of single issues, indexes, and title pages. Mutilation of copies also contributes to difficulties in management of serials. When these problems and myriad others are considered as they relate to several thousand active titles, the management problem can become very difficult indeed.

Under the manual system, access to the file for management information purposes was available only through statistical sampling techniques. Even after problems were identified through sampling, however, they could be dealt with only through great effort and expense in terms of human time. This was so because any given problem, such as those involving the retrieval of material in a narrow range of call numbers, were scattered throughout the entire alphabet. A researcher or serial worker had to read the entire file of some 38,000 titles in order to access those relating to his/her management concern. However, with the system automated, an overnight batch computer run can list the exact titles that a librarian may be questioning. Along with these titles, the computer can list any other information available to the file that may be pertinent to the question.

Claiming provides a good example of the relative benefits of an automated system. With the manual system, time for claiming was a problem because of other pressures and demands. With the automated system, every active title is automatically reviewed each week and those that may need attention are presented to serials personnel for the normative evaluations Lee Library feels are necessary.* The Library feels much more comfortable issuing too many claims than when, under the manual system, it issued too few.

Capability of managing the claiming system has produced many side benefits that allow greater efficiency in other areas. The binding program, for example, is not frustrated from lack of issues nearly as often as before. The patron—and this is the greatest benefit—can find needed serial issues more often than in times past.

Although vendor and network systems offer some useful and very interesting side products to their systems, Lee Library is quite content presently with the local control of the in-house system. Programs can easily be entered via the terminals that generate listings of information nightly. The programs are easy to devise, usually take no more than two to five minutes to develop and enter, and are input by serials personnel. These programs can be produced by keying on any of the fields, which include vendor, call number, library location, specialized collection, budget account code, geography, language, and many more. Listings involving more complex programming such as mathematical calculations are produced by the Library Systems Office.

The possibilities of management of the file presented by the automated system are many. Indeed the system has provided so many opportunities that department employees are hard-pressed to handle them all. The computer, with its regular systematic output, also exerts a constant pressure upon personnel to stay abreast of the entire serials routine. Failure to do so results in schedule breakdowns that can lead to erroneous claim production, erroneous bindery notification, and so forth. Automation of serials makes timely performance of routines extremely important—even critical.

---

*It should be noted at this point that even with human judgments on individual claims, the library still sends unnecessary claims. These unnecessary claims are being eliminated through a constant tightening process that adjusts "claim weeks" and other involved fields of the record.

## Summary/Conclusion

In summary, the main advantages of Lee Library's automated serials system are seen as the following:

1. Better patron service by making material more accessible through more timely check-in, claiming, and binding. This is significant.
2. Local control, which renders the system very responsive.
3. Access to all elements of the file for extracting management information.
4. Ability to effect changes involving large file segments relatively easily.
5. Comprehensive claiming on a timely basis.
6. Responsive bindery notification and preparation.

The disadvantages are primarily the following:

1. Difficulty in training of personnel due to technological impact of automation.
2. Cost. The current computer cost of the system is approximately $35,500 per year.
3. The records are not maintained in MARC format at this point.

The future of Lee Library's automated serials system is expected to revolve around the phenomenon of change. Change has been a major aspect of the system up to now. Once begun, there seems to be no end to development of serials automation. Although it does stabilize from time to time, in a relative sense, the system is never complete. This occasional stabilization mercifully allows the human component of the effort to catch a breath occasionally. But possibilities are endless, and the system moves on as those who control development are continually reaching for more capability. When planned and managed properly, this reaching is rewarded by increased capacity, increased productivity, and finally increased and better service to the library patron.

# CONVERTING SERIAL HOLDINGS TO MACHINE-READABLE FORMAT: AN ACCOUNT OF THE UNIVERSITY OF ILLINOIS–URBANA EXPERIENCE

Rebecca T. Lenzini
Eileen Koff

ABSTRACT. Before libraries can take advantage of automated systems, existing human-readable data must be converted to machine-readable form. The preparation for installation of LCS, an on-line circulation system, at the University of Illinois in Urbana included the conversion of 1,250,000 serial holdings. This paper documents the two-year project, describing the existing paper files and LCS, major decisions made and the rationale for them, as well as the day-to-day operations of the project. Observations and conclusions are included to aid those embarking on similar undertakings.

## Introduction

The Library Computer System (LCS) now in use at the University of Illinois is an on-line short record system which, though designed initially for circulation, also features known item searching of records and remote catalog access. LCS offers a solution to the inventory control and information retrieval problems which confront libraries today by providing immediate answers to those all-important patron questions: "Does the library own the book I want?" and "Can I get it now?"

Developed at Ohio State University by IBM during the late 1960s, LCS came up at OSU in November 1970, supporting circulation activities at their twenty-eight departmental libraries. During the early 1970s, the University Library at SUNY Albany also implemented the system.

The University of Illinois was the third institution to install the system, beginning its efforts upon the arrival of newly appointed University Librarian Hugh C. Atkinson (formerly director at OSU) in the fall of 1976. In December 1978, LCS was put into full operation at the University of Illinois Library in Urbana. The Libraries of the Health Sciences at the University of Illinois Medical Center in Chicago, as well as their branch locations of Peoria, Rockford, and Urbana, put LCS into operation in February 1979. Holdings of the University of Illinois Chicago Circle Library are now available on LCS as well.

As this paper is being written, fourteen other colleges and universities in Illinois are preparing to join LCS.

Before libraries can take advantage of any computer system, whether it is on-line or batch, locally developed or commercially vended, circulation or full catalog, existing human-readable data must be converted to machine-readable form. The ever-growing number of conversion projects in this country pays tribute to our increasing interest in and reliance on automated library systems.

Preliminary issues must be settled before conversion can begin since the end result of the conversion efforts naturally dictates the nature of the project itself. Conversion done to support a short record circulation system will differ from that necessary for a full bibliographic record system. Those planning conversions must, first, establish what the content of the desired record will be, and then search for the most cost-effective means to complete a conversion project.

Many articles have appeared in recent years on the planning of catalog conversions. Noteworthy among them are Michael Gorman's "The Economics of Catalog Conversion,"[1] which offers general strategies as well as specific instances from a conversion project which took place at the British Library; John Kountz's informal guide to the rudiments of conversions, "Shelf-List Conversion: Management Pitfalls and Opportunities"[2]; and Pat Barkalow's "Conversion of Files for Circulation Control,"[3] which forms an excellent introduction to the topic. These articles have focused primarily on conversions of monographic or bibliographic information, yet a conversion of serial holdings presents a formidable task as well and one which requires forethought and planning.

The University of Illinois Library at Urbana–Champaign represents three million titles, six million volumes, and nine million items housed in the main book stacks and thirty-six departmental libraries scattered across the campus. The conversion efforts which preceded implementation at LCS at UIUC lasted over two years. Selected pieces of bibliographic information for both serials and monographs as well as holdings for monographs were keyed commercially from shelflist cards. Conversion of serial holdings was completed locally over the course of two years. Nearly 100,000 serial titles were involved in the project; and upon completion, 1.25 million lines of serial holdings were represented in machine-readable form.

This paper represents an attempt by the authors to document this massive serials conversion project. Included in this article is a description of the existing paper files and of LCS, a history of major decisions made and the rationale for them, an account of the day-to-day operations of the project, as well as observations and conclusions. The authors participated in the project from the beginning to the end in various capacities and continue to deal with the system in its present operating format. Data included in this paper comes not only from personal experience but also from other files and from interviews conducted with those involved in the project. It is hoped that in presenting the serials conversion project at UIUC, alternatives will be offered to other about to embark on similar projects.

## Description of LCS

As presently configured, LCS records contain a call number, main entry, title, edition statement, place of publication, Library of Congress card number, and exact holdings listed by copy and location. The records are variable in length, though there are some constraints on length. On-line access to the LCS data base provides patrons with up-to-the-minute holdings and circulation information for almost all items in the Library's collection. Patrons and staff can access the data base by call number, author, title, author/title, or title number (system generated). In addition, general class number searches can be performed, thus providing one kind of subject search. The system provides complete circulation control with charge, discharge, renewal, recall, hold, and snag functions, producing all necessary library notices. In addition, a variety of management statistics are computer produced at regular intervals. Figure 1 illustrates a basic LCS monographic record and describes its various fields.

The serial holdings file in LCS provides on-line access to serial or monographic set holdings. Holdings information may be represented by a single circulatable unit (i.e., v.1) or by a summary statement representing several physically separate units (i.e., v.1-150, describing 150 actual circulatable volumes). The serial holdings field is variable in length and allows for the flexibility necessary to accurately reflect serial holdings. Figure 2 shows the LCS representation of both bibliographic information and holdings for *Time* magazine.

## Formation of the Project

During a massive conversion project such as this one, many decisions are made, some more far-reaching than others. Among the most important of those reached at Urbana was the decision to contract with a commercial firm to key the bulk of the short bibliographic records and holdings data into a machine-readable format. Sheer size, nearly three million titles, ruled out the retrospective OCLC conversion which would have produced full bibliographic records in a machine-readable form. Even had funds been available for such a massive OCLC retrospective conversion, our "hit rate" would have been unacceptably low since our pre-MARC collection is extensive.

Limits exist within vendor conversions as well. Complicated set holdings present too many problems for non-library experienced keypunchers and serve only to waste their time. In addition, the serial holding file at UIUC is physically separated from the shelflist which served as the data source for the vendor conversion. For these reasons, serial and monographic set holdings (apart from straightforward volumed sets) were eliminated from consideration for conversion by the commercial vendor.

On the other hand, bibliographic data for these titles could still be converted by the vendor from the shelflist. Since no plans for holdings conversion were set, something seemed better than nothing; the University Librarian and the Systems Analyst recommended the inclusion of bibliographic serial information as part of the commercial shelflist conversion. Assuming it was possible to convert holdings at a later date, a link between holdings and bibliographic

Figure 1.
OUTPUT FROM A DETAILED SEARCH

Operator enters:   DSC/301.4242B739W

Response:

```
        1                   2
301.4242B739W    BRAXTON, BERNARD                     3                 4      5
WOMEN, SEX, AND RACE:  A REALISTIC VIEW OF SEXISM AND RACISM$WASH DC 72-91049
        131534        1973          3    ADDED:   780221
  01      001 16-4W STX 350409081 0 CHGD    780427/780525
  02      002 3W    UGX 350409081 0 CHGD    780427/780518
  03      003 16-4W EDX 350409081 0 RCALL   780427/780504

  PAGE  1  END
            6          7         8
```

Operator enters:   DST/131534

Response:

```
      10    11
301 4242B739W    BRAXTON, BERNARD
WOMEN, SEX, AND RACE:  A REALISTIC VIEW OF SEXISM AND RACISM$WASH DC 72-91049
        131534        1973         3    ADDED:    780221 ———————————17
  01         001 16-4W STX 350409081 0 CLRET 780427/780428
9—02         002 3W    UGX 348365520 0 RLOST 780427/780428
  03         003 16-4W EDX 350409081 0 RCALL 780428/780505
                 12    13     14        15      16
  PAGE 1 END
```

| 1 | Call Number | 10 | Volume # |
|---|---|---|---|
| 2 | Author | 11 | Copy # |
| 3 | Title | 12 | Loan period |
| 4 | Place of publication | 13 | Location |
| 5 | LC card # | 14 | Patron # |
| 6 | Title # | 15 | Circulation status |
| 7 | Imprint date | 16 | Date charged/due |
| 8 | # of holdings | 17 | Date record was entered |
| 9 | Line # | | on data base |

Figure 2.
SAMPLE OF SERIAL HOLDINGS DISPLAY FROM A SIMPLE DETAILED SEARCH

```
    1           2           3    4                              5
  _____      _____      _____                               _
  051TIM                  TIME$NY      NOLC        42367        5   ADDED:   771120

        6           7
      SER         PER
  01  REX   001   2W-BU   S           CURRENT ISSUES
  02  REX   001   2W-BU               111 NO. 14-26 1978AP-JE
  03  REX   001   2W-BU               111 NO. 1-13 1978JA-MR
  04  STX   001   2W-BU               109 NO. 1-13 1977JA-MR
  05  STX   001   2W-BU               109 NO. 14-26 1977AP-JE
  06  STX   001   2W-BU               108 NO. 1-13 1976JY-S
  07  STX   001   2W-BU               108 NO. 14-26 19760-D
  08  STX   001   2W-BU               107 1976JA-JE
  8    9    10     11    12           13            14
```

| 1 | Call number | 8 | Line number |
| 2 | Author (none here) | 9 | Holding library |
| 3 | Title | 10 | Copy number |
| 4 | Place of publication | 11 | Loan period |
| 5 | Total number of copies | 12 | Holding type |
| 6 | Serial identifier | 13 | Volume number |
| 7 | Periodical identifier | 14 | Year(s) covered |

data would be necessary. The shortest unique identifier was call number, so the Library resigned itself to keying call numbers for serials twice.

Past attempts at automating serial holdings at Urbana had proven largely unsuccessful. Only one venture deserves note: production of a union serial list which was distributed to the thirty-six departmental libraries and to other library units in book format during the middle 1960s. However, the machine readable holdings information used to produce the union list was completely out of date when the LCS conversion was being considered more than ten years later in 1976. The effort to update this information and reformat it for acceptance into LCS was not deemed worthwhile. A complete conversion of serial holdings data would be necessary. However, staffing was a problem. Certainly the existing serials staff could not absorb the task, yet money for the project was tight. From two campus data-processing units, Administrative Information Systems and Services (AISS) and the Computing Services Office (CSO), came offers to convert the serial holdings at no charge to the Library. These offers illustrate the high priority which the University placed upon the entire LCS project and may suggest avenues to explore for others in this situation.

It was agreed that the serial holdings data would be prepared for entry by Library staff and then be submitted to AISS and CSO for keying, which would be done during their slack times. This arrangement presented obvious advantages: the keypunchers were on campus, within reach of library staff in case of questions or problems; and the work was free. The only major drawbacks were the lack of a schedule, since the keypunching operations were conducted entirely during slack times, and that somewhat vulnerable link to bibliographic data, the call number.

Once the data entry method was established, it was necessary to consider the source of the data. As all serialists are aware, the number of paper files representing serial holdings in a given library is not generally limited to one. At UIUC, three paper manifestations of serial holdings were considered for conversion: departmental library files, the binding file, and the Central Serial Record (CSR) in the main card catalog area. Each of these files presented advantages and disadvantages which had to be weighed.

The serial holdings files maintained by the departmental libraries at UIUC were discounted almost immediately for three reasons: the files are physically dispersed, they are of nonstandard format (some kardex, some shelflist), and no separate record exists for holdings in the main book stacks.

The binding file represented volumes as they are bound, an important consideration for ultimate entry into a circulation system since that list deals with circulatable items, not bibliographic items. However, it was a cumbersome and confusing file and would have required either much preparation prior to keypunching or time-consuming interpretation on the part of the keypuncher.

The Central Serial Record presented the most advantages since the file was centralized and straightforward, showing departmental library and bookstacks holdings for nearly 100,000 titles. However, no file is without its problems. The CSR was not complete, as it was missing many holdings for dead serials and those for a few specific locations. Some of the holdings information to be found in the CSR was not of a format LCS could accept. And most importantly, the CSR did not reflect holdings in their bound, circulatable state. Many holdings were represented by summary statements such as v.1-150, where 150 or 75 or 300 actual volumes were located on shelves. Since LCS is a circulation system, it is important to represent circulatable items whenever possible. However, the cost benefits of taking an inventory of serials in a large research library such as that at UIUC are questionable since many serial volumes will never circulate. It is assumed that the more popular items are located at departmental libraries, which tend to inventory their serials fairly frequently so that unused volumes can be weeded to make space. The logical course is to input the data at hand since the summary statements do fulfill an important informational need and correct the data as libraries inventory or as the volumes actually circulate. This is, in fact, what has been done since the system came up.

Throughout the project the Library was fortunate in having an excellent working relationship with the programming and data-processing staff, who were cooperative and responsive to its needs. One great benefit was the design of the data conversion format for serials to be used at UIUC. Although OSU's programs were available, significant modification was done to develop a local version of the serial holdings file for UIUC's conversion purposes. The original programs for building the holdings file required keying of holdings data with field tags and delimiters strung together. Proofreading of data in this format is very difficult, does not encourage easy detection of errors, and has adverse effects on the sanity of proofreaders. Considering the approximately 1.25 million volumes of holdings to be converted, the programming staff decided that a more visually hospitable format could be devised for use in proofreading and on-line editing.. Through a series of programs, data were converted into the format required for building the file. Figure 3 illustrates the original format (a) and the revised format which we used (b).

## Conversion Process

One particularly pressing question was whether or not to send actual cards from the CSR to the keypunchers. The nature of the file itself provided the answer. The CSR is more than just a holding record; it includes unit cards, cross references, temporary records, informational form cards, and the like. In

Figure 3.

ORIGINAL FORMAT (a) AND UIUC FORMAT (b)

```
a)     CN=051TIM@
       SHA C=1 L=STX U=111 NO.14-26 1978AP-JE
       U=111 NO.1-13 1978JA-MR U=109 NO.1-13 1977JA-MR
       U=109 NO.14-26 1977AP-JE U=108 NO.1-13 1976JY-S
       U=108 NO.14-26 19760-D U=107 1976JA-JE@
```

```
b)     *051TIM
       01 STX C   111 NO.14-26 1978AP-JE      B=111  Y=1978
       01 STX C   111 NO.1-13  1978JA-MR      B=111  Y=1978
       01 STX C   109 NO.1-13  1977JA-MR      B=109  Y=1977
       01 STX C   109 NO.14-26 1977AP-JE      B=109  Y=1977
       01 STX C   108 NO.1-13  1976JY-S       B=108  Y=1976
       01 STX C   108 NO.14-26 19760-D        B=108  Y=1976
       01 STX C   107          1976JA-JE      B=107  Y=1976
```

The B= and Y= fields which are displayed in (b) were generated by the programs in either instance and are used to sort the holdings in LCS and to search them. These fields do not display on the terminals.

fact, the number of holdings cards is considerably less than half the total number of cards in the file. Obviously it could not be expected of keypunchers to thumb through these drawers, recognizing the important cards and picking out the vital information on them. Therefore, it was decided to photocopy holdings cards to send for keypunching rather than sending the entire drawer. In addition, the CSR is a heavily used file and was the only public central source for serial holdings information on campus. By photocopying holdings cards it was possible to reduce the time that drawers were unavailable for public use from approximately one week to several hours. This method allowed maximum use of the keypunch time available to the library.

Data were converted into units corresponding to physical drawers of the CSR, since this was the most logical and manageable means available. Data sets were labeled by drawer number and progress charts were maintained so that the stage of conversion for each drawer could be determined at a glance. Conversion from a dynamic file necessitated duplicate maintenance; any changes to the CSR for converted drawers had to be made in the machine-readable holdings as well. For this reason it was essential for staff to know the status of conversion for each drawer in the CSR.

After the first few drawers, a definite pattern and flow developed to the project. The various stages and time involved will be described in brief. After holdings cards had been selected from each drawer, library staff photocopied three cards on an 8 x 11 inch sheet using the copy machine dedicated to the project. This phase generally required 1½ hours. Part of the Library's agreement with the data processing centers committed library staff to expend a substantial effort in date preparation. Interpretation of serial holdings data can be difficult for library staff and even more so for non-library keypunchers. Moreover, the Library's data preparation efforts helped to reduce the amount of data to be corrected after conversion. Photosheets were checked against the cards in the drawer to clarify data for keypunchers. There was a great deal of information on the holdings cards which was not to be keyed, such as the date the piece was received or notes concerning status of particular volumes. Photosheet editors were instructed to strike through data which were not to be keyed and to write over light data so that the information was legible for the keypunchers. Great emphasis was also put on call number accuracy since this was the only link to the master record containing bibliographic data.

Many items which had previously been left to interpretation had to be clearly delineated for the keypunchers. In call numbers the distinction between zero and alphabetic 0, or between lower case L and the number 1 had to be spelled out. Vague holdings notes such as "Last volume in Education" or "Last five years in Home Economics" were interpreted so that each volume was assigned to a particular location, thus eliminating the possibility of patron misinterpretation of holding records. The note "Last two years in Reference," for example, would display as in Figure 2, showing explicitly that it is 1978 and "Current issues" which are housed in Reference, while other volumes rest in the Stacks, previously an implied location. Superscripted numbers were spelled out so that v.1$^2$ became v.1 no.2, etc. As a general rule, keypunchers were told to key holdings as they appeared on the card, using standard abbreviations for the months and for terms such as number (no.), volume (v.), part (pt.), series (ser.), etc. Pre-editing of photosheets required approximately one hour per drawer.

Once pre-editing was completed, the photosheets were sent to the two campus data-processing centers. Keying of holdings data averaged seven hours per drawer. Upon completion, a print-out of formatted serial holdings for each drawer was returned to the Library along with the photosheets. At the same time a machine-readable copy of the formatted holdings was loaded on a disk for the Library to access for on-line editing and correcting. The columnar format developed for use at UIUC was a great help in the proofreading and on-line editing operations, when errors seemed to jump off the page continually.

Editing of printouts was done by library staff, often at home in the evenings. Printouts were checked against the photosheets for errors. Editors were requested to follow through on all problems so that terminal operators could work continuously without having to consult any paper files. Consistent editor formatting on these printouts was adhered to, again to increase terminal operator speed. Proofreading a printout required approximately three to four hours.

The Library was given the ability to correct keypunched holdings data on-line at the Library itself, using CRTs and a text editor named WYLBUR. This provision benefited both the Library and the data-processing centers, eliminated additional handling, and gave the Library greater control over data accuracy. In addition to correcting the data on-line, new holdings updates which had accumulated since the drawer was photocopied were added. An average terminal edit required two hours per drawer.

Each drawer then required approximately eight hours of staff time and seven hours of keypunch time. A total of 464 drawers were completed during the project.

## Observations and Conclusions

All conversion projects create similar problems and bear similar characteristics. The observations made here will apply equally well to nearly any project of this sort, be it conversion of monographs, serials, or both.

In particular, though, serial holdings conversions present the added challenge of converting extremely dynamic files. Updating the machine-readable file should be uppermost in the thinking and planning of serial conversions, since it is widely recognized that the most recent volume is often the most sought after. A computer system which lacks a record for that volume fails in its purpose. At UIUC, efforts were made to update as the conversion progressed. Staff members were carefully instructed to advise the conversion group of any changes to the existing file, including new titles, new volumes, transfers, or withdrawals. Figure 4 illustrates one of several forms used to indicate that updating was necessary. Existing forms were used as much as possible to eliminate unnecessary duplication of effort. A final three-month push for updating ensured that the UIUC serial holdings data base was as up to date as possible when added to the on-line system.

Arrangements for the continued updating of the machine file are also im-

Figure 4.

SERIALS HOLDINGS UPDATE FORM          Dr.No.____

new titles

Call No._____

☐ per.   ☐ live          ☐ Addition

☐ contin. ☐ dead          ☐ Deletion

Marking:

| Copy | Location (last vol. in?) | Holdings (As they appear in S.R.) |
|------|--------------------------|-----------------------------------|
|      |                          |                                   |

Initials:      Date:

SERIALS HOLDINGS UPDATE FORM          Dr.No.____

Call No._____

Use only those areas below which apply.

☐ Correction

☐ Transfer

|       | Copy | Location | Holdings |
|-------|------|----------|----------|
| To:   |      |          |          |
| From: |      |          |          |

Initials:      Date:

portant. Administrators must be willing to commit staff time and positions to maintenance of any machine record. At UIUC an LCS Maintenance Unit was formed in December 1978 when the system came up, and was staffed by reallocated personnel from Technical Services amounting to six FTE initially, including one .5 FTE professional.

Staffing for a conversion project of any sort is a crucial consideration. Many libraries find that they cannot afford the cost of additional staff while they are busy purchasing hardware, software, and so on. Nevertheless, the appointment of a project coordinator who is more or less relieved of all other duties will help to ensure a successful and smooth conversion. Other staff assignments and responsibilities should be made as specific as possible, and Library management must assign a priority to conversion work in relation to regular duties so that staff members know how to allocate their time.

Those who make the decisions during a conversion effort must be aware of the trade-offs which exist. The time invested in an inventory prior to conversion will save the time spent cleaning up a file. If, on the other hand, decision makers doubt the cost effectiveness of an inventory, as in the case of UIUC, adequate staffing and time must be budgeted for the clean-up which follows conversion. These cases are neither black nor white; compromises can and should be reached. For example, an inventory prior to conversion of only those titles known to be heavily used might be considered, if staff and time allow.

Above all else, conversion decisions should depend on the functioning specifications of the system. That is to say, a thorough understanding of how the system works in its finished state will ensure good decision making throughout any conversion effort. In addition, the ability to look beyond the immediate system and into the future, imagining enhancements or perhaps other systems entirely, will help those planning conversions to make the kind of decisions that are good today and will still be good tomorrow.

## REFERENCES

1. Gorman, Michael, "The Economics of Catalog Conversion." In *Proceedings of the 1976 Clinic on Library Applications of Data Processing: the Economics of Library Automation* (Urbana–Champaign: University of Illinois Graduate School of Library Science, 1977), p. 122–32.

2. Kountz, John, "Shelf-list Conversion: Management Pitfalls and Opportunities." In *Requiem for the Card Catalog*, Daniel Gore, Joseph Kimbrough, and Peter Spyers-Duran, eds. (Westport, Connecticut, Greenwood Press, 1979), p. 157–67.

3. Barkalow, Pat, "Conversion of Files for Circulation Control." *Journal of Library Automation* 12 (3) (September 1979):209–13.

# CONVERSION OF SERIAL HOLDINGS TO ON-LINE AUTOMATED LIBRARY CONTROL SYSTEM AT THE OHIO STATE UNIVERSITY LIBRARIES

Carol R. Krumm

ABSTRACT. At the Ohio State University Libraries prior to the establishment of the Central Serial Record (CSR), serial records were maintained in twelve separate files. Library faculty members serving on task forces and University Systems personnel planned for conversion of serial holdings to the Library Control System (LCS) and wrote supporting documents. Conversion procedures are described, including the use of optical scanning to input data to LCS.

After the conversion of serial holdings, it was possible to limit searches to serial only or non-serial only matches. Also, a detailed search of a serial can now be limited to a specific unique identification number, volume, year, location, copy number, holding type, or any combination of these.

At the Ohio State University Libraries more efficient library service has been made possible by the conversion of serial holdings to the on-line automated Library Control System (LCS). Master records include call number, author, title, Library of Congress card number, internal identification number or title number, date of publication, non-English indicator, monoset or serial designator, and holdings and locations for monographic and serial copies. The system provides for traditional circulation control activities (charge, discharge, renew, save, etc.) as well as access to the on-line catalog via telephone. Known items are searchable by author; by author/title (four characters of the author's last name, five characters of the first significant word of the title); by title (four characters of the first word of the title and five of the second word of the title); or by classification number. Before the conversion of serial holdings only copy number and location information were available on-line for serials.

*Maintenance of Serial Records Before Conversion*

Prior to the establishment of the Central Serial Record (CSR) in 1956, serial records were maintained in twelve separate files: public dictionary catalog, public periodical catalog, shelflist, sheet shelflist, accession book, order card, bookkeeping record, checking record, binding dummies, unclassified file, travel catalog, and continuation file. It was necessary for a patron or bibliographer to search the public periodical catalog for bound classified holdings, the checking file for unclassified material, two different files for unclassified state and local documents, and the miscellaneous file for serials received as gifts or on exchange.[1]

Presently, the Central Serial Record, housed in Acme visible files, includes a current checking file with cards for daily, weekly, monthly, annual, numerical, and irregular publications and cross references, as well as a permanent file with permanent cards and cross-reference cards.

### Planning for Conversion

Library faculty members serving on task forces and University Systems personnel planned for conversion of serial holdings and wrote supporting documents. In 1974, the Task Force on Serial Holdings prepared a document entitled "LCS Serial/Monoset Holdings File: A Proposal,"[2] which was accompanied by "Implementation Recommendations for Adding the OSU Libraries Serial and Monoset Holdings to LCS."[3] The task force envisioned that the conversion of serial holdings into machine-readable form would change the nature and concept of both the LCS and the CSR. The LCS would then not only perform a circulation function but would also assume the holdings record function of CSR. Every terminal in the system would have the capability of performing the public service provided by the Serial Division of the Acquisition Department. In order for LCS to assume the holdings record function of CSR and for every terminal in LCS to have the capability of performing the public service function of CSR, the LCS record for serial holdings would have to provide for complete and flexible circulatable unit identification, which would be clearly and consistently abbreviated and punctuated. A Summary Statement Field would be desirable for serial titles for which holdings do not circulate.[4] Unbound holdings would not usually be recorded. In 1975, the task force wrote "LCS Serial Holdings File Specifications."[5] The title of that document was changed to "LCS Serial Holdings Functional Specifications" and "Appendix A, Addenda and Corrigenda, of the LCS Serial Holdings File Specifications"[6] was added.

The Task Force on Serial Implementation in 1975 was charged with developing the policies and procedures for converting the libraries' records of serials and for implementing the serials system, both start-up and continuation. In addition, University Systems programmers prepared the "LCS Serials Control System Design Document,"[7] the purpose of which was to present a system design plan for the implementation of the "LCS Serial Holdings Functional Specifications" document. These capabilities would provide on-line entry, maintenance, access, and circulation of serial holdings through LCS.

Members of the Task Force on Serial Implementation coded holdings from the Central Serial Record for twenty-one serial titles in the LCS test file, which includes a total of more than 2,000 titles. A successful serial holdings test was conducted using those twenty-one titles.

In 1976, the libraries received from the Ohio State University a one-time special allocation of $66,000 to cover costs for the Serials Conversion Project. University Systems programmers prepared the "Serial Holdings Maintenance Procedure Manual."[8]

Since serial records in the Central Serial Record are difficult to interpret, the Task Force on Serial Implementation decided that the conversion should be done in-house rather than by a vendor. The Task Force recommended that the conversion be the responsibility of a unit apart from the Serials/Continuation Coordinating and Order Division, Acquisition Department. It was suggested that the unit be housed in the Main Library with easy access to the files for conversion.

## Conversion Procedures

The Serial Holdings Conversion Division, established August 1, 1976, was amenable to the Assistant Director of Libraries, Technical Services. Funds for special contracts and supplies, available on a one-time basis from the university administration, had to be expended by June 30, 1977. Much of the success of the project is due to the cooperative, knowledgeable, and diligent staff who worked together as a productive team.[9]

Converting serial records by using bindery records in conjunction with Central Serials Records was considered. One of several problems was that bindery records are arranged in call number order and CSR cards are filed alphabetically; in addition, only bindery records since 1960 were available. Therefore, original input of serial holdings was from CSR rather than bindery records. Holdings for serials in Main Library and more than twenty department libraries and other special locations were converted from records in CSR. Serial holdings for Health Sciences, Children's Hospital, Topaz (Optometry), and Physics Libraries were added from inventory records.

Procedures for conversion included studying in detail "The Serial Holdings Maintenance Procedural Manual," coding records from CSR trays, and discussing the coding. The 1,350 CSR trays in Acme visible files seemed endless in August 1976. The Serial Holdings Conversion Division was permitted to take from six to twelve trays at one time from the Central Serial Record. The Assistant Director for Technical Services wisely advised that a few trays in the letter "U" be coded each day rather than converting records for the United States alphabetically or at the end of the project. Conversion was completed on April 29, 1977.

An example of a simple CSR card is shown in Figure 1. The actual CSR

```
                                                                      vol.
        Z671    Library resources and technical services.
        L716
  See per.     Richmond, Va.
    check-in file

Main                    v. 13  1969
                        v. 14  1970
  v.1-3   1957-1959     v.15  1971
  v. 4    1960          v.16  1972
  v. 5    1961          v.17  1973
  v. 6    1962          v.18  1974
  v. 7    1963          v.19  1975
  v. 8    1964          V.20  1976
  v. 9    1965          v.21  1977
  v.10    1966          V.22  1978
  v. 11   1967          v. 23  1979
  v. 12   1968

Supersedes Serial slants and the Journal of cataloging and
  classification.
"Official publication of the Resources and Technical Services
  Division of the American Library Association."
  Library resources and technical services.
```

FIGURE 1. CSR (Central Serial Record) Card

cards are 4 × 6 inches and include title at the bottom of the card as well as call number and title at the top of the card. The labeling information (e.g., vol.) supplied by serial cataloguers is written on the top right corner of the card. If the note, "See per. check-in file" appeared at the top left of the card, it was necessary to check the Periodical Check-In File to convert to LCS such notes as "CURRENT ISSUES IN PERIODICAL ROOM."

Holdings for the title in the example would be coded as:

CN = 671L716n
SHA/C = 1/V = 99999,U = CURRENT ISSUES IN PERIODICAL
ROOM,HT = S/U = V1-3,Y = 1957-59,HT = S/U = V4,Y = 1960/U =
V5,Y = 1961/U = V6,Y = 1962/U = V7,Y = 1963/U = V8,Y =
1964/U = V9,Y = 1965/U = V10,Y = 1966/U = V11,Y = 1967/U =
V12,Y = 1968/U = V13,Y = 1969/U = V14,Y = 1970/U = V15,Y =
1971/U = V16,Y = 1972/U = V17,Y = 1973/U = V18,Y = 1974/U =
V19,Y = 1975/U = V20,Y = 1976/U = V21,Y = 1977/U = V22,Y =
1978/U = V23,Y = 1979n

Key words and commands used in the example are:

| CN = | Call number |
|------|-------------|
| n | Chair, end of transaction character |
| SHA | Serial holding add |
| C = | Copy number |

U =    Unique identification, the data field that gives the volume
        holdings for a specific copy of a serial title. The holdings
        may be listed as a summary (the description of several con-
        tinuous volumes), or as a circulatable unit (one physical
        volume). If the Unique Identification is for a circulatable
        unit, the information in the field should match the spine
        marking on the volume.
Y =    Year
HT =   Holding type, a code or blank that describes the kind of in-
        formation given in the Unique Identification. S indicates
        that the Unique ID is a summary statement, and blank
        (coded "P" in the conversion) indicates that the Unique ID
        is a statement of a circulatable unit.

One of the biggest problems in the conversion project was the interpretation of labeling information (i.e., the pattern of information to be placed on
the bound volume spine) on the CSR cards. At times no labeling information
was available on CSR cards, and it was often necessary to check the shelflist
for such information. Some CSR cards have no binding information, and the
shelflist indicates labeling which conflicts with the holdings pattern. The CSR
card does not always indicate changes in labeling patterns. Many CSR records
are long, involved, and difficult to interpret. Moreover, holdings for publications of state and federal governments and of universities sometimes created
problems.

*Optical Scanning*

Project staff members were trained to type the sheets to be scanned by the
IBM 3886 Optical Character Reader, which is referred to as a scanner. Requirements for optical scanning include an IBM Selectric typewriter with 10
pitch (PICA) spacing and an OCR-ASA element. The scanner scans 1,000
typed characters per second.

Weekly, op scan sheets were sent to University Systems to be scanned and
input to LCS. For conversion, input was batch rather than on-line. The highest
number of sheets sent in one week was 441. The cost of scanning was three-
fourths cents per line, i.e., twenty-one cents per page. (See Figure 2 for flow
chart for serial holdings conversion procedures.)

*Maintenance Procedures*

The serial edit report was received from University Systems once a week.
Data appeared on the edit report as it was typed on the op scan sheet. Each
call number was assigned a sequence number and each transaction for a partic-

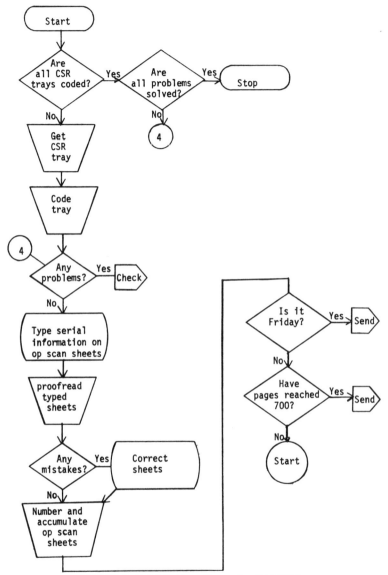

FIGURE 2. Serial Holdings Conversion Procedures

ular call number was assigned a transaction number; those numbers were retained through serial maintenance. Scan errors were underlined in the edit
report. Fatal errors caused an entire transaction to be rejected. For example,
the transaction would be rejected if "SHS" were typed instead of "SHA" for

"Serial Holding Add." Non-fatal errors caused a record unit to be rejected. For instance, if "L = MIA" were typed instead of "L = MAI" for "Location = Main Library" the message "INVALID LOCATION" would be printed in the edit report. (See Figure 3 for scanning and maintenance procedures.)

For the initial conversion of serial holdings data, there were only 1,447 scan rejects out of 386,334 unique identifications for forty batches sent to University Systems for input to LCS.

The most common problems in the weekly serial maintenance report were: "NO MASTER FOR CN" (call number), "COPY NOT IN MASTER," "RCD

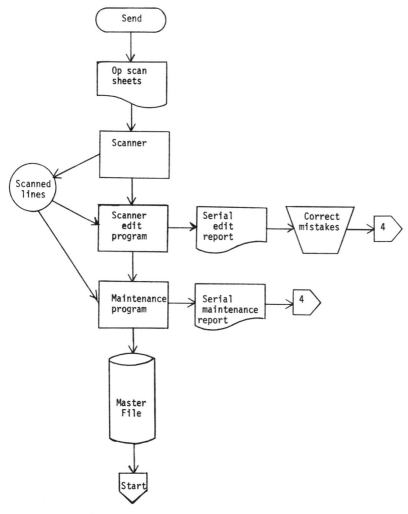

FIGURE 3. Scanning and Maintenance Procedures

(record) NOT SERIAL OR MONOSET." If a call number was not in LCS but was listed as a serial in the shelflist, an update form was sent to the Bibliographic Records Division (BRD) to be added to the LCS Master File. Another common problem was that many records, particularly for the serials which have ceased publication, were not coded "SER" (serial) in LCS. These discrepancies were sent to the Serial Cataloguing Section and then to BRD for updating in the LCS Master File. A special form was designed to describe problems with copy numbers, holdings, locations, and so on. (See Figure 4 for flow chart for problem solving.)

*Statistics*

The serial holdings conversion project progressed from an input of 2,092 unique identifications for 459 call numbers on August 26, 1976, to a cumulative total of 386,334 unique identifications for 60,306 call numbers on June 28, 1977.

*Serial Searching and Charging on LCS*

On August 2, 1977, Serials Phase II: Serial Searching and Charging became effective. It is now possible to limit general searches: author/title (ATS), title

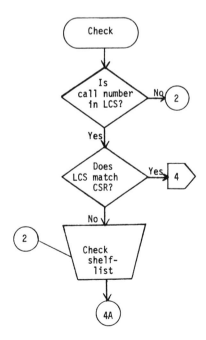

FIGURE 4A. Problem Solving

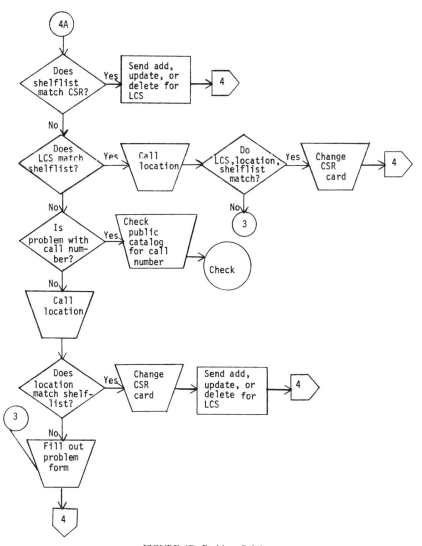

FIGURE 4B. Problem Solving

(TLS), and author (AUT) searches to serial only or non-serial only matches. For example:

    a. Author/title search for American Library Association.
        ALA...:

        ATS/AMERALA                retrieves all matches
        ATS/AMERALA/SER        retrieves only serial matches

ATS/AMERALA/MONO          retrieves only monograph
                          or monoset matches

b. Author search for American Library Association:

AUT/AMERICLIB          retrieves all matches
AUT/AMERICLIB/SER      retrieves only serial matches
AUT/AMERICLUB/MONO     retrieves only monograph
                       or monoset matches

*Detailed Search by Call Number*

Detailed searches by call number (DSC), title number (DST), and line number (DSL) have been used since 1970 to retrieve the master record of serials. The following examples are based on a detailed search by call number, but the options can be applied to a detailed search by title number or line number. A detailed search by call number retrieves all available information concerning the call number, including location, the volume holdings file, and all circulation and save records. For example:

DSC/Z671S4

Z671S4                        THE SERIALS LIBRARIAN
NOLC      2080822
01        001   MAI
02 MAI 001   S          CURRENT ISSUES IN PERIODICAL ROOM
03 MAI 001        1977-1978 V2  0 RNEWD 71036934 800712/800807
04 MAI 001        1976-1977 V1  0 RNEWD 71036934 800712/800807
PAGE  1  END

All volumes in circulation and all save information is retrieved by adding a comma or two slashes and ALLC to the search command. For example:

DSC/Z671S4,ALLC

Z671S4                        THE SERIALS LIBRARIAN
NOLC      2080822              1 ADDED: 770402
01        001   MAI
02 MAI            1977-1978 V1  0 RNEWD 71036934 800712/800807
03 MAI            1976-1977 V2  0 RNEWD 71036934 800712/800807
PAGE  1  END

*Limitation of a Detailed Search on a Serial*

A detailed search of a serial can be limited to a specific unique ID number, volume, year, location, copy number, holding type, or any combination of these.

To limit a detailed search of a serial to a specific unique ID number ",U = " and the unique ID number is added to the command. The unique ID number must match exactly the number in the volume holdings file:

DSC/Z671S4,U = V2

To limit a detailed search of a serial to a specific volume, ",V = " and the volume number is added to the command:

DSC/Z671S4,V = 1

All volumes that are volume 1 are retrieved, including those that are within the range of a summary statement. For example, if a summary statement is V1-10, it is retrieved when a search for volume 1 is performed.

To limit a detailed search of a serial to a specific year, ",Y = " and the year is added to the command:

DSC/Z671S4,Y = 1977

All volumes that have the specified year in the year field are retrieved. If there is no record of the requested year in the volume holdings file, the nearest years (both higher and lower) are retrieved, as well as all volumes charged with ERROR and the message NO EXACT MATCH-TRY ANOTHER COMBINATION OF KEYWORDS.

To limit a detailed search of a serial to a specific location, ",L = " and the three-letter location code that identifies the location is added to the command:

DSC/Z671S4,L = MAI

To limit a detailed search of a serial to a specific copy number, ",C = " and the copy number is added to the command:

DSC/Z671S4,C = 1

All information in the volume holdings file is either in summary form (summary statements indicated in the holdings file by the letter S) or listed as individual volumes (physical pieces or unique ID numbers indicated in the holdings file by a blank space in the holding type field.) To limit a search to the type of holding ",HT = " and the letter S (if summary statements only are desired) or the letter P (if physical pieces only are desired) is added to the command:

DSC/Z671S4,HT = S
DSC/Z671S4,HT = P

If there is no record of the requested volume in the volume holdings file, the nearest volumes (both higher and lower) are retrieved, as well as all volumes charged with ERROR and the message NO EXACT MATCH-TRY ANOTHER COMBINATION OF KEYWORDS.[10]

## On-Line Maintenance

On-line maintenance of the Serial Holdings File became a reality in October 1978. Staff members in the Bibliographic Records Division and in selected locations are authorized to perform on-line maintenance of serial holdings.

## Conclusion

The maintenance of serial records at OSU Libraries has progressed from the use of twelve separate files to the Central Serial Record to the automated Library Control System. Each new development has made it possible for patrons and staff to locate needed serial information more efficiently.

## REFERENCES

1. James E. Skipper, "Organizing Serial Records at the Ohio State University Libraries." *College & Research Libraries*, 14:39 (Jan. 1953), 41.

2. Task Force on Serial Holdings, "LCS Serial/Monoset Holdings File: A Proposal." (Columbus: The Ohio State University Libraries, 7 August 1974), Appendix A, B, C, D.

3. Task Force on Serial Holdings, "Implementation Recommendations for Adding the OSU Libraries Serial and Monoset Title Holdings to LCS" (Columbus: The Ohio State University Libraries, 31 August 1974).

4. Task Force on Serial Holdings, "LCS Serial/Monoset Holdings File," pp. 1–2, 16–17.

5. Task Force on Serial Holdings, "LCS Serial Holdings File Specifications" (Columbus: The Ohio State University Libraries, 3 March 1975). Appendix B, C, D. Title was changed to "LCS Serial Holdings Functional Specifications" (14 May 1975).

6. Task Force on Serial Holdings, "Appendix A, Addenda and Corrigenda, of the LCS Serial Holdings File Specifications" (14 May 1975).

7. University Systems, "LCS Serials Control System Design Document" (28 July 1975).

8. University Systems, "Serial Holdings Maintenance Procedural Manual" (23 July 1976).

9. Staff members were Elsetta R. Ervin, Supervisor of Clerical Staff; Deborah A. Cameron, Leslie K. Cox, Maurine Croyle, Sherry T. Griffin, Elva R. Griffith, Lisa Ohler, and Susan Schley.

10. Nancy Helmick et al., "LCS Staff Manual: A Guide to the Library Control System of the Ohio State University Libraries" (Columbus: Ohio State University Libraries, 1979), Sect. 2.7 - 2.7.5f.

# A COOPERATIVE SERIALS DATA CONVERSION PROJECT IN CALIFORNIA

Margaret M. McKinley

ABSTRACT. Three university libraries, the University of California, Berkeley, the University of California, Los Angeles, and Stanford University joined forces in a three-year serials data conversion project, funded by an HEA Title II-C grant. In spite of the difficulties of working with large and cumbersome files and in spite of the long distance between the two northern California libraries and UCLA, the libraries successfully converted major portions of their manually generated serials files to machine-readable form, integrated the newly created records into a single file, and also developed practical techniques which could be utilized in future cooperative activities. Some of the problems identified by project managers are reported, particularly those related to staffing, organization, and the characteristics of large, time-worn serials files.

"All scenery in California," Mark Twain commented in *Roughing It*, "requires distance to give it its highest charm. The mountains are imposing...from any point of view but one must have distance to soften their ruggedness...a California forest is best at a little distance...the trees being chiefly one of monotonous family—redwood, pine, spruce, fir—at a near view there is a wearisome attitude in their rigid arms, stretched downward and outward in one continued and reiterated appeal to all men to 'Sh!—don't say a word!—you might disturb somebody!"....Often a grassy plain in California is what it should be, but often, too, it is best contemplated at a distance because, although its grass blades are tall, they stand up vindictively straight and self-sufficient, and are unsociably wide apart, with uncomely spots of barren sand between."[1]

The uncompromising landscape that Mark Twain encountered in the late nineteenth century has been altered to a certain extent, but the vast distances, high mountain ranges, and limited number of north–south travel routes in California have contributed to the development of academic libraries in the state which might be compared to Twain's "straight and self-sufficient grass blades, unsociably wide apart." For example, the University Library at the University of California, Berkeley (UCB) is 436 or 406 miles, depending on the travel route chosen, from its sister institution, the University Library at the University of California Los Angeles (UCLA). UCB has been able to embark on cooperative ventures with Stanford University, a sociable 40 miles across the San Francisco Bay, much more easily than with UCLA and other southern California libraries.

While cooperation among the large eastern and midwestern libraries has been given much well-deserved publicity, the efforts of libraries in the far west of the United States have been less visible and have produced fewer positive results, with the notable exception of the Washington Library Network. Those unfamiliar with the history and geography of the Pacific Coast cannot fully comprehend the immense barriers blocking the paths of cooperation among research libraries in this region so that the smallest of successes must be considered a major triumph. In the past, large academic libraries in California have relied primarily on their own resources in providing access to their collections. Now modern technology, including the marvels of telecommunication, has brought the possibility of successful cooperative activities within the reach of libraries formerly separated by natural and manmade obstacles, while the ever-shrinking resources of the past decade have made such cooperation imperative.

The availability of federal funds through the provisions of Title II-C of the Higher Education Act has made it possible for research libraries to become involved in large-scale projects to improve inter-library cooperation and to make their collections more widely available. A number of libraries across the United States have seized the opportunity, provided by these funds, to convert serials records to machine-readable form and to make these records and resources available to the research library community at large. Three research libraries in California joined forces in a cooperative project funded by Title II-C and have established that weighty academic bureaucracies, large public catalogs, and unwieldy processing files are not overwhelming obstacles to successful retrospective conversion of serials records. The distances between the institutions, as well as a certain pride in fierce individualism, presented challenges rather than deterrents.

The Title II-C project undertaken by the university libraries at the University of California, Berkeley (UCB), Stanford University, and the University of California, Los Angeles (UCLA) was designed not only to convert serial records at the three institutions and to integrate these records into a single machine-readable file, but to provide, as well, opportunities for substantial and continuing cooperation. Each of the libraries also intended to make internal changes in bibliographic files and in preparation of records for those files to insure that, in the future, information about serial resources would be available on a current basis to other research libraries.

The initial grant was awarded for the 1978/79 federal fiscal year, with the possibility of continued funding for the following two years. Since the conditions and purposes of the grant, as well as the basic structure, and the interrelationships among the libraries have been documented elsewhere,[2] the present discussion will extend that account to a report of the experiences of the libraries, approaches to common problems, solutions to those problems, and prospects for the future.

Many library articles on data conversion or automation focus on technical aspects of projects or on developmental efforts. Data input forms, hardware, programming techniques, production methodology, and statistics are discussed in detail. The more elusive aspects of project management such as staff organization, interpersonal and intraorganizational relationships, staff training and development, and the impact of procedural or methodological changes are all too often ignored. With no record in the literature, libraries become involved in data conversion projects and are then forced to rediscover the same problems and solutions previously faced by others. In an effort to avoid a similar omission, this report will relate some of the human and organizational problems encountered by project managers and administrators.

## The Environment

Each of the university libraries had converted many thousands of serial records to machine-readable form and had distributed lists of serial holdings to libraries and to other research institutions in the U.S. and abroad. In each library, however, there remained thousands of records for serial titles that had not yet been converted to machine-readable form. These were generally older titles that had ceased or suspended publication before computer-based file capabilities were available. There were also many thousands of records for serial titles in special libraries on each campus which had never been converted to machine-readable form.

UCB estimated that it had about 100,000 records to be converted, including those in its Bancroft Library of Californiana. Stanford University estimated that 100,000 records could be converted, including those in the Hoover Institution of War, Revolution and Peace, as well as its government documents collection. UCLA estimated that it had 58,000 records to convert, including selected government documents.

Serials librarians and administrators in each of the libraries were aware of the impressive obstacles, in addition to those already mentioned, which could prevent successful completion of this project. Each of the libraries maintained dozens of serials files, none of which were in complete agreement with any of the others, in form or content. Serials cataloguing records in each of the libraries reflected changes in cataloguing codes and practices throughout the twentieth century as well as the chronic understaffing that appears to plague serials cataloguing operations in any large research library.

Each university library was determined, however, to build a machine-readable file of serials records and then to unite the three files into a single, integrated file. All agreed that the record conversion project should also have some lasting benefit for the libraries and that a solid base should be constructed on which to continue to publicize the serials collections.

The three libraries decided to use a major bibliographic utility as a conversion mechanism, but did not select a single utility. UCLA keyed records into the OCLC data base, while UCB and Stanford chose RLIN. The three libraries have since demonstrated that input to a single bibliographic utility is not a prerequisite for a successful cooperative data conversion project. While software development varied among the libraries, the overall project goals were, nevertheless, met.

UCB and Stanford were closely involved in developing RLIN's capabilities for handling serials records, including local holdings information. UCLA, on the other hand, developed software locally in order to utilize the machine-readable records that arrived weekly on OCLC archival computer tapes. Initially, UCLA developed programs which provided brief index listings and full register listings. Programs providing basic bibliographic control over entries were also written. These programs served the project's immediate needs while more extensive developmental work was carried out on a complete authority control system. During the project's first and second years, substantial progress was made at UCLA toward adapting its Biomedical Library's on-line serials processing system for general campus use and developing, as well, capabilities for local on-line editing of machine-readable records. Before the end of the project's second year, the staff at UCLA had the option of keying serials records into the OCLC data base or into its own, locally developed data base.

### Preliminary Planning

In the preliminary planning phase of the project, serials librarians from each of the three libraries met to discuss matters of common concern on which agreement was necessary so that the three machine-readable files could be successfully merged. Each of the libraries agreed to use the MARC-S record structure and to include all mandatory data elements as well as any additional information that might be available. The three librarians recognized, however, that if an older serial title were not catalogued, the available information might be very sketchy and that extensive searches to locate bibliographic or detailed holdings information were beyond the scope of the project. Very brief records would inevitably be included in the files being created and would remain until those records could be individually reviewed and enhanced.

The serials librarians agreed to use the standards developed in what was then Draft 7 of the American National Standards Institute's *Serials Holdings Statements at the Summary Level*. UCB managers had initially intended to carry holdings statements to the issue-specific level, while UCLA and Stanford managers decided that they would be unable to do so. During the course of the project, the staff at UCB realized that it would be unable to devote the time necessary to prepare holdings statements at this level of specificity and that this objective would have to be suspended. In each of the libraries, shelf checks would have been necessary and would have had a marked effect on the total number of records that could be converted during the course of the project.

Library administrators had decided to concentrate on the conversion of ceased or suspended serial titles in their collections. As project staff in each of the libraries gained experience, it became apparent that these were the most difficult records to convert to machine-readable form because of incomplete, faulty, and outdated information in the records and because the casual, or imaginative, display of information on old catalog cards had to be modernized and streamlined to conform to the requirements of machine-readable files. Each of the libraries eventually began to convert currently received, as well as retired, serial titles.

Each library placed its existing machine-readable file of brief serials records in new data bases in preparation for upgrading the records. Stanford placed its *Stanford Union List of Serials* (SULS), containing 70,000 titles, into the RLIN data base. UCB also read its machine-readable file of 150,000 currently received and retired serial titles into RLIN. The file which produced UCLA's *Serials Titles Currently Received at UCLA* was included in UCLA's local online edit system during the project's second year. Individual records were purged from this file if OCLC records were available and upgraded if they were not.

In the first enthusiastic months of the project, it had appeared that it might be possible to use ISSNs (International Standard Serial Numbers) as the primary mechanism to merge like titles in a three-campus listing. The project staff in each of the libraries devoted many hours to searching for ISSNs in a multitude of reference tools. The Serials Department at UCB added a step to receipt of incoming issues of periodicals by searching for ISSNs on the covers of newly received items. When staff at Stanford and at UCB had exhausted all of their available sources for ISSNs, a copy of a two-campus list was sent to UCLA to be searched through OCLC for ISSNs. As the first year of the project drew to a close, it became apparent that the effort of searching for ISSNs would not be justified by the percentage of titles for which ISSNs could be found. Many of the serial titles were too old or too obscure to have had ISSNs assigned. The error rate in ISSN assignment has been discussed elsewhere.[3,4] While project staff in the three libraries continued to include ISSNs in converted records, the plan to use ISSNs to merge the three files was given a supplementary place in the file merge strategy.

Further discussions with respect to a three-campus union listing lead to the conclusion that the proliferation of serials lists was not necessarily a boon to public service staff in any library and that access to the serials collections of the three libraries would be equally improved by including their serials files in an established union listing. The *University of California Union List of Serials* (UCULS) had been issued irregularly for ten years and software was available to include files from UCLA and UCB. In the last two editions, serials records from the California State Colleges and Universities had also been included, and it seemed reasonable to consider including Stanford's holdings as well. Stanford's serial holdings were, indeed, included in the 1980 edition of UCULS, and the listing was retitled *California Academic Libraries List of Serials*.

## Identification of Records for Conversion

Each of the libraries identified records to be converted in a slightly different fashion. UCB was fortunate in having an experienced retired cataloguer who read the Main Library's shelflist and marked titles to be converted. UCB also converted entire files, such as its newspaper collection. Stanford planned to convert the entire files of some libraries, including the Hoover Institution of War, Revolution and Peace, the Jackson School of Business Library, and the Lane Medical Library. Stanford also intended to upgrade records in SULS. At UCLA, retired titles for which the library had once had a current subscription were selected for conversion at the beginning of the project. Later, when the difficulties of working with records for retired titles became only too apparent, attention was shifted to currently received titles in selected libraries on the UCLA campus. There were plans, in the third year of the project, to begin tackling the government documents collections in each of the three libraries.

## Staff Organization

Each of the libraries decided to establish separate data conversion units that would utilize the administrative services of the three serials departments and for which the three serials librarians would have operational responsibility, each in her own department.

While there was general agreement on the overall goals of the project, each of the library administrations set short-term objectives that differed from campus to campus. Stanford, at first, concentrated on converting uncatalogued records in the Hoover Institution. These are brief records usually containing only an entry, a place of publication, and a summary holdings statement. In spite of the brevity of these records, many unique titles, not previously included in any union listing, are included in this collection. UCB began converting several different serials files, including those in the Bancroft Library, newspapers in the Main Library, and retired serial titles in the Main Library Stacks. These records at Stanford and UCB were edited prior to conversion, but without an intensive effort to upgrade the records or to alter the choice or form of entry.

The initial selection of project staff at UCB and Stanford was determined, in part, by these policy decisions. Both libraries hired less experienced paraprofessionals to key records. At UCB, these keyers worked under the direction of an experienced paraprofessional and at Stanford, under the direction of a junior librarian. The data collection work was also decentralized at UCB and Stanford with separate subunits set up in locations such as the Bancroft Library and the Hoover Insitution. Separate ISSN searching units were established at UCB and Stanford which were responsible for adding ISSNs to machine-readable records.

Later, when UCB and Stanford project staff began to upgrade records prior to conversion to machine-readable form, they discovered that this was a lengthier and more complex process than simple conversion and would require conversion staff with more skill and expertise. At that point, Stanford revised its project organization to include a MARC-S Upgrade Unit, the staff of which included two senior paraprofessionals and a librarian. UCB management, impressed with the difficulty of modifying or adding to information found in manual files, assigned record enhancement or modification work to the serials cataloguing staff. Serials cataloguers at UCB also assumed responsibility for conversion of records for titles currently received in the Serials Department and for conversion of retrospective records, as encountered.

At UCLA, short-term objectives included not only conversion, but upgrading of serials records to meet current local standards for description and establishment of entries. In developing a staff, UCLA therefore decided to employ more experienced paraprofessionals who would be expected to exercise individual judgment in selecting information to be keyed into a machine-readable file. They worked under the direction of an experienced paraprofessional and a junior, but very knowledgeable, librarian. The data collection effort was more centralized at UCLA than at the other two campuses because emphasis was placed, at first, on converting serials records in centrally located files. UCLA serials cataloguers contributed to the data conversion effort by adding summary holdings statements to newly catalogued titles. These records then became part of the new machine-readable serials file.

The project at UCLA was fortunate in being able to attract existing library staff members, some of whom resigned from career positions to accept temporary positions with the data conversion project. Both UCLA and UCB benefited from the close proximity of graduate schools of library and information science and were able to use students enrolled in these graduate programs in casual, or student assistant, positions as well as in paraprofessional positions. Stanford's staff was enriched as well, since UCB staffers transferred to Stanford from time to time. UCB and Stanford were also able to exchange staff training. Stanford staff assisted UCB staff in the use of the RLIN system and UCB reciprocated by assisting Stanford staff with learning to code records for input to RLIN. Without available pools of skilled and talented people from which to draw, it might well have been difficult for all three campuses to fill the temporary grant positions.

Each of the campuses was fortunate in having a small corps of trained serials workers, librarians and paraprofessionals, directing day-to-day operations whose organizational skills and time management abilities were tested to the fullest extent possible as various aspects of the project expanded or shifted in scope. There was, however, on each campus, a steady turnover as junior members of the conversion staff qualified for better positions as a result of their project experience or as they left to pursue alternative career objectives. The project managers resigned themselves to training a continuing series of data collectors, keyers, and coders.

### Data Collection and Conversion Methodology

The data collection and conversion techniques employed in each of the libraries were primarily characterized by change. Prior to beginning any work in data conversion, the staff in each of the libraries had designed work routines and developed strategies based upon the best estimates available concerning file sizes, contents of files, and probable time required to complete particular data conversion tasks. Project planning on each of the campuses erred in the direction of excessive optimism with respect to the number of records that could be converted in a specified time period, given the sizes, ages, and conditions of the files being converted.

As project staff became more experienced, conversion techniques were refined. The staff also discovered that the idiosyncrasies of the various files being converted demanded revision of basic procedures each time conversion of a new file was begun. In addition, the project on each of the campuses shifted in local direction and scope as administrators recognized the potential capabilities of the newly converted serials files. To capture procedures and tasks in any detail at any given time during the course of the project would be to falsely represent project operations at any other time during the project.

### Cataloguing Revisited

Each of the university libraries encountered similar deficiences in the quality of the information in the libraries' manually generated files. Bibliographic and holdings information was fragmented among a number of files. The catalog records frequently met standards of an earlier time. Many of the cataloguing practices, acceptable in former days, resulted in bibliographic records that required extensive alterations. A record might contain long, discursive notes about the history of a serial publication and that of its editor as well. On the other hand, information about the history of another publication might be very incomplete. A serial might be catalogued under its earliest entry or under an entry occurring sometime during the course of its existence, selected, apparently, at random. Even if a serial were catalogued according to successive title practices, the entries selected were sometimes questionable. Information in public and in processing records was often in conflict.

The conversion staff also found that title changes might have occurred, undetected, in retired as well as in currently received titles. Some call numbers were incorrectly recorded. Typographical errors had crept into locally prepared card sets. Added entries might not have been maintained under the most recent form of a corporate name. Linking notes might be missing or incorrect. Filing errors in card files also complicated the business of data collection preliminary to coding records for input to machine-readable data bases. All of these elements combined to make the entire data collection and conversion process much slower than had been expected.

Much of the cataloguing employed latest entries, with all holdings for a serial publication gathered together under the last title recorded for that serial, rather than successive entries in which holdings would be found under each title a given publication might have had. If the three libraries were to conform to current cataloguing standards, all catalog records in which latest entries were used would have to have been recatalogued under each of the titles carried by all of these serial publications. If this were to be done, however, the automated serials files would not agree with existing card catalogs. UCLA and Stanford decided to accept the disagreement. UCB, initially, decided that card catalogs and machine-readable files must be compatible and resolved to recatalog serial titles for the public card catalogs as well as for the new machine-readable file. This library hoped, eventually, to reduce maintenance of its manually produced files as the converted records became substitutes for card catalog records.

For each of the libraries, separating each record catalogued under its latest serial title into its various components and making individual records for every title that a particular serial may have carried created a substantial workload for the cataloguing and conversion staff. As the project neared the end of its first year, it became apparent, in each of the libraries, that the data conversion staff and the cataloguing staff would not be able to handle all of the serials records requiring recataloguing before the data could be converted to machine-readable form. UCB and UCLA faced the additional problem of integrating project objectives with plans for a machine-readable catalog. Before the end of the project's second year, UCLA and UCB planned to add trained serials cataloguers to their respective project staffs to augment the strained resources of the serials cataloguing units.

## Quality Control

Project staff in all three libraries struggled continually with quality control. While specifics of the problems varied and the solutions varied depending upon local conditions, there were a number of common elements. Rather than describing in great detail the problems uncovered and solutions found for each library, it would be as useful to concentrate on the experience of one library. UCLA has a younger library than does UCB and it is also somewhat smaller but UCLA has a larger file of centrally received serials than does Stanford. The large holdings of Stanford's special libraries present difficulties that UCLA also experienced to a lesser extent. With respect to file sizes and special local situations, UCLA is positioned midway between UCB and Stanford. UCLA's experiences with quality control have been outlined, therefore, with the understanding that these problems were also faced by Stanford and UCB to a greater or lesser degree.

Throughout the course of the project, compromise was the one word which was continually and inevitably linked with quality control. While each individual on the project staff at UCLA was vitally concerned with creating records of the highest possible quality, there was also the ever-present realization that the library was committed to converting many thousands of serial records and that one or two thousand perfectly prepared records would not meet this obligation. The project staff, therefore, concentrated its quality control work on certain critical areas in which inadequate or faulty information would have had the most impact on the public. Entries and holdings were given the most attention, with the next consideration being given to the completeness of the bibliographic data and accuracy in correctly tagging MARC-S records.

UCLA has six cataloguing centers, each of whom has built its own catalog, largely independent of any of the other centers. The project was thrust, unwillingly, into a local pioneering effort to establish consistency in form and choice of entry for serial titles. No campus-wide authority file existed, and the project was placed in the uncomfortable position of developing its own, outside the boundaries of any established cataloguing unit in UCLA's university library. Gathering together all of the holdings for a single title into a single record seemed to be of critical importance, however, since these records would eventually be merged with those converted by UCB, Stanford, other University of California libraries, and the libraries of the California State College and University system. It was clear to the project staff that lack of integrity in UCLA's file would greatly increase the difficulty of creating a useful listing.

Some cataloguers were convinced that the conversion staff was engaged in work that was most properly the province of established cataloguing units. Public and processing staff was concerned about the eventual lack of synchronization between card catalogs and machine-readable files. The conversion staff, on the other hand, felt the pressure of meeting production goals and thought that the conversion operation should take precedence over assignment of responsibility for the work done and over any corrections made to the existing card catalogs. As with any major changes in traditional library methods of displaying information and creating records and files, there was great unease among staff in established units with the methodology, goals, and products of the data conversion staff.

The project staff did not generally have access to issues or volumes and worked from public and processing records alone. Early on in the project, it became clear that consultation of physical volumes would have to be severely limited if acceptable production levels were to be maintained. Many of the project's coders, trained to strive for the highest possible degree of accuracy, were unhappy with this compromise but tried to conform to it, with only occasional lapses.

Holdings statements were drawn from public and processing records and, when these records disagreed with one another, a holdings statement was prepared based upon the coder's judgment of the most reliable data available. Coders were strongly discouraged from checking shelves or circulation records for additional information.

In transcribing bibliographic information, coders relied on information located in OCLC, local cataloguing records, and local processing files. Coders were able, in some instances, to create machine-readable records that contained more information than had been available in sketchy local catalog records. They were, however, discouraged from searching through obscure or specialized serials bibliographies for additional information.

In addition to converting records for serial titles already in UCLA's collections, the project staff developed methods for phasing newly catalogued titles into the serials file being developed. While cataloguers agreed to add holdings statements to titles they catalogued, they did not necessarily have access to records for titles catalogued by other centers at UCLA and could inadvertently add duplicate records to the file. Until centralized bibliographic control could be established, the burden of eliminating duplicate records fell to the project staff. If duplicates were displayed near one another in the file, identification and consolidation into a single record could be accomplished by workers with minimal serials experience. Identification of records for titles with differences in choice of entry required the attention of an experienced serials worker, familiar with UCLA practices, past and present, in establishing headings for corporate bodies.

### Future Prospects

The Title II-C grant has allowed each of the three university libraries to go far beyond straightforward conversion of serials records from manual to machine-readable form. A primary goal expressed by each of the libraries was to create a machine-readable data base from which various products could be generated and in which data could be altered, added, or deleted. Lasting benefits to other libraries, with respect to current information about serial holdings, could not be assured unless such data bases existed. The data bases have been developed and have been successfully integrated into a single file. Each of the libraries expects to continue to enlarge these files with additional records and to add fuller bibliographic information and more detailed holdings statements to records already converted.

Through the data conversion project, a methodology for future cooperation among the three libraries has emerged and a record of success firmly established which will encourage further cooperation. Historical and geographic obstacles have been met and overcome, demonstrating that substantial and continuing cooperation is, in fact, possible for these libraries and for others in California.

The data conversion project has also had a marked impact on technical processing operations in each of the institutions. The precise nature of the impact varied from library to library, depending upon the degree of centralization, future plans for the public catalogs, bibliographic utilities chosen, and plans for automation of technical processes. Dramatic changes in long-established methods for technical processing in large libraries or for providing access to collections rarely appear to be accomplished without some degree of organizational stress. Nevertheless, this would appear to be beneficial for an organization in order to maintain its continued good health and to prevent stagnation, boredom, and indifference from overwhelming its staff. The serials data conversion project provided an important catalyst in this evolutionary process, leading toward full utilization of recent technology.

Other research libraries will have the use of the bibliographic records converted to machine-readable form by the project and will have ready access to the unique serial holdings of the libraries, in OCLC, in RLIN, or in *California Academic Libraries List of Serials*. In addition, other libraries will be able to draw upon the experiences of the three California libraries in organizing their own data conversion projects, in planning for automation of library processes, and in development of computer-generated products.

## REFERENCES

1. Clemens, Samuel L., *Roughing It* (New York: Airmont, 1967), p. 231–32.

2. Ellsworth, Dianne J., "Serials Union Lists and Automation." *Serials Review* 6 (3) (January/March 1980);69–70.

3. Lupton, David Walker, "Tracking the ISSN." *Serials Librarian* 4 (2) (Winter 1979):187–98.

4. Sleep, Esther L., "Whither the ISSN; a Practical Experience." *Canadian Library Journal* 34 (4) (August 1977):265–70.

# CATALOGUING IN A TIME OF CHANGE

## Mary Ellen Soper

ABSTRACT. Great changes are occurring in cataloguing because of the introduction of a new set of cataloguing rules and the growth of automated cataloguing systems. The interrelationship between these two events is discussed, and possible responses to change suggested. The benefits of automated systems are considered. Cataloguing in general, with an emphasis on serials cataloguing, is covered.

The change from the Anglo-American Cataloguing Rules, 1st edition (AACR1), to the Anglo-American Cataloguing Rules, 2nd edition (AACR2), scheduled for January 2, 1981, by the Library of Congress (LC), and the far-reaching effects this change will have on library catalogs and services is not a new topic to anyone with even a modicum of interest in current events in librarianship. Reams have been written and will be written; a multitude of conferences and workshops have been held and are still to be held. Much attention has been focused on the overall effect of the new code, and attention has also been paid by many with narrower focuses to the rules covering special formats and patterns of publications. This article is concerned with some general aspects of both the new code and automation. It is quite impressionistic, with a slight slant toward serials cataloguing.

### Responses to Change

It will take time for the Library of Congress' cataloguing to reflect the rules of AACR2, but gradually we will all see the effect of the new rules, whether printed on separately ordered cards, in the *National Union Catalog, New Serials Titles*, or in machine-readable forms distributed through the MARC system to the various networks throughout the country. The cataloguing rules are going to change (some libraries adopted AACR2 before the feared date of January 2, 1981), and railing against them will do little other than offer illusionary relief.

There are various reactions possible when major changes are made in ongoing systems. The following observations are pertinent in some respects not only to changes in cataloguing codes but also to changes in other systems such as classification schemes and subject heading lists.

### 1. Ignore the New System and Continue with the Present One Indefinitely

Initially such a reaction looks alluring. There would be no need to retrain the library's personnel or users. Things would go along as they always have (assuming everything is presently going smoothly). But soon data coming from outside sources, such as the cataloguing services of OCLC, Inc., Research Libraries Information Network, Washington Library Network, or Blackwell North America, would start to conflict with the locally produced data. The library could choose to change the outside data to conform to its own interiorly produced data, but it would then lose most of the benefits of data received from other sources. The staff would undoubtedly have to be enlarged in order to make these changes, and the economic burden on the library would be great.

As far as cataloguing is concerned, I assume that the descriptive data would not have to be changed to conform to the local practices, but that only the entries and headings would be affected. I don't feel that changes in descriptive data affect either the librarian-user or non-librarian-user nearly as much as others seem to. But changes in headings are crucial. Even if new forms of headings are not changed to conform to the old forms, some sort of cross-referencing system has to be implemented or the library no longer has a catalog, but instead just has a file of unrelated bibliographic descriptions.

Some have expressed the opinion that such a file would serve the user as well as, or even better than, the "ideal" that many of us believe in—a syndetic catalog, in whatever format, with authority control of headings, and interconnections designed to lead the user to the reference he/she is seeking. The concept of main entry is not included here, as it does seem apparent that main entry, at least in on-line systems with multi-access points and choice of arrangement of descriptions, is much less important than it was in the days of the nineteenth-century printed catalogs or even with the still prevalent systems using printed unit-card descriptions with access points added. Whether the access point is main, added, or a subject heading is not really important to a user, but whether this access point will also lead to other material by or about the same name or subject is. And the only way to insure this is to control the headings used for the access points by whatever method the system permits. An on-line system, such as the Washington Library Network (WLN), does control the access points, and through its on-line authority control, permits entry on nonvalid terms by referring them to the valid terms, which can then be searched for retrieval of bibliographic items.

Lack of control of headings in a catalog of a library's collection results in increased frustration for the users. Scattering of manifestations of works under a variety of unconnected forms of the same headings would prevent a user from discovering other manifestations if he/she cannot acquire the one for which he/she is searching. Catalog use studies, plentiful if inadequate, cannot lead us to conclude a user generally wants only a particular manifestation of a work, and certainly the body of theoretical writing about catalog use, exemplified by that of Seymour Lubetzky, also prevents us from drawing such conclusions. Admittedly it is always possible to think of exceptions—the bibliographer searching for a particular state of a work comes to mind most readily—but such a user would obviously be better served by seeing all available manifestations displayed together, not just the one he/she is searching for.

Based on the previous reasoning it is difficult to imagine a library choosing to ignore completely the control of headings and just interfiling AACR2 headings in with AACR1 and earlier headings willy-nilly. The increasing burden placed on the service staff and the confusion engendered among users would not be worth the short-term benefits to the technical services staff. To repeat: a catalog without control of headings is *not* a catalog; it is an unorganized and increasingly unusable file of descriptions, serving little purpose and causing much grief.

## 2. Adopt the New Rules for All Material New to the System and Leave the Already Catalogued Material as Is

This solution, if applied to cataloguing rules, almost inevitably leads to split files of some sort. A split catalog was proposed at first by many libraries as they began tentatively to plan for the changeover in 1980 (later changed to 1981). The need for cross-references back and forth between the two files was investigated. Then libraries began to reduce the estimate of the amount of change that the new rules would necessitate, and other solutions began to emerge. The estimated percent of heading changes has steadily dropped since LC's original guess of nearly fifty percent in the existing MARC file. Now, with LC's concept of "tolerable headings" and elastic rule interpretations, the percentage of change has decreased to a much more manageable level. Arlene Dowell's report on her research done for a dissertation, made at ALA New York in June 1980, revealed that her estimate of conflicts in headings between AACR1 and AACR2 was as low as 9.5 percent in various sized libraries.[1] Similar findings from studies made in individual libraries, reported in such periodicals as *Alternative Catalog Newsletter*, have led many libraries to decide to avoid two catalogs and stay with the one file by interfiling minor punctuation and spelling differences and resorting to split files with cross-references within the one catalog only in a relatively few cases. The amount of actual recataloguing planned is minimal.

This pragmatic solution, the best choice for any ongoing system, would seem to offer the fewest problems and upsets for both the library staff and the user. Even this makeshift response to new rules would not be necessary, though, if the catalog were on-line with good authority control. In such a system, theoretically, all that would be required to change a heading to conform to the new rules would be one change in the authority file, which would then automatically affect all records indexed by that heading. The information in the description indexed by the heading might disagree with the new heading, but this should not confuse librarians, and with a little instruction, should not even cause non-librarian users any major problems. Many of us probably have doubts as to how far into a description most non-librarian users read anyway. It is certainly true that many have long questioned the usefulness of some of the items that appear in a description. If, as is believed, many users benefit little from such information, then discrepancies in the data will probably bother few.

### 3. Change All Existing Data to Conform to the New System and Use the New System for All New Material

This is an ideal, unlikely to be achieved by any but the libraries with the most rigorous weeding policies and material with short "half-lives." The large general library, with material in the humanities and social sciences that is not superseded completely by new material, will have thousands of records created under the old system that must be kept; and while it would be ideal to change everything to conform to the new system, the chaos created by such changes would be detrimental to users of all kinds. Just consider for a moment the effects on libraries of complete reclassification projects begun in the past, the effects on users, and how few of these were actually completed as originally planned.

In conclusion, changes in description brought about by AACR2 should not cause much upset in catalogs, though they will require retraining of the library staff to implement the new rules and understand their intent. The new rules for description are designed to be more consistent and understandable for all types of materials in all languages. There seems to be nothing in the new rules to cause us to believe they will not do this. I certainly have found they are easier for new librarianship students to understand. Why should not the same be true of catalog users?

Changes in entry should cause few problems in multi-access catalogs, particularly in on-line ones. An on-line catalog is particularly insensitive to the distinction between main and added entries. But changes in headings are of primary importance. These must be controlled, or the catalog is no longer a catalog.

### AACR1[2] vs. AACR2

Numerous articles and workshops have detailed the differences between the two sets of cataloguing rules.[3] As far as serials are concerned, one major change will be the discontinuance of corporate main entry for most serials, with resulting entry under titles for even those with the most nondescriptive of titles. A discussion of how this came about and a negative opinion as to the effect of this change is presented in Spalding's article.[4]

The change in entry in many corporate body issued serials may not have as great an impact as might at first be thought if the catalogs in which these entries go are multi-access. The new rules make it clear that the corporate bodies that formerly would have been main entries are now to be added entries, so access to these important bodies is not lost, and most users probably won't be aware of the change. An on-line system like WLN, which searches on names, personal and corporate, and retrieves all records to which these names are assigned as access points, whether main or added, and which permits display of retrieved records either in author order or in title order, erases any distinction between main and added entry for all but the most particular searcher. What will be new are title entries for many serials that never had such access before. We've assumed in the past that such access was worthless, but I doubt we were ever certain of this.

However, in single-entry listings, such as printed lists of holdings of a single library or union lists of many libraries' holdings, the result of the change in the new code will be primary access under massings of descriptions under such generally recognized indistinctive phrases as *Bulletin of the...*, *Journal of the...*, *Transactions of the....* Such listings of serials are new to the American library scene, but not uncommon in other printed bibliographies and catalogs, such as those produced in European countries and by nontraditional library institutions. Many are quite familiar with the citation practices of scholarly publications, which often cite serial titles in the same way. We have become accustomed to manipulating the citation titles in order to verify them in our library catalogs. After AACR2 is implemented, it may become possible to go directly, with no manipulation, from a citation to a catalog. I say "may," because the problem of what is the "real" title of a serial is not solved by the new rules. The fact that the key title derived from the International Serials Data System (ISDS) can still differ from the title proper of AACR2 illustrates this.

By changing the definition of author and excluding corporate bodies from authorship, AACR2 remains in conformity with part of the Paris Principles. Number 2.2(a) says "[The catalogue should be an efficient instrument for ascertaining] which works by a particular author...[are in the library]."[5] Though it doesn't conflict with the Paris Principles as far as the functions of the catalog are concerned, it does go against the intent of number 9: Entry under corporate bodies.[6] Some main entry under corporate bodies is allowd by Rule 21.1B2, ACCR2, but the intent is very clear that such entries should be much more limited than in previous codes, and that it is not authorship, but instead "emanation" that is involved.

Since serials by definition continue, what should be done with all the serials that began before 1981 and still continue? Most serials were entered under their titles, according to AACR1, so will not be affected. And the existing serials now entered under corporate body that the new rules would cause to enter under title will probably remain as they are unless a title change occurs and recataloguing is necessary. I am assuming a universal reluctance to recatalog existing large serial files unless absolutely necessary. The confusion will probably arise from corporate bodies which issue several serials over time. Some of these may be entered under the corporate name, while others will be entered under title, with the corporate name an added entry. Again a multi-access catalog should be able to accommodate such cases with little problem. The single-entry list, however, could present such inconsistencies to the user that he/she will be badly confused. But he/she is probably already confused over entries resulting from the application of AACR1 rule 6. Cross-references are dictated in such situations. Eventually such problems may disappear by themselves as serials cease and corporate bodies die. But it is necessary to remember the *Philosophical Transactions of the Royal Society*—still with us since 1665!

A more troublesome problem created by the change from AACR1 to AACR2 is that of the alterations in headings called for by chapters 22–25. Much discussion has centered on the changes in personal names, set forth in chapter 22. But personal name headings are not really serial problems. Geographic and corporate name headings (chapters 23–24) are.

Uniform titles in chapter 25 would not initially seem to have much to do with serials, but unique serial identifiers (necessary when the title proper is not unique and conflicts with the same or similar titles) are treated as uniform titles. This need for a kind of uniform title for serials has of course arisen because entry under a corporate body (which typically has a unique name) is no longer usually allowed. Library of Congress, in conjunction with the other ABACUS libraries, has come up with unique serial identifiers to solve the problem created by the change in definition of authorship. A current interpretation from LC appears in the *RTSD Newsletter*, under discussion of rule 25.5B.[7]

With this interpretation the unique serial identifier will be very similar to the key title of ISDS. The unique serial identifier, like uniform titles, is a manipulated title, changed from the pure title proper as it appears in the chief source of information, but it is not strictly speaking a uniform title, at least not according to the definition in the AACR2 glossary.[8] It does not usually serve to bring together manifestations of a work with differing titles, nor is it a conventional collective title. It is what its name implies—a unique construction applying to only one entity, with no collocating function.

The changes in geographic and corporate headings brought about as a result of chapters 23 and 24 in AACR2 are being illustrated clearly in the *Cataloging Service Bulletins*, which have lately contained AACR2 headings as determined by LC.[9] There are few surprises here, as many of these changes were actually called for in AACR1, but not implemented because of superimposition. The effect of these changes, primarily on added entries and subject headings where serials are concerned, will differ from library to library, depending upon the amount of corporate body–sponsored or published serials being received and catalogued. Rule 21.30E—added entries for corporate bodies[10]—continues the exclusion of corporate bodies acting solely as distributors or manufacturers from consideration for added entry, so there is no change here from the way commercial publishers have always been treated. A special library, such as a law library, will probably face great changes in its headings, as will many academic libraries. Many small public and school libraries may see little effect.

The first section of this article discussed the importance of controlling headings in a catalog. The ideal solution to the problem of changed headings was mentioned: have everything in machine-readable form with machine-readable authority control; input the AACR2 headings into the authority file in place of AACR1 headings; then the inverted authority file, with cross-references, would remove any need to alter the actual bibliographic records. All instances of the heading as an access point would be covered by the one change in the authority file.

If the catalog is in manual form, or partially machine-readable, partially manual, one or more of the various methods proposed for integrating new headings with old will be necessary. Two catalogs, split files in a single catalog, ignoring and interfiling minor changes, or even recataloguing old headings to conform to new rules are all possible. Whichever is done, cross-references seem imperative. Some of our users have become accustomed to the way we enter various names. The more alert ones will notice changes and must be helped to find our new constructions. It seems ironic that the more knowledgeable our users are, the more they could be incommoded as we change to new rules. Many other users may not even be aware of what is happening unless we make it obvious, like starting a new catalog. Past research points out the unlikelihood of the average user consulting two catalogs,[11] however, so all they may be aware of initially is that the available catalogued collection seems suddenly to have greatly decreased in size, or that no new material is being purchased by the library.

The changes in descriptive cataloguing of serials are of much less impact to a catalog than are those in the headings. There are still some unclear areas in chapter 12, AACR2, but continuing rule interpretations from LC will eventually clear these up. The old problem of what is the chief source, and hence what is the title, is not helped by the new code, nor could it be, as this is a problem created by the serial publishers and editors and, to a lesser extent, by unclear definitions.

Descriptive cataloguing is the technique of cataloguing, while entry and heading are the art. Descriptive cataloguing is mastered with practice and eventually can be done almost automatically, while determination of entry and heading continues to take imagination and intelligence in interpretation and doggedness in resolving problems. So chapter 12 may initially look formidable, but soon it should be of relatively little concern. Even the necessity of flipping between chapters, from chapter 12, which covers a pattern of publication, to other chapters which cover the format of the publication, will decrease as we all become more familiar with the chapters in part I of AACR2.

## Automation of Serials

The benefits of on-line systems governed by automated authority control have been talked about already, perhaps to excess, but I am fortunate to live where such a system is available, so I have seen the value of it and how it can help solve many of the problems a change in cataloguing rules inevitably causes. But in addition to its help in coping with change, an automated system has other important benefits. The increase in access points per bibliographic item is a major gain. Our manual systems ran into limits quickly when additional points of access were attempted. It was not possible to repeat the description, even in an abridged form, at every place access was wanted. And cross-references could not cope with the problem, because to do an adequate job a cross-reference would have to be very lengthy and complicated, thereby negating its usefulness. Cross-references work best as "see" references—blocking a term and referring to the term used. "See-also" references are not as satisfactory, as they can be misinterpreted wherever they are filed. Library of Congress' substitution of "search under" and "search also under" for "see" and "see also" may make cross-references more intelligible,[12] but the problem of where to file "search also under" instructions remains.

Some automated systems regularly provide additional search options under ISSNs, CODEN, LC card numbers, system identification numbers, and key words in titles of all kinds and in corporate names. While such systems do not yet require, or even encourage, additional added entries or subject headings, it seems likely that this will have to occur eventually. The growing use of on-line bibliographic data bases, offered by such vendors as Lockheed, System Development Corporation, and Bibliographic Retrieval Services, that contain many more access points per article, technical report or book, along with the flexible searching techniques provided, must eventually cause our on-line cataloguing data bases to enrich their access points further and provide better searching techniques.

A sophisticated cataloguing system such as WLN provides searching with truncation of names, keyword searching of titles proper and other titles, keyword searching in corporate authors and subject names, and searching with Boolean expressions, in addition to the more common searches provided by identification numbers and authors, titles, subjects, and series. Each of these latter searches can be further narrowed by authority file searches limited by type of author (personal, corporate with keywords, uniform title), type of subject (geographical and topical in addition to the list of kind of author searches), and series (personal name, corporate name with keywords, and title). These searches also incorporate access to the cross-references because they are being made in the authority file. Once a desired term is selected from the authority file, a simple command accesses the bibliographic file and retrieves the sought records.[13]

Such a searching system is infinitely superior to our old manual systems, in terms of ease of operation and speed, but the only increase in access provided is through the keyword searches (a quite valuable addition) and the various identification numbers attached to the record. Additional names and subjects are not added to enrich the record, unless a local library in the system adds some for its own use. If a connection could be made between the on-line bibliographic and cataloguing data bases, whereby a search could be made for articles in serials and chapters in books and then, with little effort, a search be made in the cataloguing system to find the location of the sought item, enrichment of the cataloging data bases may be unnecessary. Many problems exist, though. The subject access provided in bibliographic data bases differs from that provided by the cataloguing data bases. And names are not controlled in the same way. What appears to be needed is much greater cooperation between creators and managers of the two types of data bases so that they can be integrated. It is to be hoped that the existence of two basically different approaches to solve the fundamental problem of finding what is available, regardless of type of material and location, is just a manifestation of growing pains and will eventually disappear.

It seems likely that differences in approaches to names associated with records can be solved fairly easily. Perhaps the Anglo-American tradition will prevail, perhaps not. But where subject access is concerned, it seem obvious that our traditional methods of formulating and assigning subject headings will have to give way to more consistent, flexible, and accurate methods. Whether we move to descriptors and postcoordination of terms, or to a precoordinated, chain index-like system such as PRECIS, some replacement is needed. Our traditional subject headings with cross-references work in automated cataloguing systems as well as they do in manual ones—that is to say, not too well. Access to terms within the heading is needed, as are rules to insure more predictable assignment of terms and assignment of a greater number of terms. Library of Congress has already sloughed off some of the old restrictions covering subject headings, such as the rule against assigning both a general and a specific heading to certain records: now we need a complete rethinking about subject headings and a more logical, consistent set of guidelines and rules.

Our classification schemes are not often used for access to major automated systems of any kind. If the subject access is rigidly controlled, with hierarachy carefully observed, and the ability to move freely up and down the hierarchy provided with access available between chains and plentiful cross-references, alphabetic subject terms can take the place of classification. They have the advantage of permitting direct access, as access through classification usually has to be obtained by way of an alphabet index. As long as classification schemes are used primarily to provide shelf location, as they are in this country, have erratic hierarchy and little flexibility, and are not applied in depth to the contents of materials, classification will probably continue to be of little interest to data base users. Perhaps sometime in the future we will decide to dismiss our present enumerative classification systems and turn to newer syn thetic systems, governed by rigid rules of citation order that provide predictability. Then classification may take its place in our automated systems as a useful supplement to alphabetic subject access.

## *Other Benefits of Automation*

The use of automated systems, once the bibliographic data are in machine-readable form, for acquisitions, check-in of serials, fund accounting, circulation, and interlibrary loan is not new to our cataloguing data bases. Each of the major services continually adds new modules to provide more services and greater flexibility. And the future promises the final connection of citation to source, so a search will at last result in output of the sought item itself, instead of just a citation, with location, that requires further effort to retrieve what is actually the purpose of the whole operation—the text.

Before this millennium is reached, automated systems provide something else we have sorely needed in librarianship—management data. Because the computer is so efficient in counting, we can finally have accurate statistics on what is going on in our collections and how users interact with them. User studies in the past have had to rely on sometimes almost whimsically unobtrusive measures or on direct interaction of researcher and user, with the possibility of bias inherent in such contacts. Now with the computer to record all transactions, our problem will be how to interpret the mass of data finally available to us. The possibilities for research are enticing. We can stop guessing and in the future make decisions based on more reliable data.

## *Conclusion*

The Anglo-American Cataloguing Rules, 2nd edition, is a fact that will have to be faced by all libraries, if not now, than certainly in the near future. Moreover, the effects of automation will continue to expand and to enlarge our capability to provide better what our profession is all about—service to the user. Times of rapid change are always unsettling, but they also can be exciting and stimulating. Cataloguing, considered by some in the profession to be a dull, out-of-date, rule-encumbered backwater, has become an area where the action is because of automation and the new code. And since change and serials are practically synonymous words, serialists live on the cutting edge of the action. It may be dismaying out here, but it also keeps us alert and active. The challenges are great, but then, so is the fun.

## REFERENCES

1. "Order from Chaos." *American Libraries*, 11 (July/August, 1980), pp. 435–36.

2. Included with the rules of AACR1 are those from the 1949 ALA code that are still in force because of superimposition. The changes will be from ALA49/AACR1 to AACR2

3. Just one example of such articles is my contribution on "Description and Entry of Serials in AACR2," *Serials Librarian*, 4 (Winter 1979), pp. 167–76; examples of workshops are four given in Washington State during 1980–82 on AACR2 in general, two on serials in particular.

4. C. Sumner Spalding, "The Life and Death (?) of Corporate Authorship." *Library Resources and Technical Services*, 24 (Summer, 1980), pp. 195–208.

5. International Conference on Cataloguing Principles (1961:Paris). *Report*. 1969 reprint by Archon Books and Clive Bingley, pp. 91–6.

6. Spalding, *loc. cit.*

7. "LC/RTSD AACR2 Institute," *RTSD Newsletter*, 5 (July/August, 1980), pp. 46–7

8. *Anglo-American Cataloguing Rules*, 2nd ed. (Chicago, American Library Association, 1978), p. 572

9. *Cataloguing Service Bulletin*, 6 (Fall, 1979-to date).

10. AACR2, *op. cit.*, p. 323.

11. One example of such research is James R. Dwyer, "Public Response to an Academic Library Catalog." *Journal of Academic Librarianship*, 5 (July 1979), p. 132–40.

12. *RTSD Newsletter, op. cit.*, p. 48.

13. Washington Library Network, *Inquiry Reference Manual*. (Olympia, Washington State Library, 1977).

# COMPUTER CATALOGUING FOR SERIALS: RAMBLINGS OF A CURMUDGEON

Neal L. Edgar

ABSTRACT. An informal but forthright examination is made of recent changes in the cataloguing of serials, and an assessment made of the usefulness of the changes from the point of view both of the librarian and of the library user. COM catalogues and other alternatives to the conventional catalog are discussed, as are OCLC serials control and the uses of MARC and CONSER. Suggestions are made concerning the overall effectiveness of AACR2 serials cataloguing.

"Volume 7, number 3, September 1980, pages 110-112, please." Or, "7/3/9/ 80/110-112"; or, "7/-/-/80/110+"; or even less. Or perhaps the author's name and article title; or perhaps only a few letters of both; or perhaps some of the significant words of the title. Or, in some day yet to come for most of us, some aspect of a subject approach. Plus at least a part of a journal title or something that stands for the title, e.g., an ISSN.

A reader, standing at an information station, wishes to access a journal article. He can ask the questions himself, or have an attendant, who may be more familiar with the equipment, do so.

Some readers can find things easily. It does of course take some experience —just as reading in the first place does. But the operators are also pretty good, assuming they don't make keying errors which confuse the data banks.

Bigger, possibly richer, libraries have optical scanning equipment, working well with clear, block printing, but with awful results when the printing is unclear or inaccurate.

The most sophisticated libraries, not always the largest or the richest, have vocal recognition equipment, programmed for several thousand words. These should be spoken without grammatical conventions since the computer cannot yet handle little tricks like the passive or the subjunctive.

The possibility of these situations is real and hoped for. Libraries will achieve this access, perhaps even in the 1980s. But reality is not yet as sophisticated. In fact, current techniques of manipulating bibliographic information for serials are crude by comparison. This essay will present some of my thinking on the matter. Sometimes I will use the first person. Sometimes the ideas will generate disagreement. Some statements may be quite potty. But I hope one reaction will be the stimulation of discussions leading to improvements in serials control.

## Catalog Alternatives

Alternatives to present card catalogs are a topic of considerable emphasis in recent library literature. It hardly seems necessary to list even a selection of the articles and books here since the facts are so well known and understood. Book catalogs are used, but they are expensive to produce and maintain, and they immediately need supplements which generate multiple places to search. COM requires, by definition, a data base. In some cases that would require separate, duplicate input, an action which also translates into money. OCLC, for example, has no plans to produce COM. Any library desiring COM would have to re-input all entries in another data base. COM catalogs also require supplements and special equipment. COM is generally considered an interim between a manual and a fully on-line catalog, and that alone is a reason for careful consideration.

The only other alternative to a manual card catalog which has been defined through 1980 is some form of computer catalog. Direct "on-line" access is assumed. Sending postcards with inquiries to the computer, or some other manual access, doesn't appear to be an advantage. Having a minimum of the access points currently available in a manual catalog is another requirement. The obvious point here is that these access points are unevenly available in present systems; and in some systems some access points, such as subject, are not available at all. It would seem that any element of bibliographic information which has been identified in a record should be available either separately or in combinations with other elements. Multiple-term access is available in limited ways in some systems. But the approach to bibliographic information is not yet equally available in all systems. Until it is, no convincing argument about a national bibliographic access network can be made.

On an individual library basis, a fully on-line catalog cannot exist efficiently until all library records are on-line and all manual files have been discarded. Any other circumstance, such as having some exceptions, means duplication of files. Many libraries will need, or believe they need, back-up systems; and again, duplicate files and maintenance. The computer reliability of *Star Trek* is not available, and until something similar is created for libraries, on-line catalogs will remain only partially developed.

## Catalog Future

Most libraries aren't closing their catalogs, at least not in one brash move, and at least not immediately. Subject search isn't always available on-line; present manual entries haven't all been "converted"; and present records aren't all in one standard format, let alone in AACR2 form. And those aren't the only reasons. But they are enough.

What will catalogs be like in the future? That obvious question has no definite answer for a number of reasons. Prognostication is hazardous. Technical developments in information processing areas are dizzying; and libraries are generating both ideas and results, and they are utilizing these developments in the manipulation of their own information. Librarians should let imagination roam and incorporate as many new ideas as possible in their own efforts to control information.

One summary of future catalog alternatives collocates material on traditional catalog forms, machine-readable cataloguing data, computer-supported and on-line, interactive catalogs, and several comparisons of catalog formats.[1] The authors conclude that, "The form of the catalog will change, but its function will perforce remain."[2] The book is an excellent foundation and a valuable planning tool, but it does not provide an answer to the basic problem of library catalog futurity.

Two institutes on the future of the catalog held in 1975 and 1977 also covered the groundwork.[3] Many of the leading experts on cataloguing contributed to the meetings, and the collection is a solid basis for thinking about future catalogs. One of the presentations discusses the electronic catalog, and another suggests the future forms of library catalogs.

Taken together, these two books are a platform for discussions of prospects in cataloguing. A discussion of serials cataloguing as a separate subject is not covered separately; and if it must be discussed separately, these two books won't help much unless the discussion is about the general principles of all cataloguing.

One publication which does discuss computer cataloguing of serials is Osborn's new edition.[4] While the discussion is incomplete, it does imply many powerful but future developments. Possibly of even more interest is a part of one of Osborn's hypotheses, reprinted from Osborn's first edition of 1955 in which Osborn forecasts library economics in serials work "...in the comparatively near future when libraries of all kinds are linked in national networks of television facsimile reproduction machines."[5] Tantalizing. But the details aren't filled in, and the imagination is left to dream the possible.

Bibliographic utilities are working toward the provision of cataloguing services for their own groups. Charges and services vary, and the degree to which the cataloguing components of the networks provide desirable services also varies.[6,7] RLIN, UTLAS, and WLN all provide subject searching on-line, but OCLC does not.[8] This difference alone provides a weakness in the mythical national bibliographic network. So long as the potential nodes of the national network differ in their capacities to provide essential or at least the same and compatible services, the development of the national network remains an elusive dream.

## Some OCLC Considerations

Cross references are a fine tool when they are used with care and when they are designed to be helpful for library patrons. One example is to refer from a conventional title to the entry used in a library's files. The term "10-K Reports" is often used, but the entry, under the provisions of AACR is: U.S. Securities and Exchange Commission. Some libraries might use the conventional term as an added entry; but lacking that, a cross-reference is a need for helpful library service. Under the provisions of AACR2 the entry for this series will be under title since the publication as a whole does not qualify for entry under the issuing, or in this case collecting, body. An added entry should be made for the Commission; but that will not solve the "10-K Reports" access. Under AACR2 an added entry for the conventional title will be easier to justify by the wording of 21.29D, but that won't be useful for those libraries which have not changed the cataloguing for this particular publication.

A number of instances similar to this one will be on the tips of the tongues of many librarians, especially those who work with serials. The point here is that references are not currently possible in the OCLC system, and when it will be possible to install them in the system is not announced. Unless the character string which would be the "refer-from" term is tagged and accessible in the OCLC system, the records cannot be approached or found in the OCLC data base. This lack may not be a major weakness, but it is a lack, and it is one which needs to be a factor in using the OCLC system for serials cataloguing.

Bibliographic records as approved by CONSER are the records which OCLC participants are directed to use for serial cataloguing and for the construction of other files, such as the on-line serial check-in file. One of those CONSER libraries is the Library of Congress; the others are a select group of research libraries, chosen, one presumes, for the quality of their serial cataloguing. Who is to say that their cataloguing is the best in both theory and practice? Arguments have been heard that some of this cataloguing is weaker than might be expected from a select national group. Just because the cataloguing comes from the larger research libraries doesn't mean that the results are correct or accurate or that this should be the national norm. I do not propose a solution; I only observe that occasionally this cataloguing leaves something to be desired. The point is that this cataloguing is the basis of the OCLC serials cataloguing records. This ties an OCLC member library to what may be an unwanted, if not inaccurate, bibliographic record, with no recourse or options. Of course "error" reports can be filed, and other means are available to suggest a change, but serialists do not have time to spend on what should be an unnecessary task.

From an even wider perspective, another question arises. How about school, public, general, and very specialized libraries? Maybe four questions are buried there. The problem is that any library, not just a "research" library, may be tied to research-oriented records. Many times no problems will arise, but many times they will. Can this situation simply be accepted, or should alternatives be provided?

Computerized cataloguing need not be expected to accept, again without question, a system which not only does not always have universal application, but which also is incomplete, contains inadequacies, and is based on an incomplete cataloguing system.

Is MARC the only way? It is a widely used system, so why not make it the universal norm? On the other hand, why accept, without question, a system which, after all, does not have a universal application?

Why are a number of MARC standards in existence? Why do some countries which have important bibliographic distribution not adhere to the MARC concept? Answers do exist to these questions. And several groups work very hard to approach true international standards. And these groups probably have more success than setbacks.

Why ask these questions? Simply to generate additional inquiry. And the issue goes beyond serials cataloguing. But if only from that limited view, librarians are a long way from achieving an internationally accepted array of bibliographic pointers which can be sequenced and machine manipulated to control the flow of serial issues. To do so in such a way that an international record is universally available is a valid dream.

OCLC has a challenge to be a leader in this development. The profession has not yet arrived where it can be. MARC may be the answer. But it also may not be. If it is not, OCLC should use its enormous intellectual and machine resources, as well as its powerful data base, good and bad points included, to assist, if not to lead, librarians on the path toward universal bibliographic control.

## Computer Cataloguing for Serials

What problems exist for computer cataloguing of serials? The question contains the basic problem: the assumption that cataloguing of serials is different from cataloguing other materials. AACR2 dispells this problem. A few relatively minor differences exist for descriptive cataloguing, but ISBD provides a framework for describing any type of material libraries collect, and that framework is the basis for Part I of AACR2. Cataloguers have to accommodate some changes in descriptive cataloguing, but practice will bring these changes under control. The actual description of serials is easier with AACR2, and the rules make this aspect of cataloguing consistent with the description of other materials. It is as simple as that. Some people see difficulties because the techniques have changed and perhaps because they cannot believe that description is actually easier than it has been. A close study of the LC examples makes this clear.[9]

The other part of descriptive cataloguing is the application of Part II of AACR2. These are the rules for the choice and form of entry and headings. These rules apply equally to any materials; seriality is no longer a factor, and

Rule 6 of AACR is no longer a problem because it doesn't exist. If an item qualifies for personal author heading, apply those rules. If not, and if the item qualifies for main entry heading under a corporate body, apply those rules. Far fewer items, and consequently far fewer serials, will qualify under the terms of Rule 21.1B2 for main entry heading under a corporate body than qualified under the terms of AACR1 or earlier codes. If the item does not qualify for either personal author or corporate body main entry heading, only one choice remains: title. No other possibilities exist, with the sole exception of some laws which are entered under jurisdiction governed rather than promulgating jurisdiction. That's it. The same rules for everything. And furthermore, a rather neat provision exists in AACR2 for items, and consequently serials, to be entered under title. Rule 0.6 provides that if the entry begins with a title proper, the description may be given alone. This is not a change in the rules; this had been done for years. But it means that most serials will be entered in catalogues under title and with an entry which is description only.

These new rules actually simplify serials cataloguing, at least in the initial phase. The trouble for librarians arises with blending these entries in a computer system and with any given local practice at the same time. The "entry" in a computer system may derive from a MARC record or from a CONSER agency. Must it be assumed that the standards in these sources will use the standard for any given local library? Must it be assumed that a MARC record, or cataloguing from a CONSER library, is "correct"? Individual cataloguers may well disagree on statements of responsibility, series formulation, titles proper, or other information in the areas of description. If a serial is entered on a MARC/CONSER record in a way which differs from local practice, must it be assumed that local practice will change to adhere to the practice displayed in the data base being used? If so, why? If not, what accommodations will be made so that the off-line records can be found and so that the items can easily be located both in the data base and in the individual library by users?

Other questions about cataloguing serials in a computer-related system are the same as those for cataloguing other materials. It is necessary to shift viewpoints about cataloguing serials, not because of computer systems but because of AACR2. Now that the rules are the same for all materials, the questions need to be rephrased so that they relate to all materials. Perhaps that is the major, and the only important, problem for serials cataloguing, whether manual or by computer.

The issues of *The Journal of Academic Librarianship* for the past two years or so include articles on AACR2 and on serials and on automation, but the challenge of automated serials cataloguing is not specifically covered. The same is true of *International Cataloguing*, of the *Journal of Library Automation*, and of *Library Resources & Technical Services*. These are the journals where the advances appear and where the techniques are discussed. Apparently few advances are ready for discussion. But serials cataloguing remains to be done, faced with the familiar maze of challenges and difficulties.

Some items in *College and Research Libraries* come close to dealing with automated serials cataloguing,[10] but for the most part, except for a scattering of book reviews or abstracts, *C&RL* does not offer any articles in the two most recent years of publication.

The *RTSD Newsletter* in 1980 covers serials cataloguing in a number of ways. One is a series on "Serials Cataloguing Under AACR2" by Judith Cannan and Ben Tucker, already mentioned. This series is helpful in providing "hypothetical" level-two descriptions which hint at LC's positions (many not made as 1980 draws to a close). Another way in which this newsletter helps is with Jim Thompson's series on implementation studies and also with separate items such as Randolph Call's "OCLC's AACR2 Implementation and Data Base Conversion."[11]

The idea that serials ought to be done away with has great appeal. One all-too-brief position paper is a start,[12] but how can a unified action to kill publishing egomania be mounted? The appeal, or a part of it, lies in the idea that serials cataloguing problems will perforce vanish when serials no longer exist. Remember that AACR2 helps in this regard in that, except for description, the new edition of the rules does not set apart a serial as a different type of publication. Another interesting aspect of this is that the new RTSD "Goals for Action" do not specifically mention serials and that a move to have the goals specifically include serials was unanimously voted down by every group to which the change was suggested.

Serials automation, more or less from start to finish, was the topic of a September 1980 meeting held in Milwaukee and summarized in the first issue of a new journal, *Technicalities*.[13] (Interesting issue. Will the title last? Will serials librarians have another item for the volume-one-number-one file?) The emphasis seems to be check-in and Michael Gorman's position that processing should be organized by function rather than by type of material. Also, Gorman makes the point that national systems may be philosophically desirable, but local systems may be more practical.

One of the few instances of a serious attempt to solve a major serials cataloguing problem is the development of the "unique serial identifier."[14] This development is defined by Dorothy Glasby,[15] and the comments show how important this concept may be for both manual and automated systems. But a search for other specific serial cataloguing techniques applied to automation is conducted without much in the way of fruit.

## Check-In

The essential questions arising with computer check-in of serials are covered by Buckeye,[16] Corey,[17] and Kamens.[18] References to these three articles will also provide a source of opinion ranging from enthusiastic support to cautious restraint. A few comments should be sufficient to point to some important areas which may cause problems. These comments relate to some experience with the OCLC serials subsystem, but it is assumed that these conditions generally pertain to any other system.

A computer-based check-in system depends on having access to a full bibliographic record upon which the check-in record is based. This latter record will need fewer bibliographic elements than a full record, but the elements which are in both should be the same. This presents the first and a major problem. If for some reason the first elements of the two records are different, some libraries will have a problem in local procedures. One example is having a check-in record under title proper tied to a bibliographic record which has a personal or corporate main entry heading. If the library arranges this item by its title proper rather than the name entry, the library may have a control problem. If the entries are to be coordinated, decisions about spine lettering, classification, and shelf arrangement may arise.

Another problem arises with nondistinctive titles proper. In many cases these are quite impossible, or at least difficult, to search in a data base. Search algorithms have been improved in OCLC, for example, but many titles still cannot be located. Several ways around this problem exist, but these methods sometimes mean added steps, rather than the rapid efficiency which computer systems are supposed to generate.

One method is to find a check-in record by the ISSN. This works if the ISSN is on the piece being handled, and if the ISSN is a part of the record, and if the ISSN is a searchable field.

Osborn recommends the CODEN as the most reliable system.[19] This recommendation faces three problems: most serials lack CODEN even though Chemical Abstracts Service will assign them when asked; few serials print CODEN on individual pieces; and the CODEN is not a standard part of most bibliographic records. Currently, AACR2 does not have an area for CODEN, except possibly in a note, and both AACR2 and the MARC format will require modifications for this access point to be valid.

Entry to a data file can be some other identifier, such as the agent's own number. That would be fine for posting invoice information. This number does not appear on pieces, however, since they are sent from the publishers to the subscriber and seldom through an agent. The agent has no way to have his number shown on the piece. The possible exception is making the number a part of the address, but this would be no easier than having a CODEN made a part of the address. And if a library wishes to change jobbers, the library will encounter endless problems having to change access points to the data file.

Another method of dealing with nonspecific titles or entries is a second look-up in a local file to find an access point which is usable, for example, an OCLC number, or some other control number. This second look-up takes time and costs money. Both considerations are important, and both often mean computer check-in (in 1980) takes longer and costs more than a manual system. These conditions will no doubt ameliorate in the future and thus will become less important as drawbacks. The question for library administration is whether or not any shaky or incomplete system can be supported while it is under development.

One other consideration is file structure. A well-constructed manual system may have a unified file for check-in, acquisitions information, payment records, binding records, and perhaps other information as well, for example, cross-references. The OCLC system, however, cannot carry all this data now, thus requiring separate and generally duplicate records, sometimes a separate file for each aspect of the information. The question here is whether duplicate file structures, one on-line and others manual, are justified for serials control at this point in serials development.

Still one more thought on automated check-in. The use of bar codes such as the universal product code has been discussed as a means for check-in. The technique is used with some success for circulation now. Assuming some form of national (why not international?) standard on the imbedded information, such a technique should work for check-in at least as well as it does for circulation—without, it is hoped, the same per-item cost. The feelings of publishers about cover design are a problem here. Publishers won't want the bar-code box on covers just as publishers now object to including ISSNs for supposed esthetic reasons. But postal i.d. numbers were also a problem at one time, a problem which has lessened. The bar-code idea begins to approach the definite future of optical scanning and should continue to receive the serious attention of publishers and library specialists.

A limited number of articles deal with aspects of automated serials control.[20,21,22] These and other literature are helpful, but they do not solve all the critical questions involved with computer-generated serials control. The profession approaches a point when control will be satisfactory or at least as good as manual control, but that point is still beyond the horizon of development.

OCLC isn't yet the last word for serials check-in. For one thing, the display is far from user-oriented. The bibliographic record is filled with valuable information, but some users are baffled by the display. The check-in record is improved, but some way should be found to decode the information for reference purposes. One item should be changed quickly. Having the six most recently received issues displayed by a code for the date received is nearly useless. Leaving the format of the date aside, the date of the issue is the important information. Most periodical indexes are keyed to the issue date, but this date is not shown on OCLC's local data record. To argue that it is some-times possible to interpolate this date by close approximation is not a com-pelling argument.

I am sure the positions OCLC has on the serials check-in subsystem are cogent and well-founded. I am sure they are accurate and relate with the machine system insofar as its current development and capacity are concerned. But it is, I think, also true that the display and information available are de-signed more for the technical operation of libraries than they are for answering questions about holdings and other reference inquiries.

## Up to AACR2

An antecedent for serials in AACR2 is the first standard edition of the ISBD(S).[23] And before that, there was the ISBD(M).[24] The concept of interna-tional conformity in the presentation and exchange of bibliographic data is far more important than local axes to grind. Currently, little agreement exists among the many libraries not following rules which have, admittedly, been inconsistently applied by the Library of Congress.

The rules in the 1967 AACR segregate serials for different treatment on the basis of publication details and not on the basis of bibliographic detail. Many monographs do not have "authors" just as many serials do not. Now it is understood that if a publication is not "authored" it does not exist; but it is also understood that to say a publication does not have an author in the biblio-graphic sense is quite another matter.

AACR2 clarifies the concepts surrounding the bibliographic problems of the choice of the person or body having intellectual responsibility for any given item. The choice is first for one, two, or three personal authors. If more than three, "and principal responsibility is not attributed to any one, two, or three, enter under title." Lacking personal author, can responsibility be correctly at-tributed to a corporate body according to the restrictions in 21.1B2? If so, fine. The work will be said to emanate from a nonpersonal body and will be entered under that body's name given as the main entry heading. But many fewer publications will qualify under 21.1B2 than qualified for "main entry" according to the provisions of the 1967 AACR. What is left? Title. Most serials, or ongoing, open-ended publications, will be entered under title in the catalogues of the future.

A debate still exists on the use of "latest entry" as opposed to "successive entry" for serials. Latest entry works for libraries which keep the various parts of a serial together by classification. On the other hand, successive entry pro-vides an approach to the title a serial has at the time of publication. This is the approach used in indexing services; and for libraries which arrange period-icals by title, the approach is a logical one. (The rules of 1908 provide another technique, that of earliest title. That procedure would certainly give a modern library pause.)

The reason for the debate has disappeared with AACR2. These rules restate the procedure that a change in title or responsible person or body will mean a new entry. The Library of Congress has stated its intention of following this procedure. Other libraries should do the same. If this is done, successive entry for serials will become the practice in all cases.

One of the more difficult decisions cataloguers had up through 1974 was to distinguish between societies and institutions. Of course, most libraries will have entries based on this distinction for many years. This fuzziness will exist until that time when "all" entries in catalogues, no matter what the format, are changed in some mystical way to a standard which doesn't attempt the distinction. AACR2 may not be the last cataloguing code, or even the best one, but at least no one has to struggle any longer with the supposed difference between societies and institutions.

### *Personal Author Serials*

For the purposes of international cooperation AACR2 incorporates personal author for serials. A personal author is defined in AACR2 as "the person chiefly responsible for the creation of the intellectual or artistic content of a work" (AACR2, p. 568). A serial is defined, in part, as "...intended to be continued indefinitely" (AACR2, p. 570). My claim is that these two are out of phase with one another. People do not continue indefinitely; therefore, it is illogical to consider people as possible authors of indefinitely continuing serials. Perhaps the point is a small one, but I consider it a weakness in the rules for cataloguing. On the other hand, the unity of treatment and structure in AACR2 is more important than my own rather minor point. Consider the point made, however, even if it is not accepted.

One consideration is that very few "personal author serials" exist. *The Tattler* (April 1709–January 1711) was written by Richard Steele and Joseph Addison. Every indication is that the two wrote all of each issue, and the publication qualifies quite well as a periodical written by two authors. Addison and Steele also produced *The Spectator* (March 1711–December 1712), but other writers contributed to these issues. This second periodical would have to be entered under title because more than four people wrote the text. One more current example is the *I.F. Stone's Newsletter*. Other examples are Charlotte Perkins Gilman's *The Forerunner*; Mark H. McCormack's *The World of Professional Golf*; and Eunice Wilson's *Moot*. In each of these instances, an argument can be made that the "author" in actual fact did not write every word of every issue. If not, then the rules of multiple, if not diffuse, uncertain, or even unknown authorship must be considered. If any of these situations pertains, then single authorship is not the case for these periodicals, and the entry will, according to the rules of cataloguing, be under title.

However, for the sake of compromise, I admit the occasional instance of a personal author serial. In at least some of these cases, a cataloguer will be able to find grounds for title entry. What is left is a very small number of personal author entries for serials.

### Automated Serials Cataloguing

Considerable imagination is needed to cope with the possible interaction of serials cataloguing and other processing with the potentials of computer manipulation of data. Complete methods have not yet been found, although techniques can without doubt be developed. What publishers and other issues of serials do in the design and editing of their publications is probably irrelevant. Librarians decry restructuring of coverage and scope in serials; changes in title, format, frequency, and other bibliographic details; and such matters as the movement of titles from one publisher to another and mergers and splits. But these are the province of the publishers, and serials librarians have to deal with these changes as reality rather than attempting to modify the causes for the changes.

Serials librarians have to find techniques to accommodate the two basic characteristics of serials: they change, and they continue. A number of manual methods exist. Many serial experts believe that, at least in 1980, no system for serials control works as well as, let alone better than, an integrated, up-to-date, well-maintained manual serial record. This may well be the case, but it is not the point here to argue the case. That will be for another time and place.

"Automated" cataloguing results in a number of by-products which are both obvious and overlooked. First, whatever the description, and whatever the main entry heading may be for a given title, participants in an automated system are, to a degree, tied to that bibliographic description.

What are some of the results? If a library wishes to have "all" its records coordinated, each of them should be the same, to a degree, as the automated record, at least insofar as the main entry heading is concerned. One example is the payment file. But in some instances the line on the title's invoice, whether a single-line invoice or one of those massive seventy-five to 100 page invoices some libraries receive from jobbers and dealers, may not be the same as the "entry" in the library's files. In many instances a cross reference will be required. And that not only means added effort for the creation and maintenance of the reference but also means inconsistency among libraries.

Another example of coordination would arise in bindery files and on the spines of the volumes themselves. The spines *may* be less of a problem for libraries which classify periodicals, but this is relatively uncommon. Most libraries arrange bound periodicals, assuming bound periodicals, on shelves by the titles or entries the publications have when they are published. If a library wishes coordination it may have to bend local practice to the wishes, if not the whims, of a larger system which is not oriented to local needs.

A major item for serials cataloguing which utilizes the MARC format is LC's *MARC Serials Editing Guide*.[25] At this writing the second CONSER edition, with its requisite bimonthly update, is the edition for current use. (P.S. The service, updated by sheets to be interfiled in specific places, is the "classical" looseleaf format. As such, the title is a quasi-serial, often catalogued as a monograph but otherwise treated as a serial because of its "ongoing" nature. This format problem is typical of the manipulation problems for which serial librarians devise techniques and control procedures generally not needed for the control of monographs.) (P.P.S. Incidentally, looseleaf publications don't work well in the OCLC system, if the system is used correctly. The service should be catalogued as a monograph. In theory, a local data record cannot be built on a monographic record. *De facto* it can; *de jure* it shouldn't be. Therefore, no legal means exists to check in continuing shipments of a monographic, looseleaf service. Most librarians punt.)

To quote LC's news release for the MARC serials guide, it is "specifically written for CONSER Project Participants, gives instructions in the editing, or data preparation, of serial cataloging records for on-line input to the OCLC system." The document is the best editing publication currently available for creating serial bibliographic records designed for machine manipulation. A secondary document discusses the OCLC system more directly, but it is far less complete than the CONSER guide. This document, "Fixed and Variable Field Tags for Serial Records,"[26] has a brief introduction which includes OCLC-related information probably important to that system.

It is understood that the OCLC data base is the vehicle for the CONSER Project. This does explain the orientation of the LC documentation toward the OCLC system. But a valid question remains: is the OCLC system the only system? Or put another way, is the OCLC data base *the* national data base? Or is the OCLC data base, while large, only *a* national data base? If it is *the* national data base, OCLC must begin, with the understanding of distribution among regional networks, to provide comprehensive services to all libraries in the areas it serves. While this seems underway, and time will be needed for further developments, comprehensive service is by no means available at present. If, on the other hand, OCLC is only one of the national data bases, then CONSER, a national program, should be geared toward all data bases and not just to one of them. This would mean that documentation should be developed in such a way that it can be used by all the systems which manipulate serials information.

One step in this direction is a proposal made by Ryburn Ross of Cornell, which came to several groups at the 1980 ALA annual Conference, all of which endorsed the concept. Ross' idea is that

...networks, affiliates, or consortia be encouraged to establish, as an immediate priority, an electronic interconnection between their networks to provide network participants with dynamic access to each other's serial data base; provide for a more timely distribution of national level (CONSER) serial records; and promote the use of national level serial records through a carefully monitored quality assurance program.[27]

Another document which is as important for what it does not say as it is for what it does say is OCLC's Technical Bulletin no. 97.[28] The topic is the conversion of the OCLC data base to AACR2. Leaving aside the technicalities of this conversion and the degree of its success, the document is significant for serials cataloguing because it does not treat serials separately. Presumably, a bibliographic record is a bibliographic record, regardless of the format of the material. This concept is both a welcome advance in cataloguing philosophy and a development in accordance with the new edition of the cataloguing rules, AACR2.

Another step toward the light is the recommendation in "Linking the Bibliographic Utilities: Benefits and Costs," a Battelle-Columbus Laboratories paper released by the Council on Library Resources on November 10, 1980.[29] This report discusses the idea that the Library of Congress, OCLC, Inc., the Research Libraries Information Network, and the Washington Library Network should develop on-line links. An analysis of the economic and service benefits to libraries and users suggests that national improvements can be achieved in three operations: interlibrary loan, reference searching, and monographic cataloguing. It is interesting to note that the monographic cataloguing discussed is for current titles, leaving retrospective cataloguing for some other systems development. It is even more interesting to note that serials cataloguing is not discussed. "Why not?" is a good question. But at the very least, national links are recommended and discussed. Serials, I suppose, can be added later once the principles have been established.

## The End

Despite all our efforts, serials librarians and the characteristics of our work are sometimes misunderstood.[30] Perhaps we are tied too much to the traditional. A case in point is in the consideration of the elements of bibliographic description, and possibly in the fields and tags of the MARC system. It is similar to the ties most science fiction writers have to the humanoid, or at least animal, forms—two arms, one head, and two eyes for binocular vision. In the case of automated or machine-assisted cataloguing, all systems and all writing on the matter to date (1980) discuss author, or in AACR2's patois, "statement of responsibility," title, imprint, no matter what the terminology, and other bibliographic details. To achieve some form of system of wider application, new techniques have to be developed.

In this development it should be kept in mind that not all libraries will be computer-based for many years to come. That is simply a fact. Planners should accept it and realize that the wonderful world they see may not be available to all. At the same time, planners should continue to seek that muse of fire who will help us all ascend the brightest heaven of invention for serials—computer control which works.

## REFERENCES

1. Malinconico, S. Michael, and Fasana, Paul J. *The Future of the Catalog: The Library's Choices* (White Plains, N.Y.: Knowledge Industry Publications, 1979).

2. Ibid., p. 124.

3. Freedman, Maurice J., and Malinconico, S. Michael, eds. *The Nature and Future of the Catalog* (Phoenix, Ariz.: Oryx Press, 1979).

4. Osborn, Andrew D. *Serial Publications: Their Place and Treatment in Libraries*, 3rd ed. (Chicago: American Library Association, 1980).

5. *Ibid.*, p. xvi.

6. Matthews, Joseph R. "The Four Online Bibliographic Utilities: A Comparison." *Library Technology Reports* 15 (November/December 1979):665–838.

7. "Understanding the Utilities: A Special Current-Awareness Presentation." *American Libraries* 11 (May 1980):262–79.

8. Webster, James K. "Comparing the Bibliographic Utilities for Special Libraries." *Special Libraries* 71 (December 1980):519–22.

9. Cannan, Judith, and Tucker, Ben R. "Serials Cataloguing under AACR2." *RTSD Newsletter* 6 (March/April 1980):19–21, and subsequent issues.

10. Force, Ronald W., and Force, Jo Ellen. "Access to Alternative Catalogs: A Simulation Model." *College and Research Libraries* 40 (May 1979):234–39.

11. *RTSD Newsletter* 5 (November/December 1980);69–70.

12. Gorman, Michael. "Crunching the Serial." *American Libraries* 11 (July/August 1980): 416, 418.

13. Cargill, Jennifer. "A Review of Serials Automation." *Technicalities* 1 (December 1980):8–9.

14. "Unique Serial Identifiers." *Cataloging Service Bulletin* 5 (Summer 1980):4–9.

15. Glasby, Dorothy. "Serials in 1979." *Library Resources & Technical Services* 24 (Summer 1980):275.

16. Buckeye, Nancy Melin. "The OCLC Serials Subsystem: Implementation/Implications at Central Michigan University." *The Serials Librarian* 3 (Fall 1978):31–42.

17. Corey, James F. "OCLC and Serials Processing: A State of Transition at the University of Illinois." *The Serials Librarian* 3 (Fall 1978):57–67.

18. Kamens, Harry H. "OCLC's Serials Control Subsystem: A Case Study." *The Serials Librarian* 3 (Fall 1978):43–55.

19. Osborn, *op. cit.*, p. 150–55.

20. Willmering, William J. "On-line Centralized Serials Control." *The Serials Librarian* 1 (Spring 1977):243–49.

21. McGregor, James Wilson. "Serials Staffing in Academic Libraries." *The Serials Librarian* 1 (Spring 1977):259–72.

22. Kimzey, Ann C., and Smith, Roland. "An Automated Book Catalog for a Learning Resources Center Periodicals Collection." *The Serials Librarian* 2 (Summer 1978):405–10.

23. International Federation of Library Associations. Joint Working Group on the International Standard Bibliographic Description for Serials. *ISBD(S): International Standard Bibliographic Description for Serials*, 1st standard ed. (London: IFLA International Office for UBC, 1977).

24. International Federation of Library Associations. *ISBD(M): International Standard Bibliographic Description for Monographic Publications* (London: IFLA Committee on Cataloguing, 1974).

25. Bruns, Phyllis A. *MARC Serials Editing Guide.* 2nd CONSER ed. (Washington: Library of Congress, 1978).

26. "Fixed and Variable Field Tags for Serial Records," rev. (Columbus, Ohio: OCLC, Inc., 1980, Technical bulletin no. 37).

27. "New York Conference Reports." *RTSD Newsletter* 5 (September/October 1980):51.

28. "AACR2 Implementation and Data Base Conversion" (Columbus, Ohio: OCLC, Inc., 1980, Technical bulletin no. 97).

29. "Linking the Bibliographic Utilities: Benefits and Costs" (Washington: Council on Library Resources, 1980).

30. Lanier, Don, and Anderson, Glenn. "Dispelling the Serials Mystique." *The Serials Librarian* 5(4)(Summer 1981):15–17.

# COPY CATALOGUING OF SERIALS
# ACCORDING TO AACR2 USING OCLC:
# THE UNIVERSITY OF ILLINOIS EXPERIENCE

Ruth B. McBride

ABSTRACT. Copy cataloguing procedures similar to those used to catalogue monographs, utilizing bibliographic information available on OCLC data base, can also be used for serials. This paper describes the University of Illinois experience of cataloguing serials from OCLC copy and discusses the use of support staff to do so. It further describes the conversion of existing cataloguing on OCLC to AACR2, with data presented to document the actual amount of revision involved since the Illinois adoption of AACR2 cataloguing rules on November 1, 1979.

## Introduction

This paper reports a study done at the University of Illinois to analyze the effectiveness of using OCLC copy to catalog serials and to determine the effect of the adoption of the *Anglo-American Cataloguing Rules, 2nd edition* on such cataloguing.

It is economically impossible for a large research library to provide timely original cataloguing (i.e., cataloguing done without the aid of any bibliographic information drawn from outside cataloguing sources) for every title which it receives, monographic or serial. Such a practice would not only be very costly but also result in enormous backlogs since original cataloguing takes far more time than copy cataloguing. Libraries have made use of other libraries' cataloguing records, especially those of the Library of Congress (LC), for many years, using LC cards, LC proof slips, the National Union Catalog (NUC), and Cataloging in Publication (CIP).[1] Computer technology as manifested in networks such as OCLC, Inc. and RLIN (Research Libraries Information Network), among others, has made shared cataloguing even more feasible. Libraries have devised standards, guidelines, and procedures to make the most efficient use of bibliographic information available on data bases. Monographic copy cataloguing is generally practiced and accepted.

Serials cataloguing (a serial being a "publication in any medium issued in successive parts bearing numerical or chronological designation and intended to be continued indefinitely")[2] has also made use of the "shared cataloguing" concept. In the past, bibliographic information for serials was acquired and used from LC and NUC, just as for monographs. However, until quite recently, the Library of Congress was slow to catalogue many serials and the percentage of shared cataloguing available was quite small. The initiation of the CONSER (CONversion of SERials) project in 1975 has greatly increased the amount of available cataloguing. The project has been described as "a cooperative effort by the library community to build a machine readable database of quality serials cataloguing information."[3] Under the sponsorship of the Council on Library Resources, OCLC, Inc. provided the facilities for creating and maintaining a machine-readable data base. The serial holdings of the libraries participating in the CONSER project plus the Minnesota Union List of Serials and, later, the Pittsburgh Regional Library Center records were added to the OCLC data base, along with existing LC and NLC (National Library of Canada) MARC serial records.

By 1978 CONSER participants had identified and revised or updated over 200,000 serial records in the OCLC On-line Union Catalogue. Some 105,000 of these records have been "authenticated"; that is, the correctness and completeness of the bibliographic information have been certified by LC or NLC. The National Serials Data Program (NSDP), a part of the Library of Congress since 1974, is responsible for registering serial titles and assigning International Standard Serial Numbers (ISSN) to United States publications. NSDP, in cooperation with CONSER, has also been adding new serial information. New serial records are also being added to the data base by the CONSER participants, LC, NLC, and other OCLC member libraries. Library of Congress authority tapes, also available on OCLC, provide additional information valuable to serials cataloguers, sometimes including AACR2 forms of headings. The Library of Congress expects that by January 1, 1981, 350,000 records in the LC name authority file will have AACR2 forms of names.[4]

Now that cataloguing information for serials, current as well as retrospective, is available on the data base, cataloguing procedures for serials, very similar to those for monographs, can be established. Studies done in 1978 evaluating the quality and usability of such records are somewhat critical. Anderson and Melby felt their 1977/78 study revealed considerable divergence between the quality of cataloguing copy on OCLC at that time and the standards of acceptability at the University of Illinois.[5] Roughton concluded from a 1978 study done at Iowa State University that 25 percent of the OCLC records studied contained at least one error, and that 68 percent of the records studied lacked at least one field basic to the creation of a serial record.[6] Nevertheless, an increasing amount of readily usable serial information is becoming available. As with monographs, it is necessary to determine standards for acceptable records, guidelines for revising existing records, procedures for processing titles, and training of support staff to perform these tasks.

The impending adoption of AACR2 and its new rules on choice and form of entry, description, and so on, complicates copy cataloguing as well as original cataloguing. Turner is rather positive in her study predicting the effect of AACR2 on serial cataloguing records.[7] She concluded from a study done at the University of British Columbia that over 83 percent of the serial records studied would have the same entry under AACR2 rules. And, in fact, she predicted that the areas presenting the most difficulty will be (1) choice of entry for publications concerned with the activities of a corporate body, (2) distinguishing between identical titles, and (3) those forms of names which will change dramatically under AACR2. It can certainly be anticipated that the adoption of AACR2 will add to the burden of revision at least until the records on the data base reflect AACR2 rules.

Although the University of Illinois Library has long been using bibliographic information available from the Library of Congress and NUC to catalog serials, it has been only since mid-1978, when OCLC added serials to its data base, that serial copy cataloguing has been a separate operation. An administrative decision was made to close the Library's catalog on November 1, 1979, and to adopt AACR2 for all materials catalogued after that date. This paper reports on the Illinois experience of cataloguing serials from OCLC copy using AACR2 from November 1, 1979, to April 30, 1980. It describes the conversion of existing cataloguing to AACR2, with tabulation of the amount of change actually required for this conversion. The use of support staff in copy cataloguing serials is also discussed.

## University of Illinois

The University of Illinois has a serial collection of over 90,000 current titles. It is estimated that over 3,000 serial titles are added each year. "Serials" are very broadly defined at the University of Illinois and do, in fact, include periodicals, newspapers, annuals, proceedings of societies, and numbered monographic series. The cataloguing of serials for thirty-one of the departmental libraries and the General Bookstacks is done in either the Original Cataloguing Department or the Copy Cataloguing Unit of the Automated Records Department. Cataloguing of materials for the Music, Slavic and East European, and Asian libraries is done within those specialized units.

Each new title received is searched on OCLC, and if a matching record is found, a printout is made and the title is routed to the Serials section of the Copy Cataloguing Unit. If a record is not found, the title is sent to the Original Cataloguing Department. New titles are not held to be re-searched. It is estimated that 65–75 percent of new titles received at the University of Illinois are on the OCLC data base; the estimate was of 50 percent in July 1978.

All cataloguing (including serial cataloguing) at the U. of I. is done on OCLC to produce cards, to create an archival tape for a future on-line catalog, and to add new titles, extracted by program from the archival tapes, to LCS

(Library Control System), the Library's automated circulation system. Serials are provided with a full cataloguing record and classified according to *Dewey Decimal Classification, 19th ed.* Serial titles have been catalogued "successively (title changes treated as new titles even if the volume numbering is continuous) since May 1977 at Illinois. Earlier titles are not being "closed" by the Copy Cataloguing Unit except on LCS. That is, records for earlier titles are not being recatalogued to add closing date and later title information. However, patrons are referred from the earlier title to the later title (and vice versa) with information on LCS. Cards for titles catalogued since the adoption of AACR2 are filed in a new temporary public card catalogue which will be disposed of when an on-line catalogue with full bibliographic records for the entries now contained in the temporary card catalogue becomes operational, sometime in 1982.

The goal of serial copy cataloguing is to process the pieces as rapidly as possible while providing proper access points (headings and titles) and necessary bibliographic information. Every effort is made to provide accurate records; on the other hand, efforts to provide total bibliographic history or even complete descriptive records are not encouraged.

A record is acceptable for revision by the Copy Cataloguing Unit if it matches the piece as identified (where applicable) by title, place of publication, publisher, dates, numbering, and related title information. The record must also reflect the policy of successive entry. "Latest entry" cataloguing (cataloguing from the most recent issue using the latest title and describing all earlier titles in a "Title varies" note) for the new catalogue is unacceptable. A record with completed fixed fields is preferred. However, if a record is determined to be a "matching" record, it is generally acceptable regardless of the extent of revision required. For example, union list records are used despite the minimal information on them if additional information is readily available (from piece in hand). If a record is judged so sparse or inaccurate that a new record needs to be made for the OCLC data base, it is sent to Original Cataloguing. Records resulting from the NSD Program are quite brief because records are frequently added to the data base using a surrogate, usually title page information only. The physical description, that is, collation (MARC field 3xx) and subject headings (MARC fields 6xx), are usually missing from NSD records but can easily be supplied. Only subject headings from the *Library of Congress List of Subject Headings* are acceptable.

Prior to the adoption of AACR2, records were revised according to *Anglo-American Cataloging Rules, 1st ed.*[8] AACR1 specified that cataloguing be done from the most recent or latest issue available with notes describing earlier issues. Records were frequently revised to receive main entry under title instead of corporate body in cases of unique titles, provided that title did not include the name of the issuing body. Information was added to the imprint (260 field), collation (300 field), and holdings statement (362 field) if they were incomplete and the information was available. Subject headings (6xx fields) were added if they were not present. Local notes were added. Linking fields (780 and 785 fields) are considered very important in order to keep the bibliographic history accurate. According to current OCLC practice, 780 and 785 fields are in title form. It is frequently necessary to add a note describing the author/title form of earlier records in the library in the related title area (580 field). Added entries were changed to conform with already established entries. Illinois began to follow LC's policy of "desuperimposition" (changing the form of entry even though the name had not undergone any change) with "see also" references when entries in the card catalog were numerous, and changing to the new form those entries which were fewer than five in number.

Guidelines for revising OCLC records to AACR2 form were developed at the University of Illinois by using LC *Cataloguing Service Bulletins*, AACR2 itself, and decisions regarding local options. Guidelines were very much the same as for AACR1 with some important additions. Information continues to be added to those areas which are missing, for example, "physical description area" or collation (300 field), "numeric and chronological designation area" or holdings (362 field), subject headings (6xx fields), and even the "publication, distribution area" or imprint (260 field). Local notes and linking fields are still of major importance.

However, AACR2 requires cataloguing from the first issue with later issues described in notes and specifies the title page as the chief source of information (Rules 1.0 and 12.1).[9] Most entries are under title (Rule 21.1C). Corporate authorship is limited according to specific criteria (Rule 21.1B2). Title entry frequently includes "other title information" and statement of responsibility added to the title information area, as with monographs (Rules 1.1F and 12.1F). Reprints are described in the imprint and the original is described in a note (Rule 1.11 and 12.7B7). Successive title is emphasized with criteria for identifying title changes described (Rules 21.2C and 21.2A). Superimposition (LC's policy of using unchanged those headings for persons or corporate bodies which had been established prior to the adoption of AACR1 and constructing headings according to AACR1 for persons or organizations not yet represented in the catalog) is totally abandoned, and names for corporate bodies are formed according to AACR2 rules, usually as the name appears on the piece (Rule 24.1). The form of geographic names used as subject headings may also be affected (Rule 23). Punctuation requirements are spelled out for each area of the cataloguing record and follow International Standard Bibliographic Description (ISBD).

While copy cataloguing for monographs is concerned mainly with form of entry, it was decided to follow AACR2 in all respects for serials. Therefore, records for serials are revised according to choice as well as form of entry, punctuation, and description (Figure 1). However, the copy unit does adopt

UIU - FOR OTHER HOLDINGS, ENTER dh DEPRESS DISPLAY RECD SEND
OCLC: 1931129    Rec stat: n Entrd: 760116    Used: 810121
Type: a Bib lvl: s Govt pub:    Lang: ita Source: d S/L ent: 0
Repr:    Enc lvl: I Conf pub: I Ctrv: it Ser tp:    Alphabt: a
Indx: u Mod rec:    Phys med:    Cont: ^    Frequn:    Pub st: c
Desc:    Cum ind: u Titl pag: u ISDS:    Reglr: x Dates: 1953-9999

1 010
2 040    COD c COD
3 022    0485-4152
4 043    e-it---
5 090    NA4 b .R66
6 092    b
7 049    UIUU
8 ~~110 10~~ Rome (City) b Universitba. b Istituto di storia
dell'architettura.
9 245 00 Quadernix dell' Istituto di storia dell'architettura.
10 260 10 Roma: b Facolta di architettura, Università di Roma, # c 1953-
11 300    b ill. c 36 cm.
12 362 0    Serie 1- 1953-
13 650 0 Architecture x Periodicals.
14 650 0 Architecture z Italy.
15 710 20 Università di Roma. # b Istitut di storia dell'architettura.

*[handwritten:]* 720.5 #6 GUA

*[handwritten notes:]* Arch. / MC–dual / yr. / XC

*[handwritten margin notes on entries 9 and 10:]* (y ref & availity & kind (s) ... # c 1953–

Figure 1 : Example of a revised OCLC print-out

```
327.101105
ES          Estudios geopolíticos y estratégicos.
            -- No. 1 (enero/marzo 1979)-       --
            Lima : Instituto Peruano de Estudios
            Geopolíticos y Estrategicos, 1979-

                 v. : ill. ; 30 cm.
            "Organo del Instituto Peruano de
            Estudios Geopolíticos y Estrategicos."

                 1. Geopolitics--Latin America--
            Periodicals.   2. Peru--Politics and
            government--1968-        --Periodicals.
            3. Latin America--Politics and
            government--1948-        --Periodicals.
            4. Strategy--Periodicals.   I. Instituto
            Peruano de Estudios Geopolíticas y
            Estrategicos.


 IU      ns 800411 OC/TK            UITSme
```

Figure 2

some short-cuts, for example, not adding the statement of responsibility in the title field to a unique title, but making an added entry using information in the publication area, notes, and the like. Copy cataloguing for serials adds statement of responsibility to non-unique (generic) titles, however, also with an added entry. Punctuation is revised to conform to AACR2 at the time the record is added to the data base. For an example of a catalog card in AACR2 form, see Figure 2.

The principal concern is for choice and form of entry to conform to AACR2 for all access points. The first consideration is to determine the correct entry, cataloguing from the first issue's chief source of information or alternative sources, according to AACR2 instructions. This usually involves changing the main entry heading (1xx field) to added entry (7xx field) with a title main entry (245 field) because AACR2 specifies main entry under title for most serials. The form of the title may need revision to read as it appears on the piece: for example, "Quaderni dell'Istituto di Storia dell'architettura"; "Mundo nuevo: revista de estudios latinoamericanos" (subtitle added); Special liaison report/Commonwealth Geological Liaison Office (statement of responsibility added).

It may be necessary to add a note in the 570 (issuing body) field to justify an added entry. In cataloguing from the first piece, the 260 field (publisher, distribution area) is rarely corrected. If it shows a later publisher and it is necessary to make some added entries, the 260 field may be revised and a 570 field added. Records for reprints, microforms, and other reproductions are revised to follow AACR2 rules for description of the piece in hand with a note describing the original.

Form of entry probably presents the most problems, at least in the beginning. Authority files must be checked, local and LC, now on-line via OCLC.

Most entries are being established in the new catalog for the first time. An authority card file for staff use only includes authority cards and cross references. Cross references from the old form and any other variant forms to the new form are filed in the temporary public card catalog. It is anticipated that this information will be included in the on-line catalog when it becomes operational.

The University of Illinois classifies its serials according to the *Dewey Decimal Classification* (DDC). The nineteenth edition of DDC was adopted January 2, 1980. Those records with suggested DDC numbers still have to be checked against the new DDC. However, classification of serials is necessarily not as specific as for monographs. Whenever practicable, that is, if the DDC number is still accurate, "continues" titles (titles which continue the volume numbering of an earlier title) are classified by adding "1" to the Cutter number of the earlier call number ("1a," "1b," etc., for subsequent titles). This saves time for the classifier and provides for continuing titles to be shelved next to each other.

Tasks involved in processing serials are (1) searching, (2) editing, (3) classifying, (4) processing, (5) inputting, (6) proofreading, and (7) filing. Support staff of Graduate Assistant (GA), Library Technical Assistant (LTA), Library Clerk, and Clerk Typist are trained and supervised in the performance of most of these tasks.

1. "Searching" the data base is done with some bibliographic information, usually provided by the Collection Development Department or Ordering, Receiving, Claiming, and Searching Unit (from *New Serial Titles*, publisher, related records, etc.), besides the information on the piece. It is necessary to choose the proper record, provide related and authority records if needed or/and available, and make printouts. Searching requires a knowledge of the use of the terminal (search keys, etc.) and ability to identify the variety of access points for a serial search (e.g., ISSN, corporate author, title, author/title, spine title, series title, etc.). A well-trained library clerk can perform the searching duties.

2. and 3. "Editing" and "classifying" are done in the same operation at the University of Illinois. Editing involves matching the record against the piece and making revisions according to established guidelines. It may be necessary to add subject headings as well as classification to the cataloguing record. If authority work is required, it is done at this time with consultation with the professional cataloguer as needed. These tasks involve not only cataloguing and classification expertise but also a great deal of judgment. A specially trained paraprofessional, probably on an LTA or GA level, is required for these tasks.

4. "Processing" involves marking instructions, adding the 300 (physical description) field if necessary, Cuttering, and providing records and information necessary for serials to related units, such as holding cards for departmental libraries, authority cards, binding instructions, and so on. A properly trained library clerk could be responsible for these tasks.

5. "Inputting" involves adding the revised records to the data base, correct-

ing indicators to agree with the edited copy, revising punctuation to ACCR2 on-line, noting updated records, producing cards, and at the same time adding to the archival record. An understanding of tagging is required as well as skill in operating the terminal. Revising indicators on-line usually involves eliminating a title added entry (by changing 245 01 to 245 00) or changing the linking field to agree with AACR2 use of the term "continues" instead of "supersedes" regardless of numbering (by changing 780 02 to 780 00). A clerk-typist with special training could handle these tasks.

6. "Proofreading" is done by the supervisor, a professional librarian. It provides an opportunity to check on all other aspects of the operation: searching, editing, classifying, inputting, and so forth, since printouts as well as other miscellaneous records are matched to the cards. Errors can be detected, need for clarification of procedures or further information discovered, and additional instruction provided.

7. "Filing" of cards into the temporary card catalog is done by a library clerk. This task will, of course, be eliminated when the on-line computer catalog is in operation.

The above tasks can be combined in any way which fits a library's administrative plan. At the University of Illinois persons responsible for these tasks also have other responsibilities, and some function outside the Serials Unit.

In-house workshops conducted by the Principal Cataloguer (the person responsible for all Library cataloguing policy) trained the staff (professional and paraprofessional) in the use of AACR2. They were already familiar with AACR1. Training was given to provide a general understanding of serials and their unique problems as well as training in the use of the OCLC data base. Persons performing specific tasks were trained for those tasks. Also, knowledge of the unit and its relationship with other technical service units involved with serials was considered important.

## Methodology

In order to acquire some concrete data concerning the extent of revision necessary to create adequate serial cataloguing from OCLC copy, and to determine the amount of additional revision caused by AACR2, approximately 600 records which had been input on OCLC by the University of Illinois Library between November 1, 1979, and April 30, 1980, were analyzed. Additions, deletions, and changes were noted in each of the variable fields. Changes recorded were for major changes only. Few changes are made by Copy Cataloguing to the fixed fields, and these were ignored. Changes which are routinely done by the inputters and not revised on the printout were not recorded. These include punctuation, tagging changes to fit edited copy (e.g., 245 10 to 245 00 to eliminate a title added entry; 780 02 to 780 00 to read "continues" instead of "supersedes"), adding publication dates to imprint (260) field, to name a few. If the same change was made more than once on a record (e.g., geographic subject heading), the change was counted as only one revision. For purposes of this study, all notes are discussed as the "5xx" field (except local and related title notes), all subject headings in the "6xx" field, all related title information in the "78x" field, names associated with main entries in the "1xx" field, and all added entry headings in the "7xx" field.

*Data*

Of the 606 records analyzed, 277 (46%) could be used without any revision. Such records originated from a variety of sources: LC, CONSER libraries, and non-CONSER libraries. Three hundred twenty-nine records involved some editing of the copy. Five hundred eighty-one revisions were made on the 329 records, an average of 1.8 revisions per record. One hundred ninety-one (33%) of these revisions were the direct result of adopting AACR2; the remaining 390 (67%) would have been made prior to the adoption of AACR2. Table 1 shows the number of revisions made (including changes, deletions, and additions) which would have been made before the adoption of AACR2, those which were the direct result of adopting AACR2, and the combined totals.

*Revisions Made Prior to the Adoption of AACR2*

Much of the revision would have been done prior to the adoption of AACR2 anyway. For example, the field requiring the most changes prior to AACR2 was the subject (6xx) area. Eighty-one records needed subject headings added, six needed subject headings changed, and one needed a subject heading deleted.

The area requiring the next largest number of revisions was the physical description (300) area. Seventy-four records required adding information (size) and three records were closed by adding the total number of volumes. The fact that sixty-nine of the total number of records used carried the NSD symbol may explain many of these omissions, since NSD frequently adds serial information to the data base from a surrogate (without piece in hand) and, therefore, does not usually have size or subject information.

The third largest number of revisions required before the adoption of AACR2 and which would have been made in any case was to the numeric designation area (362) field. Information was added to thirty-one records, deleted from five, and changed on ten.

Forty of the revisions involved changing the main entry heading (1xx) field to the added entry (7xx) field—in other words, changing a name/title entry to a title entry according to AACR1 rules. One record involved changing the form of the main entry heading.

In the note area (5xx fields) twenty-nine records would have been revised

Table 1: Revisions Made on 329 OCLC Serial Records*

| OCLC Database Fields | Revisions Per Field | AACR1 Revisions | AACR2 Revisions |
|---|---|---|---|
| 1xx (author or main entry heading) | 131 | 41 | 90 |
| 245 (title) | 47 | 13 | 34 |
| 246 (added title) | 7 | 7 | 0 |
| 260 (imprint or publication area) | 6 | 5 | 1 |
| 300 (collation or physical description area) | 77 | 77 | 0 |
| 362 (holdings or numeric/chronological designation area) | 46 | 46 | 0 |
| 4xx (series | 6 | 0 | 6 |
| 5xx (notes) | 31 | 29 | 2 |
| 5xx (local notes) | 12 | 12 | 0 |
| 580 (related title information) | 20 | 20 | 0 |
| 6xx (subject headings) | 106 | 88 | 18 |
| 7xx (added entries) | 64 | 24 | 40 |
| 78x (linking title information) | 28 | 28 | 0 |
| Total revisions= | 581 | 390 | 191 |
|  | (100%) | (67%) | (33%) |

*Figures are for major revision only; punctuation and other minor revisions are not included.

prior to the adoption of AACR2. Twenty-four records required additional information, four changed information, and one deleted information.

Twenty-four records were revised in the added entry (7xx) field involving twelve changes, eleven additions, and one deletion.

In the linking (78x) fields, twenty-eight records were revised. These revisions stemmed largely from the fact that the University of Illinois' choice or form of entry for the earlier to later title differed from the information on the data base. If it was name/title and University of Illinois used a different form of the author, the 78x field was changed to title and a 580 note was added to give the linking information. Such notes were added to twenty records in the 580 field.

The title field (245) required thirteen revisions.

Local notes were added to twelve records in the 5xx field, usually "Bound with" or similar local information.

Other revisions were the addition of a title added entry (246 field) to six records and deleting it for one record, and adding information to the imprint (260 field) for five records.

## Additional Revisions Resulting from the Adoption of AACR2

Although the revisions discussed above were made after the adoption of AACR2, they would have been made anyway using AACR1. Additional revisions were the direct result of adopting AACR2 as the prescribed cataloguing code.

The largest number of additional revisions made involved choice of entry, changing the main entry heading (1xx) field to added entry (7xx) field—in other words, changing a name/title entry to title entry with an added entry under the name. This change was made to eighty-seven records. For three records, the corporate main entry was retained but the form of the name was revised.

The next largest number of revisions attributed directly to AACR2 was in the added entry (7xx) field. It was necessary to revise the form of the added entry heading on 40 records.

The third largest number of additional revisions occurred in the title (245) field using AACR2. Thirty-four records required revision; fourteen involved adding a subtitle, thirteen adding a statement of responsibility, six changing the form of the title entry, and one adding a qualifier.

Eighteen records required revising the subject area (6xx) fields. Changing geographic headings was the most common, but forms of personal or corporate names used as subject headings also required changing in some cases.

AACR2 was responsible for the revision of six records in the series (4xx) fields. The series were name/title and had to be revised to title entry according to AACR2 rules.

Other changes directly attributed to the use of AACR2 were revision of the publication details (260) field for one record and the note (5xx) for two records. These records involved cataloguing reproductions.

*Total Revisions Required in Editing OCLC Copy*

The area requiring the largest total number of revisions, including those changes which would have been made before the adoption of AACR2 and those made because of the adoption of AACR2, involved choice of entry: changing the main entry heading (1xx) field to the added entry (7xx) field. This was done to a total of 127 records. Four records required a change in form or some other revision.

The next largest total number of revisions occurred in the subject (6xx) fields with eighty-one additions, twenty-four changes, and one deletion, for a total of 106 revised records.

The third largest total number of revisions occurred in the physical description (300) field with seventy-seven records revised, including seventy-four additions and three changes. The adoption of AACR2 caused no additional revision to this field. (Other fields which were unaffected by AACR2 were the added title entry (246) field, holdings (362) field, local note (5xx) field, related title information (580) field, and linking entry (78x) field.)

The fourth largest number of total revisions, sixty-four, occurred in the added entry (7xx) field with fifty-two records revised, eleven additions, and one deletion.

The title (245) field was revised on a total of forty-seven records, publication area imprint (260) field a total of six times, the series (4xx) field a total of six times, and thirty-one changes were made to the note (5xx) fields.

It was necessary to make fifty-two authority records. Twenty-four would have been made anyway, and twenty-eight were made because of AACR2. Of 606 records analyzed, 212 (35%) were for titles related in some way to other titles (supplements, "continues", etc.) One hundred ninety-four (24%) had a suggested Dewey number providing helpful information for the classifiers at Illinois even though all such numbers do not reflect the nineteenth edition of Dewey.

*Summary*

Somewhat over half of the records input at the University of Illinois between November 1, 1979, and April 30, 1980, required some revision. Major revisions (e.g., choice of entry) are made on printouts by editors; minor revisions (e.g., punctuation) are made on-line by the inputters. The data collected was for major revisions only. A total of 581 revisions were made to the 329 records revised. Of these revisions, 33 percent were the direct result of the adoption of AACR2. The remaining 67 percent would have been made anyway using AACR1.

Most of the revision being done to records before the adoption of AACR2 involved adding collation (300) field and subject (6xx) information, revising information regarding linking titles (580 and 78x) to fit local information, and correcting name/title entries to title entries for unique titles. Many of the missing 300 and 6xx fields were on NSD records.

Most of the additional revision resulting directly from the adoption of AACR2 involved changing name/title entries to title entries for even more records, changing the form of the added entry (7xx) fields, and revising title (245) information.

Of the 606 records analyzed, nearly half could be used without revision. Over one-third were for titles related to other titles as supplements, or continuing titles. One-fourth of the records had Dewey information helpful to University of Illinois staff.

*Conclusion*

The University of Illinois experience indicates that serials can be dealt with efficiently in a copy cataloguing situation. Bibliographic information available on the data base is very helpful in creating accurate cataloguing records for serials with great speed. At the present time it is necessary to edit and revise much of the copy to make it usable. The need for editing increases with the adoption of AACR2, but the changes required are predictable. Predictable revisions include choice of entry (changing 1xx field to 7xx field), form of entry (revising 1xx, 245 and 4xx fields according to AACR2 rules), and changing the form of name in added entries (7xx) and subject headings (6xx) for geographic or personal and corporate names.

Cataloguing records for title entries beginning with "Vol. 1" require virtually no revision. "Continuing" titles (those with a 780 or 784 field) require special attention, partly because of discrepancies with local records for earlier titles. Since many titles are continuing, the linking fields provide important bibliographic information.

It seems likely that OCLC records will improve in the future as CONSER, LC, and NLC continue their work on the authentication of entries, adding new titles, upgrading existing records, closing entries, and eliminating duplicate records. Libraries will be adding more records for new titles, and there will be fewer wholesale conversion projects during which old records which were catalogued according to a variety of practices were added to the data base. On January 2, 1981, new records added to the data base will be arranged in accordance with AACR2 and will necessitate less and less revision.[10] It is hoped that the standardization of records with regard to choice and form of entry, which will result from the use of AACR2, will also bring about a need for less revision. If OCLC's plans to retrospectively convert records on the data base to AACR2 form are implemented, much editing will be eliminated.[11] The change from superimposition is creating AACR2-like entries.

By dividing the cataloguing process into a sequence of steps, it is possible to train support staff to catalog serials and to fit the work flow into an already established monographic copy cataloguing situation. Guidelines and procedures can be established and followed with a minimum of supervision and guidance—even for serials.

## REFERENCES

1. Dowell, Arlene Taylor. *Cataloguing with Copy: a Decision Maker's Handbook* (Littleton, Colo: Libraries Unlimited, 1976).

2. *Anglo-American Cataloguing Rules* 2nd ed. (Chicago: American Library Association, 1978).

3. *CONSER, Conversion of Serials* (Columbus, Ohio: OCLC), 1980.

4. "No delay for AACR2," *RTSD Newsletter* 5 (3) (May/June 1980):28.

5. Anderson, Sandy E., and Melby, Carol A. "Comparative Analysis of the Quality of OCLC Serials Cataloging Records, as a Function of Contributing Conser Participants and Field as Utilized by Serials Catalogers at the University of Illinois." *Serials Librarian* 3 (4) (Summer 1979):363–71.

6. Roughton, Michael. "OCLC Serials Records: Errors, Omissions and Dependability." *Journal of Academic Librarianship* 5 (6) (January 1980): 316–21.

7. Turner, Ann. "The Effects of AACR2 on Serials Cataloguing." *Serials Librarian* 4 (2) (Winter 1979):177–86.

8. *Anglo-American Cataloguing Rules*. North American text. (Chicago: American Library Association, 1967).

9. *Anglo-American Cataloguing Rules*, 2nd ed.

10. Dowell, Arlene Taylor. "Five Year Impact Study of the Effects of AACR2 on Copy Cataloging." Paper presented at Mid-winter meeting of American Library Association/Resources and Technical Services Division/Cataloging and Classification Section/Copy Cataloging Discussion Group, Chicago, Ill., January 22, 1980.

11. OCLC Steering Committee. *Memorandum FY 80-07* (February 19, 1980, Mimeographed.)

# THE AVAILABILITY AND ACCEPTABILITY
# OF SERIAL RECORDS IN THE OCLC DATA BASE

Mary Grace Fleeman

ABSTRACT. This two-part study is based upon serials cataloguing data collected during a three-month period at the University of Oklahoma Libraries. In the first part, serials for which records were available in the OCLC data base are compared with serials which had to be input locally. The second part examines more closely those records which were found to be already in the data base. LC records are compared with non-LC records to see whether there is any significant difference in acceptability. The acceptability of individual fields is considered.

## Introduction

This study examines the availability of serial records in the OCLC data base and the acceptability of these records to the serials cataloguing staff at the University of Oklahoma Libraries. It is based upon a total of 395 records for serials catalogued from October through December 1979. An assumption was made that the serials catalogued during that three-month period are representative of all serials catalogued at the University of Oklahoma.

The author recorded the following information for each title: whether it was found in the OCLC data base, when it began publication, which language(s) it is in, and whether it is in microform. For those titles which were found in the data base, she also noted whether the record represented LC cataloguing and which fields, if any, were modified in order to make the record acceptable to the University of Oklahoma.

## Part I: Availability

Of the 395 serial titles which were catalogued during the three-month period, 341 (or 86.3%) were found to be already in the OCLC data base, and fifty-four (or 13.7%) were input by the University of Oklahoma. Three factors —beginning date, language, and format (microform or non-microform)—were isolated to determine whether they are related to the availability or nonavailability of serial records in the data base.

The first factor to be examined was the date when the serial began publication. The sample was divided into three groups: (1) titles which began publication before 1970, (2) titles which began publication in 1970 or later, and (3) titles for which the beginning date was unknown. The results of this grouping are shown in Table 1.

Since the percentages shown in Table 1 are only estimates based upon a sample of 395 titles, there is some question about how close they are to the true percentages. In order to get a better idea of what the percentages are for all serials catalogued by the University of Oklahoma, 95 percent confidence intervals were constructed for Groups 1 and 2 and for the total sample. Calculation of the confidence interval for Group 1 is shown in Appendix A; intervals for Group 2 and for the total sample were calculated in a similar manner. The resulting intervals are 71.6– 84.6 percent for Group 1, 94.2–99.2 percent for Group 2, and 83.0– 89.6 percent for the total sample. In other words, assuming that the sample is representative, we can be 95 percent confident that the percentage of Group 1 serials being found in the data base is between 71.6 and 84.6 percent, the percentage of Group 2 serials being found is between 94.2 and 99.2 percent, and the overall percentage is between 83.0 and 89.6 percent.

The second factor to be considered was the language of the serial. The records in the sample were divided into the following language groups:

1. English
2. Other Roman alphabet languages
3. Cyrillic alphabet languages
4. Other languages

If a serial was published in two or more languages, it was assigned to the highest group on the list to which it could belong. For example, a serial with both English and Russian text was assigned to Group 1, rather than Group 3. The results of this division are shown in Table 2.

In examining Table 2, the author disregarded the figures for Group 4 because the group was so small. Of the first three groups, it appears that, as

|  | 1.Pre-1970 | 2.1970+ | 3.Unknown | Total |
|---|---|---|---|---|
| IN OCLC | 121 (78.1%) | 175 (96.7%) | 45 (76.3%) | 341 (86.3%) |
| NOT IN OCLC | 34 (21.9%) | 6 (03.3%) | 14 (23.7) | 54 (13.7%) |
| TOTAL | 155 | 181 | 59 | 395 |

TABLE 1:  Relationship of Publication Data to Availability of Record
in Data Base

|  | 1.English | Other 2.Roman | 3.Cyrillic | 4.Other | Total |
|---|---|---|---|---|---|
| IN OCLC | 283 (89.0%) | 35 (77.8%) | 18 (66.7%) | 5 (100%) | 341 (86.3%) |
| NOT IN OCLC | 35 (11.0%) | 10 (22.2%) | 9 (33.3%) | 0 (00.0%) | 54 (13.7%) |
| TOTAL | 318 | 45 | 27 | 5 | 395 |

TABLE 2: Relationship of Language to Availability in Data Base

|  | Microform | Non-Microform | Total |
|---|---|---|---|
| IN OCLC | 3 (20.0%) | 338 (88.9%) | 341 (86.3%) |
| NOT IN OCLC | 12 (80.0%) | 42 (11.1%) | 54 (13.7%) |
| TOTAL | 15 | 380 | 395 |

TABLE 3: Relationship of Format to Availability in Data Base

would be expected, English language serials are most likely to be found in the data base and Cyrillic alphabet serials are least likely to be found. Using the method illustrated in Appendix A, 95 percent confidence intervals were constructed for each of the first two groups. It was learned that, assuming a representative sample, we can be 95 percent confident the percentage of English language serials being found in the data base is between 85.6 and 92.4 percent and the percentage of serials in other Roman languages being found in between 65.7 and 89.9. No interval was calculated for the Cyrillic alphabet serials, because the method being used requires that the sample size be at least thirty, and the sample of Cyrillic titles was only twenty-seven.

The third factor to be isolated was whether the serial was in microform. This factor is important because a separate record is required for a microform reproduction of a serial, even if there is already a record in the data base for the serial in another form. The figures for microform and non-microform serials are presented in Table 3.

Following the method in Appendix A, a 95 percent confidence interval was calculated for the non-microform group. We may be 95 percent confident that the percentage of non-microform serials being found in the data base is between 85.7 and 92.1 percent. No interval was calculated for the microform titles since there are only fifteen titles in this group and the method being used requires that the sample size be at least thirty.

The findings in this first part of the study confirm what common sense would suggest. First, serials which began publication in 1970 or later are more likely to be found in the data base than are pre-1970 serials. Second, English language serials are more likely to be found in the data base than are serials in other languages, and Roman alphabet serials are more likely to be found than serials in the Cyrillic alphabet. Third, records for microform serials are less likely to be found than are records for non-microform serials. Perhaps the figures of most interest are the very high percentage of serials beginning in 1970 or later which were found in the data base and the relatively low percentage of microform records which were found.

## Part II: Acceptability

In the second part of the study, the 341 records which were found to be already in the data base were examined more closely. Of these records, twenty-two (or 6.5%) were accepted just as they were, while 319 (or 93.5%) had additions or changes made to at least one field. A 95 percent confidence interval for the accepted records was calculated and found to be between 3.9 and 9.1 percent.

It was expected that records with LC cataloguing would be more likely to be accepted than those catalogued by other libraries. In an attempt to examine this, the records were divided into the groups shown in Table 4.

Ninety-five percent confidence intervals were constructed for the LC group and for the non-LC group. It was determined that, assuming a representative sample, we may be 95 percent confident that LC serial records are being totally accepted between 7.4 and 25.0 percent of the time, while non-LC records are being accepted only between 1.7 and 6.3 percent of the time. As expected, LC records appear to be more often accepted without modification than do other records.

Since such a high percentage of records in the sample were modified in at least one field, the next question to be considered was in which fields all of

|          | LC              | Non-LC          | Total           |
|----------|-----------------|-----------------|-----------------|
| ACCEPTED | 11 (16.2%)      | 11 (4.0%)       | 22 (6.5%)       |
| MODIFIED | 57 (83.8%)      | 262 (96.0%)     | 319 (93.5%)     |
| TOTAL    | 68              | 273             | 341             |

TABLE 4:  Relationship of LC and Non-LC Cataloging to Acceptability of Record

| Fields | LC | | | Non-LC | | | Total | | |
|---|---|---|---|---|---|---|---|---|---|
| | Accepted | Changed | Added | Accepted | Changed | Added | Accepted | Changed | Added |
| 050/090 | 40 | 28 | 0 | 86 | 73 | 114 | 126 | 101 | 114 |
| 110/130 | 63 | 4 | 1 | 241 | 24 | 8 | 304 | 28 | 9 |
| 245 | 62 | 6 | 0 | 240 | 33 | 0 | 302 | 39 | 0 |
| 246/247 | 59 | 3 | 6 | 246 | 6 | 21 | 305 | 9 | 27 |
| 260 | 49 | 19 | 0 | 188 | 83 | 2 | 237 | 102 | 2 |
| 300 | 51 | 15 | 2 | 170 | 60 | 43 | 221 | 75 | 45 |
| 362 | 40 | 10 | 18 | 144 | 54 | 75 | 184 | 64 | 93 |
| 500/590 | 54 | 7 | 7 | 198 | 26 | 49 | 252 | 33 | 56 |
| 600/695 | 50 | 10 | 8 | 138 | 52 | 83 | 188 | 62 | 91 |
| 700/730 | 55 | 4 | 9 | 201 | 20 | 52 | 256 | 24 | 61 |
| 780/785 | 49 | 13 | 6 | 207 | 36 | 30 | 256 | 49 | 36 |

TABLE 5: Relationship of LC and Non-LC Cataloging to Acceptability
of Selected Fields

these modifications were made. Two types of modification were identified: changes made to a field already present in the record, and additions made because the field was missing from the record. Table 5 shows the number of records in selected fields which were accepted as is, changed, or added because they were missing. If one of the fields under consideration was not included in the record and it was determined that it was indeed not needed, then that field was counted as accepted.

In an attempt to make it easier to analyze the data in Table 5, each field of each record was assigned a value of 0, .5, or 1, according to the following scale:

0 = The field had to be added.
.5 = The field was present but was modified.
1 = The field was accepted.

For each block of Table 5, the sum of these values was divided by the total number of records to arrive at an average score for that block. For example, the score for the 050/090 fields in LC records was calculated as follows:

$$\frac{40(1) + 28(.5) + 0(0)}{68} = .794$$

| Fields | LC | | Non-LC | | Total | |
|--------|-------|-------|-------|-------|-------|-------|
| | Score | (s) | Score | (s) | Score | (z) |
| 050/090 | .794 | (.248) | .449 | (.426) | .518 | (8.63) |
| 110/130 | .956 | (.167) | .927 | (.215) | .933 | (1.16) |
| 245 | .956 | (.143) | .940 | (.163) | .943 | (0.80) |
| 246/247 | .890 | (.297) | .912 | (.274) | .908 | (-0.55) |
| 260 | .860 | (.226) | .841 | (.241) | .845 | (0.59) |
| 300 | .860 | (.257) | .733 | (.376) | .758 | (3.26) |
| 362 | .662 | (.436) | .626 | (.430) | .633 | (0.61) |
| 500/590 | .846 | (.326) | .773 | (.390) | .787 | (1.55) |
| 600/695 | .809 | (.346) | .601 | (.439) | .642 | (4.16) |
| 700/730 | .838 | (.350) | .773 | (.397) | .786 | (1.33) |
| 780/785 | .816 | (.322) | .824 | (.335) | .823 | (-0.18) |

TABLE 6:   Scores Assigned to LC and Non-LC Records for Selected Fields

If all the sample records had been accepted without modification in a given field, that block would have received a perfect score of 1. On the other hand, a block where the field had to be locally input for all the records would have received the lowest possible score of 0. The scores which were calculated for each block are shown in Table 6, together with their standard deviation in parentheses.

A quick glance at Table 6 shows that for all the fields except 246/247 and 780/785, the LC records received a higher score than the non-LC records. However, since most of the scores are fairly close together, it is not possible to draw any conclusions without further analysis. The LC and non-LC scores obtained for each field, or group of fields, were tested to see whether they are statistically different at the .05 level of significance. The calculations for the 050/090 fields are shown in Appendix B. Calculations for the other fields followed the same method and are summarized in the last column of Table 6. It was learned that in only three fields are the differences between the LC and non-LC scores significant at the .05 level. The scores were stastically different in fields 050/090, 300, and 600/690.

Since fields 050/090 and 600/690 are the fields for LC call numbers and subject headings, it would be expected that LC records would be superior in these fields. One reason for the difference in the 300 field is that many of the serial records input by OCLC member libraries either lacked the 300 field or, if it was present, did not include the size in subfield c. Since the University of Oklahoma requires that the size be included, it was frequently added. LC records, on the other hand, could normally be relied upon to include at least subfield c in the 300 field.

Those fields which were not statistically different at the .05 level were next tested at the .10 level. However, no additional fields were found to be significantly different at this level, where the critical region was ≤ − 1.645 and ≥ 1.645.

At this point, the findings were compared with those of Sandy E. Anderson and Carol A. Melby at the University of Illinois.[1] In a comparison of LC records with those of other CONSER libraries, Anderson and Melby have "demonstrated for certain fields that, on average, Library of Congress copy has been accepted with lesser amounts of modification than that of other participants."[2] They found statistically significant differences in more fields than were found at the University of Oklahoma. Of the three groups of fields which were found to be statistically different at Oklahoma, Anderson and Melby included two of them, the 300 and 600 fields, in their analysis. In both their Group A and their Group B, the 600 field was the one with the greatest difference between LC records and records of other CONSER libraries. In addition, the 300 field had the second greatest difference in both groups of data at Illinois.

The fields in the Oklahoma study with the least difference between LC and non-LC records included both 245 and 260. The Illinois study found that the 245 field had the least difference in Group A and next to the least difference in Group B, while field 260 had the least difference in Group B. Thus the results of this part of the present study have some similarity to the findings at Illinois.

Consideration was next given to whether the three factors which were shown in the first part of the study to be related to the availability of the record in the data base might also be related to the acceptability of the records that were found. This data was tabulated and is summarized in Tables 7, 8, and 9.

It appears from these tables that, in the three-month sample, all of the records which were accepted without modification were for English language serials which were not in microform. In addition, eighteen of the twenty-two accepted records, or 81.8 percent, were for serials which began publication in

|          | 1.Pre-1970    | 2.1970+        | 3.Unknown     | Total          |
|----------|---------------|----------------|---------------|----------------|
| ACCEPTED | 4 (3.3%)      | 18 (10.3%)     | 0 (0.0%)      | 22 (6.5%)      |
| MODIFIED | 117 (96.7%)   | 157 (89.7%)    | 45 (100.0%)   | 319 (93.5%)    |
| TOTAL    | 121           | 175            | 45            | 341            |

TABLE 7: Relationship of Publication Date to Acceptability of Record

| | 1.English | Other 2.Roman | 3.Cyrillic | 4.Other | Total |
|---|---|---|---|---|---|
| ACCEPTED | 22 (7.8%) | 0 (0.0%) | 0 (0.0%) | 0 (0.0%) | 22 (6.5%) |
| MODIFIED | 261 (92.2%) | 35 (100%) | 18 (100%) | 5 (100%) | 319 (93.5%) |
| TOTAL | 283 | 35 | 18 | 5 | 341 |

TABLE 8: Relationship of Language to Acceptability of Record

| | Microform | Non-Microform | Total |
|---|---|---|---|
| ACCEPTED | 0 (0.0%) | 22 (6.5%) | 22 (6.5%) |
| MODIFIED | 3 (100%) | 316 (93.5%) | 319 (93.5%) |
| TOTAL | 3 | 338 | 341 |

TABLE 9: Relationship of Format to Acceptability of Record

1970 or later. Unfortunately, the number of accepted records is so small that it is hard to predict with any degree of certainty how similar these percentages would be in a larger sample.

## Conclusions

The findings of the first part of this study are rather encouraging, since it was learned that roughly 83.0–89.6 percent of the serials being catalogued at the University of Oklahoma may be expected to be found in the OCLC data base. The expected hit rate is even higher for serials which began publication in 1970 or later, are at least partly in English, and/or are not in microform. Based upon these figures alone, one might tend to conclude that the majority of the serials cataloguing could be turned over to the support staff, and that a professional serials cataloguer would be needed only for the approximately 10.4–17.0 percent of the titles which are not found in the data base, and perhaps for a small percentage of other titles which have problems that cannot be solved at the clerical level.

However, as the findings of the second part of the study show, only 3.9–9.1 percent of the records which are being found in the data base are accepted without modification. Even records which represent LC cataloguing are being accepted only approximately 7.4–25.0 percent of the time. Although some of the modifications, such as adding the size to field 300, could be done at the clerical level, others, such as adding or totally changing the call number or subject heading fields, would normally require professional attention.

Further analysis of which modifications should be done by a professional cataloguer and which can be done by the support staff is desirable. In general, modifications which require the use of the LC classification schedules and subject heading list, or the interpretation of the *Anglo-American Cataloging Rules*, are considered to be professional, while more mechanical modifications can usually be handled by the nonprofessional. However, it is not possible to go very far beyond these generalizations without considering the ability and training of the support staff.

In looking at the modifications which are presently being made, it is also desirable to consider whether all of them are really necessary. In the sample under consideration, most of the modifications which consisted of adding a field not already present were necessary. For example, the field most often added was the call number field, which is essential. Field 362, which was added next most often, is always added by the University of Oklahoma, even if the beginning volume and/or date are unknown, so that there will be space to add the information later or to close the entry if it ceases publication or changes title. Other fields which were frequently added include subject headings (600/695), added entries (700/730), notes (500/590), and collation (300). All of these, with the possible exception of some notes in the 500 fields, can be considered essential. In general, most of the 534 fields which were added to the records in the sample were necessary modifications.

In contrast to the fields which were added to the sample records, many of the 586 changes which were made to fields already present in the records were not absolutely necessary. For example, the title in field 245 was sometimes expanded from a generic term to a fuller form which included the name of the corporate author. Although the title in the record as it was found was not incorrect, the record was changed to conform with the present practice of including the full title. Similarly, the 260 field was frequently modified to conform with the present practice of always including the publisher in subfield b, even if it is the same as the corporate author. Although the original 260 field was not incorrect, it was modified to make it more correct by current standards. Perhaps consideration should be given to eliminating this type of modification.

On the other hand, some of the remaining changes were necessary. Perhaps the most obvious of these are changes to the 050/090, 600/695, and 700/730 fields. Some of the changes to the 050/090 fields consisted of adjusting the author number to fit in the local shelflist, while others involved changing the entire classification number for a variety of reasons. Changes in the 600 fields were made to conform to the LC subject heading list and its supplements, and changes in the 700/730 fields were necessary to avoid conflict with forms of entry already established in the local catalog.

All of this data obtained about the current state of serial records in the OCLC data base and the way they are being modified at the University of Oklahoma will help the serials cataloguing staff improve its procedures and make plans for the future. It is also hoped that the data will be of interest and assistance to serials cataloguers in other libraries. In considering this data, one should keep in mind that the OCLC data base is constantly being expanded and upgraded. Therefore, it is expected that both the availability and the acceptability of serial records will continue to improve.

## REFERENCES

1. Anderson, Sandy E., and Melby, Carol A. "Comparative Analysis of the Quality of OCLC Serials Cataloging Records, as a Function of Contributing CONSER Participant and Field as Utilized by Serials Cataluguers at the University of Illinois." *The Serials Librarian* 3 (4) (Summer 1979):363–71.

2. *Ibid.*, pp. 368, 371.

APPENDIX A:  Calculation of 95% Confidence Interval

The confidence coefficient is .95; therefore $\alpha = 1 - .95 = .05$.

$$z_{\alpha/2} = z_{.025} = 1.96$$

For pre-1970 records, $x = 121$ and $n = 155$.

$$\hat{p} = \frac{x}{n} = \frac{121}{155} = .781$$

$$S_p = \sqrt{\frac{\hat{p}(1-\hat{p})}{n}} = \sqrt{\frac{(.781)(.219)}{155}} = .033$$

$$\pi_L = \hat{p} - (z_{\alpha/2})(S_p) = .781 - (1.96)(.033) = .716$$

$$\pi_U = \hat{p} + (z_{\alpha/2})(S_p) = .781 + (1.96)(.033) = .846$$

Therefore, we are 95% confident that the percentage of pre-1970 serials appearing in the OCLC data base is between 71.6% and 84.6%.

APPENDIX B: Test for Statistical Difference Between LC Average Score and Non-LC Average Score

Let $\mu_1$ = the true score for the field in LC records

Let $\mu_2$ = the true score for the field in non-LC records

Null hypothesis - $H_0 : \mu_1 = \mu_2$

Alternative hypothesis - $H_1 : \mu_1 \neq \mu_2$

Let $\alpha$ = .05

$z_{\alpha/2} = z_{.025} = 1.96$

Therefore, the critical region is $z \leq -1.96$ and $z \geq 1.96$

For fields 050/090, $\bar{x}_1$ = .794 and $\bar{x}_2$ = .449, and $s_1$ = .248 and $s_2$ = .426.

$$z = \frac{\bar{x}_1 - \bar{x}_2}{\sqrt{s_1^2 / n_2 + s_2^2 / n_2}} = \frac{.794 - .449}{\sqrt{\frac{(.248)^2}{68} + \frac{(.426)^2}{273}}} = 8.63$$

Since $z = 8.63 > 1.96$, $H_0$ may be rejected.

This means the LC score is statistically different from the non-LC score.

# OCLC SERIAL RECORDS: AN UPDATE

Michael Roughton

ABSTRACT. Though the OCLC data base of serial records has improved somewhat over the past two years, it is still hampered by serious problems that allow paper bibliographies to compete with it on an equal footing. A sample of forty-two cessations listed in a recent issue of *Ulrich's Quarterly* compared against the OCLC data base showed only nineteen percent of the OCLC records to be up to date. Though the data base has improved in its ability to keep pace with title changes, it has shown no improvement in supplying cataloguers with records that contain call numbers and subject headings in Library of Congress form. The system also exhibits a number of peculiarities that make it difficult to use.

Two years ago when I compiled the information for "OCLC Serial Records: Errors, Omissions & Dependability,"[1] it was clear that OCLC's data base of serial records was suffering from a carelessness that caused it to be incomplete, unreliable, and even at times wildly inaccurate. At present, the data base is much improved. Records are more complete, more accurate, and less bewildering than they were two years ago. This improvement is a testament to the diligent efforts of OCLC member libraries and the CONSER participants.

This is not to say that all is well with the serial records found in OCLC. Improvement is a relative term and here means that the data base has come from a disorderly state to something better. The data base still has problems that hinder its effectiveness to such a degree that inexpensive paper bibliographies, slow and cumbersome though they may be, can still compete in delivering certain kinds of information. The lure of any machine-based bibiographic system—that one keying will answer a multitude of questions quickly and effortlessly—is still a lure for the OCLC data base of serials records.

Evidence that this is so is not obscure. Consider the following hypothetical case: You are the Serials Acquisitions Librarian in a large university library. In your hand is the most recent issue of *The Journal of Saudi Arabian Science* you can find. It was published in January 1978. The Physical Sciences Bibliographer has decided that the journal would be a fitting addition to the library's holdings and has asked you to order a subscription. You suspect that the periodical (which was issued fitfully for three years) has ceased publication. To prove your suspicion and save yourself the trouble of typing a purchase order and the three or four claim letters that will inevitably follow, you need to find the cessation recorded somewhere. Question: Which bibliographic tool is most likely to help you? *New Serial Titles*? OCLC? *Ulrich's Quarterly*?

If you chose OCLC, you probably did so because you believe that an on-line bibliographic retrieval unit, sleek, shining, and dispensing information effortlessly at the touch of a key, could not possibly perform less well than a printed tool. In that case, you get an "A" for keeping faith with the future—but a "C" for range of experience. At the present time, *Ulrich's Quarterly* reports information on title cessations faster and more accurately than OCLC.

The evidence on which this assertion is based is the result of a simple test. In comparing forty-two titles listed as cessations in *Ulrich's Quarterly*, v.4, n.1 and 2, to the OCLC data base, I found that only eight of the records or nineteen percent of the sample showed the titles to have ceased publication. A statistic such as this may cause some to question *Ulrich's Quarterly* more than the OCLC data base. Perhaps Bowker records cessations as soon as a serial shows an irregular pattern of publication or is slow in releasing an issue. Perhaps Bowker fails to take the time to contact the publisher of a title to verify that it has ceased. In answer to the first question, it can be said that, though it does a better job than most paper bibliographies, *Ulrich's Quarterly* is anything but speedy in delivering information on cessations. Most of the titles listed as cessations in any given issue ended their lives at least one year earlier. Bowker's verification that a serial actually has ceased is dependable. The listing of a cessation in *Ulrich's Quarterly* is often the result of information supplied by publishers.[2] Some may explain Bowker's success and OCLC's failure in this area by pointing out that, as a publisher, Bowker is probably the recipient of information from other publishers that is not generally supplied to libraries. This explanation is plausible but does not explain why *New Serial Titles* outperforms OCLC almost as handily as *Ulrich's Quarterly*. Of twenty-one ceased titles listed in *New Serial Titles* the first three months of 1980, only five (23%) were recorded in OCLC as dead publications. Unless these small selections of titles are extraordinarily unrepresentative, it seems clear that *Ulrich's Quarterly* and *New Serial Titles* produce more reliable information about recent cessations than does OCLC.

The chances of locating a correct record when searching OCLC for a publication that has recently changed title are much better now than they were two years ago. A check of sixty-eight title changes listed in the "Changes in Serials" section of the January, February, and May issues of *New Serial Titles* brought fifty correct records from OCLC, or 74 percent of the sample. The remaining 26 percent of the records broke down into eleven records (16%) incomplete (dates of publication and volume designation missing) and seven records (10%) incorrect. In 1978, a check of ninety-three listings in *New Serial Titles* produced 59.1 percent correct, 23.6 percent incomplete, and 17.2 percent incorrect. Though the improvement is marked, it is overshadowed by the fact that it represents a rise from a very low point.

Of course, success in locating a record for a particular title on the OCLC system does not guarantee that the record will be of any use to a cataloguer.

Librarians using the data base on a day-to-day basis will not be impressed with the amount of information the average record contains. In the course of the past two years, OCLC has made no gain in the number of records that offer subject headings and call numbers in Library of Congress form. In the 1978 sample of 612 records, these figures stood at 75.5 percent and 64.9 percent, respectively. Based on a sample of 179 records extracted from the data base during the period March through June 1980, the present figures for subject headings and call numbers are 72.7 percent and 64 percent, a change in both instances not large enough to be called a gain or a loss. Library of Congress authenticated records lacking a call number or subject heading in LC form made up 12.8 percent of the recent sample of 179 records.

A few other spots glimmer with promise. Of the 179 records in the more recent sample, 42.5 percent showed an "lc" or "nlc" in the 042 field (authentication center), 55.8 percent showed an "nsdp" or "isds/c," and 33.5 percent showed both. The percentage of records with an ISSN has risen markedly in two years from 66.5 percent of the 1978 sample to 83 percent of the 1980 sample. These figures suggest that NSDP and its Canadian counterpart are making steady progress in assigning or authenticating key titles and ISSNs.

Other figures taken from the recent sample of 179 records may give more cause for concern. Thirty-four titles or about 19 percent of the 179 records (representing 179 distinct titles) were found to be duplicated by other records. These thirty-four titles generated forty-five duplicates, or about 1.25 duplicates per title. Most titles with duplicate records did indeed have only one duplicate, but a few had two. No title had more than two. At the present time, the duplicate records in the OCLC serials data base fall into three categories: serial records marked "DO NOT USE", monograph records (legitimate and otherwise), and serial records that are superfluous but not marked "DO NOT USE." Forty percent of the forty-five duplicate records were serial records clearly marked "DO NOT USE." About 16 percent of the forty-five duplicate records were monograph records entered by libraries that prefer to catalog individual issues of quasi-serials (annual reports, directories, irregularly issued bibliographies) as monographs. The remaining 44.4 percent were serial records that were unquestionably duplicates. Assuming that this sample is representative of the entire data base, about one out of every five title searches for a serial will elicit at least one duplicate record. In about 40 percent of the cases in which a duplicate record is elicited, the searcher will be directed from the duplicate to a superior record. In the other 60 percent of the cases, the searcher will need to puzzle out the desired record from the duplicate monograph and serial records.

An analysis of the sample of records for ninety-nine new titles taken from the OCLC data base during the period April through June 1980 does not suggest that OCLC is or is becoming the answer to librarians' prayers for one-stop preorder searching, as Kilton suggests.[3] A check of the OCLC system for ninety-nine titles which began publication in 1980 and were listed in *Ulrich's Quarterly*, v.4, n.2 and *New Serial Titles*, April–June 1980, brought forth records for only sixty titles or 60.6 percent of the ninety-nine. These sixty records brought with them seven duplicates, only two of which were legitimately input. The common explanation for the prevalence of duplicate records in the serials data base holds that the offending records are leftovers from the inception of the data base when unfortunate but unavoidable circumstances led libraries to input superfluous records. This explanation is plausible but unsatisfactory. That 8.3 percent of the records for sixty new titles should have duplicate records suggests that the problem is still very much with us.

Once you locate a record for a new serial title on the OCLC system, what can you expect to find? If the sixty records located in this sample of ninety-nine new titles searched are an indication, records will be of varying degrees of completeness. Subject headings in LC form seem to appear on records for new titles more often than do call numbers in LC form—65 percent and 43.3 percent, respectively, in this sample. On the other hand, neither a call number nor a subject heading in LC form appeared on 33.3 percent of the sixty records for new titles. Happily, 81.7 percent of the records had a complete 362 field (dates of publication and volume designation), complete in this case meaning that the volume and date of the first issue appeared in the record. The ISSN appeared on 76.6 percent of the records and the "nsdp" or "isds/c" symbol on 63.3 percent. The Library of Congress and the National Library of Canada have been less active than their authenticating counterparts, their symbols appearing on only 33.3 percent of the records. Only fifteen of the sixty new titles (25%) were fully authenticated.

In using the OCLC system, one encounters many peculiarities that make the system seem unpredictable. One of the inexplicable peculiarities of the system is the fact that the 212 field (variant title access) is not indexed. Technical bulletin No. 37 specifies that this field is to be used "when the title contains an initialism, abbreviation, numeral, symbol, non-roman character, etc." One of the most common uses libraries make of the field is to record in full form a serial title that includes an ampersand. Anyone who has searched, checked-in, or catalogued serials for any length of time knows that a serial with an ampersand in the title is not rare. Given that, it does not take much imagination to see that many searches for such a title will miscarry if a searcher innocently substitutes "and" for an ampersand. For example, a searcher may very easily search the data base for *American Arts & Antiques* using the key "ame,ar,an,a." In such a case, the system would respond with a number of records matching that key, but none of them would be for the desired title. Thus starts a train of events that could very easily lead to the inputting of a duplicate record. Whether this same sequence of events is what led the University of Tulsa to enter a duplicate (and error-ridden) record for *Criminology & Penology Abstracts* on

```
NO HOLDINGS IN OCL - FOR HOLDINGS ENTER dh DEPRESS  DISPLAY RECD SEND
OCLC: 2406009       Rec stat: c Entrd: 760831        Used: 800313
Type: a Bib lvl: s Govt pub:   Lans:   ens Source: d S/L ent: 0
Repr:    Enc lvl:   Conf pub: 0 Ctry:  ohu Ser tp:   Alphabt: a
Indx: u Mod rec:   Phys med:   Cont: i   Frequn: w Pub st:  d
Desc:    Cum ind: u Titl pas: u ISDS:    1 Resulr: r Dates: 1960-1963
    1 010      sc77-889
    2 040      COO c COO d DLC d NSD
    3 012      2
    4 022      0430-4799
    5 042      lc a nsdp
    6 090      Z7164.F5 b F49
    7 090       b
    8 049      OCLC
    9 222 04   The Financial index of corporations and industries
   10 245 04   The Financial index of corporations and industries.
   11 260 00   Cleveland [etc.] b Investment Index Co.
   12 362 0    v. 1-16; May 1960-Jan. 11, 1963.
   13 690 0    Finance x Periodicals x Indexes.
   14 785 04    t Funk and Scott index of corporations and industries
   15 936      Dec. 25, 1962 (surrogate)
```

FIGURE 1.

6-12-80 (#6414153) about two months after Fairleigh Dickinson University had entered a record for the same title (#6182742), is impossible to determine —but it might well have been.

Ampersands cause other problems as well. Figure 1 shows a fully authenticated record for the *Financial Index of Corporations and Industries* which, the 785 field tells us, was absorbed in 1963 by the *Funk and Scott Index of Corporations and Industries*. If a searcher wished to get from this record to the record for the succeeding title, he would have to use a title search key since the 785 field (succeeding title) in the record for *The Financial Index of Corporations and Industries* does not give an ISSN or an OCLC number for the succeeding title.

The search key "fun,an,sc,i" should deliver the record for the succeeding title. Unfortunately, it does not. The search key delivers only the record for the *Financial Index of Corporations and Industries*. In order to retrieve the desired record one must have the wit to realize what has happened and try instead the search key "fun,&,sc,i". That search key will yield a number of records, one of them the record shown in Figure 2. Comparing the 245 field (full title) of this record to the 785 field, subfield t (succeeding entry, full title) of the record in Figure 1, one notices that the two "and"s in the latter record have become ampersands in the former.

Concatenations of records seem to invite errors. Search the succeeding title for the record OCLC #1570321 (Figure 2) and you will receive OCLC #1079931 (Figure 3). One might expect the 780 field (preceding entry) for this fully authenticated record to refer one back to OCLC #1570321, thereby setting up an orderly link between records. Notice, however, that subfield w (control

```
Screen 1 of 2
NO HOLDINGS IN OCL  -  FOR HOLDINGS ENTER dh DEPRESS  DISPLAY RECD SEND
OCLC: 1570321        Rec stat: c Entrd: 750824          Used: 800811
Type: a Bib lvl: s Govt pub:   Lang:   eng Source: d S/L ent: 0
 Repr:    Enc lvl: I Conf pub: 0 Ctry:   miu Ser tp: p Alphabt: a
 Indx: u Mod rec:   Phys med:   Cont: i   Frequn: z Pub st:   d
 Desc:    Cum ind: u Titl pas: u ISDS:      ReSulr: n Dates: 1960-1967
  1 010       63-25278
  2 040       MUL c MUL d FUL d COO d NSD d IUL
  3 022       0532-8705
  4 035       0279918 b MULS a    PITT  NO.  3176100001
  5 035       sf97383000 b FULS
  6 050 0     HG4961 b .F8
  7 090       b
  8 049       OCLC
  9 245 00    Funk & Scott index of corporations & industries.
 10 246 10    Index of corporations & industries
 11 260 00    Detroit, b Funk & Scott Publishing Company.
 12 300       v. c 28 cm.
 13 310       Weekly with monthly and annual cumulations
 14 362 0     1960-67.
 15 650  0    Securities z United States x Periodicals.

Screen 2 of 2
 16 690  0    Finance x Periodicals x Indexes.
 17 780 05    t Financial index of corporations and industries g January 1963
x 0430-4799
 18 785 00    t F & S index of corporations and industries x 0014-567X w
(OCoLC)1079931
 19 936       Unknown a INC
```

FIGURE 2.

number) directs you to OCLC #2759914 (Figure 4). This record you will notice carries the interesting message that it is not to be used and directs you to OCLC #1570321! Similar discrepancies appear when one examines a set of records, one for a microfilm copy of a serial, the other for a paper copy. Too often the paper copy record describes the serial as dead while the microfilm record shows it to be alive and well.

Collections of statistics concerning the accuracy or completeness or dependability of OCLC serial records are one way of giving shape to the set of random impressions one develops of the data base over a period of time. The figures collected here and in the earlier study give shape to my impression that the OCLC data base of serials records does not suffer from a terminal disease, though it may be developing a chronic one. The questions and problems raised here may seem petty compared to the progress the data base has made over the course of its short existence. OCLC serials records were not born in an environment lacking in criticism, nor are they likely to improve in one. More studies of machine-readable serial records—those in OCLC or in other data bases—would be helpful in letting librarians know whether progress is real or a set of random impressions. Unfortunately, such studies are not forthcoming.

The rapid rise of machine-readable records, especially serial records, seems to have fostered a lack of critical judgment in librarians—a reluctance, perhaps, to question what is regarded as inevitable. At other times it seems that machine-readable bibliographic records have taken such hold of the collective imagination of the library world that the benefits once conceived of as being possible to deliver with a machine system—rapid delivery of accurate information, elimination of redundant work—have come to be thought of as integral parts of the system design that, like wives and washers, are inseparable from the system. In this atmosphere of uncritical acceptance, it is difficult to have a discussion in which the rather obvious advantages of paper files are acknowledged, let alone applauded. We seem to have arrived at the enviable state of mind in which we cannot be disappointed because our hopes for success are so strong as to mask all evidence of failure. Paper bibliographies can still outperform OCLC in a number of aspects of bibliographic control. This is not to say that we

```
Screen 1 of 2
NO HOLDINGS IN OCL - FOR HOLDINGS ENTER dh DEPRESS  DISPLAY RECD SEND
OCLC: 1079931        Rec stat: c Entrd: 741119        Used: 800811
Type: a Bib lvl: s Govt pub:   Lang:  eng Source: d S/L ent: 0
Repr:     Enc lvl:    Conf pub: 0 Ctry: ohu Ser tp:   Alphabt: a
Indx: u Mod rec:    Phys med:   Cont: i   Frequn: a Pub st:  c
Desc:   Cum ind: u Titl pag: u ISDS:   1 Regulr: r Dates: 196u-9999
 1 010        78-649838
 2 040        DRB c DRB d PIT d COO d NSD d IUL d DLC
 3 012        3 e s k 1 1 1 m 1
 4 022 0      0014-567X
 5 035        292515000 b PITT a 183240 b USPS
 6 042        nsdp a lc
 7 043        n-us---
 8 050 0      Z7165.U5 b F23
 9 082        016.338/0973
10 090        b
11 049        OCLC
12 212 0      Funk and Scott index of corporations and industries
13 222 00     F & S index of corporations and industries
14 245 00     F & S index of corporations and industries.
15 246 10     Index of corporations and industries


Screen 2 of 2
16 260 01     Cleveland [etc.] b Predicasts, inc. [etc.]
17 265        Predicasts, Inc., 200 University Circle Research Center, 11001
Cedar Ave., Cleveland, OH 44106
18 300        v. c 29 cm.
19 350        $325.00
20 500        Cumulation of the weekly publication.
21 650 0      Corporations z United States x Indexes x Periodicals.
22 651 0      United States x Industries x Indexes x Periodicals.
23 650 0      Commercial products x United States x Indexes x Periodicals.
24 690 0      Securities z United States x Periodicals.
25 710 20     Predicasts, inc.
26 780 00      t Funk & Scott index of corporations & industries w
(OCoLC)2759914
27 936        Unknown a 1979  (surrogate)
```

FIGURE 3.

```
Screen 1 of 2
NO HOLDINGS IN OCL - FOR HOLDINGS ENTER dh DEPRESS  DISPLAY RECD SEND
OCLC: 2759914      Rec stat: c Entrd: 770224         Used: 800807
Type: a Bib lvl: s Govt pub:    Lang:  eng Source:    S/L ent: 0
Repr:     Enc lvl: I Conf pub: 0 Ctry:  miu Ser tp: p Alphabt: a
Indx: u Mod rec: e Phys med:    Cont:  ^    Frequn: z Pub st:  d
Desc:    Cum ind: u Titl pag: u ISDS:      Regulr: r Dates: 1960-1967
  1 010        63-25278
  2 040        DLC c PIT d PIT d NSD d IUL
  3 022        0532-8705
  4 035        3176100001 b PITT
  5 043        DO NOT USE -- SEE OCLC #1570321
  6 050 00     HG4961 b .F8
  7 090        b
  8 049        OCLC
  9 245 00     Funk & Scott index of corporations & industries
 10 246 30     Index of corporations & industries.
 11 260 00     Detroit, b Funk & Scott Pub. Co.
 12 300        v. c 28 cm.
 13 310        Weekly with monthly and annual cumulations.
 14 362 0      1960-1967.
 15 650  0     Securities z United States x Periodicals.

Screen 2 of 2
 16 785 00     t F & S index of corporations and industries x 0014-567X
```

FIGURE 4.


should return to paper files and unshared cataloguing. On the contrary, we should push ahead and find ways to improve OCLC's developing data base of serials records. Though we have come a long way, we have much further to go.

## REFERENCES

1. Roughton, Michael. "OCLC Serial Records: Errors, Omissions & Dependability." *Journal of Academic Librarianship* 5 (January 1980):316–21. I will refer to this article, based on a sample of 612 records drawn from the OCLC data base in 1978, in order to draw comparisons between it and the present study.

2. Correspondence between the author and Mr. Gary Ink, Manager, Data Bases, R. R. Bowker Company. At the author's request, Mr. Ink checked Bowker's records for twenty-one cessations listed in *Ulrich's Quarterly*, v.4, n.1. In each of the twenty-one cases, the source for the cessation report was the publisher.

3. Kilton, Tom D. "OCLC and the Pre-Order Verification of New Serials." *Serials Librarian* 4 (Fall 1979):61–64.

# ISSN AND NSDP:
# A GUIDE FOR THE INITIATED*

Linda K. Bartley

ABSTRACT. This article has been prepared to help librarians and other information community members who are now using or plan to use ISSN registered by the National Serials Data Program (NSDP). This brief excursion into the policy and processing background of NSDP covers matters which may be of interest to users of the work performed by NSDP. An indication of NSDP's sources for and scope of assignments prefaces comments on interpreting MARC records containing ISSN, looking up ISSN in bibliographic sources, finding the ISSN on publications, and assisting NSDP in the administration of the ISSN for U.S. serials.

Since they have been elaborated extensively elsewhere, this discussion does not describe the International Serials Data System (ISDS), NSDP's functions and responsibilities within the ISDS and the U.S. bibliographic community, or the attributes and advantages of using the ISSN.[1]

## Requesting Sources and Scope of ISSN Assignments

NSDP currently receives documentation used in the assignment of the ISSN from the following sources: publishers, U.S. Postal Service (USPS), Library of Congress (LC) serials cataloguing sections, other ISDS centers, abstracting and indexing services, and CONSER institutions. The entire range of serial types is found among the titles for which these groups request ISSN. ISSN requests from publishers (including the USPS, which is an indirect publisher source) receive first priority for processing.

NSDP will generally register any serial for which the ISSN is requested by the publisher. If the publisher requests the ISSN directly from NSDP, upon notification of the number the publisher is asked to print the ISSN. ISSN assignments made through NSDP's cooperative work with the USPS are reported, along with instructions for their printing, to the publisher by the post office at which the serial is registered for mailing.[2] NSDP has begun to notify publishers systematically each time an assignment is made from documentation supplied by sources other than publishers or the USPS. There remain, however,

---

*This is a revised version of a piece entitled "ISSN Consumer Information" (July 1979) which was sent to all NST subscribers and is used by NSDP in response to certain kinds of requests for information.

instances where ISSN assignments have been made but publishers are unaware of them.

As already indicated, NSDP's assignments are wide-ranging: from major medical journals to hometown weeklies, from scholarly newsletters to supermarket newsstand magazines. As a result of use of the ISSN by the USPS, numerous assignments have been made to serials of a popular or commercial nature. Although priority is given to currently published serials, assignments may be made to serials which have ceased publication, particularly if they are related to active titles.

Because of file size considerations, the International Center for ISDS has requested that titles judged to be primarily of national rather than of international interest be so designated in reports sent for inclusion in the international register. Such titles are coded with "1" in the first indicator of MARC field 022 (ISSN). An abbreviated form of these records is maintained in the ISDS machine-readable international register, but the records are not included in ISDS published products. Nonetheless, NSDP processes and maintains records for these titles in the same way it does for all others.

## CONSER

A machine-readable record is entered in the CONSER data base for all current ISSN registrations made by NSDP for serials published in the United States. These records, the most comprehensive and reliable source for ISSN assigned by NSDP, are input to OCLC, Inc.'s on-line bibliographic data base. For the purpose of this discussion, CONSER records are a subset of the serials records in OCLC's data base. These records include all records either created or updated by designated CONSER institutions.

NSDP also functions as a clearinghouse for obtaining ISSN for foreign publications needed by institutions in this country. Since ISSN assignments made by ISDS/Canada are in the CONSER data base, "foreign" titles in this context refers to serials with neither a U.S. nor a Canadian place of publication. ISSNs are requested by NSDP from other ISDS centers if (1) the ISSN is not available in either the *ISDS Register* or *ISDS Bulletin* or (2) the ISSN is not printed on the serial. Bibliographic information obtained directly from an ISDS center or an ISDS publication is included in the CONSER record authenticated by NSDP. NSDP authentication of these records, then, means at least that the ISSN and key title have been confirmed by the responsible ISDS center.

The serial records examined and verified by NSDP can be identified by the presence of "nsdp" in field 042 of the machine-readable record, the field used to indicate CONSER authentication status. On the simplest level, "authentication" means that NSDP has confirmed the ISSN and key title in the record.

Such confirmation requires the examination or addition of other ISDS data elements, such as ISDS center code, alphabet of title, and key title abbreviation.

In the absence of an LC card number (LCCN) in a record already in the data base, NSDP will supply an LCCN with a "sn" prefix. Encoding level "blank" is used for all full level records authenticated by NSDP which are input to the CONSER data base by other institutions. All originally created NSDP records for ongoing and prepublication titles will have encoding level "7." Records authenticated before the above-stated conventions took effect may either be missing LCCNs or have encoding level "I"; the corrections will be made when the records are reaccessed by NSDP.

## *NSDP Records*

Only those AACR fields common to AACR *and* ISDS are checked by NSDP. However, NSDP supplies an issuing body main entry as necessary in accordance with AACR-based CONSER requirements. NSDP also supplies a cataloguing title (field 245) in all records because of the CONSER input requirement. NSDP has no responsibility for other fields, in particular for subject heading fields.

The overlay of AACR and ISDS interpretations in the same data base produces legitimate instances for "agreeing to disagree," as represented by the creation of multiple records which contain the same ISSN, for both U.S. and foreign titles. A lack of a one-to-one correspondence between ISSN and on-line records can occur for several reasons. The following examples presume entry of the same ISSN and key title in the multiple records which are created based on AACR criteria: (1) the entry is under an issuing body which has changed, even though the title has remained the same, (2) the title is issued in various formats (e.g., regular print and microfiche), (3) an AACR-based title change is judged to be minor according to the ISDS guidelines.

An ISSN in a record without NSDP authentication has generally been input by a contributing library which found the ISSN in a printed source or on the piece. If upon examination by NSDP the number is determined to be an ISSN which will be cancelled (usually a duplicate assignment), it will be placed in subfield z of field 022. Such a record will remain fully accessible by the cancelled ISSN under the conventional ISSN search. Subfield y of field 022 will generally be used for incorrect ISSNs which are associated with a particular record (e.g., the publisher has misprinted the ISSN). As part of the authentication procedure, NSDP removes the ISSN from duplicate records for the same title so that records which have been marked for deletion from the data base will not be accessible by ISSN.

Prepublication records are created on the basis of information supplied by publishers. The records are clearly designated by the presence of the expected date of publication in field 263 and the legend "PREPUB" in field 936. The records are updated as soon as an issue of photocopy confirming publication of the title is received. At that time, the key title (considered provisional until compared with the actual publication), cataloguing title, and variant titles are adjusted if necessary. Starting volume and date information, if available, is entered in field 362. The 936 field also is revised to reflect the issue received.

Several subfields in field 012, Terminal Display (LC and NSDP local use), have been defined exclusively for NSDP purposes. A full description of their application is in the *MARC Serials Editing Guide*, Second CONSER Edition (see especially the January 1979 update).[3] Of particular interest are subfields k—presence of ISSN on piece; and l (ell)—NSDP contact with the publisher. The subfields k and l of the 012 field in previously authenticated records are updated on the basis of examination of actual publications and NSDP's correspondence with publishers, initiated either by the publishers or by NSDP.

If the ISSN for a foreign serial is printed on the publication, NSDP enters the number in the CONSER record but does not authenticate the record. Field 012, subfield k will be annotated with 1 (one), however, to indicate that the ISSN is being printed on the serial. Corroboration by the ISDS center responsible for the assignment will be requested only if there is reason to suspect that the ISSN is erroneous or if there is a need for an authenticated key title.

## Bibliographic Sources for ISSNs Assigned by NSDP

All currently processed NSDP records will be included on the MARC Distribution Service-Serials tapes by the end of 1981. The NSDP records will be distributed on tape with the records authenticated by LC (many of which are also authenticated by NSDP) and the National Library of Canada. The "NSDP only" records can be distinguished by the sole presence of "nsdp" in field 042. The NSDP records are also included on the CONSER Snapshots.

All NSDP records created or updated in a given monthly cycle will appear in the editions of *New Serial Titles* prepared by automated means. As for all other entries, the full cataloguing data will be included. Earlier editions of *NST* carried only NSDP-authenticated ISSNs for titles with U.S. imprints currently catalogued by the Library of Congress.

The *CONSER Microfiche* announced in the January 19, 1979, *Library of Congress Information Bulletin* contains about 75,000 CONSER records, of which a subset have been authenticated by NSDP. This is a good printed source for earlier assigned ISSN. In addition to a title/author/series index, the publication also has an index arranged by ISSN.

Orders and inquiries for the above-mentioned tapes and publications can be sent to the Cataloging Distribution Service, Library of Congress, Building 159, Navy Yard Annex, Washington, D.C. 20541.

Most current ISSN assignments made by NSDP and the other ISDS centers are contained in the *ISDS Register on Microfiche* or *ISDS Bulletin on Microfiche*. The latter is a bimonthly publication listing approximately 4,000 new and amended records per issue and is both a tool for dissemination of current information and an updating device for the ISDS Register. It is the most authoritative and comprehensive source of ISSN for foreign titles. Orders and inquiries should be sent to CIEPS, 20, rue Bachaumont, 75002 Paris, France. Several ISDS centers have prepared catalogs of ISSN they have registered; inquiries about these should be sent to the same address.

Under an agreement between R. R. Bowker Company and ISDS to perform the early numbering of a large quantity of the world's serial publications, Bowker was authorized to assign ISSN to titles listed in the publications listed below.

— *Ulrich's International Periodicals Directory*, 14th edition
— *Irregular Serials and Annuals*, 2nd edition
— *Bowker Serials Bibliographic Supplement*, 1972
— *New Serials Titles 1950–1970 Cumulation*

NSDP routinely checks these sources when authenticating titles that began publication before 1973. Any erroneous ISSN are placed in subfield z of the 022 field. The majority of the U.S. imprints in these publications are entered as NSDP-authenticated records in the CONSER data base. Bowker obtains new ISSNs for its files from the MARC-S tapes and ISDS publications.

## Location of ISSN on the Publications

One of NSDP's goals is to have the ISSN printed on each U.S. publication to which an ISSN is assigned. The recommended position for printing the ISSN as described in the *Guidelines for ISDS* is "in a prominent position on or in each serial issue (front cover, back cover, title-leaf or imprint). On a periodical the ISSN should, whenever possible, appear in the top right hand corner of the front cover."[1] It is nonetheless acceptable for publishers to print the ISSN in other than the recommended position.

Those attempting to find ISSN already know that the location of the number on the publication is not fully predictable. The willingness of publishers to print the ISSN in the position prescribed for periodicals is strongly related to their aesthetic perception of the cover. Many publishers are understandably reluctant to print the number on the cover but are amenable to putting it in the masthead or elsewhere on the publication.

There are certain applications of the ISSN which require particular ISSN printing configurations. The U.S. Postal Service requires that the ISSNs reported to publishers from USPS files be printed immediately following or below the name of the publication in the masthead or otherwise within the first five pages of the publication. Such an ISSN printing can be omitted if the number appears on the front/cover page. Publishers complying with the USPS regulations generally print the ISSN in parentheses immediately after the title in the masthead. Those publishers participating in the services of the Copyright Clearance Center, Inc., are required to print a standardized string of information to identify each item for which special reproduction conditions apply. The first element in the code is the serial title standard number, which is generally the ISSN: for example, *0036-634X*/78/0100-0143$01.00/0.

### User-Assisted Administration of the ISSN

Users of the ISSN can help in the administration of the number. For example, when corresponding with the publisher of a U.S. serial not carrying the ISSN, the user might suggest that the publisher contact NSDP for an assignment. NSDP will make arrangements to work with groups wishing to assist in this kind of ISSN promotion.

NSDP would like to know which U.S. serials are printing the ISSN. As noted earlier, NSDP is annotating its records by use of the 012 field when the ISSN appears on the piece. For users able to do so, the OCLC data base should be checked to be certain that the record has not already been marked with this information. User reports to NSDP should be a surrogate (copy of the cover, title page, masthead) with the ISSN circled.

Also, it is appropriate to notify NSDP about the incorrect printing of an ISSN on a serial with a U.S. imprint—for example, an ISSN which applies to an earlier title; the prefix "ISBN" instead of "ISSN"; too few or many digits. The notification need consist of no more than a surrogate of the most recent issue with a brief annotation next to the incorrect number. If the surrogate does not carry the editorial address, it should be transcribed near the ISSN. NSDP will send a letter to the publisher requesting that a correction be made.

Since publishers are not always prompt in supplying NSDP with the first issue of a newly published serial, those who find a record which still reads "PREPUB" after publication has occurred should send NSDP a surrogate so that the record can be updated.

Finally, users can greatly assist in the administration of the ISSN by simply letting NSDP know: How is the ISSN being used in their institution? What must take place before the number will be used? What problems have been experienced in using the ISSN? What benefits? Written and spoken criticism and kudos are very welcome. Please direct your comments to: National Serials Data Program, Library of Congress, Washington, D.C. 20540; (202) 287-6452.

# REFERENCES

1. See for example: (a) Unesco. *Guidelines for ISDS* (Paris: Unesco, 1973). The preparation of a revised edition is in progress. (b) Mary E. Sauer. "National Serials Data Program," *The Bowker Annual of Library and Book Trade Information*, 24th ed. (New York: Bowker, 1979). (c) An "ISSN Is for Serials" brochure describing how publishers can obtain and use the ISSN is available free upon request to NSDP.

2. An article describing use of the ISSN by the USPS was published in the fourth 1980 issue of the *Unesco Journal of Information Science, Librarianship and Archives Administration.*

3. *MARC Serials Editing Guide*, 2nd CONSER Edition (Washington, D.C.: Library of Congress, 1978).

# THE ISSN AS RETRIEVER OF OCLC RECORDS

Patricia Ohl Rice
Laurance R. Mitlin

ABSTRACT. Using a random sample of periodicals checked in on the OCLC serials subsystem at Winthrop College's Dacus Library, the author studied the utility of ISSN printed on periodical issues as a retriever of local data records. While the ISSN retrieved a unique record for less than half of the titles, it was successful in retrieving almost eighty percent of the local data records when a multi-step search was used. The authors conclude that the ISSN would be an even more useful tool for serials check-in if OCLC would take certain actions including implementing additional search enhancements.

## Background of Study

The Ida Jane Dacus Library of Winthrop College (Rock Hill, South Carolina) has a small collection of approximately 2,000 current serial subscriptions. Most of these are English language titles published in the United States. The serials collection is tailored to meet the needs of a curriculum which emphasizes undergraduate and master's level professional education rather than a traditional liberal arts program. The library buys almost nothing that could be considered specialized research material.

Since 1977, the library, a SOLINET member, has been using the OCLC, Inc. serials control subsystem for check-in of all but a dozen of its currently received serials.[1] Like most users of the subsystem, Dacus Library maintains a "cheat" list, a rotary file placed next to the CRT which alphabetically lists serial titles and their corresponding OCLC numbers. It is the experience of serials checkers and reference librarians that the file is necessary to avoid dead ends or lengthy title searches through the On-line Union Catalog for serial records.[2]

During the 1979/80 academic year, the Dacus Library Acquisitions department head noticed that her periodicals checker was relying less and less on the rotary file. The checker would first examine each issue for the presence of an ISSN and, if one was found, would use it to search the On-line Union Catalog. Only if there was no ISSN on the piece in hand or if the ISSN failed to retrieve the desired record would the checker use the rotary file. The checker's subjective impression was that retrieval by ISSN was successful "at least half of the time."

The present study was designed to test that subjective opinion—to discover more precisely to what extent a periodical checker can expect to retrieve a local data record[3] as the immediate, unique response to an ISSN search, given a serials collection as described above. The investigators assume that there is a higher incidence of ISSN-carrying periodical issues in such a collection than would be the case in a larger research collection with a substantial population of obscure and foreign titles.[4]

## Methodology

The investigators identified a population of 1,707 periodicals for which a serials local data record had been created. They defined "success" as being able to retrieve a unique record from an ISSN found on the periodical issue in hand at the time of check-in.

Rather than examine all 1,707 periodicals, they selected a sample of 602, chosen randomly. This sample size was determined because it would result in an accuracy of ±4 percent at a 95 percent confidence level. To have improved the confidence level to 99 percent would have required a sample size of 1,067.[5] This procedure allowed the investigators to calculate confidence intervals for the results—that is, to indicate the ranges in which the true values for the entire collection are likely to fall.

The standard error of each of the proportions occurring in the sample was calculated using the formula

$$S_{P_s} = \sqrt{\frac{pq}{n}} \sqrt{1 - \frac{n}{N}}$$

where

$p$ = proportion of the sample meeting the desired criterion,
$q = 1 - p$,
$n$ = sample size,
$N$ = population size.

A 95 percent confidence interval was calculated by

$$p \pm 1.96 S_{P_s}$$

For example, while 20.8 percent of the sample had no ISSN, the statistical techniques described above indicate that the corresponding value for the entire collection is between 18.29 and 23.51 percent.

A current issue of each of the 602 randomly selected periodicals was examined for the presence of an ISSN. If an ISSN was found, the page carrying it was photocopied. An operator logged onto the system with a cataloguing authorization number[6] and searched each photocopied ISSN in the On-line Union Catalog, recording the results of the search on the back of the photocopy. After all 602 items had been dealt with, the results were tallied.

## Results

The investigators determined that of the 602 periodicals examined, 476 carried the ISSN and 126 did not. Two hundred fifty-one of the 476 ISSNs retrieved a unique record from the data base. The complete results are given in Tables 1 and 2.

It is apparent from these results that the Dacus Library periodicals checker can expect to find an ISSN on a majority—79.1 percent—of the periodical issues that he or she carries to the terminal. Presumably, libraries with similar serials collections would experience similar findings. But the overall success

TABLE 1

PRESENCE OF ISSN ON PERIODICAL

| ISSN on Piece | Number | Percent of 602 | Confidence Interval |
|---|---|---|---|
| No | 126 | 20.9% | ±2.61% |
| Yes | 476 | 79.1% | ±2.61% |
| | 602 | 100.0% | |

TABLE 2

RESULTS OF ISSN SEARCHES

| ISSN on Piece Retrieves | Number | Percent of 602 | Confidence Interval |
|---|---|---|---|
| No or Wrong Record | 9 | 1.5% | ±0.78% |
| 1 Record | 251 | 41.7% | ±3.17% |
| 2 Records | 169 | 28.1% | ±2.89% |
| 3 Records | 38 | 6.3% | ±1.56% |
| 4 Records | 7 | 1.2% | ±0.70% |
| 5 Records | 2 | 0.3% | ±0.35% |
| Total | 476 | 79.1% | ±2.61% |

rate as defined earlier (being able to retrieve a unique record from piece in hand *via* the ISSN) is only 41.7 percent. Thus, even for a primarily American, English language periodical collection, the ISSN is not a particularly powerful retriever of unique records from the OCLC On-line Union Catalog.

## Miscellaneous Observations

The relatively low success rate encountered during this study is a function of two factors: the failure of some U.S. publishers to print the ISSN on periodical issues, as required,[7] and the number of duplicate serial records in the OCLC data base. It is clear from Table 2 that if one were to define success simply as retrieving a desired record from ISSN found on the periodical issues in hand, with no stipulation as to how many steps retrieval should involve, the number of successful items in the population increases from 251 (41.7 percent with ± 3.17 percent confidence interval) to 467 (77.6 percent with ± 2.68 percent confidence interval).[8] Thus, an ISSN on the piece in hand almost always leads (eventually) to a desirable serial record. The question is, what accounts for the rather numerous instances of multiple response?

The investigators identified 253 instances of duplication among the 216 ISSN searches[9] that retrieved multiple responses. One hundred thirty-two instances of duplication, or 52.2 percent of the total, were caused by the presence in the On-line Union Catalog of records describing microform reproductions of serials originally published in hard copy. Since most of the hard copy records are CONSER records authenticated by the Library of Congress and most of the microform records have been input by OCLC members, a checker can often guess which record is which when an ISSN search retrieves the following sort of truncated record display:

1 Academe. ₁Washington₁ 1979 s

2 Academe. ₁Washington₁ 1979 s DLC

But a guess is not a particularly reliable form of search strategy, especially since the truncated record display may be reflecting some other type of duplication altogether.

The investigators identified fifty-two instances (20.6 percent) of successive entry-latest title duplication. Thus OCLC users continue to suffer the consequences of the initial CONSER compromise decision to permit pre-AACR1 cataloguing into the serials data base. The fact that the successive–latest problem accounted for over one-fifth of the duplications indicates the significance of that problem.

Thirty-four, or 13.4 percent of the instances of duplication involved records which CONSER has labeled "DO NOT USE" but which remain in the data base because of OCLC's failure to delete them. Users of the system have long been aware of OCLC's inability to maintain data base quality control.

Twenty (7.9%) of the duplications were the result of a title ceasing and being replaced by a new title. In these cases, an ISSN for one title can retrieve the record for the other title *via* various linking mechanisms built into the OCLC system and MARC-S format.

The remaining fifteen (5.9%) instances of duplication fell into the category "other." Most involved differences in cataloguing interpretation.

## Conclusions

James F. Corey posed the question in a recent article, "What is the contribution of CONSER to a library...building its bibliographic file for serials check-in?"[10] Since fully 88.8 percent of the records retrieved during the course of this study were found to be authenticated by the Library of Congress, the National Serials Data Program, or both (or their Canadian counterparts), the investigators conclude that CONSER's contribution to Winthrop's on-line check-in file is considerable. If Winthrop had had to create its own bibliographic file as a base for building on-line check-in records, the conversion from a manual to an automated serials control system would have been impossibly laborious. And, on a daily basis, the ability to retrieve even a portion of the on-line local data records *via* an ISSN taken from the piece in hand facilitates processing and maintenance of the check-in file.

Until OCLC, Inc. makes greater efforts in the direction of quality control, however, the ISSN cannot function in the On-line Union Catalog as the powerful retriever it was meant to be. Records that CONSER has rejected should be deleted quickly from the data base, even if the task of transferring holdings to more desirable records involves an extra effort on everyone's part. Removal of latest title records from the On-line Union Catalog (now that CONSER has repented of its initial decision) would also significantly reduce the number of duplicate records encountered.

The microform duplicate of CONSER hard copy records pose a bit more of a dilemma. It is presumably desirable that the bibliographic records for serial microform reproductions carry the ISSN, just as do the original hard copy records. If that is the case, however, a substantial number of ISSN searches will always pull up a multiple response and consequently never meet the investigator's criteria of success.

One possible remedy would be if the truncated record display were to include the value present in the fixed field Repr: area of each bibiographic record listed. The checker could then know (instead of guess) which record was the hard copy and which the microform. Retrieving the local data record would still involve two steps, but the possibility of an erroneous third step (a wrong guess) would be eliminated.

The search/retrieval enhancements installed by OCLC in September 1980 suggest another possible solution to this dilemma. A person searching the On-line Union Catalog now has the ability to modify derived search keys with certain factors taken from the fixed field area of the bibliographic record, such as "ser" (from Bib Lvl:) and date information from Date 1.[11] If OCLC were to further expand this capacity by allowing a searcher to modify *all* search keys with his or her institution symbol, the ISSN would pull up only those records, whether hard copy or microform, which had been used by the institution. Thus the checker's chances of immediate retrieval of a local data record from an ISSN on the piece in hand would be virtually guaranteed.

The authors have heard that OCLC is investigating the possibility of some such system modifications.[12] It is to be hoped that the investigations prove fruitful. Serials control subsystem users should encourage OCLC to give these enhancements a high priority.

## REFERENCES

1. At the time of writing, there are over seventy-five users of the serials control subsystem.

2. Even with the highly beneficial search/retrieval enhancements which OCLC introduced in September 1980, many serial title searches continue to pull up extensive lists of records from which the operator has to locate the desired record. The number of dead-end searches has, however, been greatly reduced.

3. In the OCLC system, serial bibliographic records are carried in the On-line Union Catalog. Local data records are the dependent check-in records created by each library that uses the serials control subsystem. When an operator who is logged on with a cataloguing authorization number uses the ISSN search, the system interrogates the On-line Union Catalog and displays the bibliographic record. When an operator who is logged on in a serials control mode uses the ISSN search, the system interrogates the On-line Union Catalog but displays the dependent local data record.

4. Within the last two years, cooperation between the United States Postal Service and the National Serials Data Program has provided a regulatory basis for the printing of ISSN on U.S. periodicals. See the United States Postal Service, *Domestic Mail Manual (DMM)*, section 461.

5. Spurr, William A., and Bonini, Charles P. *Statistical Analysis for Business Decisions* (Homewood, Ill.: Richard D. Irwin, Inc., 1967), pp. 268–70.

6. The cataloguing authorization number was used because the investigators wished to determine the reason for duplication in instances where the ISSN search retrieved more than one record. Since response to a search is based on records carried in the On-line Union Catalog, direct examination of the serial bibliographic records, rather than of the local data records, was deemed desirable.

7. Of the 126 no-ISSN periodicals in the sample, eighty-seven were U.S. titles, ten were British, two were Canadian, and twenty-seven were other.

8. The figure of 467 is obtained by adding all of the ISSN searches that retrieved one or more correct records, i.e., $251 + 169 + 38 + 7 + 2 = 467$, which is 77.6 percent of the total sample population of 602, or 98.1 percent of the 476 titles containing ISSN.

9. The figure of 216 is obtained by adding the ISSN searches that retrieved two to five records, i.e., $169 + 38 + 7 + 2 = 216$.

10. Corey, James F. "OCLC and Serials Processing: A State of Transition at the University of Illinois." *The Serials Librarian* 3 (1) (Fall 1978):65.

11. "Search/Retrieval Enhancements," *OCLC Technical Bulletin* 95 (August 29, 1980):6ff.

12. Based on a conversation with Ronald Gardner of OCLC, Inc., User Services Division, October 1, 1980.

# A REVIEW OF DEVELOPMENTS LEADING TO ON-LINE UNION LISTING OF SERIALS

Debora Shaw

ABSTRACT This paper reviews the development of the capability for on-line union lists of serials. The importance of standards, including the MARC-S format, the Conversion of Serials (CONSER) Project for serials bibliographic description, and the *ANSI Standard for Serial Holdings Statements* at the Summary Level, is stressed. The OCLC, Inc. on-line union listing capability and some of its implications are discussed.

## Introduction

The purpose of this paper is to describe current developments in the union listing of serials and to place these developments in an appropriate historical perspective. The importance of standard bibliographic description and of standard methods for recording holdings will be noted, present activities using the OCLC, Inc. system will be summarized, and predictions for the near future of union lists of serials will be proposed.

## Brief History

The compilation of union lists of serials began in earnest in the nineteenth century. The first list in the United States reported the holdings of selected libraries in Baltimore in 1876. Lists covering various other regions or particular subjects soon were created, all designed to increase access to information regarding serials holdings in various collections. By 1916 work was underway on a list of serials in major libraries of the "North-Central region" of the United States, and the defined boundaries of this region gradually expanded. The work was taken up again following World War I, with the hope of producing a single national union list.

In December 1921, H. W. Wilson approached the American Library Association with plans for a national union list of serials. Compiled under the guidance of the ALA Advisory Committee on the Union List of Serials, the resulting *Union List of Serials in Libraries of the United States and Canada* was published in 1927. Two supplements were later published to update the list, and in 1938 work began on a second edition. The list was expanded in terms of both serials included and number of reporting libraries, and the second edition was published in 1943. Again two supplements were compiled to up-date information in the union list, but by 1957 the need for a third edition was apparent. The ALA Joint Committee on the Union List of Serials appointed Edna Titus Brown as editor, and work began in 1959. With the third edition coverage was again expanded, and in 1965 a five-volume set was produced, reporting holdings of 156,499 serial titles held in 956 libraries in the United States and Canada.[1]

Meanwhile local, regional, and subject-oriented union lists were being created with increasing frequency. Huff termed this development a trend of the 1960s encouraged by increased emphasis on science and technology.[2] Other factors, such as the increasing number of serials being published, improved access to journal literature through the growing abstracting and indexing services, and the development of library networks, no doubt also played parts in this interest in union lists.

Continuing development in this area, however—namely the on-line listing of holdings from many libraries—had to await not only technical advances but also two important professional developments: (1) standards for the bibliographic description of serials and (2) standards for the reporting of library holdings.

## Bibliographic Description

The bibliographic description is the unifying part of any union list, in that a common identifier for each serial is sought, regardless of how the several agencies contributing to the union list identify the serial. In some cases the title alone might be used, though common and generic titles quickly contribute to rampant confusion, if not chaos. In this setting a "union list of uniquely titled serials" would seem an appropriate goal. The responsibility for selecting a common, unique identifier for each serial may be reserved for a union list editor or a central union list agency which collects reports of serials and their associated holdings from contributors to the list.

The development and application of common cataloguing rules have eased difficulties inherent in unifying bibliographic descriptions from several libraries. The publication of *Serials: A MARC Format* in 1969 and subsequent use of machine-readable records to create and share serials bibliographic information have also increased the possibilities for such cooperative activities as the development of union lists.[3] The intricate nature of the task, however, can be deduced from the size and detail of works written to guide serials cataloguers. The 463-page *MARC Serials Editing Guide: Second CONSER Edition*, with its eighteen appendices and bimonthly updates, is but one example.[4]

In 1975 work began on the development of a data base of serials bibliographic information through the Conversion of Serials (CONSER) Project. In this cooperative effort, initially coordinated through the Council on Library Resources, several libraries enter serials cataloguing information into the OCLC,

Inc. system, and the catalog records are later reviewed and authenticated by the Library of Congress or the National Library of Canada. (Moreover, the National Serials Data Program or ISDS/Canada reviews and authenticate elements required for the International Serials Data System.)[5] By 1980 over 200,000 serials records had been handled by CONSER participants, and more than 93,000 had been authenticated.[6] Copies of the CONSER file have been made available to the library community, and work continues toward the inclusion and authentication of still more serials cataloguing records.

Many problems of bibliographic description of serials remain, however. One essential aspect of serials is their continuance. Unlike a monograph, a serial publication can change in many subtle ways during its existence; dealing with such changes with equanimity is a challenge. Moreover, the fact that bibliographic description must not only be applied to a changing serial publication but also be handled in a changing environment creates further problems. Cataloguing rules change, and a serial needed today may have been catalogued under one of a number of cataloguing codes, requiring some historical perspective in the interpretation of the bibliographic description. The amalgamation of bibliographic information from various agencies that have applied various sets of rules to describe chronically changeable serial publications can be taxing.

The problems of different and changing cataloguing codes become even more entangling as work progresses on the conversion to machine-readable form of records of serial backfiles. Bibliographic descriptions prepared prior to the development of commonly accepted standards can require extensive and expensive review or even recataloguing. Clearly, some measure of the cost of such an undertaking and its anticipated benefits is advisable before a library commits itself to retrospective conversion of bibliographic information to machine-readable form. Nevertheless, recent work—especially in the past five years—has resulted in remarkable improvement in access to bibliographic descriptions of serials, and the resulting data provide a valuable resource on which to base a union list of serials.

## Serials Holdings

Individual libraries have traditionally kept records on serials holdings at various levels of detail and for several purposes. Most keep track of which current issues are received and which need to be claimed from publishers because of nonreceipt, and most develop a statement of the retrospective holdings for each title. Many also record volumes (or parts of volumes) missing, sent for binding, in circulation, or otherwise not immediately available to library users. On a more general level, however, union lists have traditionally recorded only a summarized statement of each library's holdings of a particular serial. Creating complete records for all holdings of all serials is probably still too expensive to be worth noting in union lists.

In 1975 a subcommittee of the American National Standards Institute Committee Z-39 was established to develop a standard for summary serial holdings statements. The subcommittee, chaired by Glyn T. Evans, reviewed serial holdings statements used around the nation and produced eight drafts of a standard. The last draft was approved in November 1979. With this agreed-upon format for reporting holdings information, the second function of the union list of serials became more manageable.[7]

*The American National Standard for Serial Holdings Statements at the Summary Level* provides for three levels of specificity in reports. The first is a hold/no hold report, simply an indication of libraries which hold any part of the given serial. The second level includes a completeness code, which allows the indication of the range of the published run the library holds (0–49%, 50–94%, or 95–100%). At the third level the standard allows report of the acquisition status, retention, policy, enumeration of volumes, and chronology of coverage.

The holdings statements are intended to be linked to appropriate bibliographic descriptions, and it is at this point that the synergistic relationship between work on bibliographic and holdings information becomes clear. With the development of a large, high-quality data base of bibliographic records and the adoption of a national standard for summary holdings information, the creation of a union list of serials could move forward more easily.

## On-line Union List of Serials

Computer-produced union lists of serials became feasible as computer speed and capacity increased. Examples of such exploitation of technology in the 1970s include the *Minnesota Union List of Serials*, the *Pennsylvania Union List of Serials*, and the serials work at Stanford University, the University of California at Berkeley, and the University of California at Los Angeles. However, a need remained for a central agency to assemble, merge, and maintain the bibliographic and holdings information from the participating institutions.

The development of telecommunications networks, allowing remote access to and modification of information, has now made on-line union lists possible. The existence of serials bibliographic information in machine-readable form and the standard for summary holdings statements which are machine-manipulable have encouraged recent interest in on-line union lists of serials. In 1979 OCLC, Inc. began work on an on-line union list of serials capability. This development, partially supported by the Indiana University Libraries under a Higher Education Act Title II-C grant, is expected to be available to the public in January 1981.

The union listing capability is part of the serials control subsystem. It will use summary holdings information in the ANSI standard format linked to bibliographic records in the MARC-S format. Libraries on-line to OCLC, Inc.

will be able to enter and modify their own holdings information, which will be retained on-line. Other libraries will be able to contract with union list centers to enter and maintain their holdings information.[8,9]

OCLC, Inc. is also evaluating support for off-line products. Machine-readable tapes of bibliographic and holdings information for various groups of libraries could be provided. Such tapes, which would reflect information as of a specific date as a "snapshot" of the files at a given time, could be used for printed or microformat union lists of serials.

## *Implications*

The days when, as Huff remarked, librarians needed "to begin shuffling 3 × 5 slips each time the phrase 'union list' is mentioned," have obviously passed.[10] The cooperative development of the CONSER data base has spread the effort needed to create more complete bibliographic descriptions of serials among several libraries.[11] Decentralized entry of holdings data eliminates the need for repeated transcription, thus reducing the chance for error. On-line access means also that changes can be recorded more rapidly. For example, a title change need be noted only once to be reflected immediately in the bibliographic record used by all participants in a union list. On-line access also makes possible the concurrent provision of union list information at several locations without the purchase of additional copies of a printed list. At the Indiana University Libraries, subject specialists and branch librarians have been quick to appreciate this prospect. Another advantage of the on-line union list is the facility with which a subset of a library's serial holdings can be reported to subject-oriented or geographically defined union lists of serials. For example, special collections, the holdings of selected branch libraries, or titles in certain classifications can be more easily reported to a subject-based union list since machine sorting of the file is possible.

The functions of union list centers are only now beginning to be explored, but they can be expected to evolve to meet the demands of the on-line environment. The union list center's role may include: resolving differences in cataloguing; entering and maintaining information for libraries not on-line; educating new participants regarding established rules and informing all participants of changes and developments; arranging for production of off-line materials; and providing the sense of cooperation necessary to make a union list work. Some union list agencies have also worked to secure funding for the conversion of bibliographic and holdings information to machine-readable form.

## *Conclusion*

The development of union lists of serials in the United States since the nineteenth century reflects the growth in interlibrary cooperation, advances in computer technology, and increased needs for access to information. The recently adopted standards for machine-readable bibliographic and holdings information and the CONSER data base have made an on-line union list of serials feasible. Continuing changes can be expected in interlibrary activity, union list agency functions, and serials work in general as libraries adapt to the on-line environment.

## REFERENCES

1. Rovelstad, Howard. Preface to the *Union List of Serials in Libraries of the United States and Canada, Third Edition* (New York: H.W. Wilson, 1965).

2. Huff, William H. "Summary of Some Serial Activities, 1942–1966." *Library Resources and Technical Services* 11(1967):301–21.

3. *Serials: A MARC Format* (Washington, D.C.: Library of Congress, 1969).

4. *MARC Serials Editing Guide, Second CONSER Edition* (Washington, D.C.: Library of Congress, 1978).

5. Ellsworth, Dianne J. "Serials Union Lists." *Serials Review* 5(1979):99–101.

6. *CONSER, Conversion of Serials* (Columbus, Ohio: OCLC, Inc., 1980).

7. American National Standards Institute. *American National Standard for Serial Holdings Statements at the Summary Level.* (New York: ANSI, 1980).

8. *Serials Control Union Listing Capability* (Columbus, Ohio: OCLC, Inc., 1980).

9. Wittorf, Robert. "ANSI Z39.42 and OCLC: OCLC's Implementation of the American National Standards Institute's Serial Holdings Statements at the Summary Level." *Serials Review* 4(1980):87–94.

10. Huff, William H. "Some Aspects of Serials Work in 1965." *Library Resources and Technical Services* 10(1966):176–98.

11. Anderson, Sandy E., and Melby, Carol A. "Comparative Analysis of the Quality of OCLC Serials Cataloguing Records, as a Function of Contributing CONSER Participant and Field as Utilized by Serials Catalogers at the University of Illinois." *Serials Librarian* 3(1979):363–71.

# IN ORDER TO FORM A MORE
# PERFECT UNION . . . LIST OF SERIALS

Marjorie E. Bloss

ABSTRACT. The Ad Hoc Committee on Union Lists of Serials is an American Library Association (ALA) Committee that was created in January 1980 at ALA's Mid-Winter Conference. The charge of the Committee will result in a publication dealing with the procedures and methods used in creating and producing a union list of serials. The publication will appear in the ALA *Guidelines* series. This paper describes the history of the Committee, the work that has been accomplished thus far on its upcoming publication, including some of the major points of discussion pertaining to union lists of serials, and some possibilities that are seen for future action by the Committee.

## Conception

Frequently, history points to almost spontaneous occurrences of ideas and inventions at the most appropriate times. To rank the creation of the American Library Association's Ad Hoc Committee on Union Lists of Serials on the same elevated plane, as, say, Darwin and Wallace is rather pompous, yet the success of seeing this Committee born after a year of discussion, coordination, and letter-writing was a heady experience.

My desire to see the existence of an ALA Committee dealing with union lists of serials came shortly after I was hired in January 1979 to create and produce a union list of serials by the Rochester Regional Research Library Council (one of nine such multitype cooperative Councils in New York State). When completed, this particular list will include the holdings of fifty-seven libraries and will contain more than 40,000 entries. I had many questions about my new position and had hoped to find all of the answers neatly packaged at the ALA Mid-Winter Conference by a committee on union lists of serials. There was one problem: there was no such committee.

I spent 1979 contacting people who also had union lists of serials interests and concerns in order to see if they, too, wished to pursue the possibility of such a committee. It was consoling to discover that there were a good number of us out there who were coming to grips with such problems as what standards to use, how holdings should be represented, and what is the most practical means of union list production and distribution. The general consensus was that there should be more formal outlets for discussion rather than numerous, groping telephone calls.

At the summer 1979 ALA Conference, I presented a resolution to the ALA Serials Section's Policy and Research Committee which would establish an Ad Hoc Committee to publish information on guidelines and procedures used in creating and producing union lists of serials. Discussion on the resolution was tabled until Mid-Winter 1980 when a report was to be made on the newly formed project of the International Federation of Library Associations, which would establish international guidelines for compiling union lists of serials.

More information on the IFLA Project was forthcoming in the fall of 1979. It was announced that Jean Whiffin, Head of the Serials Division at the Library of the University of Victoria in British Columbia, had accepted an invitation from IFLA to undertake the research and preparatory work to establish a new international standard dealing with the compilation of union catalogs and union lists of serials.

The proposed ALA Committee on Union Lists of Serials was not viewed as a committee to set standards for bibliographic or holdings information, or the machine-readable format of this information. Rather, it was seen as serving as a forum in order to share ideas on all aspects of union listing and in making the participants aware of the many choices they have and the decisions they must make when compiling such a list. So that this information could be easily shared, it would be published in the ALA *Guidelines* series.

### Birth

Prior to the ALA Mid-Winter Conference in 1980, a letter-writing campaign was headed by Dianne Ellsworth, Manager of the California Union List of Periodicals, and Jean Currie, from the South Central (New York) Research Library Council. This campaign urged support for the proposal to create a committee on union lists of serials when it would again be on the Serial Section's Policy and Research Committee's agenda. In addition, it encouraged attendance by any and all who supported the proposal. The turnout at the Policy and Research Committee meeting was tremendous. With the help of the many attending midwives, the proposal passed unanimously and was equally successful with the Serials Section Executive Committee. The Ad Hoc Committee on Union Lists of Serials was born.

The proposal creating this Ad Hoc Committee reads as follows:

— Whereas, libraries are finding it necessary to rely on each other in order to supplement their serial needs, and
— Whereas, the ability to share bibliographic and holdings information on serials is increasing dramatically which facilitates the creation of union lists of serials, and
— Whereas, inflation is reducing many libraries' ability to subscribe to as many serials as they might need, and

— Whereas, there are no readily available sources from which information and procedures on the development, production, and maintenance of union lists may be obtained, and,

— Whereas, the American Library Association has a vehicle for publishing and disseminating such information in its *Guidelines* series,

— Now, therefore, the Serials Section Policy and Research Committee recommends that the Serials Section Executive Committee establish an ad hoc committee to publish guidelines and procedures used in producing union listings of serials to be completed by December 1981.

The charge of the Ad Hoc Committee on Union Lists of Serials reads:

To solicit information from appropriate groups regarding the creation, production, and maintenance of union lists of serials. To publish these techniques and methods used in union listing of serials in the ALA *Guidelines* series by the end of December 1981.

### Beginning to Walk

In order to carry out the first charge of the Committee, namely "to solicit information from appropriate groups regarding the creation, production, and maintenance of union lists of serials," the Committee asked groups working on union lists of serials to supply the introduction of instructions on how to use the list, sample pages or copies of pages from union lists, and any internal procedures that are followed. (These procedures may include those followed within the union listing office itself, instructions to contributing libraries, etc.) The Committee will begin to analyze this material at the 1981 ALA Mid-Winter Conference. This information will be used to support and supplement a growing outline which the Ad Hoc Committee has been developing. In turn, this outline will be the basis for the Committee's future publication on how to compile a union list of serials.

As was stated earlier, the Ad Hoc Committee on Union Lists of Serials does not have the authority to set standards. The publication that the Committee plans to issue will be termed a "guideline" and will be descriptive rather than prescriptive. What the Committee hopes that its publication will do is to trace the steps in compiling a union list from its inception to its conclusion (conclusion, as all serials librarians know, is impossible because of the nature of serials). Some major aspects that will be covered include:

1. Contributors must establish the underlying principles of union lists of serials, specifically that there must be a spirit of cooperation and sharing of serial resources. There is no sense in knowing the titles and holdings of other libraries if patrons cannot acquire the materials through interlibrary loan procedures and agreements permitting them access to each other's collections. The

purposes of union lists are many, but most notably, union lists serve as finding tools. Due to current budget constraints, they may also serve as acquisitions and deselection tools.

2. Agreements must be made to assign responsibility for specific tasks in compiling the union list. This responsibility is two-fold: that of the union listing agent (i.e., the individual, group, library, etc.) responsible for the union list as a whole, and that of the contributing libraries. Before compiling the list, the union listing agent and the contributing libraries must decide whether their list is to be an internal one (for example, the serials of a main library and its branches) or an external one, listing the serials information of a group of separate libraries. Decisions must be made concerning the scope of the list: will it include all serials owned or only those on specific subjects? (Obviously, this decision is closely related to that of which libraries are to be included.)

A division of labor must be established. This includes deciding who determines which standards are to be used for cataloguing, holdings, and so on, and which fields and elements of the bibliographic record will be included or excluded. Who has the authority on resolving cataloguing and holdings conflicts? Who is responsible for creating the form to be used for reporting serials information, for sending out memos to insure uniformity, and for writing any needed manuals on union listing use? What contractual agreements, if any, need to be made among the union listing agent, the contributing libraries, and vendors? Finally, decisions have to be made concerning the format that the union list will take: book form, computer output microform, or on-line catalog. Especially when making decisions concerning cataloguing, holdings, inclusions of certain bibliographic elements, and the final form of the list, the user of the list—public services staff and, if possible, patrons—should be consulted. Although not all requests can be accommodated, compromises sprinkled with some empathy for each others' problems must be made.

From the start, thought should be given to future updating of the list. Not only does the union listing agent have to worry about title changes, but there are also changes in holdings information as libraries add new titles, discard others, and change the format of their holdings from bound to microfilm or microfiche and back again. Because of this, union lists of serials are out-of-date even before they are produced. It is wise to plan for continual updating procedures, if at all possible, from the inception of the project. The major reasons for doing this concern the time and money needed to submit a library's serials information to the union listing agent. Not all libraries have separate lists only of their serials titles and holdings. The request that those libraries without such a list compile a new one every time a new update or edition of the union list is published will probably go over like the proverbial lead balloon.

3. The content of the union list will have to be determined by the union

listing agent and the contributing libraries. This has been touched on briefly before, and includes: (a) Scope, namely what is to be included and what is to be excluded. Will this be a union list based on scientific subjects, or will it be all-inclusive? Will it include only current titles or retrospective and current? Will it cover a specific geographic area, a specific type of library, or some combination of the two? (b) Format, specifically, what bibliographic information will be included, how will holdings be represented, what filing rules will be used (assuming that you have a choice), and if you are going to use an automated system (not all union lists are produced by such means, remember), how do the procedures needed for this aspect correspond to the ones you are using for data collection? Underlying all of these decisions is the need for awareness of international and national standards and developments. While the list you are working on today may not be affected by these standards, perhaps your next edition will. A knowledge of what is developing and occurring on a variety of levels may save you the time and effort of having to redo a lot of work further down the road. If you should decide to reject *Anglo-American Cataloguing Rules,* 2nd Edition, the American National Standards Institute's *Standard on Serials Holdings at the Summary* (or, when it is published, the detailed) *Level,* or the MARC-S format, at least do so knowing the potential implications of your decisions.

4. A decision will have to be made on how to produce and distribute all of the collected serials information. In this day of the diminishing library dollar, much consideration must be given to cost. A manual list which requires a typist, a means of printing, and some method of binding might appear to be less expensive initially, but is it really cheaper if you plan to do updated editions of the list? Can a word processor be used? Would a computerized bibliographic data base be more practical in the long run even though the initial outlay may be more? If the leaning is toward a COM (computer output microform) product, how does this affect the users? Do they have the necessary equipment? Similarly, with an on-line union list, do all participants have a terminal? If they don't, some accommodation will have to be made. All of these factors must be weighed against your specific situation, needs, and financial constraints.

5. Finally, once the list has been produced and distributed, have the format, data content, and ease of use of the list critiqued, not only by the technical services staff but also by the users of the list. Does the list fulfill the needs of those for whom it is intended? Should the list be improved to meet the needs of others? If your union list is an ongoing project, reminders to contributors should go out early with regard to continual updating procedures. If possible, a schedule should be established for the frequency and time frame of union list updates and revisions.

These, then, are the major points that will be covered in the publication on compiling union lists of serials by the Ad Hoc Committee on Union Lists of Serials. Needless to say, these topics and others will be discussed more fully in the publication itself.

In addition to a guideline on creating and producing union lists of serials, the Ad Hoc Committee is also organizing an all-day workshop to be given as part of the 1981 ALA Conference in San Francisco. The workshop will focus on the decisions confronting a union listing agent; international developments, national developments, public services' needs, and the standards that can be used for cataloguing and holdings. At the conclusion of the program, reports from three union listing agents will be given, describing how they confronted these matters and eventually produced their own union lists of serials.

### Striving for Adulthood

The fact that the status of the Committee on Union Lists of Serials is ad hoc indicates that it has a specific purpose and that once that purpose has been accomplished, the Committee no longer has reason to exist. This Committee does have an ego, however, and has specific plans to broaden its scope in the hopes of becoming a standing committee. A list of long-range goals was included as part of the December 1979 letter-writing campaign that urged support for the Committee's initial existence. Future concerns of a standing committee on union lists of serials include:

1. Serving as a clearinghouse which would collect and disseminate information about union list projects.
2. Publishing further information on union list manuals, specifications, and related data.
3. Sharing information on new techniques and methods for creating union lists.
4. Presenting programs on topics of interest to union list producers and users.
5. Providing input and help with the implementation of bibliographic holdings standards.
6. Providing a forum for discussion on mutual concerns.

While the Ad Hoc Committee on Union Lists of Serials is quickly approaching adolescence, there is still much to accomplish. It appears that recently the concept of union listing has taken on greater importance. This is due to many factors, notably the advancements made in the growing standardization of bibliographic and holdings information, the ability to share this information via machine-readable records, and the fact that the serial dollar is shrinking as a result of inflation and limited library budgets. There is a definite need for communication and coordination among the producers, contributors, and users of union lists of serials at the national level. It is hoped that the Ad Hoc Committee on Union Lists of Serials will evolve as a major focal point for such discussion.

# THE CALIFORNIA UNION LIST OF PERIODICALS

Dianne J. Ellsworth
Edward Newman

ABSTRACT. The California Union List of Periodicals (CULP) contains 71,000 titles representing the holdings of over 600 public, special, community college, state and federal agency, and private academic libraries in California. It is maintained on-line using Data General's Eclipse C/330 minicomputer system.

As journal subscription prices continue to rise, and library budgets fail to keep up, the sharing of resources becomes increasingly necessary. Regional serials lists can provide useful tools for resource sharing and collection management. The California Union List of Periodicals, a product of the California Data Base for Serials Program, is one such regional list which provides access to the collections of over 600 California libraries.

*History and Background*

The California Union List of Periodicals (CULP) was originally developed by the California State Library. The State Library began the project in 1972, and by 1974, published the first edition of CULP. The first edition was published in book form, but as the number of holdings increased, the decision was made to switch to microfiche for the second and third editions.

The State Library used a computer software system called BIBCON to maintain the file. BIBCON was originally developed by the University of California and used MARC-like formats, optical character recognition, and batch updating. By 1977, the CULP data base had grown to contain nearly 70,000 records for 440 public, special, community college, state and federal agency, and private academic libraries in California. Because of the growth of the file, and the problems of managing a batch updating process, the State Library began to look for alternative methods of maintaining the list. In 1977, negotiations began with the then newly formed California Library Authority for Systems and Services (CLASS), for CLASS to take over responsibility for the maintenance and production of CULP. In July 1978, the California Union List of Periodicals project was transferred to CLASS with the intention that CLASS would develop an on-line maintenance system for CULP.

The California Library Authority for Systems and Services (CLASS), a public agency, is a statewide network for libraries of all types. Its goal is to help libraries so that they can provide better service to users by increasing library productivity and resources and facilitating resource sharing. CLASS is a membership organization; members participate in governance and obtain discounts on products and services. CLASS serves nonmember libraries in California, as well. The California Data Base Task Group, composed of representatives from public, special, and academic libraries, as well as a State Library representative, serves as an advisory group for the California Data Base Programs at CLASS. In addition to the California Data Base for Serials program (CDB-S), there is a California Data Base for Monographs program (CDB-M), which produces CATALIST, a monograph holdings list for California.

The California Data Base for Serials program at CLASS is responsible for the maintenance of the data base and the production of the California Union List of Periodicals.

In August 1978, CLASS published the fourth edition of CULP, using the data as it had been maintained by the State Library, and still using the BIBCON software. CLASS also hired programming staff and purchased a minicomputer with which to maintain the data base in-house. The editing and production systems we developed are described elsewhere in this report.

*Staff and Funding*

The maintenance of the California Union List of Periodicals is supported by Library Services and Construction Act, Title I, funds administered by the California State Library. The production and distribution of CULP is funded by sales of the product. The data base program staff consists of a manager, an editorial unit, and a data entry unit. The data entry unit has been supported in part by funding received through the Comprehensive Employment and Training Act. In addition, the Computer Services staff at CLASS provides computer systems analysis, design, development, and maintenance. The sizes of the data entry staff and editorial unit vary as program needs change.

*Size and Content of the Data Base*

The fifth edition of CULP was published in January 1980, and the sixth edition is scheduled to be published in February 1981. The file has continued to grow since its transfer from the State Library and now contains holdings for over 600 libraries. The number of records in the file is about the same, 71,000, because a massive updating and clean-up campaign, begun in 1979, resulted in the deletion of many duplicate records from the data base. There are approximately 340,000 holdings locations for the 71,000 titles. The data base is published as an alphabetical main entry/title list only; there is no subject access to CULP. The wide range of types of libraries which contribute data to CULP provides access to a broad spectrum of unique titles. The distributions of holdings across titles and libraries follow familiar exponential patterns. There are many small libraries and a few large ones. Fifty-five percent of the titles in the data base are held by only one library; ninety percent by eight or fewer; ninety-nine percent by 65 or fewer.

CULP includes holdings for all types of serials: periodicals, newspapers, transactions, proceedings, monographic series, and so on. Libraries vary in which of their serials titles they report to us. Libraries which catalog their serials may report nonperiodical serials only to other data bases such as OCLC, the Research Libraries Information Network (RLIN), or CATALIST.

## Contributors to the Data Base

As of November 1980, the data base contained holdings for the following types of libraries:

| | |
|---|---|
| Public libraries | 187 |
| State University libraries | 8 |
| Community College libraries | 84 |
| Private Academic libraries | 41 |
| Special libraries | 282 |
| Total (all contributors) | 602 |

We maintain a record on each contributor to the data base and keep track of all transactions and contacts with them as well as names of contact persons, addresses, and interlibrary loan policies. The data base contains titles from all types of libraries except for the largest academic libraries in the state. Any library in California is welcome to contribute its holdings data to the data base. We try to focus on those libraries whose collections include unique titles or subject matter, or libraries from geographic areas of the state which are not well represented. An evaluation survey was sent out in 1978, and again in 1980, to contributors and purchasers to find out how often CULP was being used and what our priorities should be for improving the union list. Currency of holdings information was a high priority for most users, and some suggestions were made as to the type of collections that should be added. We have tried to be responsive to our users: over 400 libraries have fully or partially updated their holdings records for the sixth edition, and we are trying to add some of the specialized collections that were identified in the survey.

## Data Collection

Because most of our contributing libraries do not catalog their periodicals, we get holdings reports in a wide variety of formats, including current subscription lists and other types of in-house lists, report forms, and catalog cards. We devised a report form which most of our contributors can use for reporting changes in their serials holdings. The reporting method which has worked best for us is the computer-generated "checklist." A checklist is a listing of titles and holdings currently in the data base for a specified contributor or set of contributors. We send the checklist to the library, and the library is responsible for making corrections and returning the list to us. Over 300 contributors used the checklist method of reporting holdings for the sixth edition.

There are some automated union lists of serials systems among our contributors, and we are developing systems by which we can accept machine-readable data from these systems and use it to update our data base automatically. For the fifth edition, we did such an update with records from the Central Association of Libraries, an intertype network associated with the 49-99 Cooperative (Public) Library System in central California. For the sixth edition, we are similarly updating the Central Association of Libraries holdings and also processing a file from the San Francisco Public Library, which includes libraries from the Peninsula Library System.

## Processing

We have developed routines for processing the non-machine-readable reports we get from our contributors. Every report is first screened by the editorial unit. An editor determines for each record in the report whether it matches a record we already have in the data base (that is, the report and the data base record describe the same serial publication). A record that does match is coded with the record identification number that appears in CULP and is passed on to the data entry staff for entry into the data base. Records that do not match are either titles new to the data base or titles that have changed. We verify both kinds of records by accessing the RLIN data base which now contains all MARC-S and CONSER records or by using traditional bibliographic tools such as *New Serial Titles,* the *Union List of Serials,* 3rd edition, or *Ulrich's International Periodicals Directory.* The match rate in RLIN has averaged about thirty percent during the six months we have been using it. This figure may be low because many of the titles might be too new to have appeared yet in CONSER, but we think it is because many of the titles are local California titles or house organs, which may not be catalogued by anyone.

Each month we process about 20,000 changes to the holdings records and add about 300 new titles. Because of the large amount of paper which must be processed, the maintenance of the data base is a highly labor-intensive operation. There are few machine-readable files available, and we have no simple way of providing on-line updating capabilities to our contributors at this time.

## Production

The minicomputer system in which the data base is maintained includes a Data General Eclipse C/330 processor with 512K bytes of main memory and two 190-megabyte disk drives. We use Data General's Advanced Operating System (AOS), Sort/Merge utility, PL/I compiler, and INFOS data base management system.

The first system we used to maintain the data base employed Data General's text-editing utility LINEDIT. We translated the data we got from the State Library into a format that LINEDIT could handle and divided the data base into files of a manageable size for LINEDIT. The first system was not totally satisfactory, but we had to develop one quickly, and it worked. Because LINEDIT gave the data entry staff great power to change records, we developed verification programs to read edited text files and tell us whether all the data was in legal format. The format we use has data physically divided into lines and pages; lines can be combined by their content to form fields; similarly, pages can be combined to form logical records.

We are now using our second editing system. It stores records in an INFOS data base for improved access, and we developed software that supports on-line updating of holdings data, since holdings changes far outnumber bibliographic changes to the data base. For bibliographic changes, it is still necessary to unload records from the data base, change them with LINEDIT, and then load them back into the data base. The loading process incorporates all of the checks previously done by the verification programs, plus others made possible by the existence of the INFOS data base.

We have also developed a system that extracts references from records (references are stored as rejected titles in records with the preferred title in the data base), sorts references and main records together into filing sequence, and formats the sorted data for printing. Our filing sequence ignores capitalization, punctuation, and a specified set of initial articles. This publication software system is used to produce CULP and the selected lists described below.

CULP is published in microfiche only, in two reductions, 24x and 42x. The user's guide contains lists of libraries by region, name, and city and is distributed both on microfiche and on paper with each copy of CULP. We produce a master copy of the front matter and have it photographed to make microfiche masters which are subsequently copied along with the computer-output microfiches of the list itself; the same paper master is also used for offset printing of the paper copies of the front matter.

The fifth edition of CULP contained 4,111 pages, sixty-nine microfiches in the 24x edition, twenty-one microfiches in the 42x edition. Each page or frame contains three forty-character columns. Entries are printed in a psuedo-boldface produced by overprinting. Holdings statements are sorted by geographic regions; within a region, holdings appear alphabetically by mnemonic library code. Every microfiche contains an index in the rightmost bottom frame, which gives the frame coordinates and the first entry line for each frame on the microfiche.

### Record Format, Holdings Notation, and Location Symbols

The data elements used in the data base are largely derived from the ones used in the BIBCON system by the State Library. They include:

1. Record identification number, a unique identifying number;
2. Library of Congress Card Number;
3. International Standard Serial Number (ISSN);
4. Sort title—a title which is to affect the filing order of a record, but not to be printed;
5. Title/main entry—this field may contain publisher, place of publication, or corporate author data;
6. Referred-from entry— this field is used to create references to the main entry;
7. Dates and volumes;
8. General notes;
9. Preceding entry notes;
10. Succeeding entry notes;
11. Location and holdings statements.

The notation we use for displaying location and holdings information is derived from the system the State Library used. (See Table 1.) We record both volume and chronology; issue level holdings are recorded if the issue level information clarifies the holdings statement.

### Bibliographic Considerations

Form and choice of entry is a problem which many union list producers face. Since CULP is a finding, or location, tool rather than a cataloguing tool, it does not contain full bibliographic information. For many of our reporting libraries, a title and holdings statement is all we may receive. We try to encourage our contributors to report additional information such as publisher, place of publication, ISSN, and beginning date of publication or title change, if it is available. We sometimes encounter problems in trying to match contributor records to ours. We follow the practice of successive entry, while some of our contributors use earliest or latest entry. With over 600 contributors to

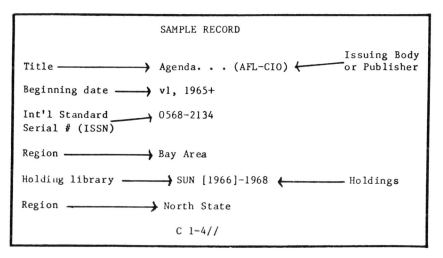

SAMPLE RECORD

Example of listing on microfiche. California Union List of Periodicals.
TABLE 1

the file, it is extremely difficult for CLASS to get all the participants to agree on a standard format. In addition, many of our contributors report to other local or regional lists, where practices may differ from ours.

## Selected Lists

The microfiche edition of CULP is only one of the off-line products of the data base. We also produce selected lists. A selected list contains data selected from the data base for a set of contributing libraries. Such a list can cover a single library and be used by that library for internal purposes; or any group of libraries can create a CULP subset union list for resource sharing. A selected list is a custom product, priced at a flat charge plus an additional charge based on the number of records selected, plus charges for reproduction. We can supply selected lists on microfiche, on paper (a camera-ready master copy is given to the library for reproduction), or on magnetic tape. We also have an arrangement with a local vendor to provide computer-output photocomposition of data from our tapes. The packaging, binding, and user guide of each selected list is arranged individually with each customer. This service has proven extremely helpful to libraries that do not have machine-readable serials records of their own.

## Relation of CULP to Other Union Lists in the State

There are other union lists of serials in the state. The University of California Division of Library Automation produces the California Academic Libraries List of Serials (CALLS), which contains over 350,000 titles and over

570,000 holdings locations representing the major academic institutions in California. The 1980 edition of CALLS (formerly the University of California Union List of Serials) includes serials holdings for the nine campuses of the University of California, the nineteen campuses of the California State University and Colleges, and Stanford University. In 1981, approximately 40,000 records from the University of Southern California will probably be included in CALLS; some USC holdings are now in CULP. The University of California Division of Library Automation gets all of the California State University and Colleges data in one machine-readable file which is maintained by the Office of the Chancellor of the State University and Colleges. The Stanford records were contributed to CALLS as part of an HEA Title II-C project among Stanford and the Los Angeles and Berkeley campuses of the University of California.

In addition to CALLS, there are many other local and regional union lists within the state. Some of the lists are subsets of the CULP data base, but most are produced independently by multitype library systems or special library groups in California. Many of these independently produced lists are merged into the CULP data base, either through the tape merge process described earlier or manually from printed lists. There is some overlap between CALLS and CULP: eight of the state university and colleges libraries are included in CULP, either by choice or because they report to a multitype library network that passes the holdings data on to us.

## Future Development

In early 1981, CLASS is planning to offer on-line access to the data base for reference use, through a vendor of on-line reference services. The availability of serials location information on the same system with indexes and abstracts of the serials literature is expected to be of great benefit to users of the system.

We are also investigating use of the CONSER data on the RLIN system to improve the bibliographic content and quality of the CULP data base. We are now matching a sample of CULP records against the CONSER records to collect data on the hit rate we might expect in a full match. If we do run a match, we plan to use ISSN as the match key when possible; over twenty-five percent of the CULP records have ISSN's assigned to them.

We would like to provide on-line updating to our contributors. One possibility might be to use the OnTyme electronic mail system which many CLASS members are using.

A related project is the microcomputer-based serials control system which CLASS is developing. CULP contributors who purchase the system may be able to have CLASS provide them with a ready-made machine-readable data base.

## The Impact of National Developments on CULP

In the past few years, there has been a great deal of activity on the national level to develop standards for both bibliographic and holdings data for serials. The MARC Serials Format, CONSER, and the standards for summary and detailed level holdings that are being developed by the American National Standards Institute all have far-reaching implications for producers of union lists of serials. The implementation of AACR2 also poses some complex problems for many union list agencies. We are planning to implement the ANSI holdings standards in the near future. Unless we use CONSER as a master bibliographic file, implementation of AACR2 would be difficult for us. CLASS is committed to following approved national standards and to making use of the work which is going on nationally to make the California data base consistent with the emerging national serials data base. The transition to the use of other standards, whether they cover bibliographic data, holdings data, or location symbols will be a considerable project because of the size of CULP and our many contributors.

## The Future of the CULP Data Base

CLASS has made certain planning assumptions that affect the future of CULP, among which are the following:

1. Very few libraries in California will be cataloguing their serials or periodicals in the next few years, so that limited information on serials will be available through the bibliographic utilities such as OCLC or RLIN for California libraries.
2. Some local systems in California will continue to publish their own union lists; other systems and libraries will become more dependent on CLASS for the generation of local or regional lists.
3. There will still be a need for a central agency to provide full information on the location of serials in California to supplement local and national lists.
4. There will continue to be two major serials union lists produced in California in the next few years: CULP and CALLS.
5. CULP may be available for on-line access by external users, but some kind of printed list (in microform) will still be required.
6. The CULP data base might be expanded to include holdings from neighboring states.

CULP continues to grow; as this article goes to press, the number of contributors has increased to 617. Regional union lists of serials will continue to provide a much needed service in support of interlibrary loan and resource sharing.

*Summary*
*(California Union List of Periodicals)*

| | |
|---|---|
| Size of data base | 71,000 titles |
| Number of contributors | 602 |
| Number of holdings statements | 340,000 |
| Number of ISSNs | 19,987 |
| Schedule | Annual |

*Production:* The CULP data base is maintained on-line on CLASS's minicomputer system.

*Output:* Microfiche (24x and 42x reduction); optional listings by library or group of libraries available.

California Union List of Periodicals

# Introduction

The fifth edition of CULP (1979) includes reports from contributing libraries received through September 1979. The User's Guide to CULP is provided both in paper copy and on microfiche proceeding each fiche set.

This is the first edition of CULP to be wholly produced and distributed by CLASS. To the hundreds of libraries throughout the state of California who willingly shared information about their collections, we express our thanks. We have tried to focus in this edition on improving the accuracy and currency of holdings data. We have made over 500,000 changes to the over 300,000 holdings records represented in CULP. A union list is necessarily an evolving process; CULP is continually updated and changes that were not included here will appear in the next edition.

We welcome suggestions for improvement. Please use the error report form included in the User's Guide to report errors in your library's holdings as well as suggestions for the list's format and entry content.

If your library is not currently reporting to CULP and wishes to, please contact the CLASS office.

STATISTICAL INFORMATION

Number of titles:       66,000
Holdings records:      335,625
Number of ISSN's:       17,481

PROCESSING

CULP is programmed in PL-1 and maintained online at CLASS in a system based on Data General Corporation's Eclipse C/330 computer.

# Selected Listings

On request CLASS can produce selected listings extracted from the CULP file for one or a group of libraries, in either hard copy or microform.

# California Union List of Periodicals
# User's Guide

## Scope

In preceding editions CULP has defined a periodical as "a publication issued . . . at more or less regular intervals at least twice a year." CULP now uses the broader definition of serials which more accurately reflects the current and future content of CULP. CULP includes periodicals, annuals, monographic series, newspapers, conference proceedings and transactions, reports and bulletins of societies, associations and other organizations, and serials in other formats (Braille, talking book, and cassette).

## Form of Entry

Generally CULP follows the practice of New Serials Titles. However, periodicals which could not be verified in standard sources may be entered as the contributing library reported them.

The practice of successive entry has been followed wherever possible. We have tried to identify title changes and create new title records when reported by libraries and verified by the editorial staff. Cross references and linking entry notes are provided. Many libraries still report latest entry and titles may be included in this form.

Entries should also be searched under both title and/or corporate entry since there may be discrepancies caused by variant reporting procedures.

## Record Format

CULP records include the following information.

(M) = mandatory (will always be present)
(O) = optional (information provided when available)

Title or Main Entry (M) Publisher/Place of Publication (O)
Beginning/Ending volume and date (O)
International Standard Serial Number (ISSN) (O)
Notes:  information about titles, including title changes, bibliographic
    history, or special notes (O)
Cross References - are provided from "not used" to "used" forms of
    entry (O)

## Library Identfiers

The library identifiers (codes) limited to five characters, are intended to be mnemonic representations of the contributing libraries' most common names. Vowels tend to be deleted unless they are necessary to aid recognition. Most community college libraries have Co or Cl in their symbols. Identifiers are the same for libraries listed in CATALIST, the monographs holdings list for California libraries produced by CLASS.

# Interpreting Holdings Statements

Holdings data may be displayed in a number of ways. CULP has attempted
to translate holdings data reported in 1979 to a format similar to that
used by the California State Library in previous editions. Holdings
may also appear in the form as reported by the library.

Holdings data consists of the library identifier, volumes and/or dates
and microform code if part or all of the holdings are in microform.
Library identifiers (codes) which are not followed by holdings data
indicate that the library needs to be contacted directly for holdings
information.

## Punctuation and Symbols Used in CULP

[ ]     BRACKETS indicate incomplete volumes or years.

-     HYPHEN is used between volume numbers or years to indicate
inclusive holdings. 1-4  1970-74. Hypen may also appear
as an indication of continuing holdings (see + PLUS).

+     PLUS SIGN indicates library is continuing to receive a title.
4+  1975+

:     COLON used to identify series notation    ns:1-5

;     SEMI-COLON  separates dates in old and new series, and indicates changes of numbering systems within a holdings statement.

,     COMMA used by CULP to indicate gaps in a library's holdings
1,3-5  1950,1952-55. Has been used in some cases to show
continued holdings:  1,1965+

#     POUND SIGN used to indicate issue numbers within volumes.
1#1-3#3

//     DOUBLE SLASH used to indicate that the publication has ceased
with the last issue of year listed.

/     SLASH indicates combined years or volumes as reported by libraries.  1978/79  1/2

( )     PARENTHESES used for reporting retention policy statements
when they are preceded by volume and date information.
1975+  (5 years + curr)

s     SERIES

ns     NEW SERIES

(M)     MICROFILM  1970+(M) 1965-1969 - portion of file in microfilm

# Library Lists

There are three lists of contributing libraries, indexed differently to permit multiple access. Each record in each list contains the following information:

> Institution name
> Address
> Telephone number (for interlibrary loan use)
> Interlibrary loan codes
> Library symbol

Libraries by Library Name – indexed alphabetically by institution name

Libraries by Library Symbol – indexed alphabetically by library symbol

Libraries by Regions – There are eight regions, each listed separately. Within each region cities are listed alphabetically; within each city, libraries are listed alphabetically by institution name.

The following is a list of regions and the counties comprising them:

| NORTH STATE | | CENTRAL COAST | SOUTH COAST |
|---|---|---|---|
| Alpine | Placer | Monterey | San Luis Obispo |
| Butte | Plumas | San Benito | Santa Barbara |
| Colusa | Sacramento | Santa Clara | Ventura |
| Del Norte | Shasta | Santa Cruz | |
| El Dorado | Sierra | | LOS ANGELES BASIN |
| Glenn | Siskiyou | | |
| Humboldt | Solano | CENTRAL VALLEY | Kern |
| Lake | Sonoma | | Los Angeles |
| Lassen | Sutter | Amador | Orange |
| Marin | Tehama | Calaveras | |
| Mendocino | Trinity | Fresno | SOUTHEAST |
| Modoc | Yolo | Kings | |
| Mono | Yuba | Madera | Inyo |
| Napa | | Mariposa | |
| Nevada | | Merced | Riverside |
| | | San Joaquin | San Bernardino |
| BAY AREA | | Stanislaus | |
| | | Tulare | SAN DIEGO |
| Alameda | | Tuolomne | |
| Contra Costa | | | Imperial |
| San Francisco | | | San Diego |
| San Mateo | | | |

# Lending Policy Code

A general indication of the periodicals lending policy of contributors to CULP has been coded and is provided with the library identifier in the following list. Such an indication can give only a very general idea of any contributor's lending policy. The codes are provided on the basis of responses to a questionnaire mailed to each contributor; no policy codes are provided for libraries from which no questionnaire was returned.

The following table outlines the policy codes. These codes follow the contributing library's name in the library location index.

| Code | Policy |
|------|--------|
| 1 | Generally does not lend periodicals. (May provide photocopies.) |
| 2 | Charges for all photocopying. |
| 3 | Provides free photocopy for short articles (about 10 pages). |
| 4 | Charges .05-.10 per page for photocopying of longer articles. |
| 5 | Charges more than .10 per page for photocopying. |
| 6 | Does not charge for any photocopying. |
| 7 | Contact Libray for lending policy information. |

If all or any part of the contributor's policy was not apparent from the questionnaire response, a question mark (?) is inserted in the code.

An asterisk (*) next to a library indicates that holdings have been partially or fully updated for this edition.

CLASS
1415 Koll Circle, Suite 101
San Jose, CA 95112

### CALIFORNIA UNION LIST OF PERIODICALS REPORTING FORM

*REPORTING LIBRARY* _____

*Date* _____ Contact Person _____ Phone _____

TITLE & SUBTITLE _____
_____

PUBLISHER/PLACE OF PUBN _____

ISSN [ ] [ ] [ ] [ ] – [ ] [ ] [ ] [ ]

Serial type [ ] Periodical [ ] Newspaper [ ] Gov't. Doc.   Medium [ ] Braille [ ] Talking Book [ ] Other (Describe) _____

#### PLEASE COMPLETE APPROPRIATE SECTIONS BELOW

1. [ ] WE ARE CHANGING OUR HOLDINGS OF THE ABOVE TITLE.

   Current Library Holdings _____

   Microform Holdings? (Please give vol./date) _____

2. [ ] WE ARE ADDING THE ABOVE TITLE TO OUR COLLECTION.

   Vol/Date of First Issue _____

   Library's Holdings _____

   Microform Holdings? (Please give vol/date) _____

3. [ ] THE ABOVE TITLE HAS CHANGED WITH: Volume _____ Date _____

   To Title & Subtitle _____
   _____

   Publisher/Place of Pubn _____

   ISSN [ ] [ ] [ ] [ ] – [ ] [ ] [ ] [ ]

   Library's Holdings: Old Title _____

   New Title _____

   Microform Holdings? (Please give vol/date) _____

4. [ ] WE ARE DROPPING OUR SUBSCRIPTION TO THE ABOVE TITLE.

   [ ] We are keeping part or all of the backfile in:
       Paper Copy (Please give vol/date) _____
       Microform (Please give vol/date) _____
   [ ] We are discarding the entire backfile

5. [ ] THE ABOVE TITLE HAS: [ ] CEASED PUBN. [ ] SUSPENDED PUBN. Volume _____ Date _____

   [ ] We are keeping all or part of the backfile in:
       Paper Copy (Please give vol/date) _____
       Microform (Please give vol/date) _____
   [ ] We are discarding the entire backfile

NOTES _____
_____
_____

THIS SECTION FOR CULP USE ONLY    Lib. I.D. Code _____ Date Processed _____

Periodical Control No. _____ Verified by _____ Date _____ [ ] ULS [ ] NST [ ] Other

(see over)

# GUIDELINES FOR THE USE OF THE CALIFORNIA UNION LIST OF PERIODICALS REPORTING FORM

The Reporting form is to be used to notify CLASS of any title changes, additions or holdings changes to periodicals.

The form has been structured to provide a means of accurately transferring information to the CULP data base.

How to use the form:

1. Although the form is multi-purpose, a SEPARATE FORM must be used for each TITLE you report.

2. Incomplete or broken holdings may be reported by using either brackets [    ] to show incomplete volumes or years, or specifying dates/issues to indicate exactly which part of the year or volume you have.

3. The data elements SUBTITLE; PUBLISHER; PLACE OF PUBLICATION are optional. This information should be reported, if readily available, to help CULP distinguish between the title you are reporting and other, similar titles in the CULP data base. If you are reporting government documents or semi-official publications, issuing agency should be identified.

4. ISSN's (International Standard Serial Numbers) should be reported if available.

5. Samples of RETENTION policy reports include the following:

    3 years and current
    Current issues only, etc. . . . .

   Some libraries report on holdings they expect to have rather than what they actually have; these holdings will appear in CULP as:

    1977 + (Five yrs. only)
    1979 + (Two yrs. only) etc. . . . .

6. The NOTES section at the end of the form should be used for reporting any change which is not covered by previous sections, and for recording additional information about the title, such as notes concerning mergers, absorption, earlier and later titles, beginning date of publication, etc. . . . .

Forms should be returned to:    CLASS/CULP

    1415 Koll Circle, Suite 101
    San Jose, CA 95112

If you have questions or problems to report, please write or call:

    Phone: (408) 289-1756
    ATSS NO.: (408) 522-1372

NEW TITLE VERIFICATION

| | | BIB LEVEL | S | SER TYPE | P | N | MED | F | T |
|---|---|---|---|---|---|---|---|---|---|
| **INDEX TITLE** | | | | | | | | | |
| **RID** | | | | | | | | | |
| **010 (LCCN)** | | 022 (ISSN) | | | | | | | |
| **045 (Sort Title)** | | | | | | | | | |
| **110 (Name Main Entry)** | | | | | | | | | |
| **245 (Title Entry)** | | | | | | | | | |
| **247 (Referred from Entry)** | | | | | | | | | |
| **260 (Imprint)** | | | | | | | | | |
| **362 (Beg vol & date)** | | | | | | | | | |
| **500 (Notes)** | | | | | | | | | |
| **780 (Preceding Entry[ies])** | | | | | | | | | |
| **785 (Succeeding Entry[ies])** | | | | | | | | | |
| **850 (Holdings)** | | | | | | | | | |

Reported Title

Notes

SOURCE

☐ ULS

☐ NST 19____

☐ ULRICH'S

☐ OTHER (specify)
_____

DATE _____

Verified by _____

# THE OCLC SERIALS CONTROL SUBSYSTEM

Pauline F. Micciche

ABSTRACT. The OCLC Serials Control Subsystem, the least known of OCLC's sub-systems, has been operational since 1975. Areas on which it impacts currently include the OCLC On-line Union Catalog, CONSER, the OCLC Cataloging Subsystem, and the world of serial publications. Soon-to-be-added capabilities include union listing, claiming, links to the Name-Address Directory, off-line products, and statistical reports. Binding control will complete the subsystem.

The future of the Serials Control Subsystem holds many possibilities including master serial records, links to all OCLC subsystems, public service displays, and on-line communication with vendors. OCLC, regional networks, and OCLC members are partners in refining the subsystem.

## Introduction

Serials operations in libraries have always been reputed to be a morass of tangled titles, numbering schemes, and publication schedules (or nonschedules). While no one method of operations can correct all of these inherent problems, the OCLC Serials Control Subsystem negotiates many of them.

The Serials Control Subsystem (SCS) is one of the six subsystems originally provided for in the overall design of the OCLC On-line System. The major function of the SCS is to provide on-line control of serial publications by offering OCLC members seven basic capabilities: inventory control, check-in, claiming, binding, union listing, management statistics, and public service displays.

## History of the OCLC Serials Control Subsystem

OCLC held the first meeting of its Advisory Committee on Serials (now the Serials Control Advisory Committee) on Friday, October 1, 1971, to begin work on the preliminary design the Serials Control Subsystem (SCS). In early 1974, OCLC member libraries began entering serial bibliographic records in the OCLC On-line Union Catalog, the data base of the Cataloging Subsystem. This entry was requisite for integrating serials control functions with cataloguing functions. Also in 1974, Ohio libraries (among them Kent State University

Acknowledgements: Graphics by Rick Limes; statistics compiled for Figure 1 by Ron Gardner.

and Case Western Reserve) began preparing to participate in the SCS. In October 1975, OCLC trained staff from nine Ohio libraries to create records for serials control. Representatives from other Ohio member libraries received preliminary training in December 1975. Staff from regional networks that contract with OCLC to provide OCLC services to their member libraries were trained in February 1976. By that time, the On-line Union Catalog contained over 90,000 serial records, which greatly facilitated the SCS inventory control capability. In late 1976, automatic check-in was added to the inventory control capability.

When the number of institutions wishing to participate in the SCS exceeded OCLC's original estimate, in January 1977, OCLC set a ceiling on subsystem use of 150 authorized institutions. Other libraries, however, were developing strategic plans for serials control. They sent OCLC urgent requests to remove this ceiling so that they could use the serials Check-in Component and other expanded capabilities as they became available. OCLC then reassessed the system processing load and was able to remove the ceiling on April 5, 1979. Although Serials Control Subsystem use accounts for only three percent of the message traffic on the OCLC On-line System, 212 institutions currently are authorized to use the Subsystem, sixty-six of which are actively checking in serial publications. See Figure 1.)

### On-line Union Catalog

The OCLC On-line Union Catalog, an integral part of the Serials Control Subsystem (SCS), has a complex structure of its own. All bibliographic information automatically displayed by the SCS is extracted from the On-line Union Catalog. This information derives from information entered in the On-line Union Catalog by over 2,300 OCLC member institutions using the Cataloging Subsystem. OCLC also adds nonserial bibliographic records produced by the Library of Congress, the National Library of Medicine, and the National Library of Canada.

The CONSER (CONversion of SERials) Project is a cooperative effort of libraries to build a data base of quality serials cataloguing information. CONSER participants modify existing serial bibliographic records in the On-line Union Catalog and add new ones.[1,2] For this reason, OCLC does not need to add Library of Congress or National Library of Canada serial bibliographic records to the On-line Union Catalog; they are added by CONSER participants. OCLC supplies the Library of Congress with a magnetic tape of all records entered or modified by CONSER participants. The Library of Congress in turn distributes the data on these tapes to subscribers to the LC-MARC Subscription Service for serial bibliographic records. OCLC also supplies the National Library of Canada with a machine-readable tape of CONSER data, from which it produces supplements to *CONSER Microfiche,* the CONSER KWOC index.[3]

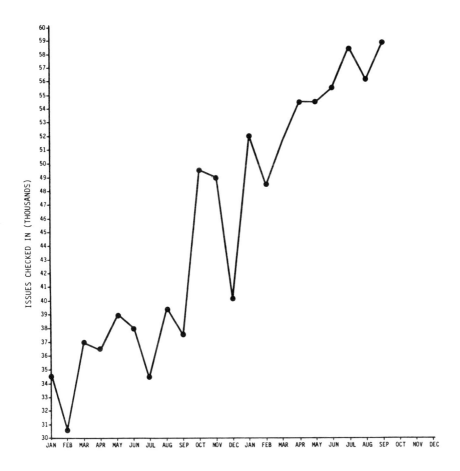

Figure 1.  Serials Control Subsystem Issues Checked-in, 1979/1980

## Subsystem Capabilities

When a Serials Control Subsystem (SCS) participating library wants to create a serial Local Data Record (LDR) for a new title, it adds its unique three-character institution symbol to the bibliographic record in the OLUC (using the Cataloging Subsystem). These symbols identify those libraries holding a copy of the serial. The library then requests a LDR workform using the "workform" command. The SCS automatically displays data from the master serial bibliographic record in the heading of the LDR workform. The library then adds desired local data to the LDR and adds the record to the on-line file, using a two-key command. If the library has more than one copy of a serial, it may create additional LDRs from existing records using the "add" command. (See Figure 2.)

The library may request a display of LDRs using the same search keys and access points available in the Cataloging Subsystem. The search, however, can be restricted to serial bibliographic records when using an author, title, or author/title search key. The search can also be restricted to serials with a certain date or dates of publication.[4] (See Figure 3.)

Once a LDR exists for a serial, any properly authorized operator in a library can check in issues of that serial, either manually or by one of two automatic methods.

To check-in serials manually, the library enters necessary check-in data into the "current holdings" or "retrospective holdings" fields and the "next expected issue" field of the LDR. Using the "update" command, the library can then replace the previous LDR with the updated LDR in the on-line file.

To check in serials automatically, the library enters the r (issue received) command. The r command instructs the SCS to add the issue to the current holdings field and to predict the next expected issue based on previously entered publication data. The library can have the LDR displayed with the check-in data after an r command or can instruct the SCS to replace the previous record in the data base with the updated record. An m (issue missing) command

```
                       ¶
American Society for Information Science.⊦
Journal of the American Society for Information Science.⊦
ISSN: 0002-8231  CODEN: AISJB6  OCLC no: 1798118  Frequn: b  Regulr: r⊦
      ¶
 ▶ Hld lib: TRNN  Copy: 1  Repr:      Subsc stat: a  Loan: 3 DAYS ¶
      ¶
 ▶ 1 CLNO     Z1007 ‡b .A477 ¶
 ▶ 2 LOCN     Faculty Library ¶
 ▶ 3 FUND     7789-2279 ¶
 ▶ 4 RMKS     Preceding entry--American documentation; a quarterly⊦
review of ideas, techniques, problems, and achievements in⊦
documentation. (0096-946X) ¶
 ▶ 5 RMKS     This record is to be used for training purposes⊦
only. ¶
 ▶ 6 DEFN     ‡v vol. ‡p no. ¶
 ▶ 7 NEXT     ‡v 30 ‡p 4 ‡d 791125 ¶
      ¶
 ▶ Date recd: ¶
      ¶
 ▶ 8 CRHD     ‡v 30 ‡p 1,3 ‡y 1979 ¶
 ▶ 9 RTHD     ‡v 23-29 ‡y 1973-1978 ¶
```

Figure 2.  Serials Local Data Record

| AUTHOR | TITLE | CODEN |
|--------|-------|-------|
| 100 | 130 | 030 |
| 700 | 222 | |
| 705 | 240 | ISBN |
| 110 | 245 | |
| 710 | 246 | 020 |
| 715 | 247 | |
| 870 | 440 | ISSN |
| 871 | 730 | |
| 872 | 740 | 022 |
| 873 | 780 | |
| | 785 | OCLC NUMBER |
| AUTHOR/TITLE | 830 | |
| | 840 | fixed field (OCLC:) |
| 1xx/240 | | |
| 1xx/245 | | GOVERNMENT DOCUMENT |
| 1xx/740 | | NUMBER |
| 240/245 when no 1xx exists | | |
| 7xx/245 | | |
| 87x/240 when indicated in record | | 086 |
| where x = 1, 2, or 3, | | |
| and xx = 00, 10, 11, or 30 | | |

Users may limit derived search keys (author, author/title, and
title) by record type qualifiers and year(s) of publication,
and retrieve up to 1,500 records per derived search key.

Figure 3.  Searchable Fields in the Local Data Record

instructs the SCS to place a comma (indicating a gap in holdings) in the
current holdings field and to predict the next expected issue. The SCS automatically displays the record after an m command so that the operator may
continue to check in issues.

## Expanded Serials Control Subsystem Capabilities

### General Enhancements

In fall 1980, OCLC will install its first general enhancements to the Serials
Control Subsystem.[5] With these changes, libraries will no longer be limited to
displays of only items previously processed by their own institutions. They will
be able to see the full bibliographic record for any serial title and attach their
institution holding symbol to the title directly from the Serials Control Subsystem, rather than through the Cataloging Subsystem. Both cataloguing and

creating the local data record will be accomplished in one operation from the Serials Control Subsystem instead of in two separate operations.

Libraries also will be able to display various lists of institutions holding a serial item. Institution holding symbols will be arranged alphabetically within state. Libraries will be able to request a display of the holdings symbols of institutions within their state, within their region (their state and the surrounding states), or for all institutions. These are the same displays of holdings symbols currently available in the Cataloging Subsystem. (See Figure 4.)

*Union Listing Capability*

OCLC will install the Serial Union Listing Capability when it installs general Serials Control Subsystem enhancements. The Union Listing Capability will provide participating libraries with a means to create, maintain, and distribute serial union list information. OCLC's implementation of the *American National Standards Serial Holdings Statements at the Summary Level* provides two new fields for holdings information in the LDR, one for institution-specific summary holdings and one for copy-specific summary holdings.[6] Any authorized user of the Serials Control Subsystem will be able to view union list group displays, regardless of whether his/her institution is part of the display. (See Figure 5.) In addition to several off-line products, such as tapes, the Serials Control Subsystem will supply union list data on-line.

```
 Screen 1 of 4        <
▶ALL LOCATIONS - FOR OTHER HOLDINGS DISPLAYS ENTER dhg, dhs, OR dhr, DISPLAY
 RECD, SEND; FOR BIBLIOGRAPHIC RECORD ENTER bib, DISPLAY RECD, SEND

 STATE       LOCATIONS <
  AL      AAA ABC ACM ADA AJB ALM mlc oak scm tal tus <
  CA      SXP <
  CO      DVP FZW <   ·
  CT      CTL CZL FAU FEM HPL HRM nwk PEM SSA TYC ub1 ub2 ub3 UCW WLU YUS yu# <
  DC      AED AFC ARL DCL DCP DDF DFC DGW DLC EAU GQG gqk gqm HNI HOU LCI NBS nsd
          SMI TRL UDI ULL <
  DE      DLM <
  FL      DZM EBC EDB EFM FBA FCM FDA FGM FHM fjd FJK fjn fjs flt fmc FNP fra FTU
          FUG ful FWA FXG FYM JPL ORL TNH <
  GA      CCL clc EMU GAS GAT GFV GGC GHA GJG GKJ GMC gom GSU GTM GUA GWC GYG mbc
          mwu pne QYM <
  IL      CGP JNA SOI SPI UIU <
  KY      KAT KHN KLG KTS KUK <
  LA      AGS dil LHA LLM LLT LNC LRU LUU LWA <
  MA      AMH AQM AZM BAN BCT BHA BJO BOS BPS bqm bwe BXM BZM CKM CUM HAM HCD HLS
          MTH MYG NED ntn rfl SNN TFW WEL WHE WPG WQM WRM wxm WZW XNL <
  MD      AGL JHE MUB NLM NSA OLA <
  ME      BBH BYN CBY MEA MMM PGP PPN <
```

Figure 4.  Holdings Symbols Arranged by State

```
                 ¶
METROPOLITAN UNION LIST OF SERIALS ¶
American Society for Information Science.l
Journal of the American Society for Information Science.l
ISSN: 0002-8231 CODEN: AISJB6 OCLC no: 1798118 Frequn: b Regulr: r ¶
ITEMS MARKED + HAVE FULLER HOLDINGS.  REQUEST LINE NO. TO VIEW THESE. ¶
¶
▶ 1  XXA (8012,0,4) 21-  1970- ¶
▶ 2+ XYZ (8012,0,4) 24-  1973- ¶
▶ 3+ YYZ (8008,0,4) 22-  1971- ¶
```

```
                 ¶
American Society for Information Science.l
Journal of the American Society for Information Science.l
ISSN: 0002-0231 CODEN: AISJB6 OCLC no: 1798118 Frequn: b Regulr: r ¶
XYZ (8012,0,4) 24-  1973- ¶
  ¶
▶ 1   XYZL 2 Z1007.A477  (8010,0,4,6  6 months only) ¶
▶ 2   XYZP 1 Z1007.A477  (8010,0,4)  24-  1973- ¶
```

Figure 5.  Union Listing Group and Institution Displays

*Claiming Capability*

With the installation of the claiming capability by spring 1981, Phase I of the Serials Control Subsystem will be complete. The Claims Component will include the ability to override the frequency reported in the bibliographic record, to provide for exceptions to regular frequency cycles, and to provide for numbering patterns. New fields will include information needed by vendors and institutions to process a claim. The Claims Component will utilize name-address records in the OCLC Name-Address Directory for processing claims. (See Figure 6.)

Libraries will have the option to specify that the Serials Control Subsystem issue claims automatically, notify them that there may be a need for a claim, or wait until they initiate a claim. Libraries will also be able to specify the number of claim cycles.

```
                        ¶
   NACN:  2244    DATE MODIFIED:  800611    DATE LAST USED:  000000 ¶
   ¶
 ▶ 1 ATTN OF:  0  ¶
 ▶ 2 TITLE     0  ¶
 ▶ 3 ORGANIZ     Central Plains Univ Libr ǂt LIBR ¶
 ▶ 4 PO/ST       12 E Campus Blvd ¶
 ▶ 5 CITY/ST     ǂc Central Plains ǂs NE ǂp 78910 ǂn US ¶
 ▶ 6 IDENTITY    ǂl main ǂn NbUnl ǂo OZY ǂo NBL ǂz OCL ¶
 ▶ 7 COMMUN      904 ǂp 333-1000 ¶
 ▶ 8 AFFIL'N     OCLC ǂa NEBASE ǂa American Libr Asn ǂa Nebraska Libr Asn ¶
 ▶ 9 POLICIES    ǂw Spec Coll: Nebraska History ***TEST RECORD*** ¶
 ▶10 MESSAGE     ¶
```

Figure 6.    Name-Address Directory Organization Record

Libraries will be able to obtain on-line summaries of outstanding and potential claims as well as cumulated statistical reports. Statistical reports will include the number of issues received, the number of claims filed, the number of issues missing but not claimed, the number of outstanding claims, and the number of outstanding potential claims.

*Binding Capability*

The last major capability, binding control, will include records of binding patterns and other binding control data. The Serials Control Subsystem will notify serials department staff of publications for future binding much in the way that it will bring potential claims to their attention. Those libraries using binding control will have access to all other components and will have the ability to search bibliographic records. Later, the Serials Control Subsystem will have more extensive links to the Acquisitions, Cataloging, Interlibrary Loan, and Circulation Control Subsystems.

*The Future of the Serials Control Subsystem*

OCLC is planning increased flexibility in the Serials Control Subsystem and increased cooperation with serial vendors, as well as the addition of new components and links with other subsystems. Talks have begun with serial vendors to determine how OCLC and vendors may cooperate better to serve OCLC members. Such cooperation may lead, not only to the increased availability of serials information, but also to on-line communication with vendors.

To further increase the availability of information about serials for library management, design of a master serial record is under consideration. This master serial record would be available to Serials Control Subsystem participants. The record would contain cross-references to related titles, names of vendors handling the publication, delays in publication or receipt, and other information of interest to all Serials Control Subsystem users.

OCLC anticipates adding special displays and capabilities for public service and creating on-line statistical reports for library management. No aspect of serials control will go unexamined. OCLC, regional networks, and OCLC member libraries are partners in refining the Serials Control Subsystem and, together, negotiating the morass of tangled titles, numbering schemes, and publication schedules.

## REFERENCES

1. "The CONSER (Conversion of Serials) Project is a cooperative effort by the library community to build a machine-readable data base of quality serials cataloging information. . . . Under the auspices of CONSER, bibliographic information is authenticated by the Library of Congress (LC) or, in the case of Canadian imprints, by the National Library of Canada (NLC). Titles and International Standard Serial Numbers (ISSN) are assigned or verified by the National Serials Data Program (NSDP) or ISDS/Canada, ensuring an authoritative data base. . . . Upon expiration of its original contract in 1977 November, OCLC announced continued sponsorship and support of CONSER and assumed managerial responsibility." *CONSER, Conservation of Serials* (Columbus, OH: OCLC, Inc., 1980).

2. Davis, Carol C. "OCLC's Role in the CONSER Project." To be published in *Serials Review*.

3. National Library of Canada. *National Library News* 12(2) (February 1980):1-2.

4. OCLC, Inc. "Search/Retrieval Enhancements." OCLC Technical Bulletin No. 95 (Columbus, OH: OCLC, Inc., 1980).

5. OCLC, Inc. "Serials Control Subsystem Enhancements." OCLC Technical Bulletin No. 96 (Columbus, OH: OCLC, Inc., 1980).

6. Wittorf, Robert. "Serials Union Lists: ANSI Z39.42 and OCLC." Serials Review. 6(2) (1980 April/June).

# THE RESEARCH LIBRARIES GROUP, INC. PROGRAMS FOR SERIALS

Lois M. Kershner

ABSTRACT. The Research Libraries Group, Inc. (RLG) is a consortium of institutions whose primary goal is to provide information to the scholarly community through cooperative programs in Shared Resources, Collection Management and Development, Preservation, and the Research Libraries Information Network (RLIN). Serials information and handling are represented in several programs through the cooperative purchase file, through the message system, and through policy statements and the on-line catalog that underpins all RLG programs.

The Research Libraries Group, Inc. (RLG) is a consortium of institutions whose primary goal is to provide information to the scholarly community through cooperative programs. RLG is perhaps most commonly known for the bibliographic data management system that supports the programs of the corporation, the Research Libraries Information Network (RLIN). However, RLG's activities are guided by four major programs: RLIN, Collection Management and Development, Shared Resources, and Preservation. Each of these programs considers the unique characteristics of serials processing and handling.

### Cooperative Purchase Decisions

A component of the Collection Management and Development Program is an on-line cooperative purchase file. This file consists of purchase decision data for serials and expensive monographs. RLG member institutions enter new serials subscriptions, as well as orders for expensive monographic material into the RLIN In Process File in the form of "CPF" (Cooperative Purchase File) records. Records are created, modified, and deleted according to policies and procedures established in the Collection Management and Development Program. Each CPF record contains bibliographic information to identify the unique item and gives the complete and up-to-date acquisition decision on that item, such as "order and date," "not ordered," or "under consideration."

The purchase decision records can be searched by all RLG members and other RLIN users before placing any orders. Material selectors at any RLG institution can then choose to defer or avert purchasing an item not required locally to which access is assured through RLG's Shared Resources Program.

RLG expects to enter serial subscription records for its members in this way only until the new RLIN network acquisition system is installed and users can enter purchase decision data in their own acquisitions records as well as search each other's records.

## Serials Loan and Access

Through the Shared Resources Program, items not available at one member institution may be requested through loan or photocopy from the resources held by another RLG library. Such loans are guided by the RLG Borrowing and Lending Policy statement. Certain materials, such as serials (unless the material needed exceeds the RLG photocopy limit), should not ordinarily be requested for interlibrary loan purposes, but may be lent at the discretion of the holding library.

Interlibrary loan requests are transmitted between RLG libraries via an on-line message system. Although not characterized as a full interlibrary loan system, the RLG message system permits members to create, send, and respond to on-line interlibrary loan requests. If a member cannot, after searching the on-line data base, identify a holding library, the seeker can direct a request to the RLG Verification Service, which will then search additional location sources like the RLG Union List of Serials and the Center for Research Libraries. If a holder is found, the Verification Service redirects the on-line request to this holding library, which can respond directly to the original requester.

In the event that serials or other materials are not available through loan or photocopy, RLG's On-Site Access Policy statement defines conditions of reciprocal access that make such materials available to all qualified faculty and students of member institutions. This statement provides for admittance to another member library by showing one's own university identification.

## The Bibliographic Data Base: Serials

The Research Libraries Information Network is the automated bibliographic network supporting the programs of RLG. The system enables users to search and catalog on-line in the U.S. MARC Books, Films, Maps, Music (Scores and Sound Recordings), and Serials formats using data bases of records already catalogued by the Library of Congress and by other RLIN users, including 74,000 records of the Stanford Union List of Serials project. The latter are brief records representing all the serials currently received by the Stanford University Libraries and all their serials catalogued since 1972. These records are being expanded and upgraded by Stanford library staff on-line in a three-year project aimed toward producing a union catalog together with the University of California's Berkeley and Los Angeles libraries.

The updates and additional serials cataloguing records issued by LC on MARC tapes are routinely added to the RLIN data base. The data base was augmented in the summer of 1980 by the addition of CONSER records and Yale University serials archive machine-readable records, the first of many member library archival tapes scheduled for loading into the data base.

RLIN Serials records are indexed and accessible by:

— Personal name
— Corporate/conference name word
— Title word
— Subject heading word
— Corporate/conference name phrase
— Title phrase
— Subject heading phrase
— Update date
— Record ID number
— Call number (local)
— Class number (numbers assigned by the Library of Congress)
— Coded Serial Name (CODEN)
— LC Card Number
— Government Document Number
— International Standard Serial Number (ISSN)
— Library Data Number (local data number, acquisition number, circulation number, local system identification number)

### Aspects of Searching

Search requests can range from single statements asking for records containing one index value to statements with boolean operators ("and," "or," "and not," "not") asking for records containing multiple or alternative values. Search requests can be made specific through combining values from one or more indexes; they can be made general through specifying one or few values.

In its simplest form the search request consists of the basic command "find," an abbreviated index name, and a search value. For example, "find t educational measurement" will retrieve all records with the words "educational" and "measurement" in their titles. One can modify a search request just carried out by specifying additional search values (and indexes if necessary), using a boolean operator. For example:

find cn [corporate name word] geological survey

the system would respond with a message like

FIND CN GEOLOGICAL SURVEY   -RESULT : 87 IN LC [i.e., in the subset of Library of Congress subscription service records in the Serials data base]

Without reiterating the "find" command, a user could then key

    and t water

and the system would respond

    FIND CN GEOLOGICAL SURVEY AND T WATER   -RESULT : 15
    IN LC

Search results may be displayed in five display screen formats: multiple, short, partial, long, and full. The display chosen depends on the type of information desired for technical processing and/or public service applications. For example, the multiple record display gives only the main entry, uniform title, title, and imprint information from each record retrieved in a search request for as many records as can be formatted on a video terminal screen at one time, so that the user can quickly scan a set of records retrieved (Exhibit 1). The full record display is a tagged list of all the data in a record. The partial

```
1) THE LIBRARY QUARTERLY. ([Chicago]) v. 1- Jan. 1931-    [32012448//R43] CS111

2) Denver Medical Society. LIBRARY QUARTERLY. (Denver.)                   CS100
                        Multiple Record Display Example
                              Exhibit 1
```

```
    The Library quarterly. v. 1-   Jan. 1931- [Chicago] University of Chicago
Press.
    v. ill. (incl. facsims.) plates, plans, diagrs. 25 cm.

    Quarterly.
    "A Journal of investigation and discussion in the field of library science.
Established by the Graduate Library School of the Universtiy of Chicago with the
co-operation of the American Library Association, the Bibliographical Society of
America, and the American Library Institute."
    Indexed by: Library literature ISSN 0024-2373  Public affairs information
service.
    Available on microfilm from University Microfilms.
    INDEXES: Vols. 1-5, 1931-35.  1 v.; Vols. 6-10, 1936-40, with v. 10; Vols.
11-15, 1941-45.  1 v.
    Editors: 1931-Oct. 1942, W. M. Randall; Jan. 1943-  L. Carnovsky.
    Key title: The Library quarterly (Chicago), ISSN 0024-2519

    1. Library science--Periodicals.  I. Randall, William Madison, 1890- ed.  II.
Carnovsky, Leon, 1903- ed.  III. University of Chicago. Graduate Library School.
IV. Key title.
    CARD: 32012448//r43              LC: Z671 .L713

                    Long Record Display Example
                           Exhibit 2
```

record display includes the owning library's holdings for the title; the long record display includes all the bibliographic data in a record, including notes and tracings, in a catalog card format (Exhibit 2).

To retrieve a broad result for bibliographic or shelflist browsing, the user can make search requests general using the truncation symbol, a pound/number sign (#). For example, "find t librar#" will retrieve all the records in the data base that have the word stem "librar" in their titles; e.g., words like "librarian," "librarians," "librarianship," "libraries," "library."

To retrieve explicit descriptive bibliographic information, the user can qualify searches of the personal name, title word, title phrase, corporate/conference word, corporate/conference phrase, ISBN, and CODEN indexes by one of four sources in the record where the information is to be found. These source qualifications are:

| | |
|---|---|
| Primary Tags | (MARC tags 020, 030, 246, & 247—for Serials records only, 100, 110, 111, 130, 210, 212, 222, 240, 242, 243, 245) |
| Series Tags | (MARC tags 400, 410, 411, 440, 800, 810, 811, 830, 840) |
| Additional Tags | (MARC tags 700, 710, 711, 730, 740) |
| Linking Tags | (MARC tags 760, 762, 765, 767, 770, 772, 775—for Serials records only, 776, 777, 780, 785, 787) |

When individual words are too common to produce usable results, RLIN offers the user an alternative approach. Titles, corporate/conference names, and subject headings are also indexed as complete phrases, without any exclusion words or stop lists. The user can search for an explicit, full phrase or a truncated phrase through these indexes; for example, "find cp american association for the united nations."

*Overview of Cataloging*

Cataloging in RLIN means the entering of bibliographic data into one's on-line catalog file from one of three sources: creating original input; deriving a record from one already in the data base; adding copies to an already created record. On a "fill-in-the blanks" formatted input screen, users key or modify bibliographic data with appropriate indicators and subfield delimiters to conform to their libraries' catalog conventions (Exhibit 3).

A catalog record, once entered, may be recalled in the catalog maintenance function to make changes necessary to improve or correct content or to keep the record up to date by adding, deleting, or altering control, bibliographic, and/or holdings information.

The holdings portion of the input screen prompts a record-level holdings structure as well as location- and copy-level structures to record the specific holdings of a title. Here one also indicates whether or not cards are to be produced and/or tape records generated, and any variations in or additions to the cards beyond the specifications of one's established catalog card profile. Serials cards may look different from books cards because of special codes that indicate what data elements are printed, what cards are produced, and whether cards reflect a union shelflist or not.

Record-level information includes the initials of the cataloguer and of the terminal operator, the call number (if there is one) for the record, holdings

```
ID:CS1755858         DF:751101  FD:05/18/80  UD:05/18/80  MS:c EL:    ISDS:1
CC:111  REC:as   MOD:    DCF:    CSC:      ALPH:a    CON:     TP:u
CP:ilu   L:eng   SL:0    GPC:    CPI:0     INDX:u    CMI:1    TYP:p
PC:c      PD:1931/9999   FRQ:q   REG:r     PMDM:     REP:     IS:
010     32012448//r43
022     0024-2519
040     ‡cMUL‡dCtY‡dDLC‡dNSDP
042     lc‡ansdp
050  0  Z671‡b.L713
082     020.5
222 14 The Library quarterly‡b(Chicago)
245 04 The Library quarterly.
260 00 [Chicago]‡bUniversity of Chicago Press.
265     The University of Chicago Press, 11030 S. Langley Ave., Chicago, IL 60626
300     v.‡bill. (incl. facsims.) plates, plans, diagrs.‡c25 cm.
350     $16.00 (U.S. institution)‡a$12.00 (U.S. individual)‡a$9.60 (U.S.
        student)‡a$17.00 (foreign institution)‡a$13.00 (foreign individual)‡a$10.60
        (foreign student)
362  0  v. 1-  Jan. 1931-
500     "A journal of investigation and discussion in the field of library
        science. Established by the Graduate Library School of the University of
        Chicago with the co-operation of the American Library Association, the
        Bibliographical Society of America, and the American Library Institute."
510  0  Library literature‡x0024-2373
510  0  Public affairs information service.
530     Available on microfilm from University Microfilms.
555     Vols. 1-5, 1931-35. 1 v.; Vols. 6-10, 1936-40, with v. 10; Vols. 11-15,
        1941-45. 1 v.
570     Editors: 1931-Oct. 1942, W. M. Randall; Jan. 1943-  L. Carnovsky.
650   0 Library science‡xPeriodicals.
700  11 Randall, William Madison, 1890-‡eed.
700  11 Carnovsky, Leon,‡d1903-‡eed.
710  20 University of Chicago.‡bGraduate Library School.
871  10 ‡j710/1‡aChicago.‡bUniversity.‡bGraduate Library School.

LSI     ‡a041962A‡bMULS‡a  U1p   No.  4734900001‡aPITT NO.
        4752000008‡a311940‡bUSPS
PUC     ‡aUnknown‡aApr. 1976 (surrogate)
```

Full Record Display Example
Exhibit 3

on a multivolume edition, instructions to the system on whether or not to produce cards for the record, and specific information needed to govern whether or not tracings, local notes, and/or footnotes will appear on cards. Immediately after these record-level fields, local data fields may be input, such as ANSI Standard Serial Holdings Summary Statement, identification of the piece used for cataloguing, and private local information.

Location-level information includes the permanent shelving location, instructions to the system on whether to produce cards for the local catalog, and holdings in this location of a multivolume edition.

Copy-level information includes the copy number and volume number, if applicable, of an item held in a specific location, as well as copy-specific information. Users may key values for a number of different locations and copies in just one location field and one copy field, and the system will expand their input into the correct number of unique, associated data fields to represent each copy in each location (Exhibit 4).

## Summary

Serials information and handling are represented in several programs and activities of the Research Libraries Group; in Collection Management and Development through the Cooperative Purchase File; in Shared Resources through the message system as well as the lending and borrowing policy statements; in technical processing through use of RLIN for cataloguing; and in public services through the various RLIN indexes and record display formats. The on-line RLIN serials data base, which provides bibliographic and holdings information for the member libraries, is an on-line catalog that underpins all RLG programs.

# AUTOMATED SERIALS ACQUISITIONS IN THE WASHINGTON LIBRARY NETWORK

David E. Griffin
Bruce Ziegman

ABSTRACT. This article discusses automated serials acquisitions in the Washington Library Network. The general features of WLN's Acquisitions Subsystem are first presented, followed by a more specific analysis of the Subsystem's serials features. The implementation of the Subsystem by the Washington State Library's Serials Section is then reviewed, with particular attention to the issues, problems, and solutions of the first few months of automation.

Flexible fund accounting, automatic claiming, multiple access points to orders in-process, links to bibliographic data base for preorder searching, the ability to monitor payments for all types of serials—these are some of the important features librarians look for in an automated acquisitions system. Since the Summer of 1978 the Washington Library Network (WLN) has provided an Acquisitions Subsystem which includes these capabilities and many more. In this article we will discuss the general features of WLN's Acquisitions Subsystem, look more specifically at the ways in which it handles serials, and then review the implementation of the Subsystem by the Washington State Library Serials Section.

## Background

In 1972, WLN began providing automated services to Pacific Northwest libraries with the production of the Resource Directory, a book catalog which included the holdings of nine Washington libraries. Rapid growth of the catalog forced an early change to a microfiche format, and the Directory has now grown to over one-half million titles. In mid-1977, the nine libraries were brought on-line. They were provided with on-line access to a bibliographic data base for shared cataloguing and catalog maintenance, featuring an Authority File and rigorous quality control standards, as well as a holdings file complete with local library call numbers. One year later the Acquisitions Subsystem was made available on-line.

Of the 60* libraries now on-line to WLN, over one-third are using the Acquisitions Subsystem. Acquisitions users range in size from large and medium-sized university libraries such as the Washington State University and Boise State University libraries, to medium-sized public libraries such as the Timberland and Sno-Isle Regional Libraries. Both the Washington and Idaho State Libraries use the Acquisitions Subsystem, as do several private colleges, universities, and community colleges.

## General Features of WLN's Acquisitions Subsystem

Preorder searching and verification have always been time-consuming elements in the acquisitions process. Acquisitions Subsystem users have access to WLN's bibliographic data base of nearly 2 million titles, which consists of the LC MARC, COMARC, and GPO records, supplemented by the original cataloguing of WLN participants. The data base can be searched by author, title, subject, series, LC card number, ISBN, and ISSN, including "boolean" search combinations. Key word searches can be done on all corporate headings (name, subject, and series) and on title searches.

Because of the numerous access points, preorder searching can often be done successfully with incomplete or imprecise order information. Once a title is verified on the bibliographic data base and selected for ordering, the terminal operator generates an acquisitions record in the "In-Process File," WLN's on-line order file. Since it is linked to the bibliographic record, the acquisitions record can be retrieved by all the above-mentioned bibliographic access points (author, title, ISSN, etc.) as well as by a unique "Purchase Order" number. In addition, all WLN libraries can use the bibliographic access to view brief order information (such as vendor selected, list price, order date, and receipt date) input by the Acquisitions users. Selected bibliographic fields are automatically printed on Purchase Order form and rarely need to be typed.

The automatic claiming option is also flexible. Libraries establish their own claiming intervals. If an order does not arrive within the allotted time, a claim letter is automatically printed and mailed to the library for review. The claiming intervals are established as "profile" options, but can be easily altered, over-ridden, or entirely suspended for individual orders or for the library as a whole. Issue-by-issue claiming of serials is not currently provided.

A variety of accounting features are available. The number of individual accounts which a library can create is virtually unlimited (the current number of accounts per library ranges from five to well over 500). Encumbrance, liquidation, and disbursement transactions are recorded for each order and are summarized for each account as well as for the library budget as a whole.

---

*WLN participants are located in Alaska, Idaho, Montana, Oregon, and Washington. WLN has one participant in Arizona.

The balances for each account are available on-line, and weekly summaries are available on printed reports. The system automatically calculates sales tax, when necessary, and produces printed vouchers for payment. A paper accounting trail is provided for each accounting transaction.

Other noteworthy features of WLN's Acquisition Subsystem are: (1) a permanent archival or history file on magnetic tape (microfiche copy is also provided) of all past acquisitions activity; (2) end of year/beginning of year processing which automatically brings outstanding encumbrances forward to the new fiscal year; (3) complete order processing for nonbibliographic items such as office supplies; (4) processing of prepayments and partial payments; (5) a variety of printed products including Purchase Orders, Claim Letters, lists of In-Process File records and serial records, notification and "vendor report" cards, an "Exceptional Conditions Report" which detects problems in individual orders, and other management reports.

## Serials Features

The Standing Orders File is the second major on-line file in the WLN Acquisitions Subsystem. Virtually any type of material that is received on an ongoing basis can be maintained in this file, including periodicals of any frequency, monographic series, annuals, and items received on an irregular basis. All the bibliographic access points (author, title, ISSN, series, etc.) are available for searching this file. Standing Orders File records need not represent an individual bibliographic item; blanket orders, depository accounts, membership accounts, and the like can also be established and monitored as Standing Order records.

The basic purpose of the serials feature is to process and monitor payments. Each time an invoice is received for a Standing Orders File record, the record is copied to the In-Process file for payment. When payment is completed, the In-Process File record is in turn copied to the archival History File and the accounting transactions are copied back to the Standing Orders File creating an on-line payment history for all Standing Orders File records. Approximately twenty payment records can be maintained on-line for each Standing Orders File record. Remarks can be added to each accounting transaction so that years later the payment history will reveal the exact dates, volumes, and so forth, covered by each payment as well as the account number used to pay for it. Thus, the fact that the library subscribes to a particular serial can be quickly verified and its payment history made readily available on-line.

A number of reports are available which are of importance to serials acquisitions: (1) The Renewal List reports Standing Orders File records which are overdue for automatic renewal by the vendor, according to an overdue interval determined by the library. (2) The Reorder List alerts a library to records which must be reordered periodically. The warning can be produced as far in advance of the reorder date as the library chooses. (3) The Mail Room Distribution List specifies branch locations for titles in the Standing Orders File to aid a library's mail room in distributing issues. (4) The Standing Orders File Title Index lists all records in the file in title order. (5) WLN is now beginning to produce management reports from the Standing Orders File. The first is the Costcenter Report, which subdivides titles according to a predetermined scheme (e.g., subject or department). Invoice information is included for each title and category.

One of the most difficult areas in serials acquisitions is duplicate control for monographic series. Since the payment record is maintained under the series in the Standing Orders File, there is no automatic indication in the In-Process File of which titles have arrived. An In-Process File record can be established for each title in the series to help prevent duplication, but this is an additional procedure. This problem, as well as better methods of tying together items which arrive on monographic series and memberships, is currently being studied.

Also under consideration for development are the direct placement of orders with vendors (either by magnetic tape or on-line connection) and the ability to process serials invoices received on magnetic tape so that the information need not be keyed in manually.

## Implementing the Subsystem

In January 1980, the Serials Section of the Washington State Library began converting all currently received serials—some 5,500 titles—to the WLN Acquisitions Subsystem. At first thought, the project seemed staggering, but the Serials Staff took some comfort from the fact that the State Library's Acquisitions Section had been ordering books and other materials on the new system since June 1978, and that after two years' experience the automated ordering and invoicing process was running very smoothly.

Still, the new demands of the automated Standing Orders File, the multiplicity of order plans used by the library, and the necessity of consolidating three separate manual check-in files posed new problems. It was not surprising that the first month was spent in discussions between the WLN Acquisitions Services Librarian and various members of the State Library's Technical Services staff, and in training of Serials Section staff members.

A number of questions had to be answered before the project could begin: How many and what types of serials should be converted to the new system— should just those publications traditionally defined as "standing orders" be placed into the Standing Orders File, or should all currently received serials, including periodicals and newspapers, also be placed in the new system? Should the project be limited to the placing of titles into the In-Process File as each new invoice arrived, where they would automatically copy to the Standing Order Files at the copy-to-history point, or should the titles be keyed directly into the Standing Orders File? How could the two large annual invoices from the Library's two subscription agents best be handled under the new system?

These problems were further compounded by the existence of three separate manual check-in files: a "serials file" that was on the way to becoming a single central serials check-in record, and two other files, a periodical kardex and a "direct file" of standing orders, that were gradually being phased out as their titles were converted to the serials file. The direct file was particularly vexing to most staff members; shifting back and forth between the Serials and Acquisitions Sections, it has grown like Topsy over the years. Worst of all, unlike the other files, it was not arranged by title; instead, the standing order cards were filed every which way—although, admittedly, title or issuing agency were the two most likely starting points in finding a particular standing order. In addition, separate payment record cards for all but those orders in the direct file had already been created and established in the serials file. In considering all of this, it became obvious that the project would be dual in nature and that a large part of it would involve streamlining and consolidating the manual files as the orders were being converted to the automated system.

Some of these issues quickly resolved themselves as staff members became familiar with the WLN Acquisition Subsystem's capabilities. As previously mentioned, the system is actually designed to accommodate all types of serial orders, whether standing order or subscription, membership, blanket order, or depository account. The traditional standing orders or subscriptions are placed in the In-Process File by linking an order screen to a record from the bibliographic files. Memberships, depository accounts, and blanket orders are entered by creating an "unlinked" record—a record solely for use in the Standing Orders File with no link to the bibliographic files, such as "American Library Association institutional membership" or "NTIS depository account." It was therefore quickly decided to convert all currently received serials to the new system, regardless of type or order scheme.

The five staff members of the Serials Section, together with the Serials Librarian, did much of the subsequent planning and eventually worked out a system that fell neatly (and perhaps too neatly) into existing job descriptions. In order to complete the conversion as quickly as possible, a Clerk-Typist III who was responsible for serial acquisitions would enter the serial orders into the In-Process File with the arrival of each new invoice. Her assistant, a Clerk-Typist I, would begin with the first drawer of the serials file and enter titles directly into the Standing Orders File. At the same time, two of the three staff members on the bibliographic side of the Section would concentrate on converting the manual files to a single check-in file. In addition, one of the three, a Library Technician II, would assist in some of the bibliographic aspects of the automated conversion, such as locating particularly hard to find titles in the data base and entering interim records (brief cataloguing records for titles not found in the data base).

*Problems and Solutions*

The work plan looked logical enough on paper, but some problems quickly surfaced as the project got underway. It soon became apparent that the neatly divided responsibility owed as much to a rivalry between two of the serials staff members and the resultant territorial imperatives than to any independently rational plan of operation. Each was on guard against the possibility that any of her new automated duties might resemble too closely the previous manual duties of the other. This fairly common library problem was eased through a series of staff meetings and conferences and solved through the chance resignation of one of the two (for reasons unrelated to the question at hand). It soon became obvious, though, that regardless of what personnel problems might exist, conversion to an automated acquisitions system signals a whole new day—that old responsibilities and divisions of duties need complete reevaluation. In particular, it seems critical that all members of a serials staff understand a new automated system and have a stake in it and that all be expected to have a solid, well-rounded knowledge of the entire system. From a practical point of view the "all hands" approach is necessary anyway, at least during the first stages of the conversion, if progress is to be made. The cost of continuing traditional divisions of labor at the onset of an automated system is likely to be a slow rate of progress in converting to the new system and a resultant lack of faith among the staff in what the new system can accomplish.

The first six months of the project, in retrospect, went rather smoothly, in spite of the usual day-to-day difficulties that seemed earthshaking at the time. Most often, problems encountered were a matter of insufficient knowledge of system capabilities that a quick conversation with the WLN Acquisitions Services Librarian would solve: how to handle a depository account or membership on the system, for example, or the difference in accounting functions between a new and existing standing order. A few of the problems concerned coordination between the Library's Business Office and the Serials Section, such as how often to order Receiving Reports (the system produced voucher form) or how many accounts to establish in the automated files for the State Library and its branches. These, too, were not difficult to resolve, but they did underline the fact that close cooperation between a business office and a serials section is essential for any library in the early stages of serials automation.

*The Faxon Invoice*

By August 1980, thanks to help from the Acquisitions Section staff, all currently received serials from "A" to "H" were in the Standing Orders File. At this point, the 1981 quotations from the F. W. Faxon Company arrived— the precursor to the State Library's largest annual invoice for materials, a

$50,000 invoice for renewal of some 1,450 titles. Faced with the problem of putting the Faxon invoice into the system, the staff decided to drop the strictly alphabetical approach for the time being and key the titles from the quotations directly into the Standing Orders File. Upon arrival of the invoice, titles entered in this way could merely be copied to the In-Process File for payment rather than being keyed in as new orders (a process that takes considerably longer). In the four weeks that followed, with as many staff keying in orders as could be spared, nearly seventy-five percent of the 1,450 titles had been entered into the Standing Orders File. With invoices in hand, three staff members began copying the records into the In-Process File for payment as the others continued the first phase of the project. Altogether, the Faxon invoice took the three staff members five working days to complete, an interval that compares favorably to the nearly two weeks the invoice had taken the previous year. Once all of the titles are in the system, the process will be considerably shortened, so even more time will be saved in succeeding years. The other large subscription invoice, from the Ebsco Company, will be processed in the same way, and the staff will then return to the manual serials file and proceed alphabetically. Altogether, the entire conversion of all currently received serials should take about one year, the corresponding consolidation of the separate files into a single check-in file an additional six months.

Halfway into the project, how would we evaluate our progress? What did we do right (on purpose or inadvertently) and what would we have done differently? In retrospect, the decision to involve all serials staff members in the planning and implementation of the project has proven well worth the extra time and effort necessary at the outset. No staff member has been pigeon-holed into one small facet of the project, and all have been given a chance to learn the entire system. This has kept morale high, and even during times when problems occurred, the approach has generally been one of finding the solution together rather than assigning the responsibility to a single person. On balance, it would have been better to start keying in titles from Faxon and Ebsco from the outset and then go back to pick up what was left; this would have saved some time later on. In other respects, the conversion has gone as smoothly as we hoped for: orders are being processed and invoices paid more quickly than before, and (for the past three months) with one less staff member than when we started. Even the one staunch holdout on the staff is grudgingly admitting the benefits of automated serials acquisitions and is no longer anxious to return to the typing of field orders and voucher distribution forms. No one suggested that all problems would disappear with the new system, and in fact they haven't, but we are doing more with fewer people and doing it more accurately.

# NATIONWIDE NETWORKING AND THE NETWORK ADVISORY COMMITTEE

Lenore S. Maruyama

ABSTRACT. The activities of the Network Advisory Committee, which was established to advise the Library of Congress on issues related to network planning, are described in terms of three phases: (1) its first year of existence from 1976 to 1977; (2) a transition phase from 1977 to 1979; and (3) a third phase from 1980 onward. The advisory committee has made substantial progress toward the goal of a nationwide library network but in a way quite different from its original intent.

## Introduction

The year 1976 ushered in a new player in the networking arena: the group that eventually became known as the Network Advisory Committee. Although its entrance had not been heralded by fireworks and universal acclaim as other events had been during that Bicentennial Year, it did generate considerable interest in the library and information communities as well as some concern. This article provides the highlights of the advisory committee's activities and attempts to describe these activities in terms of the broader framework of a nationwide network for library and information services.

The concepts of networks and networking were not new to the library and information profession, but by the mid-1970s, the period in which the Network Advisory Committee was established, the library network organizations had started to use computer and telecommunications facilities to perform many of their services. There was also a proliferation of network organizations, virtually all of which were referred to by their initials or acronyms and were unique in their governance structure, services, membership, and so forth. In other words, no two organizations were exactly alike. Also, no mechanism existed by which the network organizations or the libraries themselves could coordinate their activities and work toward common goals.

The idea for an advisory committee for a nationwide library network can be traced to two reports. The first, entitled *Toward a National Program for Library and Information Services: Goals for Action,* was issued by the National Commission on Libraries and Information Science (NCLIS) in 1975. This report recommended that a nationwide network of library and information services be planned, developed, and implemented "to tie together information systems at all levels: federal, multistate, individual state, and local, as well as compatible systems found in the private sector."[1] The NCLIS program document assigned specific responsibilities to the organizations at all of these levels, including the Library of Congress for whom the following statement was made: "The participation of the Library of Congress is crucial to the development of a National Program and to the operation of the nationwide network because it has the capacity and the materials to perform many common services in both the areas of technical processing and reference and because it can set the national bibliographic standards for the program."[2]

To provide further detail on its responsibilities, the Library of Congress commissioned a study in 1975 resulting in the report *The Role of the Library of Congress in the Evolving National Network*. The study attempted to identify in what areas and how the Library could support the activities of the network organizations and larger resource libraries that were potential participants in the national network. One of the principal findings of the study was that the "Library of Congress should assume leadership of network development activities by performing the major coordinating role in applying technology and acquiring funding for the technical and standards-related tasks required to link federal, multistate, state, and local systems into the national network."[3] The report also contained two recommendations related to this topic: "Meetings should be held with appropriate individuals to develop the specifications for the telecommunications and computer architecture of the distributed computer processing system required by the national network...and with appropriate individuals to determine the organizational structure of the national network so that the levels and the access routes by which individual libraries are served by the network can be defined."[4]

Another event that had a direct effect on the Network Advisory Committee occurred in early 1976 when the Library of Congress established an office for the Special Assistant for Network Development (later named the Network Development Office) headed by Henriette D. Avram, a long-time leader in library automation, to allow the Library to participate more actively in national network planning. The stage was now set for the entrance of the new network planning group.

The following sections describe briefly the activities of the Network Advisory Committee in terms of three phases, roughly the periods 1976–77, 1977–79, and 1980 onward. The actual chronology of events is given in Appendix I, and other reports can be consulted for specific details.[5]

### The First Year

On April 12, 1976, senior representatives from several of the major network organizations attended a meeting at the Library of Congress at the invitation of the Deputy Librarian of Congress, William J. Welsh. Different networking issues were discussed, and the participants agreed that such a gathering was a useful vehicle for the exchange of ideas related to networking and should be continued. For the next meeting, the Network Development Office staff was requested to prepare a working paper incorporating the major points discussed earlier to provide a focus for the group's deliberations. Funding for this meeting and all but one of the subsequent ones was provided by the Council on Library Resources.

At the second meeting on August 9, 1976, Mr. Welsh asked that the attendees, as representatives of their organizations, act in an advisory capacity to the Library's Network Development Office as the Network Advisory Group. Having received a name, the group began its review of the working paper prepared by the LC staff and, with the assistance of several ad hoc subcommittees, started the refinement process that continued through the following two meetings. By the time the third meeting was held on December 3–4, 1976, the paper, which was viewed as an initial blueprint for nationwide library network planning, contained sufficient detail for specific tasks to be started. These tasks concentrated on a subset of the total network, namely, the library bibliographic component, whose purposes are to facilitate the sharing of bibliographic resources and to reduce the rate of increase of per-unit costs for bibliographic services. This component constitutes that part of the network encompassing a bibliographic service system and portions of a communications system but excludes for the time being a resource system to deliver needed items to a user.

The advisory group recommended that: (1) a task force of technical experts from the network organizations with operating automated systems be established to undertake the initial design work of the network architecture; (2) the Library of Congress conduct a study to determine the hardware configuration and resources required to operate a network bibliographic service; and (3) a subcommittee of the advisory group be assigned the task of investigating future network organization and management. The Library also announced that steps were being taken to establish the advisory group as an official Library of Congress committee.

The fourth and last meeting of the "original" Network Advisory Group took place on April 11–12, 1977, exactly a year after that first informal gathering of network representatives. Shortly after this meeting, the Librarian of Congress, Daniel J. Boorstin, established a Network Advisory Committee to advise the Library on matters related to nationwide network planning.

Although a limited distribution of the working paper had been made to members of the advisory group and their constituencies before this April 1977 meeting, only a few comments were received at this point. To give the paper greater prominence, the advisory group decided to hold a briefing at the annual conference of the American Library Association that June. It recommended that the comments received be incorporated into a revised version to be made available for the briefing. Thus, the paper *Toward a National Library and Information Service Network: The Library Bibliographic Component* was introduced to the library profession.[6]

Even with such short notice, the briefing attracted a standing-room crowd. A panel composed of Network Advisory Group members discussed the different sections of the paper and attempted to convey to the audience an appreciation of the complex issues involved. The advisory group had successfully cleared the first hurdle and was ready for the next one.

## The Second Phase

The newly constituted Network Advisory Committee met for the first time on November 28–29, 1977. Although the core of members of the Network Advisory Group remained the same under the new organization, some new members were added at this point. (The membership of the advisory group and the advisory committee is given in Appendix II).

Several things were set in motion, resulting in a completely different emphasis for the committee by the end of 1979. At the November 1977 meeting, the advisory committee approved a motion to create a steering committee to establish the agenda for the advisory committee's meetings and articulate the issues to be brought before the full committee. Before these tasks could be accomplished, the steering committee attempted to resolve some fundamental issues such as the credentials, goals, and objectives of the Network Advisory Committee.

Concurrently, the Council on Library Resources, an independent, nonprofit body established with Ford Foundation funds to support research and development activities to solve library problems, was in the process of preparing a five-year development plan for a comprehensive, computerized bibliographic system for review by several foundations that had an interest in library services. The council, whose representatives had been active participants in the work of the Network Advisory Committee, derived many of the key elements for the proposed program from the advisory committee's planning paper and the work performed by the Library of Congress Network Development Office. The council received funding for this plan, and its Bibliographic Service Development Program (BSDP) was officially established in November 1978.[7]

Discussions at the Network Advisory Committee's meetings during 1978 and 1979 indicated considerable confusion vis-à-vis the relationship of the committee and its activities to the BSDP. These issues were eventually resolved, as described below.

Other activities were also in progress. Following the advisory committee's recommendations, a task force of technical experts (which became known as the Network Technical Architecture Group) from the network organizations with operating automated systems was established to design the network architecture.

The group met several times during 1977 and 1978 and produced a general requirements document entitled *Message Delivery System for the National Library and Information Service Network,* which was reviewed and approved by the Network Advisory Committee at its May 1978 meeting. The advisory committee instructed the Network Technical Architecture Group to proceed with the specifications for detailed requirements of the message delivery system. The technical group prepared a request for proposal to obtain these detailed requirements with contractual support, and the proposal was submitted to the Council on Library Resources for possible funding. This project was eventually subsumed by activities conducted by the Council's Bibliographic Service Development Program, which is using the general requirements document mentioned above as a starting point.

Another task identified during the initial stages of the advisory committee's deliberations was to investigate network organization and management. A subcommittee had been established to work on this issue; its report, in the form of a work statement, was submitted to the advisory committee at its meeting in May 1978. The advisory committee subsequently recommended that the latest version of the work statement be turned over to the Council on Library Resources for consideration in its Bibliographic Service Development Program.

Dissemination of the advisory committee's paper *Toward a National Library and Information Service Network: The Library Bibliographic Component* triggered many responses from the profession. In terms of the work of the advisory committee, the response from the Association of American Publishers was important in that it recommended investigating the potential role of the nonlibrary sector in the proposed network. Two meetings were held in 1978 and 1979 with individuals representing the organizations in this sector, resulting in a formal proposal to establish a subcommittee to bring together the different parts of the nonlibrary sector and to involve them more actively in the planning and development of the network. The subcommittee presented a plan for action to the advisory committee, but since this presentation occurred at a point when the advisory committee itself was in a transition stage, the plan was not acted upon. The advisory committee, however, did recommend that the four principal organizations involved in this effort, the American Society for Information Science, the Association of American Publishers, the Information Industry Association, and the National Federation of Abstracting and Indexing Services, be given member status in the Network Advisory Committee.

The September 25, 1979, meeting was a watershed in that it resulted in a new statement of goals and objectives, including as a key provision that the Network Advisory Committee should serve as a focal point for the identification of issues and formulation of recommendations with regard to nationwide network planning and policy. The other goals and objectives were to advise the Librarian of Congress on the role of the Library in a nationwide network, provide information to the Council on Library Resources on the design and development of a nationwide network, provide a forum for the several segments of the library and information communities to contribute to the development of network specifications, serve as a coordinating body for networking activities, keep informed through status reports provided by operating entities in networking, and publicize networking activities to interested persons.

The advisory committee compiled a list of topics for discussion and picked one as a prototype for the new mode of operation. A planning subcommittee was then appointed to work out the details for the program. Thus, the second and most difficult phase of the Network Advisory Committee's existence came to a conclusion.

## The Third Phase

In its first program session on March 4–5, 1980, the Network Advisory Committee tackled the topic of the ownership and distribution of bibliographic data. This issue was of great concern to all parties in the public/private, and for-profit/not-for-profit sectors because the unprecedented growth of machine-readable bibliographic files and the uses and services derived from them have created relationships for which precedence and ground rules do not exist.

The advisory committee concluded that access to bibliographic information must be granted in a way that preserves the economic incentive of those providing the records while at the same time preserving the tradition of wide dissemination of bibliographic information. It also recommended that a six-month project be undertaken with contractual support to identify the current and potential creators, modifiers, and possessors of machine-readable bibliographic information and to get their endorsement of this meeting; to determine their current plans for shared access to bibliographic data; and to determine their requirements for fair compensation or other recognition for their data so that mechanisms for shared access to bibliographic information could be established.

While this discussion only scratched the surface of the issue, it did bring together the diverse interests in the library and information communities and provided a meaningful structure in which to explore complex problems. The meeting was a success not only in terms of its results but also as a framework for the operations of the Network Advisory Committee. In its meeting on October 1–2, 1980, the advisory committee will be addressing the problem of governance in a nationwide network.

In terms of an administrative structure, the Network Advisory Committee now has separate subcommittees to plan the individual program sessions. The structure was left flexible enough to allow discussion of the issues to take place over several meetings if necessary, and the selection of the issues to be discussed would be based on wide appeal, interest, or concern to the entire membership. In addition, a subcommittee was appointed to establish membership criteria for the advisory committee.

## In Retrospect

The accomplishments of the Network Advisory Committee have been considerable, particularly viewed from the standpoint of the complex nature of the problems for which it sought solutions, the relatively short period of time in which it has been operating, and the informal structure of the group. Putting "flesh" on the "skeleton" that comprises the full-scale nationwide network of library and information services envisioned by the National Commission on Libraries and Information Science was not an easy task. One approach taken by the advisory committee was to limit the scope of its initial efforts to the library bibliographic component so that tasks to provide tangible results over a three-year period for a smaller constituency, specifically the part of the profession concerned with bibliographic control, could be accomplished. While the initial efforts may have involved only a subset of the total profession, dissemination of the results of this work (in the form of briefings, articles, papers, etc.) was made to everyone. The advisory committee itself organized sessions at two annual conferences of the American Library Association to describe its work, and the staff of the Library of Congress Network Development Office presented papers and talks at numerous meetings of other professional organizations and library networks. The success of this approach can be seen in the fact that the profession began to think more actively of how the resource component, that is, the capability to share materials and get desired items to the ultimate users, would fit into this framework, and in the further fact that the nonlibrary sector gained a vehicle whereby common problems faced by it and the library sector with regard to networking could be tackled.

In terms of an organizational structure, the Network Advisory Committee is essentially a volunteer group whose continued existence indicates the support and commitment of the members' parent organizations. Although the Council on Library Resources has provided funds for a portion of the members' travel expenses, the parent organizations have supported this effort by allowing their personnel to attend the advisory committee meetings and spending time on specific projects.

In reviewing the activities of the Network Advisory Committee over the last four years, one dominant feature appears: the committee's evolving character.

A few notable developments:

— Its membership started off with primarily representatives from library network organizations, expanded to include representatives from professional library associations, and finally included representatives from the nonlibrary sector.

— Its planning paper *Toward a National Library and Information Service Network: The Library Bibliographic Component* presented an initial blueprint for only one component of the total nationwide network, and its activities were geared toward this narrower path. By 1980, its scope was broadened to reflect the interests of its diverse membership.

— During its first year, the advisory committee acted as an operating entity in that it produced a planning paper, and under its general direction several of the tasks outlined in the paper were begun. But by 1980 other groups took over such functions, and the Network Advisory Committee took on the role of a catalyst and forum.

As time passed, the role of the Network Advisory Committee has changed. It should be noted, however, that during its four-year history, the advisory committee had been performing a unique role by bringing together different segments of the profession to address some very complex issues in the area of networking. Few, if any, other groups can make that claim. What will happen in the 1980s? My guess is that many of the same problems, such as ownership and distribution of bibliographic data or governance of the nationwide network, will still exist, but technological advances, improvements, and the like will have added a new wrinkle that no one had considered before. The Network Advisory Committee now has the appropriate mechanism with which to identify problem areas and to begin the analysis and discussion that will lead to their resolution. It is hoped that as these problems are discovered, they will be given the attention they deserve.

## REFERENCES

1. National Commission on Libraries and Information Science. *Toward a National Program for Library and Information Services: Goals for Action* (Washington, D.C.: 1975), pp. 48-49.

2. *Ibid.*, p. 67.

3. Buckland, Lawrence F., and Basinski, William L. *The Role of the Library of Congress in the Evolving National Network* (Washington, D.C.: Library of Congress, 1978), p. 4.

4. *Ibid.*, p. 5.

5. Summaries of the meetings of the Network Advisory Committee have been included in the *Library of Congress Information Bulletin* as follows: April 12, 1976, meeting in the June 4, 1976, issue, p. 325; August 9, 1976, meeting in the September 24, 1976, issue, p. 585; December 3-4, 1976, meeting in the January 14, 1977, issue, pp. 18–19; April 11–12, 1977, meeting in the May 27, 1977, issue, pp. 347–48; November 28–29, 1977, in the January 20, 1978, issue, pp. 64–66; May 18–19, 1978, meeting in the July 7, 1978, issue pp. 398–400; November 20, 1978, meeting in the March 2, 1979, issue, pp. 73–76; April 10, 1979, meeting in the June 22, 1979, issue, pp. 232–33; September 25, 1979, meeting in the November 23, 1979, issue, pp. 483-84; and March 4–5, 1980, meeting in the May 30, 1980, issue, pp. 186–88.

6. Network Advisory Group. *Toward a National Library and Information Service Network: The Library Bibliographic Component,* Prelim. Ed. (Washington, D.C.: Library of Congress, June 1977).

7. Description of the overall program can be found in C. Lee Jones and Nancy Gwinn, "Bibliographic Service Development: A New CLR Program." *Journal of Library Automation* 12 (June 1979): 116–124. Specific aspects of the program are described in occasional articles such as "An Integrated Consistent Authority File Service for Nationwide Use." *Library of Congress Information Bulletin* 39 (July 11, 1980): 244–48.

8. Webster, Duane E., and Maruyama, Lenore S. *Ownership and Distribution of Bibliographic Data* (Washington, D.C.: Library of Congress, 1980). In press.

## Appendix 1

### Chronology

| | |
|---|---|
| April 12, 1976 | First meeting of network representatives at the Library of Congress |
| August 9, 1976 | Second meeting of network representatives; formally named Network Advisory Group |
| December 3–4, 1976 | Third meeting of Network Advisory Group |
| April 11–12, 1977 | Fourth meeting of Network Advisory Group |
| April 26, 1977 | Establishment of Network Advisory Committee announced |
| June 1977 | *Toward a National Library and Information Service Network: The Library Bibliographic Component* published |
| June 18, 1977 | Briefing at ALA annual conference, Detroit |
| November 28–29, 1977 | First meeting of Network Advisory Committee |
| May 18–19, 1978 | Second meeting of Network Advisory Committee |
| June 25, 1978 | Briefing at ALA annual conference, Chicago |
| November 20, 1978 | Third meeting of Network Advisory Committee |
| April 10, 1979 | Fourth meeting of Network Advisory Committee |
| September 25, 1979 | Fifth meeting of Network Advisory Committee |
| March 4–5, 1980 | First program meeting of Network Advisory Committee |

## Appendix II

### Network Advisory Committee Members

The following list of organizations represented on the Network Advisory Committee covers the period from April 1976 to the present. If the organization became a member after April 1976, the date of the beginning of its membership is noted. In addition to the official representative, some of the staff personnel from certain organizations who provided considerable support to the work of the committee are listed.

| *Organization* | *Representatives* |
|---|---|
| American Library Association, 1977– | Robert Wedgeworth<br>Carol Henderson<br>Joseph Shubert |

American Society for Information Science, 1979–

Ward Shaw (Colorado Alliance for Research Libraries)

AMIGOS Bibliographic Council

James Kennedy

Association of American Publishers, 1979–

Sandra Paul

Association for Research Libraries, 1977–

Richard Dougherty (University of Michigan)
William Studer (Ohio State University)

BALLOTS, 1976–78

David Weber (Stanford University)
Edward Shaw

Bibliographical Center for Research, 1977–

Donald Simpson
JoAn Segal

California Library Authority for Systems and Services, 1977–

Ronald Miller

Chief Officers of State Library Agencies, 1978–

Anne Marie Falsone
Patricia Broderick
Anthony Miele

Council for Computerized Library Networks 1976–1980?

James Dodson (University of Texas, Dallas)
Mary Jane Reed (Washington State Library)
Barbara Markuson (Indiana Cooperative Library Services Authority)

Council on Library Resources

Fred Cole
Lawrence Livingston *
Warren Haas
Lee Jones

Federal Library Committee

James Riley
Alphonse Trezza

Information Industry Association, 1979–

Paul Zurkowski
Robert Willard

Library of Congress

William Welsh
Henriette Avram
Carol Nemeyer
Lenore Maruyama

Medical Library Association, 1978–

Erika Love (University of New Mexico)

Midwest Region Library Network

John Metz
Joseph Treyz (University of Wisconsin)
James Skipper

National Agricultural Library, 1977–

Richard Farley
Wallace Olson
Samuel Waters

National Commission on Libraries and Information Science

Alphonse Trezza
Ruth Tighe
William Mathews
Andrew Aines
Toni Bearman

| | |
|---|---|
| National Federation of Abstracting and Indexing Services, 1979– | Toni Bearman<br>Lynne Neufeld<br>James Wood |
| National Library of Medicine, 1977– | Davis McCarn<br>Grace McCarn<br>Lois Ann Colaianni |
| New England Library Information Network | Ronald Miller<br>John Linford |
| OCLC, Inc. | Frederick Kilgour<br>Paul Schrank (University of Akron)<br>James Rush<br>Mary Ellen Jacob |
| Research Libraries Group | James Skipper<br>Edward Shaw<br>John Heyeck |
| Southeastern Library Network | James Govan (University of North Carolina)<br>James Boykin (University of North Carolina at Charlotte)<br>Charles Stevens *<br>Lee Handley |
| Special Libraries Association, 1978– | Irving Klempner (SUNY, Albany) |
| University of Chicago | Stanley McElderry<br>Charles Payne<br>Martin Runkle |
| Washington Library Network | Roderick Swartz<br>Ray DeBuse |
| Western Interstate Library Coordinating Organization, 1976–1977 | Eleanor Montague |

| *Observers* | *Representatives* |
|---|---|
| American Association of Law Libraries, 1979 | Betty Taylor (University of Florida) |
| Carnegie Corporation | Richard Sullivan |
| National Endowment for the Humanities | Margaret Child |

*Deceased.

# AUTOMATION AND THE SUBSCRIPTION AGENCY

F. F. Clasquin

ABSTRACT. This article traces the history of electronic data processing in the U.S. subscription business from the F. W. Faxon Company viewpoint. The motivation for changing the style and quality of subscription services is reviewed, and attention is given to the computer state of the art and how computers are used to meet the needs of agencies and libraries. Productivity which relates to costs of agency services, is traced over a twenty-five-year period, 1965–1980.

Mechanical methods for handling large volumes of cyclical financial transactions to support the permanent and temporary clerical staff were used by subscription agencies long before electronic data processing was an affordable alternative. These methods were organizational batch systems, manually operated, and assisted by simple mechanical devices which used multipurpose forms. The labor-intensive costs flowing from such a system limited the basic services of the subscription agency to ordering new and renewing journal subscriptions either for an individual or for a library.

Before 1960, most subscription agencies in the United States had a considerably greater interest in selling magazine subscriptions to individuals through local agents. Door-to-door sales labor was the most effective method of increasing circulation and was then only a very minor cost in the magazine publishing system. As a result, there were many catalog agencies represented by field agents selling subscriptions. A catalog agency is an enterprise which uses a field selling force and a catalog of prices for each magazine. Publishers required such an agency to publish a special "agents price" catalog (see Figure 1) from which the local agent could extract the price and properly remit payment for sold subscriptions to the agency represented. Some independent agents were able to sell and service library facilities such as small public or school libraries.

Once pictured as the twelve- to fifteen-year-old juvenile selling *Liberty* magazine and others to earn a bicycle, this sales force changed to adult representatives who could produce enough revenue to earn a living wage in the 1950s and 60s. As the cost of labor increased, a tragic turn in representation took place. Con artists drifted into the field and the physically handicapped were encouraged to act as representatives, taking advantage of the social con-

| | Pub. Price | Agts. Price | For. Post. | Can. Post. | P.A. Post. |
|---|---|---|---|---|---|
| **Canadian Med. Assn. Journal** | | | | | |
| Canadian Medical Association Journal W. | 12.00 | 12.00 | no | | no |
| Canadian Mining & Metallurgical Bulletin M. | 10.00 | 9.60 | | | |
| —, In U.S.A. and British Comlth .. | 12.00 | 11.60 | | | |
| —, Elsewhere | 15.00 | 14.60 | | | |
| Canadian Mining Journal (Canada) ..M. | 5.00 | 4.50 | | | |
| —, U.S.A. & Br. Commonwealth | 15.00 | 14.50 | | | |
| —, 2 years | 25.00 | 24.00 | | | |
| —, Foreign, P.A. & P.I. | 20.00 | 19.25 | | | |
| —, 2 years | 30.00 | 28.75 | | | |
| Canadian Modern Language Review .Q. | 4.00 | 4.00 | no | | no |
| Canadian Nurse (in Canada) ..M. | 3.00 | 2.80 | | | |
| — (In U. S. A.) | 3.50 | 3.30 | .50 | | .50 |
| Canadian Patent Office Record (in U.S.A. and Canada) ..M. | 40.00 | 40.00 | 15.00 | | 15.00 |
| Canadian Poetry Magazine ..Q. | 2.00 | 1.75 | no | | no |
| Canadian Statistical Review ..M. | 5.00 | 5.00 | 1.75 | | 1.75 |
| Canadian Surveyor .. 5 Nos. | 5.00 | 5.00 | no | | no |
| Canadian Textile Journal ..B.-W. | 6.00 | 5.60 | 4.00 | no | 4.00 |
| —, 2 years | 10.00 | 9.50 | 5.00 | no | 5.00 |
| —, 3 years | 14.00 | 13.25 | 6.00 | no | 6.00 |
| Canadian Transportation (in U. S. A.) M. | 10.00 | 18.00 | | | |
| — (in Canada) | 0.00 | 6.00 | 19.00 | | 19.00 |
| Canadian Welfare .. 7 Nos. | 2.50 | 2.50 | no | | no |
| Cancer ..B.-M. | 15.00 | 13.50 | 2.00 | no | no |
| Cancer Research, by Vol. ..M. | 15.00 | 14.50 | 1.00 | .50 | .50 |
| Candy Industry and Confectioners' Journal B.-W. | 5.00 | 4.50 | 2.00 | no | 2.00 |
| —, 3 years | 10.00 | 9.00 | 6.00 | | 6.00 |
| Canner/Packer ..M. | 5.00 | 4.60 | 5.00 | no | 5.00 |
| —, 2 years | 8.00 | 7.40 | 8.00 | | 8.00 |
| —, 3 years | 10.00 | 9.20 | 10.00 | | 10.00 |
| Canning Trade (1) ..W. | 5.00 | 4.60 | 2.00 | 1.00 | 2.00 |
| Capper's Weekly ..W. | 2.00 | 1.75 | | | |
| —, outside U.S.A. | 3.00 | 3.00 | | | |
| **CAR CRAFT** ..M. | 3.00 | 2.50 | 1.00 | no | 1.00 |
| —, 2 years | 5.00 | 4.50 | 2.00 | | 2.00 |
| —, 3 years | 7.00 | 6.50 | 3.00 | | 3.00 |
| Carnegie Magazine .. 10 Nos. | 2.00 | 1.75 | no | | no |
| Carolina Quarterly .. 3 Nos. | 1.25 | 1.25 | .50 | | .50 |
| —, 2 years | 2.25 | 2.25 | 1.00 | 1.00 | 1.00 |
| Catholic Art Association Membership includes Good Work ..Q. | 5.00 | 5.00 | 1.00 | no | 1.00 |
| Catholic Biblical Quarterly ..Q. | 5.00 | 4.85 | no | | no |
| Catholic Boy (1) .. 10 Nos. | 3.00 | 2.65 | no | | no |
| —, 2 years | 5.00 | 4.60 | 1.00 | | |
| —, 3 years | 7.00 | 6.50 | 1.50 | | |
| Catholic Bulletin ..W. | 3.00 | 2.90 | 2.00 | 1.00 | no |
| Catholic Charities Review .. 10 Nos. | 1.00 | 1.00 | .50 | .25 | .25 |
| Catholic Choirmaster ..Q. | 2.75 | 2.65 | no | | no |
| **CATHOLIC DIGEST** ..M. | 4.00 | 3.50 | no | no | no |
| —, 3 years | 10.00 | 8.00 | | | |
| (See advertisement, page 111.) | | | | | |
| Catholic Educational Review .... 9 Nos. | 5.00 | 4.60 | no | no | no |
| Catholic Educator .. 10 Nos. | 4.00 | 4.00 | .75 | .25 | .75 |
| Catholic Historical Review ..Q. | 6.00 | 5.50 | no | | no |
| Catholic Lawyer ..Q. | 5.00 | 5.00 | no | | no |
| Catholic Library World .. 8 Nos. | 6.00 | 6.00 | 1.00 | no | no |
| Catholic Life .. 6 Nos. | 2.00 | 1.60 | .50 | .25 | .25 |
| —, 3 years | 3.00 | 2.50 | .75 | .50 | .50 |
| Catholic Mind ..B.-M. | 3.00 | 2.70 | .50 | .50 | .50 |
| —, 2 years | 5.00 | 4.50 | 1.00 | 1.00 | 1.00 |
| —, 3 years | 7.00 | 6.30 | 1.50 | 1.50 | 1.50 |
| Catholic Miss (1) .. 10 Nos. | 3.00 | 2.65 | .50 | no | no |
| Catholic News (2) ..W. | 5.00 | 4.40 | 1.50 | .50 | 1.00 |
| Catholic Review ..W. | 4.00 | 3.60 | 1.00 | .50 | 1.50 |
| Catholic School Journal (1) .. 10 Nos. | 4.00 | 3.90 | 1.00 | no | 1.00 |
| —, 2 years | 6.50 | 6.25 | 2.00 | | 2.00 |
| —, 3 years | 8.75 | 8.40 | 3.00 | | 3.00 |
| Catholic Universe Bulletin ..W. | 3.50 | 3.20 | 1.00 | .50 | |

| | Pub. Price | Agts. Price | For. Post. | Can. Post. | P.A. Post. |
|---|---|---|---|---|---|
| **Catholic U. of A. Law Review** | | | | | |
| Catholic University of America Law Review .. 2 Nos. | 4.00 | 4.00 | no | no | no |
| Catholic Worker .. 11 Nos. | .25 | .25 | .30 | .30 | .30 |
| Catholic World (1) ..M. | 6.00 | 5.25 | 1.00 | no | 1.00 |
| —, 2 years | 10.00 | 9.00 | 2.00 | | 2.00 |
| —, 3 years | 14.00 | 12.75 | 3.00 | | 3.00 |
| Cattleman ..M. | 3.00 | 2.75 | 3.00 | 3.00 | 3.00 |
| —, 3 years | 7.50 | 6.60 | 7.50 | 7.50 | 7.50 |
| **CAVALIER** ..M. | 3.00 | 2.40 | 3.00 | 1.00 | 3.00 |
| —, 2 years | 5.00 | 4.00 | 7.00 | 2.00 | 7.00 |
| —, 3 years | 7.00 | 5.60 | 11.00 | 3.00 | 11.00 |
| Ceramic Age (2) (3) ..M. | 4.00 | 3.50 | 4.00 | 1.00 | 4.00 |
| —, 2 years | 7.00 | 6.00 | | | 2.00 |
| —, 3 years | 10.00 | 8.75 | | | 3.00 |
| Ceramic Industry ..M. | 4.00 | 3.75 | 4.00 | no | 4.00 |
| —, 3 years | 8.00 | 7.50 | 8.00 | | 8.00 |
| Ceramics Monthly .. 10 Nos. | 5.00 | 4.70 | 1.00 | .50 | .50 |
| —, 2 years | 9.00 | 8.60 | 2.00 | 1.00 | 1.00 |
| —, 3 years | 12.00 | 11.60 | 3.00 | 1.50 | 1.50 |
| Cereal Chemistry (4) ..B.-M. | 15.00 | 14.50 | 1.00 | 1.00 | 1.00 |
| Cerebral Palsy Review ..B.-M. | 3.00 | 2.80 | .50 | .50 | .50 |
| Chain Store Age ..M. | 3.00 | 2.75 | 9.00 | 1.00 | 3.00 |
| —, 2 years | 5.00 | 4.50 | | | |
| —, 3 years | 7.00 | 6.00 | | | |
| Challenge Magazine .. 10 Nos. | 2.50 | 2.00 | no | .60 | no .60 |
| —, 2 years | 4.25 | 3.50 | 1.20 | | 1.20 |
| —, 3 years | 6.00 | 5.00 | 1.80 | | 1.80 |
| —, Schools | 2.00 | 1.60 | | | |
| **CHANGING TIMES**, The Kiplinger Magazine M. | 6.00 | 4.75 | 1.00 | no | 1.00 |
| —, 2 years | 10.00 | 8.00 | 2.00 | | 2.00 |
| —, 3 years | 14.00 | 11.00 | 3.00 | | 3.00 |
| Channels .. 20 Nos. | 12.50 | 12.00 | no | no | no |
| —, 2 years | 22.50 | 22.75 | | | |
| —, 3 years | 32.00 | 29.75 | | | |
| Chemical Abstracts Service with Indexes | | | | | |
| —, School, College & Univ. Librs. .. | 200.00 | 200.00 | 7.00 | 2.20 | 4.30 |
| —, All Others | 925.00 | 925.00 | 7.00 | 2.20 | 4.30 |
| Without Indexes | | | | | |
| —, School, College & Univ. Librs. .. | 170.00 | 170.00 | 6.00 | 1.00 | 3.60 |
| —, All others | 800.00 | 800.00 | 6.00 | 1.00 | 3.60 |
| Chemical Bulletin ..M. | 2.00 | 2.00 | .50 | no | no |
| Chemical & Engineering News (4) ..W. | 6.00 | 6.00 | | | 2.00 |
| —, 2 years | 10.00 | 10.00 | | | 4.00 |
| —, 3 years | 14.00 | 14.00 | | | 6.00 |
| —, Foreign | 15.00 | 15.00 | 5.00 | | 3.30 |
| **CHEMICAL ENGINEERING** ..M. | 3.00 | 3.00 | 22.00 | 4.00 | 12.00 |
| (See advertisement, page 124.) | | | | | |
| Chemical Engineering Progress ..M. | 6.00 | 5.40 | 2.00 | .50 | 1.50 |
| —, Libraries | 5.40 | 4.80 | 2.00 | .50 | 1.50 |
| Chemical Reviews ..B.-M. | 12.00 | 12.00 | 1.25 | .50 | .50 |
| **CHEMICAL WEEK** ..W. | 3.00 | 3.00 | 22.00 | 4.00 | 12.00 |
| (Indexes $1.00 per year) | | | | | |
| (See advertisement, page 124.) | | | | | |
| Chemist ..M. | 4.00 | 3.25 | no | no | no |
| Chemistry .. 8 Nos. | 4.00 | 3.70 | 1.00 | 1.00 | 1.00 |
| —, 2 years | 7.00 | 6.50 | | | |
| —, 3 years | 10.00 | 9.30 | | | |
| —, 2 or more 1 year to same address, each | 3.50 | 3.25 | | | |
| Chemistry in Canada ..M. | 6.00 | 5.50 | 2.00 | | 2.00 |
| (U.S.A. add $2.00 postage.) | | | | | |
| Chemurgic Digest (Schools and Libraries) (1) M. | 5.00 | 5.00 | no | no | no |
| — (Others) ..M. | 6.00 | 5.50 | no | no | no |
| Chess Review ..M. | 6.00 | 5.50 | no | no | no |
| —, 2 years | 11.00 | 10.00 | | | |
| Chester White Journal ..M. | 1.00 | 1.00 | .50 | .50 | .50 |
| —, 3 years | 2.00 | 2.00 | 1.00 | 1.00 | 1.00 |
| Chicago Art Institute .. 4 Nos. | 1.00 | 1.00 | no | no | no |
| Chicago Daily Drovers Journal (3) 5 Issues Per Week | 9.00 | 8.50 | 12.00 | no | 9.00 |
| — (In Chicago) by carrier .. | 12.00 | 11.50 | | | |

FIGURE 1a. Faxon's Trade List 1960

cerns of that era. Manipulation by the poor in spirit for profit was not, however, confined to this industry.

The popular or shelter magazine publishers granted a sufficient margin off the published price to support such a system.

As labor costs increased and libraries learned that library subscription agents could handle not only their popular titles but scientific and scholarly journals as well, the library subscription agency became an important factor as a service organization to libraries. Libraries further discovered that the agencies were willing to handle their subscriptions at a discount off the published subscription rate. However, it was not until the mid-1960s that agencies, searching for greater volume to replace the diminishing business from the labor-intensive costs of the local agent, aggressively solicited library business.

With this new source of revenue came more service demands, requirements, and expectations. Furthermore, the publisher margin or discount on technical, scientific, and scholarly journals was considerably less than than offered by the popular magazine publisher. Even in the early 1960s, when the popular magazine publisher offered fifty percent off the published rate to the agency, the publisher of scientific journals granted an average of twelve to fifteen percent. Since 1960 the average margin granted by all publishers of all classes of journals has diminished by fifty percent, explaining the vanishing discount on scholarly journals by agents to libraries.

The financial relationship between the agency and the publisher is not negotiable, because each publisher unilaterally sets its rates for both the subscriber

## Leader In The Catholic Field

It is the only magazine of its kind in the entire Catholic publishing field. Each monthly issue contains from 25 to 30 complete articles screened from newspapers, magazines and books from all over the world. The *best* of human experiences from general and religious fields.

**FOR EVERY MEMBER OF THE FAMILY**

A family magazine and also makes the ideal gift for clergy, nuns, teachers, students, weddings, graduations, Mother's Day, Father's Day. Now read by millions and growing fast.

1 yr. **$4.00**
3 yrs. **$10.00**

| Ca | | Subs. Pays | Agent Pays | Add For'gn | Add Can. | Add PanA |
|---|---|---|---|---|---|---|
| Catholic Biblical Quarterly | Q. | 5.00 | 4.85 | No | No | No |
| Catholic Book Merchandiser | B.M. | 4.00 | 3.85 | 1.00 | No | No |
| Catholic Book Reporter | B.M. | 4.00 | 3.85 | 2.00 | — | — |
| Catholic Boy | 10 Nos. | 3.00 | 2.65 | .50 | No | No |
| Catholic Business Education Review | Q. | 3.00 | 2.75 | — | — | — |
| Catholic Charities Review | 10 Nos. | 1.00 | 1.00 | .50 | .25 | .25 |
| Catholic Choirmaster | Q. | 2.75 | 2.65 | No | No | No |
| **CATHOLIC DIGEST** | | | | | | |
| Monthly—with millions of readers in several languages. Of interest to everyone interested in religion. | | | | | | |
| —1 year | M. | 4.00 | 3.50 | No | No | No |
| —2 years | M. | 7.00 | 6.30 | No | No | No |
| —3 years | M. | 10.00 | 9.00 | No | No | No |
| Catholic Educational Review | 9 Nos. | 5.00 | 4.60 | No | No | No |
| Catholic Educator | 10 Nos. | 4.00 | 4.00 | .75 | .25 | .75 |
| Catholic Historical Review | Q. | 7.00 | 6.50 | No | No | No |
| Catholic Lamp | M. | 3.00 | 2.40 | .50 | No | .25 |
| Catholic Life | 6 Nos. | 2.00 | 1.60 | .50 | No | .25 |
| —2 years | 12 Nos. | 3.00 | 2.40 | 1.00 | No | .50 |
| Catholic Mind | B.M. | 3.00 | 2.70 | .50 | .50 | .50 |
| —2 years | B.M. | 5.00 | 4.50 | 1.00 | 1.00 | 1.00 |
| —3 years | B.M. | 7.00 | 6.30 | 1.50 | 1.50 | 1.50 |
| Catholic Miss of America | 10 Nos. | 3.00 | 2.65 | .50 | No | No |
| Catholic News | | 5.00 | 4.00 | 1.50 | .50 | 1.00 |
| Catholic Preview of Entertainment | M. | 5.00 | 4.00 | 1.50 | 1.00 | 1.00 |
| Catholic Review (Baltimore) | W. | 4.00 | 3.75 | 1.50 | .50 | 1.50 |
| Catholic School Journal | 10 Nos. | 4.00 | 3.90 | 1.00 | No | 1.00 |
| Catholic Transcript (Hartford) | W. | 3.50 | 3.30 | 2.00 | 2.00 | 2.00 |
| Catholic World | 6 Nos. | 6.00 | 5.25 | .50 | No | .50 |
| —2 years | | 10.00 | 9.00 | 1.00 | No | 1.00 |
| —3 years | | 14.00 | 12.75 | 1.50 | No | 1.50 |
| Cats | M. | 4.00 | 3.00 | No | No | No |
| —2 years | M. | 7.00 | 5.25 | No | No | No |
| —3 years | M. | 10.00 | 7.50 | No | No | No |
| Cattleman | M. | 3.00 | 2.75 | 3.00 | No | 3.00 |
| Cavalier | M. | 7.50 | 7.00 | 7.50 | No | 7.50 |
| —2 years | M. | 3.00 | 2.40 | 1.00 | 1.00 | 3.00 |
| —3 years | M. | 5.00 | 4.00 | 7.00 | 2.00 | 7.00 |
| Ceramic Age (Trade only) | M. | 7.00 | 5.40 | 11.00 | 3.00 | 11.00 |
| Ceramic Arts and Crafts Monthly | M. | 4.00 | 3.50 | 4.00 | 1.00 | 4.00 |
| —2 years | M. | 3.00 | 2.85 | .50 | .50 | .50 |
| —3 years | M. | 5.00 | 4.65 | 1.00 | 1.00 | 1.00 |
| | M. | 7.00 | 6.45 | 1.50 | 1.50 | 1.50 |

| Ce | | Subs. Pays | Agent Pays | Add For'gn | Add Can. | Add PanA |
|---|---|---|---|---|---|---|
| Ceramic Industry | M. | 4.00 | 3.75 | 4.00 | No | 4.00 |
| Ceramics Monthly | 10 Nos. | 5.00 | 4.75 | 1.00 | .50 | .50 |
| —2 years | 20 Nos. | 9.00 | 8.60 | 2.00 | 1.00 | 1.00 |
| —3 years | 30 Nos. | 12.00 | 11.50 | 3.00 | 1.50 | 1.50 |
| Cereal Chemistry | B.M. | 18.00 | 17.25 | 1.00 | 1.00 | 1.00 |
| Chain Store Age | | | | | | |
| (State edition desired) | M. | 3.00 | 2.75 | 9.00 | 1.00 | 3.00 |
| Challenge, The magazine of economic affairs | 10 Nos. | 3.00 | 2.40 | .80 | No | .80 |
| —2 years | 20 Nos. | 5.00 | 4.00 | 1.60 | No | 1.60 |
| Challengers Unknown | B.M. | .75 | .70 | .75 | .75 | .75 |
| Champion Crosswords | 9 Nos. | 3.00 | 2.75 | .45 | .45 | .45 |
| **CHANGING TIMES, The Kiplinger Magazine** | | | | | | |
| "The Magazine Of Ideas On Money, Job and Living." | | | | | | |
| —1 year | M. | 6.00 | 4.75 | 1.00 | No | 1.00 |
| —2 years | M. | 10.00 | 8.00 | 2.00 | No | 2.00 |
| —3 years | M. | 14.00 | 11.00 | 3.00 | No | 3.00 |
| Channels | S.M. | 12.50 | 11.50 | No | No | No |
| Chatelaine | M. | 2.50 | 2.15 | — | — | — |
| Chemical Engineering Progress | M. | 6.00 | 5.40 | 2.00 | .50 | 1.50 |
| Chemical Reviews | B.M. | 12.00 | 12.00 | 1.25 | .50 | .50 |
| Chemistry | 8 Nos. | 4.00 | 3.70 | No | No | No |
| Chef Magazine | M. | 3.00 | 2.40 | No | No | No |
| Chess Review | M. | 6.00 | 5.50 | No | No | No |
| Chester White Journal | M. | 1.00 | 1.00 | .50 | .50 | .50 |
| —3 years—Subs NA | M. | 2.00 | 2.00 | 1.00 | 1.00 | 1.00 |
| Cheyenne—Subs NA | | | | | | |
| Chicago Daily News (in Ill., Ind., Iowa, Mich., and Wisc.) | 6 Iss. | 16.50 | 15.50 | — | — | — |
| —Other states, Canada, and Pan America | 6 Iss. | 20.00 | 18.80 | — | — | — |
| —Foreign | 6 Iss. | 33.00 | 31.00 | — | — | — |
| Chicago Daily Defender | W. | 8.00 | 7.25 | 1.50 | 1.00 | 1.50 |
| —Monday thro' Thursday | W. | 14.00 | 12.50 | 3.00 | 2.00 | 3.00 |
| —1 year | 4 Iss. | 6.00 | 5.40 | 1.50 | 1.00 | 1.50 |
| Chicago Drovers Journal—Now: Drovers Journal | | | | | | |
| Chicago Packer | W. | 7.00 | 6.30 | NA | No | NA |

**SELL THEM**

*Changing Times*

THE KIPLINGER MAGAZINE

This unique monthly service will help your customers live better . . . and bring you good commissions as well.

1 year $6 you make **$1.25**
2 years $10 you make **$2.00**
3 years $14 you make **$3.00**

FIGURE 1b. McGregor Wholesale List 1961

| Canadian Historical Review | Pubs. Price | Agts. Price | For. Post. | Can. Post. | P.A.U. Post. |
|---|---|---|---|---|---|
| *Canadian Historical Review ...........Q. | 4.00 | 3.65 | No | No | No |
| *Canadian Journal of Economics & Political | | | | | |
| Science (1) (Subs. must begin Feb.) Q. | 6.00 | 5.50 | No | No | No |
| Canadian Nurse (In Canada) (2) .....M. | 3.00 | 2.80 | | | |
| Same—(In U.S.) (1) ..............M. | 3.50 | 3.30 | No | No | No |
| *Cancer (1) ........................B-M. | 15.00 | 13.50 | 2.00 | | No |
| (Subscriptions must begin January or July.) | | | | | |
| *Cancer Research (1) (No March) ..11 Nos. | 15.00 | 14.50 | 1.00 | .50 | .50 |
| Candy Industry & Confectioners Journal (2) (8) | | | | | |
| B-W. | 5.00 | 4.00 | 2.00 | No | 2.00 |
| Canner/Packer (8) ................13 Nos. | 5.00 | 4.60 | 5.00 | No | 5.00 |
| Canning Trade (1) ..................M. | 5.00 | 4.60 | 2.00 | 1.00 | 2.00 |
| CAR & DRIVER .....................M. | 5.00 | 4.00 | 1.00 | .50 | .50 |
| Same—2 years ....................M. | 9.00 | 7.20 | 2.00 | 1.00 | 1.00 |
| Same—3 years ....................M. | 12.00 | 9.60 | 3.00 | 1.50 | 1.50 |
| Special Gift Rates (To Jan. 30, 1962) (11) | | | | | |
| Two 1-year Gift Subscriptions ........ | 9.00 | 7.20 | | | |
| Each additional 1-year Gift Subscription | 3.00 | 2.40 | | | |
| CAR CRAFT comb. with Kart ........M. | 3.50 | 3.00 | 1.00 | 1.00 | 1.00 |
| Same—2 years ....................M. | 6.00 | 5.50 | 2.00 | 2.00 | 2.00 |
| Same—3 years ....................M. | 8.00 | 7.50 | 3.00 | 3.00 | 3.00 |
| CAR CRAFT comb. with Kart—No short terms except 2 mos. for | | | | | |
| schools in U. S. only ..........9 Nos. | 2.75 | 2.25 | | | |
| Special Gift Rates (To January 31, 1962) (11) | | | | | |
| One 1-year Gift Subscription ...... | 3.00 | 2.50 | | | |
| Each additional 1-year Gift Subscription | 2.00 | 1.75 | | | |
| (Publishers require donor's name and address.) | | | | | |
| Car Life ...........................M. | 4.00 | 3.50 | 1.00 | No | 1.00 |
| *Carrows & Travel Times ...........M. | 1.00 | .85 | 1.00 | No | .50 |
| Carolina Israelite ................B-M. | 3.00 | 2.40 | 1.00 | 1.00 | No |
| Same—2 years ....................M. | 5.00 | 4.00 | 2.00 | 2.00 | No |
| *Catholic Biblical Quarterly .........Q. | 5.00 | 4.85 | No | No | No |
| *Catholic Boy (1) (Sept.-June) ..10 Nos. | 3.00 | 2.65 | .50 | .50 | .50 |
| *Catholic Charities Review .....10 Nos. | 1.00 | .90 | .50 | .25 | .25 |
| (Published Sept.-June.) | | | | | |
| *Catholic Choirmaster .............Q. | 2.75 | 2.60 | No | No | No |
| Catholic Counselor (1) ..........3 Nos. | 1.50 | 1.50 | No | No | No |
| (Published February, May and November.) | | | | | |
| CATHOLIC DIGEST (2) ............M. | 4.00 | 3.50 | No | No | No |
| Same—(New or Renewal) ........9 Nos. | 2.50 | 2.15 | No | No | No |
| Same—2 years ....................M. | 7.00 | 6.30 | No | No | No |
| Same—3 years ....................M. | 10.00 | 9.00 | No | No | No |
| Same—4 years ....................M. | 12.50 | 11.25 | No | No | No |
| Same—5 years ....................M. | 15.00 | 13.30 | No | No | No |
| Special Gift Rates (To Jan. 31, 1962) (11) | | | | | |
| Two 1-year Gift Subscriptions ........ | 7.00 | 6.30 | | | |
| Three 1-year Gift Subscriptions ...... | 10.00 | 9.00 | | | |
| Each additional 1-year Gift Subscription | 2.50 | 2.15 | | | |
| (Publishers require donor's name and address.) | | | | | |
| CATHOLIC DIGEST—To active members of | | | | | |
| U.S. Armed Forces (12)—1 year only M. | 3.00 | 2.50 | | | |
| Catholic Educational Review (9) ..9 Nos. | 5.00 | 4.60 | No | No | No |
| (Published September-May.) | | | | | |
| *Catholic Educator (Sept.-June) ..10 Nos. | 4.00 | 4.00 | .75 | .25 | No |
| *Catholic Historical Review (9) .....Q. | 7.00 | 6.50 | No | No | No |
| Catholic Mind—To Jan. 1, 1962 ..B-M. | 3.00 | 2.70 | .50 | .50 | .50 |
| Same—After Jan. 1, 1962 ......B-M. | 4.00 | 4.50 | .50 | .50 | .50 |
| Catholic Miss (Teen Age Girls) ..10 Nos. | 3.00 | 2.65 | .50 | .50 | .50 |
| (Published Sept.-June.) | | | | | |
| *Catholic News ....................W. | 5.00 | 4.40 | | | |
| Catholic School Journal (1) ......10 Nos. | 4.00 | 3.90 | 1.00 | | 1.00 |
| (Published Sept.-June.) | | | | | |
| *Catholic Standard & Times .......W. | 3.00 | 2.70 | | | |
| Catholic World ...................M. | 6.00 | 5.25 | 1.00 | No | 1.00 |
| Same—2 years ....................M. | 10.00 | 9.00 | 2.00 | No | 2.00 |
| Cats ..............................M. | 4.00 | 3.25 | No | No | No |
| CAVALIER .........................M. | 5.00 | 4.00 | 1.00 | 3.00 | 3.00 |
| Same—3 years ....................M. | 7.00 | 5.60 | 11.00 | 3.00 | 11.00 |
| Centennial Review of Arts & Science (3) | | | | | |
| 1 Nos. | 3.00 | 3.00 | No | No | No |
| Ceramic Arts & Crafts Monthly (2) ..M. | 3.00 | 2.85 | .50 | .50 | .50 |
| Ceramic Industry—To Jan. 1, 1962 ..M. | 1.00 | 3.75 | 1.00 | No | 1.00 |
| Same—After Jan. 1, 1962 .........M. | 5.00 | 4.60 | 5.00 | No | 5.00 |
| Ceramics Monthly (Sept.-June) ..10 Nos. | 5.00 | 4.75 | 1.00 | .50 | .50 |
| Same—2 years ..................20 Nos. | 9.00 | 8.75 | 2.00 | 1.00 | 1.00 |
| Same—3 years ..................30 Nos. | 12.50 | 11.75 | 3.00 | 1.50 | 1.50 |
| Cerebral Palsy Review ...........B-M. | 3.00 | 2.80 | .50 | .50 | .50 |
| Chain Store Age (1) ...............M. | 3.00 | 2.75 | 9.00 | 1.00 | 3.00 |
| Same—2 years ....................M. | 5.00 | 4.50 | Ask | No | Ask |
| Same—3 years ....................M. | 7.00 | 6.25 | Ask | No | Ask |
| Challenge Magazine of Economic Affairs (2) | | | | | |
| (Published Oct.-July) ..........10 Nos. | 3.00 | 2.40 | .80 | No | .80 |

*Send Your Orders Promptly*
*At Least Twice-a-Week*

| Changing Times | Pubs. Price | Agts. Price | For. Post. | Can. Post. | P.A.U. Post. |
|---|---|---|---|---|---|
| CHANGING TIMES, The Kiplinger Magazine | | | | | |
| 1 year ..........................M. | 6.00 | 4.75 | 1.00 | No | 1.00 |
| Same—2 years ...................M. | 10.00 | 8.00 | 2.00 | No | 2.00 |
| Same—3 years ...................M. | 14.00 | 11.00 | 3.00 | No | 3.00 |
| (Subscriptions for less than 3 months not accepted.) | | | | | |
| (See advertisement on Page 25.) | | | | | |
| Year Round Gift Rates (11) | | | | | |
| Two 1-year Gift Subscriptions ...... | 10.00 | 8.00 | | | |
| Each additional 1-year Gift Subscription | 5.00 | 4.00 | | | |
| (Publishers require donor's name and address.) | | | | | |
| For Christmas Season (Oct. 1, 1961-Dec. 31, 1961) Free Bonus Book | | | | | |
| "Family Success Book" sent with gift subs. | | | | | |
| Chemical Abstracts Service (1) (4) (9) 22 Nos. To Schools, Colleges, Univer- | | | | | |
| sities (all teaching insts.) and their libraries and depts.— | | | | | |
| With Indexes | 200.00 | 200.00 | 7.00 | 3.20 | 4.30 |
| Without Indexes | 170.00 | 170.00 | 6.00 | 1.00 | 3.60 |
| Same—To all other Libraries (Public Libraries, private libraries, etc.) | | | | | |
| With Indexes | 925.00 | 925.00 | 7.00 | 3.20 | 4.30 |
| Without Indexes | 800.00 | 800.00 | 6.00 | 1.00 | 3.60 |
| (Subscriptions for more than 1 year not accepted.) | | | | | |
| Note: Sub. without Indexes available only to subscribers to a complete sub. | | | | | |
| with Indexes. | | | | | |
| Chemical & Engineering News (1) (9) W. | 6.00 | 6.00 | | No | 12.30 |
| Same—2 years ................W. | 10.00 | 10.00 | 27.50 | No | 24.10 |
| Same—3 years ................W. | 14.00 | 14.00 | 41.00 | No | 35.90 |
| Chemical Engineering (1) (8) .......M. | 3.00 | 3.00 | Ask | Ask | Ask |
| (Official title or position of subscriber, name of company and product pro- | | | | | |
| duced or type of service performed required by publisher.) | | | | | |
| Chemical Engineering Progress (6) (8) .M. | 6.00 | 5.40 | 3.00 | 1.50 | 1.50 |
| Same—To school & public libraries ..M. | 5.40 | 4.80 | 2.00 | 1.50 | 1.50 |
| Chemical Reviews (Vol. 62 in 1962) 1 Vol. | 20.00 | 20.00 | 1.25 | .50 | .50 |
| (Subscriptions must be entered for Vol. beginning Feb.) | | | | | |
| (Subscription. for more than 1 year (1 volume) not accepted.) | | | | | |
| Chemical Titles (1) (4) (Published Semi-Monthly) | | | | | |
| To Teaching insts.—1-10 Subs. ...Each | 50.00 | 50.00 | 2.80 | 1.80 | 2.00 |
| Same—To all others—1-10 Subs...Each | 65.00 | 65.00 | 2.80 | 1.80 | 2.00 |
| To all subscribers—11-25 Subs. ..Each | 45.00 | 45.00 | 2.80 | 1.80 | 2.00 |
| To all subscribers—26 and more Subs. | | | | | |
| Each | 30.00 | 30.00 | 2.80 | 1.80 | 2.00 |
| Chemical Week (1) (8) ..............W. | 3.00 | 3.00 | Ask | No | Ask |
| (Subscriptions for more than 1 year not accepted) (No subscriptions ac- | | | | | |
| cepted for high schools, new or renewal.) | | | | | |

FIGURE 1c. Goldberger Wholesale List 1961

and the agency. A publisher's degree of interest in agency services is determined by its cost and methods of soliciting subscriptions, new and renewal, and its fulfillment procedures. Naturally, the benefits to the publisher of agency services should dictate the financial arrangement. The modern agency does not try to promote the circulation of one journal over another to the library because the labor cost of doing so would be excessive. Therefore, the publishers will not relate the quantity of orders received from agents to the discount margin. Few if any publishers have translated the service benefits into cost-reduction factors.

Field selling agencies, using door-to-door or telephone solicitation, continue as a separate business to boost circulation of popular magazine publishers and therefore receive special rates for this service.

Before the 1960s the service concerns of the library subscription agency were narrow in scope compared to those of the present day. At that time the library community was satisfied with a title selection base of approximately 3,000 titles available from less than 1,000 publishers (excluding foreign language journals). Perhaps only one-fourth as many libraries used the subscription agencies' services then as do now. Subscription agency services before 1960 were primarily concerned with timely order entry; that is, getting prepaid orders to the publishers early enough so that the publishers could deliver all issues of the volume year ordered. Also, the order date was not as critical then because print runs were calculated to build up back issue stocks, particularly

| Canadian Jour. Economics | Pub. Price | For. Post. | Can. Post. | P.A. Post. |
|---|---|---|---|---|
| Canadian Journal of Economics & Political Science ...Q. | 6.00 | no | | no |
| Canadian Journal of Mathematics ....Q. | 10.00 | no | | no |
| Canadian Journal of Medical Technology Q. | 3.00 | no | | no |
| Canadian Journal of Microbiology .B.-M. | 6.00 | no | | no |
| Canadian Journal of Physics .....M. | 9.00 | no | | no |
| Canadian Journal of Plant Science ...Q. | 4.00 | 1.00 | | no |
| Canadian Journal of Psychology ....Q. | 6.00 | no | | no |
| Canadian Journal of Public Health (Canada) (4) ...M. | 3.00 | | | |
| —, U.S. & Elsewhere ...........M. | 5.00 | | | |
| Canadian Journal of Soil Science .S.-A. | 2.00 | .50 | | no |
| Canadian Journal of Zoology ....B.-M. | 5.00 | no | | no |
| Canadian Machinery (Canada) .....M. | 5.00 | | | |
| —— (In U.S.A., and Great Britain) ... | 10.00 | | | |
| —, Elsewhere ................ | 20.00 | | | |
| Canadian Medical Association Journal W. | 12.00 | no | | no |
| Canadian Mining & Metallurgical Bulletin M. | 10.00 | no | | no |
| Canadian Mining Journal (Canada) ..M. | 5.00 | | | |
| —, U.S.A. & Br. Commonwealth .... | 15.00 | | | |
| —, 2 years ...............| 25.00 | | | |
| —, Foreign, P.A. & P.I. ..........| 20.00 | | | |
| —, 2 years ...............| 30.00 | | | |
| Canadian Modern Language Review ..Q. | 3.00 | no | | no |
| Canadian Nurse (in Canada) ......M. | 3.00 | | | |
| —— (In U. S. A., For., P.A., & P.I.) . | 3.50 | .50 | | .50 |
| Canadian Patent Office Record (in U.S.A. and Canada) ...........W. | 25.00 | 15.00 | | 15.00 |
| Canadian Poetry Magazine ..........Q. | 2.00 | no | | no |
| Canadian Statistical Review .......M. | 5.00 | 1.75 | | 1.75 |
| Canadian Surveyor ...........5 Nos. | 5.00 | no | | no |
| Canadian Textile Journal ......B.-W. | 6.00 | 1.00 | | 1.00 |
| —, 2 years ...............| 10.00 | 2.00 | | 2.00 |
| —, 3 years ...............| 14.00 | 3.00 | | 3.00 |
| Canadian Transportation (in U. S. A.) M. | 3.50 | | | |
| | 3.00 | 22.00 | | 22.00 |
| Canadian Welfare ..........7 Nos. | 2.50 | no | | no |
| Cancer ................B.-M. | 15.00 | 2.00 | no | no |
| Cancer Research, by Vol. ........M. | 15.00 | 1.00 | .50 | .50 |
| Candy Industry and Confectioners' Journal B.-W. | 5.00 | 2.00 | no | 2.00 |
| —, 3 years ...............| 10.00 | 6.00 | | 6.00 |
| Canner/Packer ............M. | 5.00 | 5.00 | no | 5.00 |
| —, 2 years ...............| 8.00 | 8.00 | | 8.00 |
| —, 3 years ...............| 10.00 | 10.00 | | 10.00 |
| Canning Trade (1) ..........W. | 5.00 | 2.00 | 1.00 | 2.00 |
| Cappers' Farmer ...........M. | 1.00 | | | |
| —, Outside U.S.A. ..........| 1.50 | | | |
| Capper's Weekly ............W. | 2.00 | | | |
| —, outside U.S.A. ..........| 3.00 | | | |
| Car Craft ....................M. | 3.00 | 1.00 | no | 1.00 |
| —, 2 years ...............| 5.00 | 2.00 | | 2.00 |
| —, 3 years ...............| 7.00 | 3.00 | | 3.00 |
| Carnegie Magazine ..........10 Nos. | 2.00 | no | | no |
| Carolina Quarterly ........3 Nos. | 1.25 | .50 | .50 | .50 |
| —, 2 years ...............| 2.25 | 1.00 | 1.00 | 1.00 |
| cludes Catholic Art Quarterly ....Q. | 5.00 | 1.00 | no | 1.00 |
| Catholic Art Association Membership includes | | | | |
| Catholic Biblical Quarterly ......Q. | 5.00 | no | no | no |
| Catholic Boy (1) ..........10 Nos. | 3.00 | .50 | no | no |
| —, 2 years ...............| 5.00 | 1.00 | | |
| —, 3 years ...............| 7.00 | 1.50 | | |
| Catholic Bulletin ............W. | 5.00 | 1.00 | 1.00 | no |
| Catholic Charities Review ....10 Nos. | 1.00 | .50 | .25 | .25 |
| Catholic Choirmaster ..........Q. | 2.75 | no | | no |
| CATHOLIC DIGEST ........M. | 4.00 | no | no | no |
| —, 3 years ...............| 9.00 | | | |
| —, 5 years ...............| 15.00 | | | |
| (See advertisement, page 109.) | | | | |
| Catholic Educational Review ....9 Nos. | 5.00 | no | no | no |
| Catholic Educator .........10 Nos. | 3.50 | .75 | .75 | .75 |
| Catholic Historical Review ......Q. | 6.00 | no | .40 | no |

| Catholic Lawyer | Pub. Price | For. Post. | Can. Post. | P.A. Post. |
|---|---|---|---|---|
| Catholic Lawyer ...........Q. | 5.00 | no | no | no |
| Catholic Library World .........8 Nos. | 6.00 | 1.00 | no | no |
| Catholic Life .................6 Nos. | 2.00 | .50 | .25 | .25 |
| —, 2 years ...............| 3.00 | .75 | .50 | .50 |
| —, 3 years ...............| 5.00 | 1.00 | .75 | .75 |
| Catholic Mind ............B.-M. | 3.00 | .50 | .50 | .50 |
| —, 2 years ...............| 5.00 | 1.00 | 1.00 | 1.00 |
| —, 3 years ...............| 7.00 | 1.50 | 1.50 | 1.50 |
| Catholic Miss (1) ..........10 Nos. | 2.00 | 1.00 | 1.00 | 1.00 |
| Catholic News (2) ............W. | 5.00 | 1.50 | .50 | 1.00 |
| Catholic Review ............W. | 4.00 | 1.00 | .50 | 1.50 |
| Catholic School Journal (1) ...10 Nos. | 4.00 | 1.00 | no | 1.00 |
| —, 2 years ...............| 6.50 | 2.00 | | 2.00 |
| —, 3 years ...............| 8.75 | 3.00 | | 3.00 |
| Catholic Universe Bulletin ......W. | 3.50 | 1.00 | .50 | |
| Catholic University of America Law Review ...2 Nos. | 4.00 | no | no | no |
| Catholic Worker ..........11 Nos. | .25 | .30 | .30 | .30 |
| Catholic World (1) ..............M. | 6.00 | 1.00 | no | 1.00 |
| —, 2 years ...............| 10.00 | 2.00 | | 2.00 |
| —, 3 years ...............| 14.00 | 3.00 | | 3.00 |
| Cattleman ..................M. | 3.00 | 3.00 | 3.00 | 3.00 |
| —, 3 years ...............| 7.50 | 7.50 | 7.50 | 7.50 |
| **CAVALIER** ................M. | 3.00 | 3.00 | 1.00 | 3.00 |
| —, 2 years ...............| 5.00 | 7.00 | 2.00 | 7.00 |
| —, 3 years ...............| 7.00 | 11.00 | 3.00 | 11.00 |
| Ceramic Age (2) (3) ..........M. | 4.00 | 4.00 | 1.00 | 4.00 |
| —, 2 years ...............| 7.00 | 2.00 | | |
| —, 3 years ...............| 10.00 | 3.00 | | |
| Ceramic Industry .............M. | 4.00 | 4.00 | no | 4.00 |
| —, 3 years ...............| 8.00 | 8.00 | | 8.00 |
| Ceramics Monthly ..........10 Nos. | 4.00 | 1.00 | .50 | .50 |
| —, 2 years ...............| 9.00 | 2.00 | 1.00 | 1.00 |
| —, 3 years ...............| 12.00 | 3.00 | 1.50 | 1.50 |
| Cereal Chemistry (4) ........B.-M. | 15.00 | .50 | .50 | .50 |
| Cerebral Palsy Review ........B.-M. | 3.00 | .50 | .50 | .50 |
| Chain Store Age ............M. | 3.00 | 9.00 | 1.00 | 3.00 |
| —, 2 years ...............| 5.00 | | | |
| —, 3 years ...............| 7.00 | | | |
| Challenge Magazine ..........10 Nos. | 2.50 | .60 | no | no |
| —, 2 years ...............| 4.25 | 1.20 | | |
| —, 3 years ...............| 6.00 | 1.80 | | |
| —, Schools ...............| 2.00 | | | |
| **CHANGING TIMES,** The Kiplinger Magazine M. | 6.00 | 1.00 | no | 1.00 |
| —, 2 years ...............| 10.00 | 2.00 | | 2.00 |
| —, 3 years ...............| 14.00 | 3.00 | | 3.00 |
| (See advertisement, page 110.) | | | | |
| Channels ................20 Nos. | 7.50 | no | no | no |
| —, 2 years ...............| 12.50 | | | |
| —, 3 years ...............| 17.50 | | | |
| Charm merged into Glamour, which see | | | | |
| Chemical Abstracts Service with Indexes | | | | |
| —, School, College & Univ. Librs. .. | 150.00 | 3.00 | 1.00 | no |
| —, All Others ...............| 570.00 | no | no | no |
| Without Indexes | | | | |
| —, School, College & Univ. Librs. ... | 130.00 | 2.40 | .80 | no |
| —, All others ...............| 540.00 | no | no | no |
| Chemical Bulletin ..........10 Nos. | 2.00 | .50 | no | no |
| Chemical & Engineering News (4) ..W. | 6.00 | 1.00 | | |
| —, 2 years ...............| 10.00 | 2.00 | | |
| —, 3 years ...............| 14.00 | 3.00 | | |
| —, Foreign ...............| 15.00 | 3.00 | | no |
| **CHEMICAL ENGINEERING** ........M. | 3.00 | 22.00 | 4.00 | 12.00 |
| Chemical Engineering Progress ......M. | 6.00 | 2.00 | .50 | 1.50 |
| —, Libraries ...............| 5.40 | 2.00 | .50 | 1.50 |
| Chemical Reviews ........B.-M. | 12.00 | 1.25 | .50 | 1.25 |
| **CHEMICAL WEEK** ............W. | 3.00 | 22.00 | 4.00 | 12.00 |
| (Indexes $1.00 per year) | | | | |
| Chemist ................M. | 4.00 | no | no | no |

FIGURE 1d. Faxon's 1960 Librarian Guide

of scholarly journals. Only rarely would a publisher not be able to fulfill all issues of a new late-placed order or a renewal which arrived late. An average library order at Faxon then, from all classifications, was seventy-five titles or approximately $1,000. A 3,000-title order from a large university was a rare occurrence.

Most claims for missing issues were then handled by the libraries directly with the publishers, and the agency became involved only if the publisher insisted on proof of payment.

In the 1950s the F. W. Faxon Company elected to concentrate its service efforts in the field of library subscriptions. By 1958 the number of complex financial transactions with a large number of publishers prompted the owner, Mr. A. H. Davis, Jr., to find a more efficient and accurate method of managing the business. With the purchase of a 305 Ramac, having a print speed of seventeen lines per minute, and assistance from IBM, the basic programs were developed, and the transfer of records to data processing cards was begun. The underlying notion of timely renewal action centered on a common expiration month, which was the heart of the library service concept. Then, as today, the most popular volume year was the calendar year. A common expiration time target is vital to reduce the number of financial transactions to a minimum. Direct subscription renewal, which is the alternative to the use of an agency, invites publisher invoices one year from the starting date, which causes large volumes of payments throughout the year. The programming of the rate structure had to deal with single issue rates and parts-of-a-year billing for those titles which were not published on a fixed volume year or had other order restrictions. The intensive study of the automation of the records and methods of management of the agency dealing in periodicals focused on the repetitive nature of the business. This repetitive data settled the basic record design of a fixed field system, which subsequently developed into relational data files. This concept simplified the programer's tasks by eliminating the need for duplicate or non-unique information.

The programing and records transfer took two years of manual effort to complete. Since the system was cardbound, any errors introduced had to surface through human review of invoice documents by the agency or the library staff. An alternate source of error detection was the arrival of an unwanted journal at the library. In general, check-in methods and procedures at libraries then were wholly inadequate and undependable by current-day standards. Although only a two percent error factor was introduced (the wrong title was ordered or a title was not ordered at all), it took at least four years to track down this small number of errors in the original 225,000 orders handled during the first year of automation at Faxon. The library community had the patience to tolerate this error performance, while other improvements in the quality of the total service moved into place. The routine tasks of prompt renewals and efficient handling of new orders, together with accurate financial payment records reproducible on a timely basis, seemed worth the price of introductory error.

In the twenty years or so since electronic automation first appeared, the number of titles in service has grown at an average of eleven percent per year. In order to respond to this service growth, the title data base grew at the rate of approximately twenty percent per year over this same period.

The ratio of titles in service to the selection base vividly portrays the unique construction of library serial collections. Once the core journals in a discipline have been selected, the "spice of life" in collection development begins.

By 1965, the 305 Ramac no longer had the power to handle the larger volume of business, nor could services be expanded because of the card-bound mode. Of even greater significance was "down time," which became prohibitive due to the weakening of the electronic tube system. That Central Processing Unit (CPU) was replaced by a 1401, which continued to rely on card input, but the record storage onto tape replaced the millions of cards. Microfiche was introduced as a means of distributing necessary record information to the service staff. It was an excellent medium for keeping needed service information reasonably current. The 1401 had its limitations as well because it was a batch-bound processor and imposed priorities on the service system which seemed intolerable, particularly when a small manual effort could easily meet the performance specifications of an urgent service request. However, the record keeping and reproduction capacity of the 1401 gave superior service for the majority of libraries.

At the close of the 1960s, the 360/30 replaced the 1401, and disc storage replaced tape as the primary data medium. Storage on tape as a backup of the records before alteration added a special dimension for accurate reconstruction in the event of a system malfunction. This permitted the option of immediate or random access to records, which heretofore could be recovered only in a print mode. However, to take advantage of this option Faxon had to develop its own unique teleprocessing monitor which would display the data stored on disc.

The microfiche records were then replaced by CRT displays for maintenance and use in the title and rate publisher files. Search strategies were developed to retrieve needed records for all basic files, and upon this, a data base management system was developed for historical file preservation. Although in the late 1960s and early 1970s the specific information value of the data passing through the system had not been defined, Faxon elected to build an archival record base. This concept formed the foundation of the data bases which are now so valuable in the peripheral services needing retrospective support for forecast validity.

The programing language used to translate systems into active data processing is important to realize maximum efficiency and productivity from a programing staff. At this time, assembler language was the vogue in the business environment, but it was inefficient and expensive, and narrowed the selection of hardware alternatives. After a study of the options, Faxon selected PL1 as a high-level language. This decision improved productivity and proved to be an efficient choice in this particular situation.

Recognizing the high capacity of on-line data processing and with a consistent increase of service demands in all areas, the hardware changed from a 360/30 to a 360/40, then from a 370/145 to a 370/158, all within a four-year period. In 1979, a 3032 replaced an upgraded 370/158, substantially increasing CPU power by two and one-half times; print speed remained constant at 1,800 lines per minute. With this additional power, on-line systems were developed for all of the basic files. Sophisticated search strategies were then needed to retrieve selectively constructed records, as this would allow the service staff to perform its tasks based upon service requests from libraries in specific service areas.

The history of data processing in the subscription agency business is perhaps very vividly expressed in terms of the labor needed to perform the services delivered. In 1958, it took twenty-three people for each million dollars of sales and, interestingly enough, the same number of people to service each each 100,000 subscriptions. However, the quality and range of service brings each 100,000 subscriptions. However, the quality and range of service beings another dimension to service performance as anyone active in the serials librarian field will attest. A conservative translation of the quality and quantity of services of today into the number of people required to perform those functions in 1958 would mean at least doubling of the 1958 staff. Since 1975, however, productivity gains have been negligible. Today fourteen people are needed for 100,000 service lines and slightly less than four people per million dollars in sales.

This can be interpreted in terms of the financial value to libraries as follows. Serving 3,000 libraries in 1960 took about sixty full-time and thirty part-time people. Assuming one person in each library to carry the workload performed by agencies, that would mean that the 3,000 libraries would have had to pay for the services of forty times as many employees than Faxon had if direct ordering were to have taken place (3,000 ÷ 75). Similarly, calculated labor costs for 1980 indicate that direct ordering would require the employment in libraries of 18,000 people or about fifty-eight times as many as there are at Faxon now (18,000 ÷ 310).

A search for the first users of electronic computers to perform the tasks of a library subscription agency turned up a company in Riverside, California, which will remain unnamed. It published what is believed to be the first computer-printer produced catalog intended for use by libraries for the selection of titles to be ordered from the agency. The catalog also served as a source for the complete name of each title listed on the itemized invoice (see Figure 2).

With such an advanced system of record manipulation this company should have grown rapidly; however, this was not the case. The data processing technology, system design, and programs for records control must be matched with sound business practices. The unnamed company became financially insolvent in about 1962 or 1963, causing some severe financial losses to be sustained by a large number of libraries. Unfortunately, this financial disaster was accompanied by a scheme to defraud, in that cashed payment checks sent to multiple title publishers were used to claim payment when no payment had been made. The scheme was simple enough in that the back (endorsed side) of a payment which had been through the bank system was photocopied and attached to a photocopy of the front side of a check not disbursed as proof of payment. The principal rushed to Canada when the scheme was fully exposed.

This sketchy view of automation in the subscription business does not describe the radical changes in agency service concepts. All subscription agencies competing for their market share of all classes of library business would not necessarily follow the same changes or selection of hardware as they expanded services to lower costs in this labor-intensive field. However, the drift toward handling more bibliographic elements would not have been possible without the introduction and application of electronic data processing.

The flow charts which follow (Figures 3, 4, and 5) show the transition of how data is collected and manipulated starting with the card-bound data process, through batch and tape systems, to the present on-line technology.

| Title Code | Title of Periodical | Title's Address Code | How Title Is Invoiced | Issues In One Year | 1 Year Price | 2 Year Price | 3 Year Price |
|---|---|---|---|---|---|---|---|
| 263468 | CAREER INDEX | 2384 | CAREER INDEX | 8 | 8.00A | | |
| 351006 | CAREER NEWS | 1767 | CAREER NEWS | 6 | 1.00A | 1.75A | 2.25A |
| 207010 | CARNEGIE MAGAZINE | 0334 | CARNEGIE MAG | 10 | 2.00C | | |
| 376072 | CARNETS VIATORENS | 1276 | CARN VIATORIENS | 4 | 2.50B | | |
| 323036 | CAROLINA QUARTERLY | 0256 | CAROLINA QTRLY. | 3 | 1.25C | 2.50C | 3.75C |
| 263241 | CARROUSEL | 1530 | CARROUSEL | 6 | 1.50G | | |
| 228073 | CARTEL | 1184 | CARTEL | 4 | 1.50C | | |
| 286020 | CARTOGRAPHY | 2253 | CARTOGRAPHY | 2 | 2.10A | | |
| 206024 | CASABELLA | 1526 | CASABELLA | 12 | 20.00D | 30.00D | |
| 247004 | CASH BOX | 1978 | CASH BOX | 52 | 15.00C | | |
| 280004 | CASKET & SUNNYSIDE | 2412 | CASKET & S/SIDE | 12 | 4.00F | | |
| 406040 | CATALOG OF UNITED STATES CENSUS PUBLICATIONS | 0482 | CAT US CENSUS | 4 | 1.25C | 2.50C | 3.75C |
| 041009 | CATHOLIC ACTION | 0228 | CATHOLIC ACTION | 52 | 3.00C | | |
| 261019 | CATHOLIC BIBLICAL QUARTERLY | 1610 | CATHOLIC BIB.QT | 4 | 5.00B | 10.00B | 15.00B |
| 261022 | CATHOLIC CHARITIES REVIEW | 0228 | CATH CHARITIES | 10 | 1.00C | | |
| 041010 | CATHOLIC DIGEST | 0029 | CATHOLIC DIGEST | 12 | 4.00C | 7.00C | 9.00C |
| 261101 | CATHOLIC DOCUMENTS | 2598 | CATH.DOCUMENTS | | 1.65B | | |
| 295099 | CATHOLIC EDUCATIONAL REVIEW | 1768 | CATH EDUC REV | 9 | 5.00C | | |
| 320029 | CATHOLIC HISTORICAL REVIEW | 1768 | CATH HISTORICAL | 4 | 5.00C | | |
| 041115 | CATHOLIC LIBRARY WORLD | 1956 | CATH.LIB.WLD. | 9 | 6.00A | | |
| 261057 | CATHOLIC MIND | 0293 | CATHOLIC MIND | 6 | 3.00C | 5.00C | 7.00C |
| 041018 | CATHOLIC SCHOOL JOURNAL | 0571 | CATHOLIC SCH JL | | 3.75B | 6.00B | 8.25B |
| 041011 | CATHOLIC WOMANS JOURNAL – NEW | 0854 | CATH.WOMANS JL. | 11 | 1.25B | | 3.25C |
| 261012 | CATHOLIC WOMANS JOURNAL – RENEWAL | 0854 | CATH.WOMANS JL. | 11 | 1.25B | | 3.25B |
| 014001 | CATHOLIC WORLD | 0588 | CATHOLIC WORLD | 12 | 6.00D | 10.00C | 14.00C |
| 430026 | CATS MAGAZINE | 0230 | CATS MAGAZINE | 12 | 4.00F | 7.00F | 10.00F |
| 377031 | CATTLEMAN | 0589 | CATTLEMAN | 12 | 3.00C | | 7.50C |
| 001081 | CAUCASIAN REVIEW – ENGLISH EDITION | 1078 | CAUCASIAN REV. | 12 | 1.50E | | |
| | CAVALIER | 0999 | CAVALIER | 12 | 3.00E | 5.00E | 7.00E |
| 216111 | CELLULE | 3154 | CELLULE | 3 | 12.00A | | |
| 267057 | CEMENT & LIME MANUFACTURE | 1360 | CEMENT & LIME M | 6 | 1.50D | 3.00D | 4.50D |
| 263498 | CENTENNIAL REVIEW OF ARTS & SCIENCES | 3155 | CENT REV ARTS S | 4 | 3.00A | | |
| 021437 | CENTRAL AMERICA & MEXICO | 3073 | CENTRAL AM MEX | 4 | 2.50A | | |
| 377097 | CENTRAL ASIAN REVIEW | 2919 | CENTRAL ASIAN R | 4 | 4.80B | | |
| 377022 | CENTRAL EUROPEAN FEDERALIST | 1193 | CENTRAL EUROPEAN F | 4 | 1.00A | | |
| 259011 | CENTRAL PHARMACEUTICAL JOURNAL | 0317 | CENT.PHARM.JL. | 12 | 3.00A | 6.00A | 9.00A |
| 234002 | CERAMIC AGE | 0231 | CERAMIC AGE | 12 | 4.00B | 7.00D | 10.00D |
| 234004 | CERAMIC INDUSTRY | 0188 | CERAMIC INDUST | 12 | 4.00B | | 8.00B |
| 242002 | CERAMIC NEWS | 2041 | CERAMIC NEWS | 12 | 2.50C | | 5.50C |
| 242006 | CERAMICS | 0538 | CERAMICS | 12 | 5.00A | | |
| 234007 | CERAMICS MONTHLY | 0335 | CERAMICS MTHLY | 10 | 5.00B | 9.00B | 12.00A |
| 237063 | CEREAL CHEMISTRY | 1769 | CEREAL CHEMISTRY. | 6 | 15.00B | | |
| 332021 | CEREBRAL PALSY REVIEW | 0232 | CEREBAL PALSY R. | 6 | 3.00B | 6.00B | 9.00B |
| 021435 | CERVIS JOURNAL | 2912 | CERVIS JOURNAL | 52 | 12.00D | 22.00D | |
| 325057 | CHAIN SAW AGE | 1355 | CHAIN SAW AGE | 12 | 5.00F | | 8.00F |
| 335002 | CHAIN STORE AGE | 0233 | CHAIN S.AGE | 12 | 3.00C | 5.00C | |
| 259038 | CHAIN STORE AGE, DRUG EXECUTIVES EDITION | 0233 | CHAIN S.AGE D.E | 12 | 3.00C | 5.00C | |
| 284025 | CHAIN STORE AGE, EXECUTIVES COMBINATION | 0233 | CHAIN S.AGE E.C | 12 | 3.00C | 5.00C | |
| 299025 | CHAIN STORE AGE, GROCERY EXECUTIVES EDITION | 0233 | CHAIN S.AGE G.E | 12 | 3.00C | 5.00C | |
| 390015 | CHAIN STORE AGE, RESTAURANT & FOUNTAIN EXECUTIVES EDITION | 0233 | CHAIN S.AGE G.E | 12 | 3.00C | 5.00C | |

Index of serial publications (CHAIN STORE AGE — CHEMISCH WEEKBLAD):

| No. | Title | Ref | Abbrev. | Freq | | | |
|---|---|---|---|---|---|---|---|
| 284026 | CHAIN STORE AGE, VARIETY STORE COMBINATION | 0233 | CHAIN S.AGE VSC | 12 | 3.00C | 5.00C | 6.00F |
| 262048 | CHALLENGE | 2468 | CHALLENGE | 10 | 2.50F | 4.25F | |
| 228012 | CHAMBERS JOURNAL. - CEASED PUBLICATION | | | | | | |
| | CHANGING TIMES | 0234 | CHANGING TIMES | 12 | 6.00E | 10.00E | 14.00D |
| 200033 | CHANGING TIMES TO SCHOOL ADDRESSES - SAME AS ABOVE | | | | | | |
| 200038 | CHANNELS | 1183 | CHANNELS FULL | 20 | 12.50C | 22.50C | 32.50C |
| 200034 | CHANNELS FULL SERVICE | 1183 | CHANNELS FULL | 20 | 37.50A | | |
| | CHANNELS LIMITED SERVICE | 1183 | CHANNELS LTD.. | 20 | 25.00B | | |
| | CHARM NOW INCORPORATED IN GLAMOUR | | | | | | |
| 267122 | CHARTERED MECHANICAL ENGINEER | 2629 | CHART.MECH.ENG. | 12 | 8.25B | 16.50B | 24.75B |
| 267165 | CHARTERED SURVEYOR | 3615 | CHART.SURVEYOR | 12 | 14.50A | | |
| 047010 | CHATELAINE | 0006 | CHATELAINE | 12 | 3.00C | 6.00C | 9.00B |
| 008255 | CHECKAWAY | 1531 | CHECKAWAY | 24 | 1.00A | | |
| 236014 | CHEMICAL ABSTRACTS | 0294 | CHEMICAL ABSTR. | 24 | 925.00A | | |
| 236127 | CHEMICAL ABSTRACTS - WITHOUT INDEXES | 0294 | CHEMICAL ABSTR. | 22 | 800.00A | | |
| 237052 | CHEMICAL ABSTRACTS SCHOOLS AND LIBRARIES | 0294 | CHEMICAL ABSTR. | 22 | 200.00A | | |
| 237055 | CHEMICAL ABSTRACTS TO LIBRARIES WITHOUT INDEX | 0294 | CHEMICAL ABSTR. | 24 | 170.00A | | |
| 236040 | CHEMICAL AGE | 2637 | CHEMICAL AGE | 52 | 9.00D | | |
| 236011 | CHEMICAL AND ENGINEERING NEWS | 0294 | CHEM.ENGIN NEWS | 52 | 10.00B | 10.00B | 14.00B |
| 236005 | CHEMICAL & ENGINEERING NEWS INDEX | 0294 | CHEM.EN.N.INDEX | 4 | 6.00B | | |
| 348019 | CHEMICAL & PROCESS ENGINEERING | 1020 | CHEM.& PROC.ENG | 12 | 6.00D | | 15.00D |
| 236041 | CHEMICAL AND RUBBER | 0042 | CHEMICAL RUBBER | 12 | 1.50C | | |
| 236004 | CHEMICAL BIOLOGICAL COORDINATION CENTER REVIEW-CEASED | | | | | | |
| 236003 | CHEMICAL ENGINEERING | 0011 | CHEMICAL ENGIN | 12 | 3.00B | | |
| | ABOVE TO SENIOR COLLEGE OR PUBLIC LIBRARIES | 0011 | CHEMICAL ENG | | | | |
| 337051 | CHEMICAL ENGINEERING & MINING REVIEW | 3695 | CHEM.ENG.MINING | 12 | 3.00B | 4.00B | 5.00B |
| 336028 | CHEMICAL ENGINEERING PROGRESS | 1000 | CHEM.ENG.PROG. | 12 | 5.10A | | |
| 336033 | CHEMICAL ENGINEERING SCIENCE | 1181 | CHEM.ENGIN.SCI. | 12 | 6.00C | 10.00C | 14.00C |
| 237173 | CHEMICAL INDUSTRY & ENGINEERING | 3696 | CHEM.IND.& ENG. | 12 | 60.00B | | |
| 236044 | CHEMICAL MARKET ABSTRACTS | 2776 | CHEM.MARKET ABS | 12 | 4.50A | | |
| 236019 | CHEMICAL PROCESSING | 2281 | CHEM.PROCESSING | 12 | 240.00A | 450.00A | 650.00A |
| 236036 | CHEMICAL REVIEWS | 0294 | CHEMICAL REV. | 6 | 10.00A | | |
| 237035 | CHEMICAL REVIEWS USSR ENGLISH TRANSLATION | 3418 | CHEMICAL REVS. | 12 | 12.00B | | |
| 237036 | ABOVE TO COLLEGE & UNIVERSITY LIBRARIES | 3418 | CHEMICAL REVS. | 12 | 36.00B | | |
| 236024 | CHEMICAL SOCIETY JOURNAL & PROCEEDINGS. | 0818 | CHEMICAL SOC.JL | 12 | 27.00B | | |
| 237133 | CHEMICAL SOCIETY OF JAPAN BULLETIN | 0035 | CHEM S JAPAN B | 12 | 60.00B | 120.00B | |
| 237152 | CHEMICAL SOCIETY OF JAPAN JOURNAL - INDUSTRIAL CHEMISTRY SECTION | 0035 | CH.SOC.JAP.ICS | 9 | 12.00C | | |
| 237007 | CHEMICAL SOCIETY OF JAPAN JOURNAL - PURE CHEMISTRY SECTION | 0035 | CH.SOC.JAP.PCS | 12 | 10.00C | | |
| 236001 | CHEMICAL TITLES - 1ST-10TH SUBSCRIPTIONS | 0294 | CHEMICAL TITLES | 12 | 10.00C | | |
| 236119 | CHEMICAL TITLES - 11TH-25TH SUBSCRIPTION | 0294 | CHEMICAL TITLES | 24 | 65.00B | | |
| 236130 | CHEMICAL TITLES - 26TH & SUCCEEDING | 0294 | CHEMICAL TITLES | 24 | 45.00B | | |
| 236131 | CHEMICAL TITLES - TO TEACHING INSTITUTIONS | 0294 | CHEMICAL TITLES | 24 | 30.00B | | |
| 237131 | CHEMICAL TRADE JOURNAL & CHEMICAL ENGINEER | 3203 | CHEM TRADE JL | 52 | 9.00C | 18.00C | 27.00C |
| 236006 | CHEMICAL WEEK | 0011 | CHEMICAL WEEK | 52 | 3.00B | 4.00B | 5.00B |
| 236007 | ABOVE TO SENIOR COLLEGE OR PUBLIC LIBRARIES | 0011 | CHEMICAL WEEK | 52 | 3.00B | | |
| 237027 | CHEMICKE LISTY | 2108 | CHEMICKE LISTY | 52 | 15.00A | | |
| 237095 | CHEMIE INGENIEUR TECHNIK | 2632 | CHEMIE ING.TECH | 12 | 23.00A | | |
| 237041 | CHEMIKER-ZEITUNG/CHEMISCHE APPARATUR MIT CHEMIE-BORSE | 3017 | CHEMIKER ZEITU. | 24 | 17.20C | | |
| 237029 | CHEMISCH WEEKBLAD | 2764 | CHEMISCH WEEKBL | 52 | 7.56B | | |

FIGURE 2

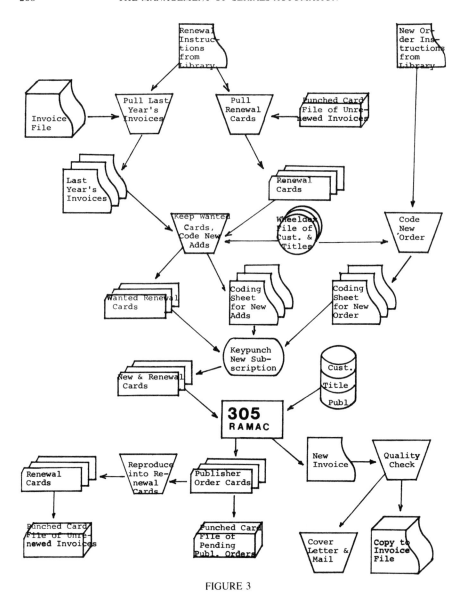

FIGURE 3

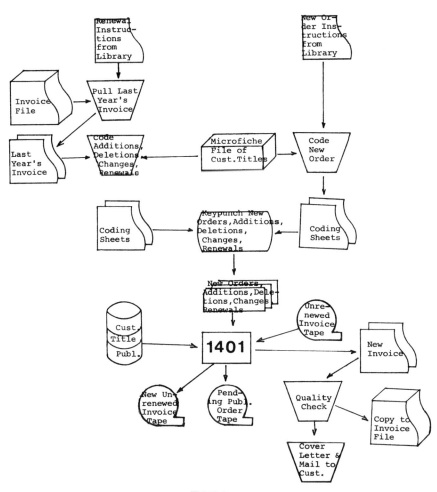

FIGURE 4

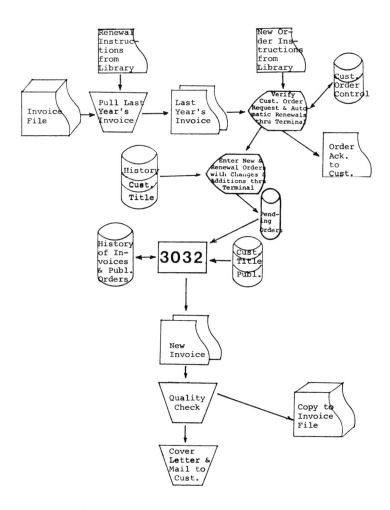

FIGURE 5

| File Description | Record Count | No. of Cylinders | % |
|---|---|---|---|
| Title Data Base | | | |
| Title Alpha Search | 137,012 | 52 | 1.3 |
| Title Price & Biblio | 111,453 | 374 | 9.3 |
| | | | |
| Publisher Data Base | | | |
| Publisher Locator | 49,663 | 5 | .1 |
| Titles within Publ. | 157,466 | 4 | .1 |
| Publisher Name & Addr. | 49,758 | 35 | .9 |
| | | | |
| History Data Base | | | |
| Scan | 6,784,833 | 172 | 4.3 |
| Customer Info. Search | 2,278,805 | 137 | 3.4 |
| Invoice Cross-Reference | 222,542 | 25 | .6 |
| Check | 690,828 | 128 | 3.2 |
| Mini-Check | 2,206,984 | 45 | 1.1 |
| History | | | |
| Invoices | 180,336 | | |
| Billing Lines | 6,770,833 | | |
| Complete File | 17,301,514 | 1,771 | 43.9 |
| Quotes awaiting confirmation | | | |
| Quotes | 4,500 | | |
| Lines | 170,000 | 129 | 3.2 |
| | | | |
| Customer Data Base | | | |
| Customer Alpha Search | 614,588 | 61 | 1.5 |
| Accounts Receivable | 1,472,837 | 301 | 7.5 |
| Name and Address with Order | | | |
| & Sales Stats. | 31,251 | 273 | 6.8 |
| Claims | 1,357,007 | 365 | 9 |
| | | | |
| Miscellaneous Files | | | |
| Cancellations | 109,979 | 24 | .6 |
| Refunds | 128,990 | 22 | .5 |
| Serials Update | 87,060 | 12 | .3 |
| Serials Check-in | 66,179 | 9 | .2 |
| Customer Address Change | 150 | 10 | .2 |
| Document Request | 4,815 | 4 | .1 |
| Order Entry | 17,214 | 9 | .2 |
| Panvalet | N/A | 70 | 1.7 |

Reserve for annual growth
  Production Files                                       949
(Reserve cylinders not included in % calculations)

Recap of total disk space
(Sixteen 3350 Disk Drives with a total capacity
to store 5,080,000,000 char. of information)

| | | |
|---|---|---|
| Production files | 9 Disk | 56.3 |
| Systems Files | 4 Disk | 25 |
| Programming Test Files | 1/2 Disk | 3.1 |
| Data Dictionary (allocated) | 1/2 Disk | 3.1 |
| Operations Work File | 2 Disk | 12.5 |

(Systems file include MVS, CICS, TSO, IMS, DATA DICTIONARY, PANVALET, etc.)
hdc:1B5

FIGURE 6. Faxon-File Construction 1980

# CHANGE OR DECAY?
# NEW PATTERNS IN SERIALS PUBLISHING

Peter W. Lea

ABSTRACT. Various pressures are causing many publishers to consider alternatives to the conventional serials publication. These pressures are identified together with their effects. New ventures include simultaneous microform publishing, synoptics, in-house composition, and the on-line journal. Types of the latter are identified together with some current examples. The influence of new technology on the information community is discussed, and suggestions are made about possible future patterns of serials publishing.

The scholarly journal has had a relatively unchanged existence, both physically and in type of content for the past 300 years, and if there are plans to change even a small part of this well-established information system, the reason must be socially, and/or economically, quite powerful. Even to consider change is an enormously radical step to take, causing much soul searching and retrenchment of attitudes on the part of the protagonists. Sir Arnold Bax, late Master of the Queens Music, said, in his book, *Farewell to My Youth,* "One should try everything once, except incest and folk dancing," to which could be added "and changing the scholarly journal," so strong, at times, is the lobby for the retention of this traditional medium of communication.

Herschman suggested that the scholarly journal provided archival, current awareness, and social functions,[1] and it is essential that these features are borne in mind when change is considered. Any new or relatively new system should provide the means of storing information for posterity, should allow current dissemination of knowledge, and should give the author the prestige and recognition he deserves for his intellectual efforts. The majority of scholarly journals attempt to fulfil these requirements, some with greater success than others. Any new dissemination system which neglects to provide any one of them, particularly the third—the social function—will find acceptance by the information community difficult to attain; and without authors there is no information community.

The past five years has seen the scholarly journal widely examined and reappraised as a communication medium. There are three separate but related reasons for this reassessment and for the consideration of innovations and developments which would improve, complement, or even at times replace some conventional journals.

The first reason, and one most familiar to librarians, is economic. The golden goose of the 1960s laid the inflationary egg of the 1970s. This act proved painful for all concerned. Production costs for journals rose dramatically, followed by the inevitable increase in subscription prices as publishers attempted to keep revenue at a reasonable level. A number of publishers searched for ways to reduce their costs or to put their organization on a more businesslike footing. Some were less effective than others. One enthusiastic but misguided editor of a society journal decided to accept advertisements for his publication as a means of raising income. His more efficient successor later discovered that it had been costing the society considerably more to include the advertisements in the journal than had been received in income from the advertisers. Other editors, more successfully, attempted to effect savings by using camera-ready copy and other expedients in an attempt to keep annual rises to an acceptable level, but often the economic pressures were on a global scale and beyond their control. As prices rose, the number of subscriptions tended to drop, particularly those of individuals as opposed to institutions such as libraries. Even here, reassessment of serials holdings was taking place and a number of titles were cancelled as perceived use became the main criterion for selection and retention, which many would claim was an exercise long overdue in a number of research libraries.

The second cause of the current reassessment of the scholarly journal is the availability of new technology. The computer has been used for many years for various aspects of journal production, such as computer photocomposition, but during the past few years its application has been directed toward the total electronic transmission of information. This has provided us with completely new concepts to consider, such as the electronic journal and the *editorial processing center*. With computer costs falling, some organizations are seriously examining the role of the computer in providing alternatives to the conventional journals or improving the current editing and production processes.

Together with economic and technological causes for considering change came a desire to improve the existing system of information transfer, or at least parts of the system. Dissatisfaction has been felt for many years over such problems as the overproduction of journal papers, delays in publishing them, the quality of authorship, refereeing, copyright, and the low amount of use made of the published research paper. The latter point is probably one of the least regarded but possibly one of the most significant factors when criticism is made of the present method of disseminating current information. It is well-known that a very high percentage of research workers are already familiar with the contents of the typical research paper, and have been so for some time prior to its publication. The actual readership, therefore, is likely to be very low. In 1970 it was estimated that no paper in the core journals of psychology would be read by more than seven percent of the subscribers to the host journal.[2] Studies on other subjects such as chemistry, physics, and geology have produced equally condemning sets of statistics regarding the low relevancy of journal content. When this criticism is added to Rossmaster's claim that "the system does a good job of assembling knowledge into packages which are about 90% mismatched to the needs of users,"[3] the question might be asked is the system or at least the package ready for change? Many feel that this is the case.

A direct result of the economic pressures facing journal publishers and the desire to improve the primary dissemination of information has been the introduction of the synopsis journal. There is little new about the concept; indeed, it was first discussed nearly fifty years ago. However, in recent years renewed attention has been focused upon this type of publication, eventually culminating in its legitimation in an American National Standard in 1978.[4]

The essential features of a synoptic publication are that it contains concise primary papers and allows access to the back-up full length paper for users who require complete versions of the work described. The size of the concise paper varies. It may be either one or two pages in length or about one-fifth of the original. The complete paper may be supplied in microfiche or miniprint with the synopsis or obtained from the publisher, author, or other sources on demand.

What has been learned about this type of publication from the various examples so far produced? It has been shown that the synopsis journal can fulfill the three requirements of the scholarly journal, namely, providing a current awareness service, insuring an archival record, and conveying the prestige and recognition which the author desires, since the papers continue to be refereed by experts. Synoptic publishing has been less successful in the United States than in Europe, mainly due to author resistance. There still exists considerable pressure to publish in the most prestigious journals, and American authors have yet to be convinced that traditional status and prestige will be forthcoming for papers published in nonconventional sources. It has also been suggested that as economic pressure to innovate is less acute in the United States than in Europe, the larger American publishers have shown an obvious reluctance to change from the current accepted and profitable system. One exception to this is the Geological Society of America, which introduced a synopsis/microfiche format for the *Bulletin of the Geological Society of America* in 1978. Initially, author reaction was to desert the *Bulletin* and offer the papers to an alternative journal, but when it was discovered that rapid publication and other benefits resulted from the change, authors started to return to the *Bulletin*. The suggestion is that given the right circumstances there may be a brighter future for synopsis publishing in the United States. Readers on both sides of the Atlantic tend to be reasonably enthusiastic about synopsis publishing, which may be considered paradoxical since these are often the same persons who produce the papers in the first place. There are inevitable criticisms, but on the whole, user reaction has been favorable.

Subjects which appear to be best suited to synoptic treatment are the pure and applied sciences rather than conceptual subjects. In Britain, experiments have been carried out with varying degrees of success in chemistry, production engineering, management research, and mechanical engineering. A report on a recent experiment with *Engineering Synopses* was fairly optimistic about the value of this type of publication, suggesting that it had a useful role to fulfill in future information transfer.[5] The most successful new service has been *Journal of Chemical Research.* This is a joint international venture which was carefully planned and implemented from the outset, providing benefits to the information community at all levels. The publisher has speedier production, his costs are reduced, and an improved system of communication is achieved. The user benefits by gaining access to a publication of a manageable length, easily browsable, and at a price which is not as prohibitive as so many of the full-length scholarly journals. The packaging of information in synoptic form could have an advantage to the librarian of reducing the demand on his interlending services which increasingly will become overloaded as the use grows of on-line bibliographical retrieval systems.

Present abstracting and indexing services, although invaluable, do have a number of weaknesses. A major one is the inevitable problem of not providing enough information in the abstract to enable the user to request a document with more than a fifty percent chance of the documents meeting his needs. Synoptic papers by virtue of their length and nature, being complete in themselves, could help alleviate this deficiency. The conciseness and completeness which characterize synoptics could well be exploited in future on-line information systems. There can be little doubt that users of an electronic journal would benefit greatly from a synoptic-length text store rather than one based on bibliographical references or on full (i.e., complete) text. The former would produce too little and the latter too much information. The synoptic could provide a potential economic and effective store of manageable size for the producer and a retrieval service which would not give the user mental indigestion.

A second major feature of current serials publishing is the growing availability of microforms as alternatives to hard copy. We are familiar with the use of microfilm for archival records of newspapers and back runs of serials, but during the past few years an increasing number of publishers are providing microform issues of journals simultaneously with current hard copy. The main attraction of this service to librarians appears to be the amount of storage space which would be saved by keeping journals in this format. The subscription prices are either the same as the hard copy version, or reduced by about twenty percent, and that only if both formats are purchased. The reason for the high cost of microforms is perfectly understandable when one considers that if librarians purchased large numbers of microforms at a low, attractive price instead of conventional current issues, the financial rock on which the traditional journal stands would be liable to collapse. In a curious attempt to retain both the status quo and to encourage purchase of microforms, a variety of trade-in schemes are available where, for example, exchanges of back runs of printed issues can be made for microform versions, so reducing the price of the latter. Although the provision of microform alternatives is very widespread among publishers, it appears that very few titles in this format are sold in comparison with the printed issues. Indeed the only successful type of publication sold as microforms in competition with printed versions are some of the major secondary services.

Heavier use of microforms has been observed in libraries in recent years and there has been a decline in user resistance. However, many librarians still display a reluctance to purchase material in this format if it is available in hard copy. Maurice Line appears to sum up the typical attitude of many of his professional colleagues, describing microforms as "the unreadable in the form of the illegible," and "the ideal medium for publishing materials that nobody wants to read."

Color microfilm and fiche is now well established as a publishing medium for serials. Among the well-known journals available in color are *National Geographic, Studio International,* and *Wildlife Diseases.* The last title has been published as an original journal on microform since 1959, and has been produced in color since 1972.

The quality of color microform varies from publisher to publisher, and while some good examples of the format exist, others are of an indifferent standard. There are also other technical problems which have yet to be solved such as that of the permanence of the medium itself.

There is little original publishing on microform, with less than a dozen journals produced solely in this format throughout the world. A recent British journal produced exclusively on microfiche is *CORE (Collected Original Resources in Education).* It is issued three times per annum and consists of fifteen fiche in a full-size journal cover complete with printed contents list and index. It has the advantage of being able to be shelved with the normal journals in a library so does not suffer from the problems caused by separation from the main sequence and subsequent lack of use experienced with microform publications in many libraries.[6] However, it would be interesting to hear the comments of readers who, when expecting to be able to read *CORE* in full size text, are faced with a microfiche and its attendant disadvantages.

The future of microforms in libraries is very much in the hands of librarians. As microform collections of serials, government publications, reports, and other information sources grow, so librarians might direct more thought to the improvement of reading environments, acquiring better equipment and generally attempting to make an uncongenial format more convenient to use. With greater user acceptance and increased demand by libraries, producers may be encouraged to provide a technically better product with a more rational pricing structure than currently exists, ultimately benefiting the total information community. Unfortunately, some cynics suggest that microforms as a totally accepted and integrated library service will be made obsolete by new technology before this situation occurs.

When looking at new patterns in serials publishing, the technological advances experienced in the 1970s have offered some of the most stimulating and revolutionary ideas. Some of the advances are already well established, others are in their infancy, although proving so precocious that we may find that today's new technology has been made redundant almost overnight. One major development in printing which has made a significant impact in some countries, especially in the United States, is computer photocomposition. Its use is continuing to grow as more printers and publishers become aware of its advantages and are able to afford the necessary capital investment. A recent report on computer composition claims that by the mid-1980s, ninety percent of traditional hot-lead typesetting machinery in the United States will be replaced by automated phototypesetting. A large future market is forecast for in-house systems linking word-processors to typesetting and reproduction services.[7] The changeover is already well under way in the newspaper industry, and when the saturation point is reached here, manufacturers will turn to commercial printing and finally to society publishers, some of whom have already established their own in-house computerized composing units.[8]

In-house composition utilizes a word-processing unit, which is basically an electric typewriter incorporating a text-processing device. It is possible with normal typing skills to edit, correct, and update without need to key in more than the actual alterations. The author need not have any inhibitions about last-minute changes (which can be expensive using a conventional printing system), and thus can have the script perfectly typed and error-free at the latest possible time before publication. The potential benefits are the cost saving of a single keyboarding (as opposed to possibly six or seven keyboardings), the advantages of almost immediate turnaround in typesetting, and the production of error-free texts without the need for proofreading. The capital cost of the equipment could be offset against savings in typing the original. It is important to remember that in periodical work with large areas of text the typesetting will represent about fifty percent of the total cost of production. Input for photocomposition can also be made from optical character recognition (OCR), where typed texts are scanned by a photoelectric cell and translated into codes (usually on punched paper tape) compatible with the phototypesetter. In the systems which offer compatibility between word processing and phototypesetting, a disc or cassette can be sent from the publisher to the printer for conversion prior to the printing process. Phototypesetting via word-processing input is well established in the United States and Germany, but the criterion for acceptance by the British print unions appears to be whether it is taking work away from their members. There are instances of word processing and

OCR output to phototypesetting being acceptable, if it results in work being produced that otherwise would not have been printed.

Most of the word-processing equipment available in the United Kingdom is currently advertised for basic office use, but a growing number of organizations are also using it as an in-house composing unit for multiple copies of documents of various types, such as reports. Word processing may be capital intensive in its creation, but with a high volume of input, plus its use as an efficient office typing system, it could be regarded an an economical proposition. It may be seen that a society publishing a low-circulation specialist journal, which at present has a precarious future, could use word-processing equipment to compose the journal in-house, either independently or cooperatively with other societies, with a possible increase in subscriptions, and a longer life for the journal. Once cooperation between societies or institutional publishers is achieved and the necessary equipment installed, we can think in terms of the establishment of the *editorial processing center* (EPC). This concept has been described and discussed in considerable detail for the National Science Foundation in the United States[9] and Aslib[10] in the United Kingdom. The EPC is a cooperative venture between society publishers where a computer is used to undertake as many of the editorial and publishing functions as feasible. The results of the assessment by various experts show that the technology is available and the concept could work admirably, but social and economic difficulties militate against its adoption in its broadest terms. Currently, it appears to be regarded as a creator of even greater problems for publishers than as a method which could solve them.

A relatively recent innovation which has caused much interest in the information community is the electronic journal. This term embraces three technologically related but functionally varied types of "publication": specialist research journals, newsletters, and videotex- and teletext-based systems.

The concept of the electronic research journal emanated from the U.S. National Science Foundation in the early 1970s, and a number of partial and full-scale experiments have taken place since that time to test the practicality of the technology and its possible applications.

One recent experiment involving researchers at the Jersey Institute of Technology, the University of Toronto, and Stirling University in Scotland illustrated some of the difficulties facing innovators of the on-line research journal. *Mental Workload* was to provide, among other advantages, efficient retrieval facilities, a great reduction of publication delay, and interactive communication between users. In the event, the problems encountered in the experiment caused the main researcher to deliver the ambivalent announcement that the operation had been a success but unfortunately the patient had died. Much of the success was of a negative nature, identifying some of the social, psychological, and technological barriers which will have to be overcome in the future by other innovators in this area. Some of the difficulties encountered were small but frustrating, such as authors' inability to cope immediately with complex command structures. Others were international in scope, and fundamental in nature, such as the obstructiveness of the British Post Office in not allowing, more or less at the last minute, the trans-Atlantic telecommunication link. However, John Senders of the University of Toronto is positive about the future of the research journal in electronic form. He is convinced that it will appear, and that it will be successful if properly planned and organized.[11]

Currently, the British Library Research and Development Department is negotiating with various organizations in the United Kingdom in order to establish an electronic research journal in which authors would transmit papers via their own terminals to a central computer where the editorial functions would take place. Facilities would also be available for refereeing and computer conferencing.[12]

The subject coverage of the British journal is likely to be very narrow and therefore of interest to a minority of researchers, as was *Mental Workload*. This suggests that the future of this type of communications medium will most probably follow this pattern of being based on a very narrow specialist subject with a readership of less than a hundred individuals worldwide. This will inevitably preclude access by research workers in countries without sophisticated telecommunications links, leading to charges of elitism and restriction on the unimpeded flow of scientific information. However, to judge from the experiences of Senders et al. with their attempts to establish an international electronic journal, it will be many years before some countries, even though possessing the appropriate technology, will be able to set up a system which crosses national telecommunications frontiers without encountering difficulties imposed by unenlightened bureaucracies.

An already established and fairly fast-growing example of a newsletter type of electronic journal was available for examination at the recent Aslib/Eurim Conference held in Brussels. *Extemplo*, provides information about scientific conferences, lectures courses, and the like, in the Nordic countries via the Scannet telecommunications network. It appears biweekly from an institution in Stockholm to which items can be sent by mail, telex, or telephone.

A simple on-line journal has been developed at Manchester Polytechnic. *On-line Education News* (OLEN) is available on-line to possessors of teletype-compatible terminals as a newsletter for lecturers at library schools concerned with teaching computer systems. It is available daily, and users can request the full contents of the main file, up-to-date details of news from individual library schools, or general news from subfiles. A hard copy version is reproduced at the end of each term directly from the stored text. At the moment input is made at Manchester, but it is hoped that in the future users will be able to input news directly. It must be stressed that this is a very simple system which grew from a distaste for the inconvenience of producing a hard copy newsletter with the requirements of proofreading, retyping, duplicating, distribution, and accounting. We also wished to see how the theory would work in practice.

The moderate success of OLEN is causing attention to be turned to increasing the news content and perhaps expanding the scope and consequently the readership. Inevitably this potential growth will create some of the problems experienced by experimenters with the specialist research journals, and some of the advantages which a short-item newsletter possesses may be lost. It may be that an optimum size of on-line newsletter already exists, and an increase in size or scope will produce diminishing returns of value and effectiveness.

Electronic publishing using videotex and teletext has been developed in various forms in many countries. The former system uses the telephone network for transmission of signals and the latter uses broadcast signals. Both can be received on domestic television screens or on computer display terminals. The British Post Office's *Prestel* makes available a wide range of information services, including a number of general journals such as *Exchange and Mart,* a weekly magazine of classified advertisements and *Scitel,* the Institute for Scientific Information's source of new information on science, technology, medicine, and related topics.

The potential mass market for this type of service is causing some observers to speculate on what longterm effect electronic publishing may have on the more popular serial publications and newspapers. These groups rely very heavily upon advertising revenue and any swing, however marginal, toward electronically based advertising would affect the balance upon which the newspaper industry, particularly, is delicately poised. Already, on-line newspapers exist, although they have not yet made much impact on the user community. They may be available to any member of a locality possessing a terminal or home computer with communicating facilities, as is the case with the *Columbus Dispatch* of Columbus, Ohio. Alternatively, the newspaper may form part of a news searching service such as Mead Data Central's *NEXIS,* which includes in its data base the *Washington Post.* This newspaper will be produced totally by computer photocomposition by the end of 1980 and will be able to transmit its content on-line to the host computer at M.D.C. It is significant that the *Washington Post* has imposed a twenty-four-hour delay on the appearance of news on NEXIS, suggesting that it is conscious of the possible competitive nature of a current electronic news service.

Another area which is currently exciting some attention in the communications world is the digitized transmission of information. It is early to speculate how this may affect serials publishing and libraries, but an experiment in Britain between the British Library Lending Division and two libraries in London suggests that on-demand publishing could possibly rival the transmission of photocopies through the post as the main method of information transfer for urgently needed items between large research libraries. If this technique develops economically and efficiently, and there is every indication that this will be the case, we could see the fruition of Bernal's idea of a central depositary of scientific papers, with separates, not sent through the post, but transmitted electronically.

When considering the implications of new technology and its potential use in serials publishing, it would appear that we are facing a revolution as fundamental as that which resulted from the introduction of printing by movable metal type in Europe over 500 years ago. However, there are other innovations concerned with the transmission of information which suggest that we are facing, not only *one* revolution, but a whole series of them. Recent advances in the technology of light have presented us with a number of discoveries which could affect our future.

Holography with its immense storage capability, fiber optics, and laser printing all provide new methods of storing and transmitting information. The latter technique, for example, can print over 400 pages per minute. When a user can push a button to retrieve a complete research paper plus accompanying data and a copy of *War and Peace* in under two minutes, who needs libraries? Even the old argument about the convenience of handling single items of print on paper, either as research journals or books, begins to look a little thin when confronted with the prospect of a battery-powered reading tablet with a bubble memory.

Undoubtedly, new technology will progressively affect serials publishing and information transfer methods, but in the short to medium term, as parallel development to traditional methods of communication. These are too convenient to use, too well established, and too profitable for the larger publishers to be easily replaced. The traditional serials will continue and will be improved upon as new production techniques and management skills are employed in their creation, but it is equally true that alternative forms will grow because of the pressures discussed earlier. For example, one large commercial publishing group, Butterworths, has been investigating for many years all new methods of publishing and disseminating information. The immediate results of these studies were improvements and changes made to the various areas of printing and distribution of publications. However, the amount of material which has been discovered is so enormous to handle and examine that a special research and development department has been set up. This R and D group has been testing new equipment and systems, and as a result a new company has been formed known as Butterworths (Telepublishing) Ltd. This company now offers to the UK legal and accountancy professions a fast computerized information system as well as other services such as microfiche journals and information on audio cassettes. In announcing the new company, the Chairman and Chief Executive of the Butterworth Group, Gordon Graham said: "We believe that Butterworths, as the UK's leading legal publisher, and as a publisher also in the fields of science, technology and medicine, has both a major opportunity and a major responsibility to launch into that form of publishing in which the computer replaces the printing press. As the name Telepublishing indicates, we believe that this is a proper role for traditional publishers and should not be left to governments, electronic corporations or user groups." However, Mr. Graham also pointed out, no doubt to the relief of many of his customers, "that folio publishing will be the dominant medium for transmitting professional information, but that computer-assisted publishing will be a valuable new dimension."

A longer term view might see society evolving away from the tradition publication and communications systems toward a totally paperless system. The first areas to be replaced completely would be the information-intensive services such as abstracting and indexing publications. Some of the larger of these services are already experiencing a decline in total numbers of subscriptions due to the growth of on-line data bases. Other information sources which may be available only in electronic form in the future could include highly specialized primary publications, reference books, and other data stores. These changes would present us with totally new concepts of information transfer, and it is important that we consider them with an open mind as well as analytical judgment. Changes and innovations will need to be carefully monitored and their potential effects judged on all three groups which make up the information community: the suppliers, the users, and librarians. All depend upon each other for the successful formal supply of information. Consideration must be given by each group to others in the system when a change is planned, if the innovation is to work most efficiently. All the groups have supposedly the same aim—that is, the effective transfer of information, regardless of the package in which it comes.

## REFERENCES

1. Herschman, A. "The Primary Journal: Past, Present and Future," *Journal of Chemical Documentation* 1 (1) (Feb. 1970):37–46.

2. Wooster, H. "The Future of Scientific Publishing," *Journal of Washington Academy of Sciences* 60 (2) (June 1970):41–45.

3. Rossmassler, S. A. "Scientific Literature in Policy Decision Making." *Journal of Chemical Documentation* 10 (3) (Aug. 1970):163.

4. *American National Standard for Synoptics.* A.N.S.I. Z39.34-1977 (New York: A.N.S.I. Inc. 1978).

5. Millson, R. J. *An Experiment in Synopsis Publishing in the Field of Mechanical Engineering.* British Library Research and Development Department, Report no. 5498 (London: British Library 1979).

6. Osborn-King, R. "Current Research Communication through a Microfiche Journal." *Reprographics Quarterly* 12 (1) (Winter 1979):12–14.

7. *Computer Composition: Automated Phototypesetting and Copy Processing* (San Jose, CA: Creative Strategies International 1978).

8. Lea. P. W. *Trends in Scientific and Technical Primary Journal Publishing in the U.S.A.* British Library Research and Development Department, Report no. 5272 HC (London: British Library 1976), pp. 6–7.

9. Aspen Systems Corp. and Westat Inc. *Editorial Processing Centers: Feasibility and Promi*

(Rockville: Aspen Systems Corp. and Westat Inc., for U.S. Office of Science Information Service, National Science Foundation, 1975).

10. Woodward A. M. *Editorial Processing Centres: Scope in the United Kingdom.* British Library Research and Development Department, Report no. 5271 HC (London: British Library, 1976).

11. Senders, J. W. *The Electronic Journal.* Paper given at *Eurim 4: a European Conference on Innovation in Primary Publication,* (Brussels, Belgium, March 1980).

12. "Electronic Journal Plan for British Library." *Outlook on Research Libraries* 1 (13) (Oct. 1979):13.

# CONTRIBUTORS

**Anne Marie Allison** is the Assistant Director for Library Services at Florida Atlantic University in Boca Raton, Florida.

**Linda K. Bartley** is Head of the National Serials Data Program at the Library of Congress in Washington, D.C.

**Marjorie E. Bloss**, MLS, is the Union List of Serials Project Director for the Rochester (New York) Regional Research Library Council and Chairperson of the American Library Association's Ad Hoc Committee on Union Lists of Serials.

**F. F. Clasquin**, now retired, was Vice President for Research & Development at the F. W. Faxon Company.

**Roberta Corbin** is a systems analyst at the University of California, San Diego Library. She is a graduate of Michigan State University and has been at UCSD for eleven years.

**Janice E. Donahue** is Head of the Library's Collection Organization Department at Florida Atlantic University in Boca Raton, Florida.

**Neal L. Edgar** is Research Librarian at the University Libraries at Kent State University in Kent, Ohio.

**Dianne Ellsworth** is Program Manager for the California Data Base for Serials at the California Library Authority for Systems and Services (CLASS).

**Mary Grace Fleeman**, MSLS, MSM, is Senior Cataloguer at George Washington University Law Library, National Law Center, in Washington, D.C.

**David E. Griffin** is Serials Librarian at the Washington State Library in Olympia.

**K. Paul Jordan**, MLS, is Assistant Director of Technical Services at the Harold B. Lee Library, Brigham Young University in Provo, Utah.

**Lois M. Kershner**, MLS, MBA, is Director for Library Services at Research Libraries Group, Inc. in Stanford, California. She has been involved in the installation and management of automated systems in academic libraries for the past fourteen years. She holds a Master in Library Science degree from the University of Wisconsin and a Master of Business Administration degree from Pepperdine University.

**Tom D. Kilton** is Humanities Bibliographer at the University of Illinois Library at Urbana, Illinois.

**Eileen Koff**, MSLS, is a Library Associate at the National Library of Medicine in Bethesda, Maryland. She worked as a graduate assistant on the Serials Conversion Project at the University of Illinois at Urbana.

**Carol R. Krumm**, BS in LC, is Librarian for Technical Services Planning and Special Projects and Assistant Professor of Library Administration at the Ohio State University Libraries in Columbus, Ohio.

**Peter W. Lea**, MLS, ALA, MIInf Sci, is a Senior Lecturer in Information Services at Manchester Polytechnic, Department of Library and Information Studies in Manchester, England.

**Rebecca T. Lenzini**, MSLS, is Coordinator of OCLC Cataloguing at the University of Illinois in Urbana and was formerly Head of Automated Records Maintenance there.

**Lenore S. Maruyama**, MALS, is a Senior Information Systems Specialist in the Library of Congress Network Development Office, which provides the secretariat for the Network Advisory Committee.

**Ruth B. McBride** is an Assistant Professor of Library Administration, Automated Records Department, at the University of Illinois in Urbana-Champaign.

**Margaret M. McKinley** is Head of the Serials Department at the University of California in Los Angeles.

**H. Kirk Memmott**, MLS, is chairman of the Serials Department at the Harold B. Lee Library, Brigham Young University in Provo, Utah.

**Pauline F. Micciche** is the Manager of the Resource Management Services Department of OCLC, Inc., in Columbus, Ohio.

**Laurance R. Mitlin**, MLS, is Assistant College Librarian for Public Services at the Dacus Library at Winthrop College in Rock Hill, South Carolina.

**Edward Newman** is Manager of Computer Services at the California Library Authority for Systems and Services (CLASS).

**Patricia Ohl Rice**, MLS, is the former Head of Acquisitions at Winthrop College in Rock Hill, South Carolina.

**Michael Roughton** is Serials Acquisitions Librarian at the Iowa State University Library.

**Debora Shaw**, MALS, was Project Manager for the On-Line Union List of Serials Project at Indiana University Libraries. She is now a doctoral student at the Graduate Library School of Indiana University in Bloomington, Indiana.

**Mary Ellen Soper** is an Assistant Professor at the School of Librarianship at the University of Washington.

**John R. Taylor**, MLS, is Library Systems Analyst at the Harold B. Lee Library, Brigham Young University in Provo, Utah.

**William J. Willmering** was formerly Head of the Serials Department at the Northwestern University Library in Evanston, Illinois.

**Bruce Ziegman** is Acquisitions Services Librarian of the Washington Library Network at the Washington State Library in Olympia.

# INDEX

# DATE DUE